INSIGHT GUIDES

BULGARIA

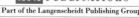

Part of the Langenscheidt Publishing Group

██ INSIGHT GUIDE
BULGARIA

Editorial
Editor
Dorothy Stannard
Editorial Director
Brian Bell

Distribution

UK & Ireland
GeoCenter International Ltd
Meridian House, Churchill Way
West Basingstoke, Hants RG21 6YR
Fax: (44) 1256 817988

United States
Langenscheidt Publishers, Inc.
36–36 33rd Street 4th Floor
Long Island City, NY 11106
Fax: 1 (718) 784 0640

Australia
Universal Publishers
1 Waterloo Road
Macquarie Park, NSW 2113
Fax: (61) 2 9888 9074

New Zealand
Hema Maps New Zealand Ltd (HNZ)
Unit D, 24 Ra ORA Drive
East Tamaki, Auckland
Fax: (64) 9 273 6479

Worldwide
Apa Publications GmbH & Co.
Verlag KG (Singapore branch)
38 Joo Koon Road, Singapore 628990
Tel: (65) 6865 1600. Fax: (65) 6861 6438

Printing

Insight Print Services (Pte) Ltd
38 Joo Koon Road, Singapore 628990
Tel: (65) 6865 1600. Fax: (65) 6861 6438

©2007 Apa Publications GmbH & Co.
Verlag KG (Singapore branch)
All Rights Reserved

First Edition 2007

CONTACTING THE EDITORS
We would appreciate it if readers
would alert us to errors or outdated information by writing to:
Insight Guides, P.O. Box 7910,
London SE1 1WE, England.
Fax: (44) 20 7403 0290.
insight@apaguide.co.uk
NO part of this book may be reproduced,
stored in a retrieval system or transmitted
in any form or means electronic, mech-
anical, photocopying, recording or otherwise, without prior written permission of
Apa Publications. Brief text quotations
with use of photographs are exempted
for book review purposes only. Information has been obtained from sources
believed to be reliable, but its accuracy
and completeness, and the opinions
based thereon, are not guaranteed.

www.insightguides.com
In North America:
www.insighttravelguides.com

ABOUT THIS BOOK

The first Insight Guide pioneered the use of creative full-colour photography in travel guides in 1970. Since then, we have expanded our range to cater for our readers' need not only for reliable information about their chosen destination but also for a real understanding of the culture and workings of that destination. Now, when the internet can supply inexhaustible (but not always reliable) facts, our books marry text and pictures to provide those much more elusive qualities: knowledge and discernment. To achieve this, they rely heavily on the authority of locally based writers and photographers.

Insight Guide: Bulgaria is structured to convey an understanding of the country and its people as well as to guide readers through its many attractions:

◆ The **Features** and **History** sections, indicated by an orange bar at the top of each page, cover the natural and cultural history of Bulgaria as well as its array of recreational opportunities in a series of informative essays.

◆ The main **Places** section, indicated by a blue finder bar at the top of the page, is a complete guide to all the sights and areas worth visiting, organised by area. Places of special interest are coordinated by

ABOVE: Nessebar Waterfront.

The contributors

This book was produced by **Dorothy Stannard** in Insight Guides' London office, using two authors with specialist knowledge of Bulgaria.

Her first task was to commission the travel writer and journalist **Craig Turp**, the author of *Berlitz Guide Bulgaria*, to write the history and features, as well as the Places chapters on Sofia and the surrounding region and the Pirin and Plovdiv mountains. Craig, who is a regular visitor to Bulgaria from his home in Bucharest, has seen enormous changes in Bulgaria in its run-up to join the European Union, captured in his essay on The Rural Dilemma.

The UK-based writer and photographer **Jane Egginton**, who has previously written about South America for Insight Guides, wrote the rest of the Places chapters, including the two chapters on the Black Sea Coast. As the owner of holiday properties on the coast, Jane was well-placed to write a feature on buying property in Bulgaria, an increasingly popular investment for foreigners. In addition, she went off the beaten track to cover the remote areas of the Danubian Plain and the Balkan Mountains, and wrote features on skiing, food and drink, religion, music, monasteries, festivals and the essay on The Bulgarians. Lastly, she produced the fact-packed Travel Tips.

Insight Guide Bulgaria is brought to life by its exceptional photography, most of which was produced by **Gregory Wrona**, who has visited many different destinations on behalf of Insight Guides, and **Pete Bennett**. The book was proof-read by **Sylvia Suddes** and indexed by **Helen Peters**.

number with the maps. At the end of each Places chapter is a listing of the best restaurants in that area.
◆ Three picture stories highlight particularly interesting aspects of Bulgaria, from its strong folk traditions and festivals to its monasteries.
◆ The **Travel Tips** listings section, with a yellow bar, provides all the practical information you will need for a trip to Bulgaria. It is divided into four key sections: transport, accommodation, activities (including nightlife, shopping and outdoor activities) and an A–Z listing of practical tips. Information may be located quickly by using the information on the back cover flap.

Map Legend

—— - -	International Boundary
———	Regional Boundary
– – – –	Province Boundary
⊖	Border Crossing
—•—	National Park/Reserve
– – – –	Ferry Route
✈ ✈	Airport: International/Regional
🚌	Bus Station
●	Metro
●	Tourist Information
✉	Post Office
† † †	Church/Ruins
†	Monastery
☾	Mosque
✡	Synagogue
🏰 🏚	Castle/Ruins
∴	Archaeological Site
∩	Cave
𝟏	Statue/Monument
★	Place of Interest

The main places of interest in the Places section are coordinated by number with a full-color map (e.g. ❶), and a symbol at the top of every right-hand page tells you where to find the map.

Contents

Introduction

Land of Future Hope and
  Past Glory **17**
Geography and Landscape **19**

History

Early Days..............................**23**
Bulgaria Since Independence ..**32**
Decisive Dates **38**

Features

The Bulgarians **43**
The Rural Dilemma **51**
Bulgarian Voices **56**
A Balkan Stew........................**59**

Information panels

Religion **47**
Wine, Beers and Spirits **63**
Hiking in the Rila **134**
Skiing **144**
Buying Property **224**
The Spa Industry **250**

Places

Introduction **71**
Sofia **77**
Around Sofia and
  the Northwest **109**
The Southwest and Rila
  Mountains........................**125**
The Pirin Mountains **141**
Plovdiv **155**
The Rhodopes **173**
The Balkan Range................**191**
The Danubian Plain **209**
Varna **221**
The Northern Black Sea
  Coast **231**
The Southern Black Sea
  Coast **245**

Insight on...

Festivals................................**48**
Monasteries and Icons **138**
Bird-watching in Bulgaria **188**

OFF THE BEATEN TRACK

● **Iskar Gorge**
Follow the long and spectacular course of the gorge. *See page 109.*

● **The Rila and Pirin Mountains** South of Sofia, the Rila and Pirin ranges offer hiking trails in summer, and skiing in winter. *See page 125–152.*

● **The Shipka Pass**
This is the main route between the River Danube and Turkey. *See page 201.*

● **The Rhodopes Mountains** This remote area has picturesque villages and dramatic mountain scenery with waterfalls and caves. *See page 173.*

● **The Rusenski Lom National Park**
The dramatic gorges here attract hikers and climbers. *See page 214.*

● **Belogradchik**
Unusual limestone formations tower over this town on the Serbian border. *See page 119.*

● **Arda Gorge**
This nature reserve near the Turkish border is known for its birdlfie. *See page 186*

● **The Strandzha**
Old traditions are very much alive in the southeast corner of Bulgaria. *See page 261.*

ABOVE: view in the Rhodopes Mountains.
RIGHT: hiking is one of the best ways of exploring rural Bulgaria.

TOP MONASTERIES, CHURCHES AND MOSQUES

● **Rila Monastery**
A UNESCO World Heritage site on account of it magnificent frescos, Rila also has a spectacular setting. *See page 128.*

● **Bachkovo Monastery**
Covered in glorious frescos, Bachkovo, in the Rhodopes, is also a World Heritage Site *See page 177.*

● **Boyana Church**
This fresco-covered church on the edge of Sofia dates from the 10th century. *See page 96.*

● **Prebrazhenski Monastery**
The highlight here is the Monastery of the Transfiguration with its *Circle of Life* fresco. *See page 196.*

● **Dragalevtsi Monastery**
Set in the woods of Mount Vitosha, this picturesque monastery is easily accessed from Sofia. *See page 99.*

● **Assenovgrad** The area around the Assen Fortress is packed with monasteries and churches. *See page 176.*

● **The Rock Churches of Ivanovo**
Settled in the 13th century, the Rusenski Lom valley is dotted with churches hewn out of the rock by monks. *See page 214.*

● **The Banya Bashi Mosque** This Ottoman-style mosque is the last functioning mosque in Sofia and one of its loveliest buildings. *See page 82.*

● **The Dzhumaya dzhamiya** This nine-domed mosque in Plovdiv is one of only a few survivors in a city that once contained some 500 mosques. *See page 163.*

BELOW: church of the Virgin Mary, Assenovgrad.

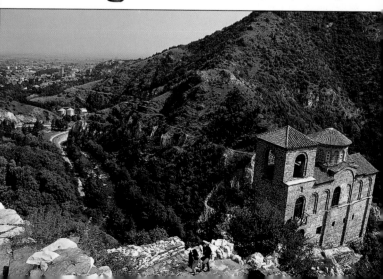

OUTDOOR ADVENTURE

● **Skiing**
Bulgaria's burgeoning ski industry centres upon Vitosha, near Sofia, Bansko, Pamporovo and Bovorets. *See page 144.*

● **Cycling and Mountain Biking**
More and more areas are setting up trails of varying difficulty. You can often rent bikes at hotels and tourist offices. *See page 286.*

● **Caving**
There are nearly 5,000 caves in Bulgaria, some with ancient cave paintings and many with extraordinary stalagmites and stalactites. There is a museum of speleology in Chepelere in the Rhodopes. *See page 285.*

● **Climbing**
As part of the Alpine-Himalayan mountain range, Bulgaria has lots of geological variations. Its two Alpine mountain ranges are Rila and Pirin, both reaching more than 2,900 metres above sea level. *See page 285.*

● **Diving**
Prime diving spots along the Black Sea Coast are Kavarna, Nessebar, Varna and Sozopol. *See page 286.*

● **Hiking**
There are many hundreds of miles of marked trails. Pirin, Rila and the Rhodopes Mountains are the three main walking areas. *See pages 134 and 286.*

● **Horse riding**
Bulgaria has a strong equestrian tradition and seeing the countryside on horseback is an excellent way of experiencing rural Bulgaria. Some ranches are offering horse riding holidays. *See page 287.*

● **Canoeing, Kayaking and Rafting**
Spring, when the rivers swell with meltwater, is the time for this. The best rivers are in the Rila and Pirin ranges. *See page 285.*

ABOVE: watching the wildlife, Martisa river.

BEST FOR BIRDWATCHING

● **Maritsa river**
Attracts hundreds of species of migratory and resident waterfowl. *See page 189.*

● **Shabla Lake**
This area is the wintering site of around 60 percent of the world's red-breasted goose population. *See page 189 and 242.*

● **Kaliakra**
This coastal headland towards the northern end of the Black Sea coast is a good place to spot Mediterranean shag, long-legged buzzard and wheatears. *See page 189 and 240.*

● **Around Bourgas**
The extensive reed beds of Lake Pomorie and the Poda Lagoon on the Black Sea coast attract a wide range of birds year-round. *See page 189 and 261.*

● **Trigrad Gorge**
This gorge in the Western Rhodopes Mountains is known for golden and short-toed eagles, peregrine falcons, as well as black woodpecker, kingfisher and grey wagtail. One of the specialities here is the wallcreeper. *See page 189.*

LEFT: winter wonderland on Mount Vitosha.

TASTES OF BULGARIA

● *Gyuvech*
A tasty stew of peppers, aubergines, beans and meat, served in an earthenware pot. *See page 60.*

● **Grilled meat**
Simple but often delicious, this is found on every menu. Choose from succulent lamb chops to first-rate kebabs *(kebapche)*. *See page 61*

● **Ponichki**
You will find these deep-fried doughnuts being cooked and sold on street corners in towns and villages all over the country. *See page 213.*

● **Yoghurt**
Bulgarian yoghurt is hard to beat. *See page 61.*

● **Baklava**
Dripping with honey and stuffed with nuts, this Turkish sweetmeat (and variations on a theme) is delicious. *See page 62.*

● **Hearty soups**
Thick soups of many kinds are very popular, even for breakfast. *See page 62.*

● **Wine and Rakia**
Bulgaria produces a wide range of excellent and inexpensive wines, including Cabernet, Melnik, Güzma and Mavrud.
Reds are best. The national firewater is Rakia. *See page 63.*

ABOVE: *Gyuvech*, a tasty Balkan stew.

ABOVE: dancers at the Pirin folk festival

BEST FESTIVALS

● **Rose Festival**
Held in the Kazanlak region during the first week of June. *See page 203.*

● **Varna Summer**
This is one of Bulgaria's best arts festivals. *See page 226.*

● **Fire Dancing**
Held on 21 May in some rural villages. Dancers perform on burning embers. *See pages 48–9.*

● **Kukeri festivals**
These spectacular processions are held all over Bulgaria to mark the passage of the seasons, especially spring and autumn. *See pages 48–9.*

● **Pirin folk festival**
Bulgaria's folk music and dance are celebrated throughout Bulgaria but one of the best festivals is the Pirin festival held in Sandanski. *See page 148.*

● **Horse Easter**
Young bachelors race horses to celebrate the animals' good health and to impress the young women of the village. *See pages 48–9.*

TOP TIPS FOR TRAVELLERS

● **Don't judge a hotel by its star rating**
The star-rating system for accommodation has been inherited from communist times and has not been updated. As a result, star-studded older establishments often prove inferior to newer business hotels or even family B&Bs. If you are doubtful about an establishment, ask to see the room first.

● **Travelling Around**
Public transport is limited, slow and fairly unreliable (cancelled services, breakdowns, etc), so be sure to leave plenty of time for journeys by train or by bus. If time is tight, and you don't want to rent a car, consider hiring a taxi for the day. Negotiate with the driver directly and be clear about whether petrol is included. It is usual to pay for the driver's meals.

● **Money**
If you are travelling in rural areas you will need to take cash (*leva*, the local currency, or euros), as banks are rare. Leva notes pre-dating 1999 (when the currency was devalued) are obsolete.

● **Yes or no?**
It is essential (but quite difficult) to remember that a shake of the head means yes while a nod means no.

LAND OF FUTURE HOPE AND PAST GLORY

Bulgaria has come a long way since 1990, the year of its first post-Communist election. As the new kid on the EU block, it is on the brink of a radical and hopefully life-enhancing transformation

When Bulgaria joined the European Union on 1 January 2007, it entered a brand-new chapter in a long and eventful history. Having proved itself a stable democracy for more than 15 years, it was at last allowed into an exclusive club, with labour rights (more limited than hoped), trading opportunities and foreign investment.

As a country whose power peaked in the Middle Ages, and which has been suppressed in one form or another almost ever since, Bulgaria has high expectations of its new status. Throughout the country, New Year parties in 2007 were ecstatic. Thousands of ambitious migrant workers were reported to be speeding west by plane or bus within hours of the clock striking midnight.

But with opportunities come dangers, the chief of which are the possible loss of Bulgaria's unique rural culture and the certain brain drain as the young are lured abroad. Bereft of teachers, doctors, engineers and builders, how, it is argued, can the country prosper? Change is desired and needed, but will it be carefully managed and will heed be taken of the problems inherent in rapid development? Unfettered construction of holiday villas and apartments on previously pristine stretches of the Black Sea coast does not bode well.

Such worries may underestimate the Bulgarians' considerable pride in their culture and love of their undeniably beautiful land. Most commentators predict that migrant workers will return home once they have earned enough to build a home and business there.

It is harder, though, to see how Bulgaria's rural way of life can ultimately survive, ecotourism initiatives notwithstanding. For that reason it is best to see it soon, limiting your impact by using local guesthouses and *mehanas* (inns), travelling independently and perhaps getting off the beaten track by hiking. Bulgaria is a fascinating destination with beaches and ski slopes, monasteries and mountains, with rare birds and dazzling displays of wild flowers. And for the time being at least, it is a country where Thracian treasures are regularly turned up by farmers tilling their fields with a horse-drawn plough. ❑

PRECEDING PAGES: off the beaten track in the Stara Planina: the Roman Theatre in Plovdiv; ceiling frescos in Rila Monastery.
LEFT: the Assen Monument, commemorating the mighty Assen dynasty, at Veliko Tarnovo, capital of the Second Bulgarian Kingdom.

GEOGRAPHY AND LANDSCAPE

When it comes to geography, Bulgaria has everything –
high mountains, wide plains, lakes, marshes
and long golden beaches

One of the joys of visiting Bulgaria is the fact that it is all things to all people. In winter, many skiers enjoy the guaranteed snow of the country's mountain resorts; in summer, not five hours' drive away, hundreds of thousands of holiday-makers of a different kind sun themselves on the country's beaches. Likewise, the wet grasslands and marshes of the Kaliakra Peninsula on the Black Sea are very different in nature and in their appeal from the dry plain of Thrace that stretches from the Stara Planina to the Danube. Bulgaria may be a small country, but it has the most diverse landscapes in Europe.

Describing the country

Bulgaria comprises portions of ancient Moesia, Dacia, Thrace and Macedonia. Vaguely rectangular in shape, it is described by natural barriers on all four sides: to the north the Plain of Thrace and the Danube; to the east the Black Sea; to the south the Rhodope Mountains; to the west the Rila and Pirin ranges. The interior is split in two by the Stara Planina, a sweeping range of mountains that stretches from west to east and is punctured with thousands of tiny highland lakes. Much of the country is covered with forest, the source of many myths and legends. A history of folklore in any country is tied inextricably to the history of the land: in Bulgaria the two are often one and the same.

The country extends over an area of roughly 111,00 sq. km (42,850 sq. miles), making it roughly equal in size with Ireland, or the US state of Tennessee. Besides its better known topographical features it also has deep river valleys,

LEFT: the Pirin Mountains in winter.
RIGHT: a lush valley in the Rhodopes.

thrusting gorges, highland plateaus and shallow basins. Bulgaria has a total border of 2,264 km (1,400 miles), of which almost 640 km (400 miles) is accounted for by the River Danube and 400 km (248 miles) by the Black Sea.

The concertina effect

Topographically it is often said that Bulgaria is structured like a concertina. From north to south lowland and highland areas give way to each other at regular intervals: the Danubian Plain, the Stara Planina, the central Thracian Plain, and the Rhodope Mountains. The easternmost sections near the Black Sea are also hilly, often collapsing abruptly into the sea. The country is therefore split almost 50:50 by mountains and plains. More than 40 percent of the country lies at an altitude above 600 metres (2,000 ft), while the country's average altitude is 470 metres (1,550 ft).

The highest mountain in the country is Mount Moussala, in the Rila range, not far from the ski resort of Borovets. At 2,925 metres 9,596 ft), it is the tallest mountain on the Balkan Peninsula.

Caves and rock formations

Travelling around Bulgaria, you will come across many dramatic rock formations, from the sandstone pyramids around Melnik in the southern Pirin to the Belogradchik rock formations in the western foothills of the Balkan range. Bulgaria also has some of the finest cave systems in Europe,

Hot summers, cold winters

Bulgaria's climate is as varied as its topography. A land of extremes in every way, Bulgaria offers freezing winters – especially in the high Rila – and hot, stifling summers, particularly across the length of the Stara Planina. Average temperatures in Sofia in January range from -4–2°C (25–26°F), while in July and August the average temperature in the capital is a soaring 28°C (83.2°F).

FLORA AND FAUNA

Bulgaria's rich variety of landscapes, and the fact that they are relatively unspoiled, make it a haven for many species of flora and fauna that are rare or extinct elsewhere in Europe. It has one of Europe's largest populations of brown bears, wolves, roe deer, red deer, wild boar and wild goats, not to mention amazing bats, butterflies and other insects.

There are also year-round opportunities for birdwatching, especially in the marshlands around Bourgas (known as the Strandzha), and the Madzharovo nature reserve in the Rhodopes (see page 186). Spring (May) and autumn (September) are good for migratory birds, as two of the main migratory routes – the Via Pontica and Via Aristotelis – cross Bulgaria. Early summer is the time to see the wallcreeper, an elusive bird prized by ornithologists, which is often seen in the Rhodope Mountains, especially the Trigdad Gorge. Even winter has its spectacles, including almost the entire world population of red-breasted goose, a beautiful species which winters on the Black Sea coast.

Wildflowers, alpine and lowland varieties, are profuse in spring, especially in the remote Pirin and Rila Mountains, but also in Vitosha National Park, on the very doorstep of the capital, which contains a UNESCO Biosphere reserve, as well as being a habitat for brown bears.

You best chances of seeing any kind of wildlife is to join an organised tour. Several operators specialise in this (see page 287 of Travel Tips for details).

Bulgaria does not want for rainfall: the nation-wide average is 630 mm (24 ins) of rain per year. Much of this falls during the summer (July is the wettest month). The one exception is the far east along the Black Sea coast, which in summer enjoys a Mediterranean climate: warm and very dry. In winter however, the continental climate of the interior stretches its icy fingers to the sea, creating windy, cold and very wet conditions. Violent storms are common. The driest part of the country is the Plain of Thrace.

Bulgaria's climate makes it perfect for agriculture. Cultivated agricultural land occupies about 44 percent of the total territory of the

much for the economy of the areas in which they are situated, the effects on the environment – which saw areas once popular with migrating birds flooded – went unreported.

The biggest environmental problem in Bulgaria, however, was caused not by the construction of a dam, but by the draining of the Danube floodplain for agricultural use in the late 1940s. What was once marshland and spawning ground for Danube fish became bone dry in summer, and the link with the Danube – on which thousands of locals depended – was lost. A programme to restore the marsh, and the link with the Danube, is now underway. ❑

country. Viniculture is especially well suited to the concertina-like topography, the hills and troughs creating microclimates which, when combined with good-quality soil, produces ideal conditions for growing the finest-quality grapes.

Conservation matters

Much of the Bulgarian environment was ravaged by the rush to industrialise during the 1960s and '70s. Though the huge hydroelectric dams at Belmeken and Iskar – to name but two – generate much-needed power and did

---

LEFT: landscape near Svishtov, the Danubian Plain.
ABOVE: where the wild things are, near the Black Sea.

EARTHQUAKE ZONE

Much of Bulgaria is prone to earthquakes, especially the border lands north of Pleven, the centre of the country around Veliko Tarnovo, and the Western Rhodopean Fault, extending through the Rila and northern Pirin regions to Plovdiv. Tremors can also occur along fault lines running between Skopje in Macedonia and Razgrad in northeast Bulgaria, and from Albania eastward to Plovdiv. Though 16 quakes registering more than 5.0 on the Richter scale have occurred since 1900, there has been no loss of life since two major quakes hit Plovdiv within four days of each other in April 1928. The modern trend appears to be towards frequent but very short tremors which do little damage.

EARLY DAYS

Bulgaria – land of the Bulgars – is something of a misnomer, as the roots of the modern country are found in the intricately intertwined stories of many different peoples

A ny history of modern Bulgaria must begin with the Thracians, the original Balkanites. Yet for a people who are legendary both for their steadfastness in battle and their manipulation of the elements – the Thracians created some of the earliest gold jewellery so far discovered – it remains a mystery to historians as to why such a clearly advanced people did not come up with any form of writing system.

People of Thrace

The prehistoric origins of the Thracians therefore remain obscure. It is generally thought that they developed from a mixture of invading Indo-Europeans (who migrated throughout Europe from an area east of the Caucasus Mountains from 4000–2000 BC) and indigenous peoples already populating the Balkans. This development took place over a lengthy period of many centuries, from around 2500–1500 BC.

The identity of the indigenous peoples living in the Balkans when the Indo-Europeans arrived remains another of history's mysteries, though it is widely assumed that Minoans and other Proto-Greek tribes had planted settlements as far north as the Danubian Plain by at least 2500 BC.

In *The Iliad*, Homer relates how one of these groups, from around the Hellespont, fought on the side of Troy in the final years of the Trojan Wars. Thracians make a further appearance in *The Odyssey*, though as the geography of Odysseus's epic journey is at best confused, the reliability of such evidence is called into doubt by scholars. Though Homer wrote his epics

around 700 BC, the stories were based on oral legends at least 1,000 years old.

That there were many Thracian tribes is clear from the writing of Greek historian Herodotus, who points out the differences in the habits of the many Thracian groups in Book 5 of his *Histories* (written in around 440 BC). According to Herodutus, the Thracians could not even decide on which gods to worship: while most were polytheist, "the Gods they worshipped were three: Mars, Bacchus and Dian", some were monotheist, worshipping Mercury alone

Hellenic Thrace

The Thracians remained separate and often warring tribes until the beginning of the 5th

LEFT: item from the 4th-century BC Vratsa Treasure.
RIGHT: silver plaque from a Thracian tomb near Lovech.

SPARTACUS

The most famous Thracian is probably Spartacus, the gladiator who led a slave revolt against the Romans in 73 BC, famously celebrated by Stanley Kubrick's epic film of 1960, starring Laurence Olivier and Charles Laughton.

century BC, when the first recognisable state, sometimes called the Odrysian State after the most dominant Thracian tribe, emerged on the Danubian Plain, hereafter the Plain of Thrace.

A Persian invasion in the 6th century appears to have acted as a wake-up call, and the Odrysians became the first Thracians to adopt Greek habits

and practices; its upper-echelons eventually – though far later – adopted the Greek language. The Thracian State covered almost all of present-day Bulgaria, including much of sub-Carpathian Romania and northern Greece.

Teres (reigning 450-431 BC) was the first King of Thrace. His successors, Sitalkes and Suethes, succeeded in keeping the Thracian tribes united through a policy of pre-emptive warmongering. Sitalkes attacked the Triballi (an Illyrian people to the north), while Seuthes launched wars against both Athens and Macedonia. Its downfall came when Philip of Macedonia conquered Thrace in 346 BC, and began colonising the area.

Under Philip's son, Alexander the Great, the Thracian interior was fully opened up to Greek settlers and merchants, who over the next 200 years fused with the Thracians to form a Hellenistic ethnic group, distinct from those Thracian tribes north of the Danube.

Roman Thracia

During the long Macedonian Wars (250–150 BC) between Rome and Thrace the Macedonian elite gradually saw its hold over Thrace diminish, and tribal leaders once again became the most powerful authority. After the battle of Pydna in 168 BC, Macedonia lost its last grip on Thrace, though the newly enfranchised tribal leaders were not yet ready to submit power to Rome. As a result, a number of rebellions against Rome took place over the next century. The Andriscus Revolt of 149 BC, begetter of the Third Punic War that led to the fall of Carthage, drew the bulk of its support from Thracia. Later the slave Spartacus, a Thracian,

THRACIAN TREASURE

Reaching its heyday around 380 BC, Thrace was a rich state that produced gold coinage, built roads and demanded vast sums in tribute from a number of Greek cities. The capital was Seuthopolis, present-day Kazanlak, the centre of the so-called Valley of the Thracian Kings *(see page 202)*, a vast necropolis containing thousands of tombs, only a few of which have so far been excavated. Treasure, usually in the form of gold jewellery, weaponry, masks and horse tackle, is being discovered all the time, but archaeologists struggle to keep one step ahead of the tomb robbers, which have proliferated since the end of Communism.

Evidence of Thracian settlements can be found all over Bulgaria. Among the most significant sites are the following:

•**Perperikon**. Hewn out of the rock on a hill top 15km (9 miles) from Kurdzhali, this Thracian city includes an oracular temple to Dionysus *(see page 186)*.

•**National Museum of Archaeology**, Sofia. Superb examples of Thracian gold work *(see page 80)*.

•**Kazanluk Tomb, Kazanluk**. Listed by UNESCO, this tomb dates from the late 4th to the early 3rd century BC. The real tomb cannot be visited but a replica of the beautifully decorated tomb is close by *(see page 202)*.

•**Thracian Tomb at Sveshtari**. This elegantly decorated three-chamber tomb is also listed by UNESCO.

•**Rogozen Treasure**. A cache of 5th-century BC silverware displayed in the History Museum, Vratsa *(see page 114)*.

carried the battle to the Italian peninsula itself, leading an army of 120,000 in the Third Servile War of 73–72 BC, ultimately won by Rome.

Rome finally conquered Thrace in AD 46 after the last Thracian king, Roimitalkes III, was murdered by his wife. Following the tried and trusted policy of divide and conquer, the Thracian kingdom was split into three: Dacia in the north (corresponding almost exactly to present-day Romania); Moesia across the Balkan Mountains and the Plain of Thrace; and Thracia in the south.

All three provinces were heavily colonised, and economically the region prospered. New towns were settled, including Serdica (Sofia),

Byzantine) authority was again fully imposed over all of present day Bulgaria.

The Slavs and the Bulgars

Though Justinian encouraged culture and education to flourish, fortified the cities of the border lands and settled Serdica and Philipopolis with great numbers of people, the continued vacuum in Dacia to the north meant that Thrace remained susceptible to invasion. Though barbaric, ill-organised tribes such as the Pechenegs did not get far, a much larger tribe, the Slavs, swept all before them on their march into the Balkans in the latter part of the 5th century.

Augusta Traiana (Stara Zagora) and Durostorum (Silistra). Yet once Dacia was abandoned to the Barbarians by Emperor Aurelian, in 260, as too costly to defend, Moesia and Thracia came under constant Barbarian attack.

By the time the Roman Empire was split between Rome and Constantinople in 395, Rome had all but given up defending Moesia and Thracia too, and Germanic Goths and Ostrogoths settled unhindered throughout the provinces. It was not until the reign of Emperor Justinian I (the Great, 527–565) that Roman (by now

LEFT: a 1st-century face mask with helmet, found at Silistra, an important Roman base.
ABOVE: Justinian the Great, Holy Roman Emperor.

The original Slav homeland was in eastern Ukraine. They migrated south along the coast of the Black Sea, first settling – in the 6th century – in the Wallachian lowlands (Dacia), before moving to the eastern and southern Balkans 50 years later. After early skirmishes the Byzantine authorities – buoyed by the Slav interest in Christianity – allowed them to settle throughout the empire. They quickly became the most powerful people in the Balkans, though their hegemony did not last: in the second half of the 6th century the Bulgars, arrived.

Politically astute and quite brilliant horsemen, the Bulgars pitched up on the Plain of Thrace speaking an Asian language of either Turkic or Iranian origin (historians and linguists have yet to reach a definitive verdict). They came originally from Central Asia, and migrated to the European continent in the 2nd century, settling on the plains west of the Caspian Sea. Here they created what is known as the Old Bulgarian Kingdom.

Bulgars took part in the Hun raids on Central and Western Europe in around 400 and fought against the Ostrogoths as allies of Byzantium. In the middle of the 6th century, war broke out between the two main Bulgar tribes, the Kutrigur and Utigur. The Kutrigur, led by a leader called Kubrat, who called himself a *khan* (king), won the power struggle.

appear to have pursued a policy of enlightened rule, actively assimilating the two peoples.

Although the state was ruled by the khan, whose title was hereditary, the Slav princes retained much of the autonomy they had enjoyed under Byzantium, paying annual tribute to the khan. The Bulgarian nobility adopted the Slavic language and practices, and encouraged their subjects to do likewise. There was much intermarriage and interbreeding between the Bulgars and the Slavs, and as early as 750 it can be said that the direct ancestors of the modern Bulgarian nation had been formed.

In 679 Kubrat's youngest son, Khan Asparuh, moved the entire tribe (around 250,000) westward, defeating a Byzantine army near Balchik on the Black Sea coast in 680. He then conquered Moesia and part of Thrace, territories that were recognised as an independent state under a treaty signed with Constantine IV Pogonatus in 681. The state was called the Parvo Bulgarsko Tsarstvo (the First Bulgarian Kingdom), and the capital was at Pliska (see page 216).

The First Bulgarian Kingdom

Though the Bulgars were in the ascendancy, the vast majority of the new state's population was Slav. Eager not to foment revolt, the Bulgars

External enemies

While interior consolidation was therefore relatively easy, defending the exterior boundaries of Bulgaria proved increasingly difficult. Bulgaria fought with Byzantine forces against invading Arabs in 717, assisting in their defeat at Constantinople. However, with the Arab threat temporarily subdued, the belligerent and iconoclastic Leo III (reigning 717–741) set about recovering lost Byzantine territory in the west.

Though Leo III never attacked Bulgaria, his successor, Constantine V, did, in 756. There were no territorial gains, however, and the attacks served only to convince the Bulgarians that they needed to expand their kingdom. Allying themselves with the Franks of Charlemagne, they first kicked the Avars out of central Europe, occupying much of southern Romania before heading south and southeast at the beginning of the 9th century. Under Khan Krum (reigning 803–14) they reached the gates of Constantinople in 813 before withdrawing to Adrianople.

Krum's successor, Omurtag (reigning 814-831), spread the Bulgarain wars of expansion far and wide, attacking even his erstwhile allies, the Franks. Pannonia (much of modern-day Hungary) and Macedonia were conquered in 829, their absorption into Bulgaria recognised de jure in the Treaty of Pannonia (831), which restored peace between the Bulgarians and the Franks. Omurtag also acted to reduce the influence of the remaining Slav princes, reorganising the entire country and abolishing the old principalities.

Consolidating Christianity

Though much of Bulgaria – as part of the Roman Empire when Constantine made Christianity a state religion – had taken to the Christian faith early, the subjects of the Bulgarian Kingdom worshipped a panoply of gods and held innumerable belief systems as late as the mid 9th century. Such religious pluralism was anathema to the khans' wish to consolidate power, and so a great effort was made to convert the population to Christianity en bloc.

Khan Boris I ascended to the Bulgarian throne in 852 and began petitioning the Byzantine Emperor Michael III to appoint a Bulgarian patriarch. Michael never complied, but his successor, Basil the Macedonian, in agreement with Pope Adrian II, created a Bulgarian archbishopric at the Fourth Ecumenical Council of Constantinople, in 870. The archbishopric was placed under the jurisdiction of the Patriarch of Constantinople and had its seat at Pliska; its diocese covered the whole of the Bulgarian state.

Boris I had already – in 863 – declared Christianity the state religion, and had begun a fierce campaign of conversion. Pagan gods were outlawed, and the liturgy was conducted solely in Greek. The problem was that many Bulgarians did not speak Greek, and even those who did could certainly not read it. The need to create a

Slavonic liturgy therefore became acute, and to the rescue rode two Bulgarian monks: the brothers Cyril and Methodius *(see box below)*.

Simeon the Great

Armed with the Cyrillic alphabet the greatest of all the early Bulgarian leaders, Simeon the Great (reigning 893–927), further expanded the Bulgarian kingdom, creating the largest empire on the continent. At its zenith, around 920, Bulgarian territory stretched from Greece to Ukraine, and from the Black Sea to the Adriatic.

Simeon's first act upon taking the throne was to move the capital of Bulgaria from Pliska to

LEFT: the court of Tsar Simeon of Bulgaria.
RIGHT: portrait of Sebastocrator Kaloyan, the 13th-century ruler of the Bulgarian state, and his wife Desislava, patrons of Boyana church, near Sofia.

Preslav. The Slav nobles of Pliska had organised a pagan revolt in 892, and Simeon sought protection in the Christian environs of Preslav.

Simeon had been schooled in Constantinople and was the first Bulgarian leader to be brought up a Christian. He knew well the value

of a good education and used the newly created Cyrillic alphabet as a means of uniting the Slavs who were incorporated into his empire. Something of a prototype Renaissance man, he patronised the arts, ordering the translation into Slavonic of every Greek classic, and the writing down of Old Bulgarian and Slavic oral histories. He created the Preslav Writing School in 896 and Slavonic quickly became the third great body of literature in the world, exceeded only by Greek and Latin. The capital also became a centre of icon painting, and Simeon oversaw a prolonged period of church and monastery building.

He was also careful not to neglect his armed forces, for despite the monicker of Simeon the

Peaceful (of which he apparently encouraged the use), Simeon harboured dreams of being crowned Byzantine Emperor, and in 913 invaded Thrace, the first of his territorial gains. He marched unopposed to the gates of Constantinople, where he demanded to be named Emperor. The patriarch, however, convinced him to settle for the title "Emperor of the Bulgarians and Romans", and despite further military success against the Serbs, Croats and Byzantium, his ambition remained unfulfilled.

Though a heavy defeat in 926 against the Croats of King Tomislav in Bosnia marked the end of Simeon's expansionist wars and resulted in the loss of the far western part of his empire, Bulgaria survived Simeon's death in 929, and the succession of his son, Peter, heralded a 40-year period of relative peace and much prosperity. By the time of Peter's death in 969 however, the pendulum had swung back in favour of Byzantium, resurgent under Basil II.

The Byzantine Wars

The Byzantine Wars marked the bitter and rather rapid end of the First Bulgarian Kingdom. Bulgaria was turned into a battleground upon which two foreign powers, the Kyivan Rus and the Byzantine Empire, fought a long and protracted war for Balkan supremacy. The Bulgarians, caught in the middle, attempted to play one power off against the other, but the poor diplomatic skills of the young King Boris meant they instead found themselves as little more than whipping boys.

By 1004 Byzantine forces had taken land as far east as Skopje in Macedonia. But it took another decade, and one of history's greatest battles, the Battle of Klieidon (Belashtitsa, 1014), before all of Bulgaria would fall under Byzantine control.

The Byzantines ruled Bulgaria for the next two centuries. Though it initially resisted, the Bulgarian nobility eventually withdrew its objections to Byzantine rule in exchange for titles and guarantees of security. There were revolts – not least one launched by Peter II in 1040, designed to take advantage of the death of Basil II – but none succeeded in recovering more than token pieces of Bulgarian territory.

The Byzantines ruled Bulgaria benignly, viewing its peasantry as good Christian stock fit to fight the growing Turkish menace in the east. The most repressive measures were taken against those members of the Bulgarian Church who refused to recognise the authority of the Constantinople Patriarch. By the time of the Great Schism between Rome and Constantinople in 1054, however, all of Bulgaria's clergy had sworn allegiance to the Eastern Church.

Second Bulgarian Kingdom

After the death of John II Komnenos (John the Good (reigning 1118-43), considered one of the finest Byzantine rulers, Byzantium quickly fell into chaos. The folly of Manuel Komnenos, fourth son and chosen heir of John the Good, who launched pointless wars against Hungary and Serbia, allied to the anarchy caused by the Crusaders, meant that by 1180s the empire faced bankruptcy and annihilation. After more than half of the Byzantine army was killed by the Turks in Asia Minor, in 1176, Bulgarian nobles sensed that the time was again ripe for rebellion.

Cleverly, however, the two brothers credited with leading the successful Bulgarian rebellion of 1185–6, Peter and Assen, did not at first overplay their hand. They repeatedly appealed to Constantinople for land privileges, which were sometimes granted, and sometimes not. After one such rejection, early in 1185, Peter and Assen went in person to see the Byzantine Emperor, by now Isaac Angelos, to plead their case. After Angelos allegedly slapped Peter across the face for his impertinence, the brothers returned to Bulgaria to prepare for war.

Mustering support amongst the peasantry – who were fed up with high taxation and Byzantine conscription – the brothers attacked the seat of Byzantine power in Bulgaria, Preslav, which quickly fell. By the spring of 1186 most of present-day Bulgaria was back in Bulgarian hands. Peter had been crowned King of Bulgaria late in 1185, at Veliko Tarnovo, the capital of the new Bulgarian Kingdom. Ill health forced him to abdicate in 1189, however, and Assen, regarded as the most powerful of the brothers, was crowned king. He took the name Ivan Assen, and spent the rest of his reign restoring the Bulgarian Kingdom. He defeated the Serbs in 1195, occupying Belgrade, before dying in 1196.

The early achievements of the nascent Assen

LEFT: a Russian force, hired by the Byzantine emperor, defeats the Bulgarian army in 968.
RIGHT: statue of Ivan Assen at Veliko Tarnovo, the new capital of the Second Bulgarian Kingdom.

NATIONAL HEROES

The nationality of the Assen brothers is disputed: Romanians claim that the brothers were Vlachs (Romanians), as they probably came from the Wallachian Plain north of the Danube. Bulgarian historians usually accept that the brothers originated from Wallachia, but then insist that they were strictly of Bulgarian descent.

Dynasty was compounded by Ivan Assen's son, Kaloyan, who further restored Bulgaria, recapturing Varna in 1204, the year the Crusaders took Constantinople and declared their Holy Eastern Empire. Kaloyan then set about the

Crusaders and defeated them – the first leader to do so – close to Adrianople in 1205. Crusader Emperor Baldwin I was captured and killed by Kaloyan's forces, earning him the nickname John the Dog among his opponents.

Sadly for Kaloyan, he was murdered in a palace coup while besieging Thessaloniki in 1207, and replaced by his nephew Boril, who misruled for 11 years before being overthrown by Ivan Assen II (son of Ivan Assen I), who had been in exile in Constantinople.

Assen II was to the Second Bulgarian Kingdom what Simeon had been to the First. During a glorious reign of 23 years he restored Bulgaria to its size under Simeon, restored the Bulgarian patriarchate, modernised commerce and

EASTERN INSPIRATION

It is often argued that the National Revival was a manifestation of Bulgarian integration into and not out of the Ottoman Empire. The eastern, Moorish influences and squiggles that characterise the architecture of the period are evidence to support this theory.

introduced gold coinage, and kept court politics peaceful. He also managed to placate the Catholic Church through a number of nominal but diplomatic alliances with key Catholic kings.

Though the Assens ruled Bulgaria until 1396, the death of Ivan Assen II marked the Second

sader support, failed. Known as the Ottoman Yoke, Turkish occupation would last for the best part of 500 years.

The list of atrocities committed by the Turks during the Yoke is a long one, though most occurred in the early days of Turkish domination. At least half the Bulgarian population was killed or left to starve in the first 50 years after the conquest, and many of those that survived were forced to convert to Islam. Arabic replaced Bulgarian as the language at court, and Greek became the language of the Church, at once disenfranchising many of the Bulgarian faithful.

The Ottomans named the Bulgarian territories

Kingdom's zenith. The Mongols devastated most of the Balkans in 1242, Bulgaria included, and by the 1250s the country had been reduced to a small rump of land around Veliko Tarnovo.

A mini-revival under Ivan Alexander (reigning 1331–371) restored Bulgaria to something approaching its present borders, but the imminent expansion westwards of the Ottomans meant the kingdom was ultimately doomed.

The Ottoman Yoke

It was the notorious Serb defeat at Kosovo Polje in 1389 that tolled death for the Balkans. In 1393 Veliko Tarnovo was captured by the Turks, and the Battle of Nicopolis, a last-ditch attempt to push back the Ottomans with Cru-

the Beyerlik of Rumili, ruled by a *beylerbey* (governor) from Sofia. The Beyerlik was sub-divided into several sanjaks, each ruled by a *sanjakbey* accountable to the *beylerbey*. Most of the Bulgarian lands became the private possessions of the sultan or of the Ottoman nobility, called *mülk*. The Bulgarians were squeezed for every penny, paying taxes not just on things such as land and livestock, but also on weddings and funerals. As Muslims paid lower tax rates, some Bulgarians converted to Islam.

Occasionally, the pips were squeezed too hard, and the Bulgarians revolted. There were uprisings at Veliko Tarnovo in 1598 and 1686, for instance, but they never succeeded in bringing about anything resembling real change.

The National Revival

It was the dominance of Greek priests, appointed by Turkey to oversee the Bulgarian Church, that galvanised a number of Bulgarian intellectuals into ensuring the Bulgarian language and history survived, though many, such as Bogdan Bakshev, were forced to publish their works outside of Bulgaria. Bakshev's *History of Bulgaria* caused a furore when published, as did Pasius of Hilendar's *History of the Slav-Bulgarians*.

Both writers contributed to the Bulgarian renaissance – the National Revival – and were to inspire many a revolutionary. Economics also played its part, as an increasing number of Bul-

garian Revolutionary Committee (BRCK) in Bucharest in 1869 (in 1859 Romania had rid itself of the Turks with Russian help) was the first time that Bulgarian nationalists managed to unite under one group and one leader, Vasil Levski (1837–73). Levski had been influenced by George Rakovski (1821–67), a writer turned revolutionary credited with being the first to politicise the goals of the Revival movement, in his 1861 pamphlet, *Plan for the Liberation of Bulgaria*.

Levski did not live to see Bulgarian independence, but his capture and execution by the Turks in 1873 was the catalyst for it. The inde-

garians were able to travel and trade in areas not dominated by Turkey, returning with new liberal ideas that were anathema to the Porte.

If Hilendar's *History* (published in 1792) marked the birth of the National Revival, it came of age after the Greek revolt against the Turkish Empire of 1821. The increased freedom that the Turks allowed their subjects gave wind to a renaissance of architecture and art.

While Bulgarian independence may not have been a goal of the Revival movement, it was a product of it. The creation of the Bul-

LEFT: the Battle of Nicopolis in 1396 marked the beginning of the Ottoman Yoke.
ABOVE: the Treaty of Stefano, 1878, marked its end.

pendence movement now had a martyr, which boosted its support. In April 1876 it was ready to launch a full-scale uprising against the Turks.

Known as the April Rising, the rebellion against the Turks was a military disaster but a public relations coup for the BRCK. More than 30,000 rebels died, mostly in awful revenge attacks by the Turks.

It was this huge loss of life that provoked the great powers into action. Russia, with its own anti-Turkish agenda, declared war on Turkey in 1877, and after a year of heavy fighting, the Ottoman Empire was thrown out of Bulgaria, and forced to sign the humiliating San Stefano Peace Treaty. On 3 March 1878, Bulgaria declared independence. ❑

BULGARIA SINCE INDEPENDENCE

After finally casting off the shackles of the Ottoman Empire, Bulgaria
tasted freedom for the first time in 500 years. But this didn't last
long. It was soon playing second fiddle to Germany in two
world wars and then became a satellite of the Soviet Union

N o sooner had the ink dried on the Treaty of
San Stefano than four of the Great Powers
were conniving in its undoing. The problem was Russia, and its apparent hold over the
Bulgarian elite, both secular and religious. Not
without reason therefore, Britain, France, Germany and Austria-Hungary felt that a large and
independent Bulgaria would be a powerful
vassal for Russian influence in the Balkans.

At the infamous Congress of Berlin, July
1878, the British Prime Minister, the newly
ennobled Earl of Beaconsfield, Benjamin Disraeli, and German Chancellor Otto von Bismarck personally supervised the drawing up of
a new treaty. While recognising the complete
independence of Romania, Serbia and Montenegro, the treaty clipped the new Bulgarian
state's wings, reversing much of the San Stefano Treaty. Macedonia was returned to Turkey,
while the rest of the country was divided into
two provinces: the Principality of Bulgaria in
the north and west, and Eastern Rumelia in the
south and east. While notionally independent,
both of these provinces would still be required
to pay annual tribute to the Sublime Porte.

Search for two rulers

The Principality of Bulgaria, though encom-
passing Sofia, was at first still ruled from the
old Bulgarian capital at Veliko Tarnovo. The
head of state was to be a foreign prince chosen
by an assembly of Bulgarian nobles, though at
the express request of Bismarck, Russian
princes were discounted. In trawling Europe for
a monarch considered decent, the Bulgarian
assembly chose Alexander Battenberg, a German, the son of Prince Alexander of Hesse's
marriage to a commoner (a fact which had dis-
qualified him from inheriting any of his father's
titles). Alexander was chosen primarily for his
youth (he was 22 when elected *knyaz*, or
prince), though the Bulgarian politicians who
chose him also admired his pro-Russian stance
on European affairs. Alexander was a frequent
visitor to St Petersburg, and was well liked by
the Russian Tsar, Alexander II, his uncle.

Eastern Rumelia was ruled by a Governor
General – who under the terms of the treaty had
to be a Christian – appointed by the Turks. They
chose Alexander Stefanov Bogoridi, a liberal
Turkish politician of Bulgarian descent.
Bogoridi had been born and educated in Constantinople, and had played a leading role in
the creation of the Ottoman Empire's first con-

stitutional government in 1876; he was thought trustworthy by Sultan Abdul Hamid II.

Unification

The first Bulgarian constitution of 1879 was a model of liberalism and tolerance, which allowed for generous suffrage, and strictly limited the actual powers of the prince. Most authority rested with the General Assembly, now moved to Sofia, which was dominated by the Liberal Party of Stefan Stambolov, a former leading member of the BRCK. Alexander, however, quickly fell out with Stambolov, and grew unhappy with his limited authority. In

rid himself of his Russian advisors by hastily restoring the old constitution in 1883. Though the shock tactics worked, the Russians retaliated by withdrawing all of their military personnel, leaving the Bulgarian army fragile and rudderless. Nevertheless, though Serbia invaded Bulgaria in 1885 in an attempt to take advantage of these weaknesses, Alexander personally led the army to a surprisingly crushing victory at Slivnitsa.

By then, the two halves of Bulgaria had been unified. That had happened in September 1885, when a coup in Plovdiv, the capital of Eastern Rumelia, had deposed the Governor General,

1881, ostensibly to head off a minor parliamentary crisis between the Liberals and opposition Radicals, Alexander annulled the constitution and declared himself absolute ruler. Russian generals arrived to advise Alexander; the lower ranks of the army had long been dominated by Russian officers.

Alas for Alexander the Russians were less than discreet and undermined any remaining sympathy he held in the eyes of the Bulgarian public. Realising his error, and that he was somewhat out of his depth, the prince tried to

LEFT: the 1868 Congress of Berlin reorganised the Balkan states. **ABOVE:** Prince Alexander signs his abdication in the Palace in Sofia.

Gabriel Krstevic. Though Turkey opposed unification, it was powerless to prevent it.

The main opponents to the unification were in fact the Russians, who feared that their waning influence over the prince would now be entirely eradicated. As a result they organised his dethroning: in August 1886 they persuaded pro-Russian officers to seize him in his palace and bring him to St Petersburg. The Russians then installed a puppet government, which did not see out the year: Stefan Stambolov organised a coalition of the democratic political parties and with the help of non-Russian partisans in the army managed to oust the Russian regime. Stambolov immediately brought Alexander back to Bulgaria, but fierce Russian opposition persuaded the prince that it would be wise to abdicate once and for all. He did so and retired, at the age of 29, to Austria, where he died under mysterious circumstances four years later.

The Balkan Wars

Unified but headless, Bulgaria in 1887 was a country once again searching Europe for a suitable head of state. The Bulgarians – led by king-maker Stambolov – this time plumped for the Austrian prince, Ferdinand Saxe-Coburg-Gotha. Though young, Ferdinand had spent much time at court and was considered a natural politician. He worked well with Stambolov and the other

Independence Day, while 3 March 1878, is celebrated as Liberation Day.

Having finally rid itself of the Turks, Bulgaria now wanted to kick the Turks out of the rest of the Balkans. Macedonia for example – claimed by Bulgaria, Serbia and Greece – was still under the direct rule of the sultan. In 1912 Bulgaria made secret alliances with Serbia, Montenegro and Greece, and the three allies attacked Turkey in October, starting what has become known as the First Balkan War. The war-weary and demoralised Turkish Army was crushed almost immediately, and by early 1913 the allies threatened even Istanbul. Anxious to

main politicians, generally respected the constitution and was adored by the military. Though Stambolov was assassinated in 1895 after a quarrel with the prince, it is considered unlikely that Ferdinand played any role in the assassination. Russia, which had always detested Stambolov, remains the likely culprit.

Though Bulgaria was now unified and a de facto an independent country, Ferdinand was keen to make Bulgaria's status de jure, something he achieved on 22 September 1908 when he declared Bulgaria to be entirely independent of the Ottoman Empire, and himself as Tsar of Bulgaria. Under pressure from the other Great Powers, Turkey immediately recognised the new state. Bulgarians commemorate the day as

avoid the complete collapse of their empire, the Turks sued for peace in March and agreed to hand over almost all of their European territories: they were left with the rump around Istanbul that closely relates to modern European Turkey.

Having suffered the greatest casualties, Bulgaria demanded that Macedonia be awarded to it: Serbia and Greece refused, so in June Bulgaria declared war on its erstwhile allies (known as the Second Balkan War). The war started well for Bulgaria, but after Romania and the Turks speculatively attacked it in July 1913, it all went badly very quickly. A peace treaty was signed in Bucharest in August: Macedonia was retained by Serbia, Adrianople went back to Turkey, and the southern Dobrudja was lost to Romania.

World War I and after

At the outbreak of World War I the majority of the Bulgarian population sided with Russia and its allies. Its government, however, led by Vasil Radoslavov, was a sworn enemy of Serbia, Russia's ally, and having been swayed by German promises of Macedonia in the post-war carve up, decided to back the Axis powers. The result was carnage, and defeat in September 1918, after which deserting soldiers attempted a coup, which though unsuccessful, forced Ferdinand to abdicate in favour of his son, Boris III. In the aftermath of the war, Bulgaria lost more territory, along its Aegean coastline, to Greece.

Macedonian nationalists in the guise of the Macedonian Revolutionary Organisation (IMRO) were a thorn in Bulgaria's side throughout the early 1920s. Refugees from – and opposed to – the newly created Yugoslavia (which included Macedonia), IMRO were opposed to the prime minister Alexander Stamboliski *(see box)*, some suggesting that he even wanted to take Bulgaria into Yugoslavia. In alliance with military officers who also opposed Stamboliski, IMRO staged a coup in 1923, killing Stamboliski and creating a right-wing coalition called the Democratic Accord, with Boris still nominally the head of state. Alexander Tsankov served as prime minster. The immediate aftermath of the coup saw something resembling a White Terror, in which many supporters of Stamboliski, his now banned Agrarian Party and the Communists were killed.

The 1920s were marked by terrorism, including two attempts on the Tsar's life, and the infamous bombing of St Nedelya church in Sofia in April 1925, which killed General Konstantin Georgiev *(see page 81)*. By 1931 the King had had enough, and forced Tsankov to resign. The moderate Andrei Lipachov took over. The Agrarian Party was brought back into mainstream politics, though the Communists remained outlawed. A relatively democratic election later in the year comfortably confirmed the return of the Agrarians to power.

Alas for the Agrarians, and for Bulgaria, the global depression that followed the Wall Street Crash of 1929 meant that the soft loans which had propped up the Bulgarian economy

throughout the 1920s were called in. Living standards plummeted, and in November 1934 Boris decided he had had enough of politicians and created an absolute monarchy. All political parties were banned, and Boris was increasingly attracted to Fascist Italy and, especially, Nazi Germany. Economic ties between the countries were developed, but Boris repeatedly managed to resist calls to tie his foreign policy to that of his new allies.

World War II

At the outbreak of World War II, Boris ostentatiously declared Bulgaria's strict neutrality.

The dominant politician in the years following World War I was Alexander Stamboliski, the liberal leader of the Agrarian Party who had been imprisoned during the war for his opposition to both the war and Tsar Ferdinand. As prime minister, working with King Boris (who was incidentally the first Orthodox Bulgarian monarch since the Middle Ages), Stamboliski became the champion of Bulgaria's large peasant population. He pursued a modernising agenda, which included land reform, reduction in the size of the army and reaching a compromise with the newly created Yugoslavia over the status of Macedonia. He was assassinated in a right-wing coup in 1923.

FAR LEFT: the Bulgarians bombard the Turkish city of Adrianople (now Erdine). **LEFT:** Tsar Ferdinand.
RIGHT: cartoon depicting Bulgaria's relationship with Germany in World War I.

RUSSIAN SYMPATHIES

While Bulgaria had declared war on the United Kingdom and the United States in December 1941, King Boris still refused to get involved in the war against the Soviet Union, invoking his people's overwhelming sympathy for Russia.

He had recently concluded an agreement with Yugoslavia over Macedonia (all but renouncing his claim to that disputed territory) and was keen not to be forced into war. However, after a Hitler diktat known as the Vienna Award of 1940 restored Bulgarian sovereignty over southern Dobrudja, Bulgaria sent troops to occupy the

area. Tempted also by German promises of Macedonia, Bulgaria officially sided with Germany and the Axis Powers in April 1941.

In effect, however, the country picked its battles: it sent troops to occupy Macedonia and took part in the invasion of Greece, but refused to send forces to the Russian front. So angry was Hitler that he summoned Boris to Berlin in August 1943 to protest against his failure to commit forces to the eastern front.

Boris died of apparent heart failure shortly after returning to Sofia, and his death has been the subject of myth and legend ever since. Many claim that Hitler had him poisoned; others allege he was the victim of Communist assassins. He was replaced as king by his six-

year-old-son Simeon, but real power resided in the hands of the regent, Prince Kiril, the young king's vehemently pro-German uncle.

By spring 1944, with the war inexorably going the way of the Western Allies, Bulgaria's politicians were desperate to ditch the Nazis. In the end Bulgaria followed Romania's lead: it unilaterally withdrew from the war on 26 August 1944. The withdrawal was not recognised by the Soviet Union, however, which declared war on Bulgaria on 5 September. Anxious not to incur pointless loss of life, Bulgaria allowed the Red Army to occupy the country unopposed, three days later.

Communist accession

With the Red Army in control of the country it was impossible for Bulgaria to avoid a Communist takeover after the war. The gradual Communist accession to power followed the classic model used all over Eastern Europe: the Communists were at first minor partners in a broad coalition, then majority partners, then absolute rulers. In a rigged referendum in September 1946 the monarchy was abolished and many of its supporters arrested. The king was taken into exile in Switzerland by his mother.

The Communists who now controlled Bulgaria were made up primarily of those who had fled to Moscow in the 1920s. They were led by Georgi Dimitrov, who as leader of the Comintern during the purges of the 1930s had a lot of blood on his hands. Elected in a mockery of an election as prime minister in November 1946, Dimitrov immediately had a Communist Party-dominated parliament rubber-stamp a new constitution based on that of the Soviet Union, which created the People's Republic of Bulgaria. All political parties except the Communists and Agrarians were banned; in 1947 even the Agrarians were outlawed and their leaders arrested.

Dimitrov died in 1949 and was replaced by Valko Chervenkov, who continued Dimitrov's work by eradicating all opponents (most of whom perished in the death camps of Belene, on the Danube). Chervenkov fell out of favour with Moscow after Stalin's death in 1953, however, and was replaced by Todor Zhivkov, who remained Bulgaria's absolute ruler until 1989.

Zhivkov's legacy

Zhivkov's period in office is marked by little except utter Bulgarian subservience to the Soviet Union, and economic stagnation. In foreign policy he was an active member of the Warsaw Pact, fully supporting the repression of the Hungarian and Czech revolutions of 1956 and 1968 respectively. Domestically, however, he was less of a Stalinist that Dimitrov or Chervenkov. He closed the labour camps his predecessors had set up, and rehabilitated a number of executed former liberal politicians.

Economically the country was misruled, however. Though there was never anything like the rationing that had to be introduced in neighbouring Romania, consumer goods were always in short supply, and there were occasional shortages of many basic foodstuffs.

ENJOYING THE GOOD LIFE

While his people endured hardships Todor Zhivkov revelled in the good life. His excesses are legendary: the luxurious modernist palace he built for himself in the Sofia suburb of Boyana is now open to the public as the National History Museum *(see page 97)*.

Unsurprisingly – given it retained a monopoly on state-controlled media – the Communists (renamed the Socialist Party) won Bulgaria's first post-Communist elections, held in June 1990. Since then governments of left and right have traded office, with no party managing to retain power for more than a single term. Yet given the

The return to democracy

When it came, the end was swift. Though 1989, Eastern Europe's year of revolutions, looked at first to have passed Bulgaria by, Zhivkov was finally undone by reformers inside the Communist Party, who on 10 November arrested him on charges of embezzlement and fraud. The reformers, who had overseen small but significant changes in Bulgaria's economy since the mid-1980s, elected Peter Mladenov as the new head of the Communist Party's Central Committee.

LEFT: a labour brigade awaits orders in the 1950s.
ABOVE: pro-democracy demonstrators in 1989.
RIGHT: Simeon Saxe-Coburg-Gotha, once Bulgaria's child monarch, now prime minister.

problems that the country has had switching from a planned to a market economy, it is remarkable that it has remained politically stable: each handover of power has been peaceful.

In 2001 the National Movement Party of Simeon Saxe-Coburg-Gotha – the same Simeon who as a boy was briefly king in the 1940s – was elected on a centre-right ticket with a mandate to enact drastic reform. It did so, but social pressure saw the party lose ground to the Socialists in 2005. With no party able to create a working majority, the two agreed to form a Grand Coalition to see Bulgaria through the final stages of its accession to the European Union. On 1 January, 2007, Bulgaria – despite reservations in Brussels – was admitted to the EU. ❑

Decisive Dates

THRACIAN AND ROMAN ERA

Circa 2500–1000 BC Thracian tribes establish a civilisation in the southeast of the Balkan peninsula.

600–400 BC Thrace is heavily colonised by Greek settlers and traders. In 450 BC the first recognised Thracian state emerges with Teres I as its king.

346 BC Philip of Macedonia conquers Thrace.

168 BC Macedonia loses its grip on Thrace, as the Macedonian-Roman wars rage around it.

73–72 BC Thracian slave Spartacus leads the Third Servile Revolt against Rome

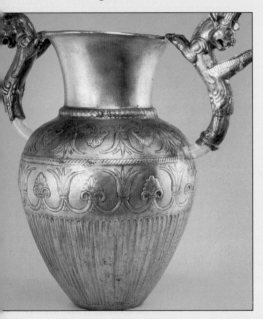

AD 46 Thrace incorporated into the Roman Empire as three provinces: Dacia, Moesia and Thracia.

MIGRATION PERIOD

Circa 400 Rome's grip on Thracia and Moesia diminishes in the wake of Germanic attacks.

Circa 500 Slavic tribes first begin to settle Thracia and Moesia (comprising most of modern Bulgaria).

527 Emperor Justinian I restores imperial Byzantine rule.

Circa 635 Khan Kubrat unites two warring Bulgar tribes in their Caspian homeland.

679 The Asiatic Bulgars leave their Caspian homeland and invade Moesia. In 681, after striking a peace deal with Byzantium, Khan Asparuh establishes the first Bulgarian kingdom.

FIRST BULGARIAN KINGDOM

813 Khan Krum attacks Byzantium, reaching Constantinople before withdrawing to Adrianople.

863 Christianity becomes the official religion.

920 The kingdom reaches its zenith under Simeon the Great.

969 Russians invade Bulgaria, but are driven back in 976 by the Byzantines. By 1018 Bulgaria is part of the resurgent Byzantine Empire led by Basil II.

MEDIEVAL BULGARIA

1185 After a successful revolt against Byzantium the kingdom is re-established in 1185 under the Assen Dynasty. It remains an important power in the region for 150 years.

1330 Bulgaria is defeated by the Serbs. Large parts of the kingdom come under Serb rule.

1370 Under Ivan IV Serb rule is ended, but Bulgaria is left divided into rival states; the two largest and most powerful are based at Veliko Turnovo and Vidin.

OTTOMAN BULGARIA

1389 The Ottoman Turks invade Bulgaria. In 1396 it becomes part of the Ottoman Empire.

1400s Christians are made subordinate to Muslims. Many Bulgarians choose to convert to retain property rights.

1767 The Bulgarian Patriarchate is abolished; the Bulgarian Church falls under the command of the Patriarch of Constantinople.

NATIONAL REVIVAL PERIOD

1830s A revolutionary movement for independence grows around Bulgarian intellectuals influenced by the Greek revolt against the Turks of 1821.

1870 The Bulgarian Patriarchate is re-established.

1873 Influential revolutionary leader Vasil Levski is executed by the Ottoman authorities.

1876 The largest ever revolt against Ottoman rule, the April Rising, fails. Some 15,000 Bulgarians are killed in Turkish reprisals.

1877 Russia invades the Balkans ostensibly to protect Bulgarian Christians, marking the start of the Russo-Turkish War.

1878 After several Turkish defeats. Russia occupies much of Bulgaria. At the Treaty of San Stefano the Turks agree to independence for Romania, Serbia and Montenegro, and autonomy for Bulgaria. Two autonomous principalities: Bulgaria and Eastern Rumelia are established within the Ottoman Empire.

1885 Eastern Rumelia (the south of present-day Bulgaria) is incorporated into the autonomous principality of Bulgaria. The Serbo-Bulgarian War begins when Serbia opposes what it terms the annexation of Rumelia. Serbia is defeated in 1886.

1908 Under pressure from all of the Great Powers, Turkey finally awards full independence to Bulgaria. The Kingdom of Bulgaria is established with Ferdinand of Saxe-Coburg declared tsar.

THE 20TH CENTURY

1912 Bulgaria makes alliances with Serbia, Greece and Montenegro. In October Montenegro declares war on the Ottoman Empire, starting the First Balkan War.

1913 After the Ottoman fortress of Adrianople falls to Bulgarian forces, a peace treaty divides the remnants of the Ottoman Empire among the victors. Macedonia remains occupied by Bulgaria despite Serb and Greek claims to it. In July Serbia and Greece declare war on Bulgaria, starting the Second Balkan War. In August Macedonia is partitioned into three parts, shared by Bulgaria, Serbia and Greece.

1915 Bulgaria declares war on Serbia, entering World War I on the side of Germany.

1916 Bulgaria switches from the Julian to the Gregorian calendar.

1918 Bulgaria surrenders to the Allies after the Serbs, British, French and Greeks break through on the Macedonian front.

1919 Under the Treaty of Neuilly Bulgaria loses its Aegean territories to Greece, the Dobrudja to Romania and most of its Macedonian territory to the new state of Yugoslavia.

1920 The Agrarian Party, which had opposed the war, forms the first genuinely democratic government.

1923 A military coup backed by the tsar deposes the Agrarian government.

1931 Losing faith in the military, the tsar restores democratic rule. The Agrarians win free elections.

1934 An authoritarian regime headed by Kimon Georgiev is established with the backing of Tsar Boris. It lasts less than a year before Boris appoints a government of "national regeneration", little more than a royal dictatorship.

1939 Bulgaria declares strict neutrality at the outbreak of World War II.

1941 Bulgaria signs the Axis Tripartite Pact, and German forces invade Greece and Yugoslavia from Bulgarian bases; Bulgaria declares war on Greece and Yugoslavia, and occupies Macedonia and

Aegean Thrace. In December Bulgaria declares war on Britain and the US.

1944 Bulgaria declares itself neutral in the conflict, but this is not recognised by the Allied Powers. In September the USSR occupies Bulgaria.

1945 Control of Macedonia is transferred to Yugoslavia, while Thrace is awarded to Greece and southern Dobrudja to Romania.

1946 Elections are held under the supervision of the Soviet army. The Communist Party wins.

1947 The People's Republic of Bulgaria is established, led by Georgi Dimitrov.

1949 Dimitrov dies and is replaced by ultra-Stalinist Vulko Chervenkov.

1954 Todor Zhivkov ousts Chervenkov. Under his rule Bulgaria is regarded as the Soviet Union's most loyal eastern European satellite.

1980 Zhivkov launches a "Bulgarianisation" campaign, forcing the country's ethnic Turks to change their names to sound more Bulgarian.

1989 The Communist Party votes itself out of office. Zhivkov is placed under house arrest but lives on – in great comfort – until 1998. The Social Democratic Party (the renamed Communist Party) wins the first post-Communist election.

1991 Bulgaria elects its first non-Communist government.

2001 Simeon Saxe-Coburg wins elections.

2004 Bulgaria joins NATO.

2007 Bulgaria joins the European Union. ❏

LEFT: Thracian silver vase from the 5th century BC.
RIGHT: the Soviet liberation of Sofia in 1944.

THE BULGARIANS

Fiercely proud of their rich history and culture,
yet keen to put their past behind them, the
Bulgarians are full of contradictions

The term "Bulgarian" dates back to the Asian Turkic tribes who settled in the eastern part of the Balkan Peninsula during the 7th century. The Bulgarian nation is also made up of Armenians (concentrated in the cities), Tartars (who migrated from the Crimea to the Dobrudja area), Greeks (found mostly in the south, near the Greek border) and a myriad of small minority groups. Bulgarian people are essentially Slav and therefore close relatives of the Serbs, Croats and Slovenians, but they are Balkan too, sharing many common traditions with the Greeks, Romanians and Turks.

Neighbourly interference

In some ways the national consciousness has been whittled away on all sides. Many of the country's powerful neighbours have shaped the country's culture, but it is the Turks who have had most influence. Over five centuries of Ottoman occupation, thousands of Bulgarians converted to Islam, some forcibly, others by choice. Many were promising young men who were groomed to be civil servants in the Ottoman Empire. Other Bulgarian converts to Islam became known as Pomaks, as they are today. You will find Pomak villages all over Bulgaria, especially in the Rhodopes and the northwest.

By the 17th century, the Ottoman Empire was on the wane, and Bulgarians began to return to the towns, bringing with them the religious and cultural identity that had survived in the remote parts of Bulgaria ignored by the occupiers. Trade along the Danube

increased, and western social and political ideas gained a toe-hold, but by the mid-1800s Turks still outnumbered Bulgarians.

When a Bulgarian revolt in 1876 was brutally suppressed by the Turks, Bulgaria attracted great sympathy in Europe. Russia, sharing Bulgaria's Slavic roots and looking to expand its own influence, declared war on the Muslim occupiers, and as a result the tide turned. Within five years, some 500,000 Turks had fled Bulgaria, and a further quarter of a million were dead. It was a death knell for Ottoman rule, but it also marked the beginning of increased interference from the Great Powers of Europe, which went on to dominate Bulgaria for most of the 20th century *(see history, page 31)*.

PRECEDING PAGES: shady tryst in Stara Zagora.
LEFT: hanging out in Pleven.
RIGHT: national pride is engendered at a young age.

Bulgaria's great dictator

Todor Zhivkov ruled Bulgaria for 35 long years from 1954 to 1989. A Communist dictator in the mould of Khrushchev and Brezhnev, he introduced many limitations on the individual freedoms of Bulgarians, but particularly minorities. Turks and other Muslims were denied the right to use their own names, speak their language in public or even wear traditional clothes. Zhivkov went so far as to claim there were no Turks in Bulgaria, when international estimates put their number at over one million. Many ethnic Turks fled to Turkey during this period, urged on their way by Zhivkov, who readily issued them with passports – normally so difficult to obtain in Communist Bulgaria. When he was forced from power in 1989, Bulgarian minorities breathed a collective sigh of relief.

Gradually, as Bulgaria modernises and looks towards a new future as a member of the European Union, minorities are rediscovering their voice, organising themselves into pressure groups and publishing their own newspapers.

The Roma

The Roma, often disparagingly called Gypsies, have lived in Bulgaria since the 14th century. This nomadic people were forced with govern-

ILL AT EASE WITH ITS PAST

To this day, the long history of Ottoman occupation is a bitter collective memory for Bulgarians. This is apparent in government-produced tourism brochures, which tend to make oblique and gloomy references to the Ottoman period while taking any opportunity to eulogise the National Revival movement. Similarly, while grandiose monuments to Bulgarian heroes are well patronised and cared for, many historic Ottoman buildings are locked up and dilapidated. Ottoman influences, obvious to anyone who has visited Turkey or its former colonies, are often denied and instead ascribed to the National Revival movement, including, most audaciously, carved sun-burst patterned ceilings, a trademark of Ottoman design.

ment "assistance" to settle in designated neighbourhoods – effectively ghettoes – cut off from society. Some Roma are Orthodox Christians, others Muslim; some speak Bulgarian, others Romany, and there are a number of dialects.

Official estimates suggest the Roma make up five percent of the population, but the real figure may be 10 percent. Despite this, they are almost absent from public life. Literacy rates are low, partly because their language has no alphabet or written literature, but also because of bullying of Roma pupils and distrust of the state machine. Although a small number have made it as musicians, writers and professionals, education and welfare for the Roma are woefully lacking, and prostitution and criminality are big problems.

Earning an honest euro

Bulgaria remains a paradox, with policemen driving Porsche convertibles (confiscated from the mafia), while peasants still use horse-drawn carts. Some Bulgarians live like kings, but the average monthly salary in Sofia is just 300 euros. Despite increases in foreign investment, one in 10 Bulgarians is unemployed, and one in seven lives below the poverty line.

Entrepreneurs are finding their feet but are still regarded with a certain amount of suspicion, as the shadow of organised crime looms large. Its protagonists are deeply entrenched in society. Communist-era wrestlers, a tightly-knit

the European Union. Visitors arriving at Bulgarian passport control will notice the "No Money Here" signs on customs booths, symptomatic of the government's attempts to stamp out the bribery culture that was once all-pervasive.

group that was once idolised, formed a criminal brotherhood that runs motels as brothels and monitoring posts for the smuggling trade. Former state security agents work as heavies for the old Communist bureaucrats, who were quick to reinvent themselves as "legitimate businessmen", snapping up all the most promising concerns when the old regime fell.

Although there is still a long way to go, small steps have been made in controlling organised crime, particularly during the run-up to joining

LEFT: girls in Plovdiv, much like young teenagers anywhere in the world.
ABOVE: moving to a modern, leisure-loving society from one governed by hard work and stoicism.

Women and children

Under Communism, the sexes were treated equally under the law. As a result, women made up half the workforce, a statistic that still stands today, in spite of a lax approach to equality since the end of Communism. In 2004, in the run-up to EU membership, workplace sexual discrimination was explicitly outlawed and legal definitions of sexual harassment were set down. Critics point to the low number of prosecutions since the act was enabled, and call it EU window-dressing.

Until 1944, divorce in Bulgaria was rare, but by 1983 it had reached 16.3 percent. This,

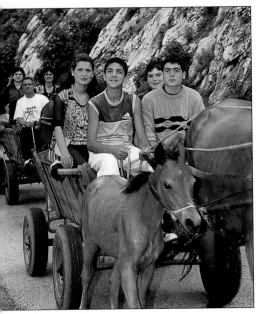

combined with a tumbling birth rate, prompted the Zhivkov regime to introduce the 1985 "Family Code" under which Bulgarians had to pay three months' wages for a divorce, and each application was subjected to a thorough investigation. The measures did nothing to halt the rise in divorce. The law has been amended twice since the collapse of Communism, giving increased rights for single parents and better protection for children. Today, around 30 percent of all marriages end in divorce, and Bulgaria's population is still shrinking by around 1 percent annually.

By law, children must attend school from the age of 7 to 16. At the height of the Communist era, the country was proud of its education sys-tem. Nowadays, those who can afford it choose private schools. Nonetheless a respectable 30 percent of students go on to higher education.

Making ends meet

Bulgaria's population became increasingly urbanised after 1945, partly as a result of forced industrialisation, yet even today only 70 percent of people live in cities – compared with 90 percent in the UK and Germany. The average Bulgarian family is made up of two adults and two children, but extended families often live together to save on housing costs. It is common to see the grandmother of a household perched outside the front door, knitting in hand, one eye on the children, and chatting to her neighbours, all the while on the lookout for tourists to buy her wares.

Although unemployment has fallen from 18 to 10 percent over the last five years, wages are still low, so the typical family will have their own vegetable patch or use of an allotment and these will often double as home to the family chickens. Fresh fish, when they can catch it, is a bonus, while tinned and packet goods are unobtainable luxuries. Bulgarians save their money to pay their way through the bureaucracy. The free health-care system that was built up under Communist rule has suffered under the market economy. Bribes to officials are routinely required for doctor's appointments, medicines and hospital referrals.

The Bulgarians abroad

Around 3 million Bulgarians live abroad in countries such as the US and Turkey, the equivalent of 40 percent of the Bulgarian population. The exodus that followed the collapse of the Communist regime is chiefly to blame, but many commentators believe EU membership will lead to another population spiral.

Many young people are looking to western Europe and the US for work opportunities, with large numbers learning English and studying business and tourism. But even the younger generation takes pride in its culture, perhaps because it has survived despite years of foreign occupation. The older generation is wary of external influences, of anything "non-Bulgarian" and of change in general, but there are clearly huge changes ahead. Democracy is still relatively new for Bulgarians and they have an exciting future ahead. ❏

Religion

Although only 10 percent of Bulgarians attend church on a regular basis, around 85 percent describe themselves as Orthodox Christians. The **Bulgarian Orthodox Church** has always been an important part of the national consciousness, and often the only means of preserving the country's identity.

From 1396 until the end of Ottoman occupation 500 years later, priests hid books and icons in remote villages. In the mountain monasteries, knowledge was passed from monk to monk, and valuable texts were stored in secret libraries.

With the National Revival and the decline of the Ottoman Empire, the Bulgarian Orthodox Church was declared the national religion. After World War II, however, the newly formed Communist government embarked upon a programme of repression. The clergy was forbidden to speak out on social issues, all church property was seized and monasteries, including Rila, the largest in the country, became museums.

After the fall of Communism in 1989, religious holidays were observed once more (Christmas was celebrated for the first time in nearly 50 years), bibles were published, and some church property was returned. Bulgaria re-established relations with the Vatican.

In recent years, the Orthodox Church has been battered by infighting, conflict dating back to the Communist-era appointment of Maxim as patriarch. In the 1990s, the church split in two, with Maxim's opponents alleging he had colluded with the dictatorship. Angry protests and shouts of "Red Garbage" still accompany Maxim whenever he appears in public, and the two camps are still arguing over control of Church assets.

Muslims in Bulgaria make up a little less than 13 percent of the population. Around 700,000 are of Turkish descent, and the remaining 230,000 are split between Muslim members of the Roma and enclaves of Pomaks – native Bulgarians who converted to Islam under the Ottomans. There are around 1,000 functioning mosques, and many more that are in disuse.

Bulgaria's once thriving **Jewish** population is now much reduced. There are now only about 4,000 Jews in Bulgaria, two-thirds of whom live in the capital, where synagogues have existed since the 10th century. The first Jews in Sofia were of Greek origin, but they were soon joined by others escaping from the Crusades. In the 15th century, thousands of Jews expelled from Christian Spain and Portugal found their way to the comparative safety of Ottoman-controlled Bulgaria, where, under Islamic law, the Jews were recognised as a separate nation, and allowed to coexist. In helped that the Jews were shrewd businessmen who enhanced the wealth of the Ottoman territory.

In the battles that ended Turkish domination, the Jewish community in Sofia fought in self-defence against the retreating Turks, but in other

cities and town, Jewish homes and businesses were looted in the belief that their owners were Turkish collaborators.

After independence, anti-Semitism festered below the surface, and in the 1920s, Fascist and openly anti-Semitic organisations sprang up. In World War II, persecution of Bulgaria's Jews was enthusiastically fostered by pro-Nazi elements in the government. However, the king, with the support of the clergy and the common people, managed to prevent mass deportations to death camps, in stark contrast to what happened in neighbouring countries.

After the war nearly 90 percent of Bulgaria's Jews emigrated, mainly to the new state of Israel. Those few who remained became almost totally secularised under pressure from the Communist regime. ❏

LEFT: the school run in rural Bulgaria. RIGHT: the vast majority of Bulgarians are Bulgarian Orthodox.

FESTIVALS – A YEAR OF SERIOUS FUN

Tradition is important in Bulgaria, but so is having fun, and there are plenty of opportunities to combine both in a packed calendar of festivals

Nothing epitomises this mix better than the *kukeri* festival, a well-loved tradition that is practised in many towns and villages, but most famously in Pernik, Blagoevgrad and Shiroka Luka. In winter, the dead are risen and the men of the village must fight them off, so that spring life may blossom. With fearsome masks, drums and noisy bells, these sheepskin-clad mummers dance their way down village streets towards the inevitable feast.

Bulgaria has festivals for the wine harvest, maidens coming of age, for roses blooming, and even the invention of the Cyrillic alphabet. Bulgarians even celebrate their birthdays twice; once on their own birth date and again on the national day of their namesake saint.

ABOVE: in the Kukeri Festival, the sound and fury of the dancing mummers is designed to ward off evil winter spirits to make way for the new life of spring.

BELOW: the feast of St Konstantin is an excuse for some trance-like fire-dancing in several Bulgarian villages, especially in the Strandzha on the Black Sea coast. The skill of fire-dancing is handed down from father to son.

Many old festivals revolve around courtship and marriage. On St Todor's Day, for example, a young woman in her first year of marriage will bake a loaf for her mother-in-law. After bowing to the matriarch three times, she is no longer bound to silence in front of the older woman. The same day is known as Horse Easter, when young bucks would rise early for ritual races in the saddle. To the winner the spoils: a full pot of wine and his pick of the village maidens.

LEFT: to scare away the dead, each man of the village makes his own fierce mummer (face mask), dresses in sheepskin and wears a bell. Mummers are a feature of many festivals.

ROOTED IN NATURE

A nation of farmers who depend on the land, Bulgaria's biggest festivals are inevitably rooted in nature and the natural patterns of the year, from planting to harvest. When the blooms are fullest in the Valley of Roses, in Kazanlak, women and girls rise before dawn to gather the precious flowers. Once the harvest is in, processions take place on the first Sunday in June to celebrate youth and beauty and a successful year, with villagers garlanded in roses, pageants to find the "flower of the valley", and a great deal of revelry.

Another Bulgarian tradition related to the land is *Peperuda* ("Prayer for Rain"), an all-female ritual during a period of drought in which a male doll is adorned in flowers and leaves and then ceremonially buried. After a decent interval, the figure is exhumed and cast into the river, and this is said to banish drought and bring rain.

A different element plays a part in perhaps the strangest of all Bulgarian traditions. In certain remote villages, the holiday of St Konstantin on 21 May is a fiery affair. After church, mystic music is played while a bonfire is lit. A certain villager, who has learnt this trick from his forefathers, will fall into a trance, and when the flames have dropped and the embers are red, he will dance on them barefoot. It is said that the fire-dancer speaks with the saint, is cleansed of his sins, and can then interpret omens for his neighbours.

LEFT: a morning of horse races is the prelude to a romantic date with destiny in Horse Easter, when young men compete for the attentions (if no longer the hand) of the fairest single women in their village.

BELOW: girdles of enormous bells, called *kukers*, are an essential part of the Kukeri festival: the more *kukers*, the more noise can be made.

TOP: rain-making rituals are part of Bulgarian folklore.
RIGHT: a month of celebrations and dressing up culminates in the pre-dawn harvest of Bulgaria's valuable rose crop in Kazanlak.

THE RURAL DILEMMA

Bulgaria represents one of Europe's last rural idylls, but it badly needs to modernise. Can this be done without damaging the environment or sacrificing traditional values?

Bulgaria is nothing if not a land of extremes – a place where the very rich and the very poor live side by side. Yet in the dynamic and modern bubble that is Sofia, or on the golden sands of the Black Sea coast, any such dichotomy of wealth is barely noticed by visitors. It is only when visiting rural Bulgaria that the real scale of the chasm between the haves and the have-nots becomes apparent. Even then, some of the more Potemkin-like villages of the tourist trail (for example, Koprovshtitsa and Melnik) can leave visitors envying and even dreaming of emulating the idyllic lives of Bulgaria's happy peasants. Many take the dream a step further by actually buying houses in remote Bulgarian villages.

In truth Koprovshtitsa and Melnik are as far removed from the day-to-day existence of the average Bulgarian peasant as is a Sofia factory worker from a wealthy businessman living in a penthouse overlooking the Alexander Nevski Cathedral. For most rural Bulgarians life is a daily struggle based on hard labour and subsistence farming. Though almost a third of Bulgarians still live in the countryside, and are actively involved in farming, the fact that agriculture accounts for just 16 percent of the country's output demonstrates the inefficiency and hopelessness of the situation.

The European Union's pre-accession programme for agriculture (Sapard) has brought some investment, and much change for the better (Bulgaria does at least now have a positive agricultural trade balance), but this has been almost exclusively at the sharp end of the agri-

cultural sector: smallholders have seen little or no improvement in their standard of living.

Before transition

Under Communism, almost all Bulgarian agricultural land was confiscated by the state, and subsequently collectivised, in a two-stage process carried out between 1946 and 1952. By the latter date more than 90 percent of the country's arable land was in state hands, and all peasants and farmers were state employees. Though in general paid a living wage, and encouraged to produce surplus on tiny plots of land (usually gardens) for their own use or to sell on the open market, most people found the rigidity of the collective farm stultifying. Nor

LEFT: horses are still vital to the rural economy.
RIGHT: high on a hill in the Rhodopes.

SELF-SUFFICIENCY

Throughout much of rural Bulgaria running water, plumbing and central heating are unattainable luxuries. For the majority of people water is raised from a well and carried short but often hilly and difficult distances.

was it efficient: the poor distribution network often saw crops rotting before they could be taken to the cities. This was one of the main reasons behind food shortages throughout the Communist bloc.

After Bulgaria dispensed with Communism in 1989–90, the subject of what to do with col-lective farms and the people who worked on them came to the fore. The first idea was to retain the farms' basic structure, but to privatise them, offering shares to employees. When this proved to be unpopular, ex-collective farm work-ers were offered small plots, usually around half a hectare in size. Some non-agricultural workers were also offered plots. This land was then sold (often instantly) to large agricultural companies who continue to hold it to this day. Former col-lective farm workers returned to their homes to tend their gardens and exist as subsistence farm-ers. Today, just 16 percent of Bulgaria's agricul-tural land is in the hands of smallholders.

A DELICATE BALANCE

Selo, an association of Bulgarian villages, was set up in 2005 to tackle the problems involved in reconciling the need to preserve tradition with the desire to modernise, and to progress. Selo, which means, simply, villages, is more than a collection of well-meaning but misguided environmentalists. Instead it is a genuine from-the-ground-up movement that recognises that the only way to prevent young people from leaving Bulgaria's villages – and to attract those who have left to return – is to offer them more than a future in subsistence farming.

The association – which currently has around half of Bulgaria's 10,000 villages as signed-up members – is actively attempting to attract direct investment (both local

and foreign) in a wide range of fields into rural Bulgaria. Slowly, but surely, Selo is drawing up investment pro-files of every village, a long-term project designed to identify those villages best suited for viniculture, for organic farming, for light industry, for mining and for tourism. In doing so, and in directing investment in the places best suited to accept and use it, Bulgaria's vil-lages will continue to function and offer their inhabitants a decent future.

Should the Selo project fail, however, it is to be expected that Bulgarian villagers will continue to vote with their feet, and that many of the traditions which once appeared to be eternal will be lost for good.

Rural inequalities

Though life on a collective farm was tough, it offered a number of certainties that disappeared with the end of Communism. As a result, many peasants swear that life is no better now than it was under Communism. The good soil does at least guarantee a plentiful supply of basic food, but low winter temperatures make raising livestock difficult.

Health is also a problem in rural communities. In many villages poor diet results in poor health, which is exacerbated by the lack of decent medical care. Few newly qualified doctors and dentists are prepared to take up poorly

In a number of bizarre but strangely common cases throughout the Balkan Peninsula, ironies abound: in many rural areas brand-new or newly renovated school buildings stand empty for want of teaching staff. Local children are therefore forced to attend what are often far less salubrious schools in nearby towns. When these distances become too great many parents simply refuse to send their children so far. In many cases children are expected to help out on the family farm, and having them travel two hours to and from school every day deprives their families of much-needed labour.

paid posts in remote villages, where tips – on which most Bulgarian medical workers depend – are liable to be negligible or non-existent. While an urban Bulgarian can expect to live to the age of 73, life expectancy plummets to below 65 in parts of rural Bulgaria. Yet the rural population is ageing: the average urban dweller is 39; in the countryside that average rises to nearly 46.

In education too there are serious problems. For reasons similar to those given by health-care workers, it is all but impossible to attract good, young teachers to Bulgaria's villages.

LEFT: selling raspberries to passing trade.
ABOVE: working in Bulgaria's vineyards.

Urban migration

As many as one million Bulgarians now live outside Bulgaria, and the vast majority of these emigrants are men from rural areas. Ironically, their preferred destinations are Spain and Italy, where they often end up working in the agricultural sector – albeit on much higher wages. The women they leave behind are forced to carry out ever more demanding work, often without modern machinery or equipment.

The effect that these migrants have on their home villages is multifarious. While their remittances (which totalled more than €6 billion in 2006) provide a boost to the economy of the whole country, many return to build expensive holiday homes near their home villages, driving up the cost of living for those who live there year round. Immigrants from western Europe (*see below*) have a similar effect.

The EU's direct aid for farmers – designed to reduce the incentives to move abroad – kicked in on 1 January 2007, but did little to stem the tide as families simply organised themselves, as they had done for decades, so that some members take care of the farm while others work for higher wages elsewhere, which in the days of budget airlines usually means abroad.

In 2006 the UK's *Financial Times* reported that at current economic growth rates it could take 20 years before Bulgarians reach the living standards of today's western Europeans, and even longer in the countryside.

Far from charming

Though a trickle compared with the tide going the other way, some western Europeans (Britons especially) are choosing Bulgarian villages as a retirement location. With its laughably low property prices, and far from the rat race of western Europe, it is not difficult to understand how rural Bulgaria can look so enticing. Its often unspoiled landscapes and simple way of life are seductive.

The problem is that the very things which

serve to attract western Europeans are the ones that drive many locals away. Interviewed by the French News Agency Agence France Presse in 2006, one English couple said that their new home in the village of Gostolitsa, near Dryanovo, either "had running water or electricity; never both at the same time." That, they said, was the charm of living there. For Britons escaping the modern world that may be so, but for locals who want the things western Europeans take for granted it is not. A lack of access to electricity and running water is a sign of poverty, and poverty is not charming.

Similarly, the development of skiing in a number of Bulgarian villages is being actively opposed by many foreign environmentalists.

While locals unanimously want the development and jobs that ski resorts will bring, environmentalists are concerned that pristine landscapes and centuries-old lifestyles will be spoiled, completely missing the point that an end to centuries of poverty is exactly what local people are hoping for.

Rural tourism takes off

Indeed, tourism as a whole has long been viewed as the saviour of the Bulgarian countryside. On closing the agricultural chapter of its entry negotiations with the EU in 2004, Bulgaria was given the task of developing its

the most out of the boom in tourism are the more savvy and business-oriented villagers for whom life may well have been more than merely tolerable already.

Secondly, while a certain number of people will always be able to make a decent living opening their homes as *mehana* (rustic inns) or bed and breakfasts, or as stores for home-made treats and crafts, it goes without saying that not every house in every village can become a restaurant, hotel or shop. There are not, and – even using the most optimistic projections – never will be enough visitors to go round. Neither are support-service industries an option:

rural tourism sector; funds were made available for it to do so. As a result the sector has seen its popularity shoot up in recent years, as word of the beauty of the Bulgarian interior gets out, and an increasing number of good places to stay attracts visitors. In 2006 alone rural tourism saw visitor numbers increase by 25 percent, signalling the sector's most successful year ever.

Yet while a number of villages have been helped by the development of tourism, all is not well. For a start, the people who have made

LEFT: rural scenes such as these are pretty as a picture in summer sunshine, but bleak in the midwinter snow. **ABOVE:** transport in the northwest.

rural holiday-makers (agrotourists) tend to be extremely low-spenders.

Thirdly, the kind of agrotourism that visitors want is usually a watered-down version of the genuine Bulgarian experience. The areas that have seen a boom in visitor numbers are those closest to existing tourism centres (especially around the ski resorts) which offer folklore shows and other "traditional" experiences in many cases far removed from local realities. Instead of plugging in to local knowledge, craft and traditions, modern agro-tourism can in fact displace it. In any case, poor villagers are the least likely to benefit from such tourism. The Bulgarian countryside therefore needs a far more sustainable plan to prevent its total demise. ❏

BULGARIAN VOICES

Bulgaria's musical voices are many and strong,
drawing on centuries-old folk traditions,
national pride, politics and sex

The powerful, resonant melodies and harmonies of the *a cappella* band Le Mystère des Voix Bulgares first propelled Bulgarian music on to the world stage 20 years ago. This all-women's choir was acclaimed by critics and loved by the public, topping music charts around the world. The band even won a Grammy in the United States.

The band's collection of recordings may seem like simple folk music to some ears, but is actually the result of musical experimentations informed by a thousand years of musical traditions. The singers constrict their throats in order to amplify the sound – oddly, a technique known as "open-throated".

Tradition versus politics

Bulgarian folk music is far from simplistic. Constructed from elaborate melodies and a wide range of often furious-sounding rhythms, it makes use of traditional instruments such as the bagpipe (the *gaida)*, string instruments such as the *rebec* and *pandore,* and the drum.

Folk music accompanies almost every aspect of everyday life in Bulgaria, at home, in the village square and at celebrations from Christmas to christenings. Land workers living closely with nature often play music in small bands in their spare time. Performed largely by memory and passed down, the women sing, the men play, and everyone dances.

When Bulgaria became a Communist state in 1944, music, along with many other aspects of life, became subject to state control. Music for its own sake was no longer valid; it had to serve the nation. In an attempt to erase 500 years of Turkish occupation, the new nationalists repressed the oriental influences and looked instead to a

pre-Ottoman medieval period. Because of its deep-bedded roots in remote villages, folk music had been relatively unaffected by Ottoman rule, and so for the Communists, this "pure" music fitted their ideals. At the same time, the urban elite turned to Paris and Moscow, adopting orchestral and operatic styles.

Wedding music

But sanitised, state-sponsored folk ensembles were not what most people wanted to hear. It was this fact that made "wedding music" – which was more expressive and representative of Bulgaria's ethnic diversity – so popular. Today, Bulgaria's "wedding music" can be heard in London cafés and chic New York

MUSIC OF THE GODS

According to myth, Orpheus, the Greek god of music, was born in Bulgaria's Rhodope Mountains in the 6th century BC. He could supposedly lure the wildest animal and even charm rocks to dance. When his ship passed the island of the Sirens, it was Orpheus's music that saved the crew from certain death in the famous myth.

eateries. It was the clarinet player, Ivo Papasov, who introduced most Westerners to this form of music, which also uses saxophones, guitar, accordion, bass and drums. He takes traditional folk forms and infuses them with high-energy rock and fast dance rhythms, transforming Bul-

Nina, Petra — stereotypically blond and big-breasted, and representing an aggressive Western form of sexuality. The instrumentalists were relegated to the background, or even replaced by synthesizers and drum machines. Part of the reason for *chalga*'s popularity was that it allowed Romas, Turks and others on the margins of Bulgarian society to express themselves.

The likes of Gloria have since been replaced by Azis, a transsexual and highly flamboyant Roma singer of *chalga* music. While popular music in Bulgaria becomes increasingly influenced by Western styles, it continues to maintain its very distinct identity. ❑

garia's traditional repertoire into something jazz-inspired and improvisational.

Chalga, from the Turkish word *calga*, meaning music, is an eclectic mix of Turkish and Greek pop, Roma and Arab rhythms, and contemporary electronic dance and rock. It is eastern rather than Slavic in origin. Appreciated mostly in bars and discos, it is characterised more repetitive and synthesised rhythms.

When Communism collapsed, *chalga* was one manifestation of the massive changes in society. Its musical stars were mainly women – Gloria,

LEFT: performer at one of Bulgaria's many folk festivals. **ABOVE:** a performance of the internationally acclaimed Le Mystère des Voix Bulgares.

OPERA LOVERS

Bulgarian opera, part of a rich Balkan tradition, is known throughout the world. The first companies were established after liberation from the Turks in 1878. Strongly influenced by the National Revival movement, the operas they sang were inspired by national epics such as *Siromachkinya* (The Poor Woman), written by Emanuil Manolov and first performed in 1900.

Bulgarian opera continues to thrive. Several cities have opera houses *(see page 282 of Travel Tips for details)*, and music festivals such as Varna Summer *(see page 227)* allow you to see top international performers, such as Boris Hristov and Nikola Gyuzelev at very reasonable cost.

A BALKAN STEW

Bulgarian food is a delicious melting pot flavoured
by the culinary contributions of its many
neighbours, both eastern and western

Bulgaria's cuisine is a colourful reflection of its history and geography. The country's position at a crossroads in the Balkans means that many different nationalities have passed through it over the centuries, adding their own particular influences to the food.

The 500-year occupation by the Ottomans has clearly left its mark, but Greece, Italy and other Mediterranean countries have also been important influences. Sitting down to a Bulgarian meal could mean eating Turkish kebabs, Greek moussaka or Italian pasta, with shiny red peppers and aubergines, bulbous courgettes and glistening olives that might seem more fitting in the Mediterranean than in the Balkans.

And there is another reason why Bulgarian food can be described as a melting pot. At its core is a traditional stew cooked in an earthenware pot known as a *gyuvech*, which is brought to the table for serving. Meat and vegetables are slowly simmered over a low fire or charcoal embers, a method of cooking that preserves the goodness of the ingredients, tenderises the meat and ensures the aromatic melding of flavours. The result is a hearty, rich stew not unlike the Hungarian goulash.

The eldest woman in the house, usually the grandmother, is the head of the kitchen. These matriarchs pass recipes down through the generations and play a key role in cooking for celebrations and festivities.

Home-grown

Bulgarians have not yet embraced the western European way of importing green beans from

LEFT: a *mehana* (inn) beckons.
RIGHT: alcohol is never served without food.

Kenya and jet-lagged pineapples from the Caribbean; even pasta and mayonnaise are relatively recent imports. Bulgarian cooking makes use of fresh, simple ingredients, almost always locally produced and often organic; pre-prepared, packaged foods are rare, and there is a long tradition of home-grown fruit and vegetables. Most households have their own vegetable patch and even vineyard.

A Bulgarian's larder may not differ greatly from your own shopping basket. Beef, lamb and chicken are the most commonly eaten meats, with staples of rice and beans and sometimes pasta. Potatoes, carrots, tomatoes, peppers, aubergines, onions, spinach and mushrooms are popular vegetables. Fruits are particularly tasty, with raspberries, cherries, strawberries, apricots and all kinds of melons in plentiful supply from spring through summer.

Bulgarians are essentially gatherers. Although sheep, pigs and hens are bred for consumption in the plateaus and mountains, the country is one of the lowest consumers of meat per capita in Europe, with meat eating tending to be reserved for high days and holidays. When you choose meat in poorer areas, pork, which is almost always outdoor-reared, tends to be the safest option, as beef and lamb (often mutton) can be tough.

Harvesting is a big part of local life, with

mushrooms, other vegetables and wild fruits picked by old and young alike in rural areas. Individuals fishing for the pot are common along the Black Sea, as well as on the Danube River and from the shores of local lakes.

Seasoning is usually quite subtle. A pinch of salt in Bulgaria is actually *Balkanska sharena sol*, Balkan mixed salt, made up of fenugreek, red pepper and other spices. The herb *chubritsa*, which is rather like oregano, is widely used. Its leaves are dried and added to soups and stews, or sometimes ground and eaten on bread. Parsley – both fresh and dried – is another common ingredient, chiefly in soups and salads. Thyme, sometimes called "shepherd's basil", is used as general seasoning in a wide range of dishes, both meat and vegetable.

Local specialities

Although Bulgaria is a small country, historically dominated by its larger neighbours, there are some distinct variations in terms of its cuisine, thanks to its varied geography and climatic regional traditions. Those travelling to the north, for example, may come across dishes never heard of in the south, and there are many specialities only found in a single village.

Authentic *kapama* – a meat, vegetable and rice stew made in a clay pot – comes from the mountain region of Bansko, although versions are found throughout the country. *Chomlek*, a potato and meat stew, and *katino meze* – fried pork with garlic and mushrooms and a particular kind of sausage known as *staretz,* are other Bansko delicacies. The town of Elena in the north of Bulgaria is famed for

---

WHAT'S ON THE MENU?

Chushki burek Fried peppers stuffed with egg and cheese.

Gyuvech Slowly cooked lamb and sliced vegetables.

Kashkaval pane fried, breaded cheese.

Kebapcheta Spicy minced meat or grilled sausages.

Kavarma The national dish, this is a spicy stew of meat, peppers, tomatoes and paprika.

Kyufte Spicy meat balls or hamburgers.

Mish Mash Baked potatoes, tomatoes, onions and cheese.

Riba plakiya A baked fish dish, often carp or perch, flavoured with lemon, onion, garlic and tomato.

Shopska The salad section on a Bulgarian menu *(listata)* can run for several pages. Almost every meal will include a salad, usually as a starter and accompanied by an aperitif such as *rakia*. The most common version is *shopska*, generally known as Greek salad. It's a delicious combination of crumbling, creamy white cheese, beef tomatoes, crisp cucumbers and tangy onions.

Sirene po shopski White cheese with egg and tomatoes baked in a pot.

Yoghurt Bulgarian yoghurt is delicious. It is usually made from cow's milk, but you will also find versions (generally considered inferior) made from buffalo and sheep's milk. It is served with almost every meal, either added to a dish or served on the side.

Elenski pork leg (a leg of pork processed to a particular recipe). In the south, the historic coastal towns of Nessebar and Sozopol are known for their fish soup, made with the pick of local catches. All along the coast you will find street vendors selling *tsati*, delicious sardine-like fish fried in batter and generously sprinkled with salt.

Wherever you go, you will find fast food. Although you will find hamburger chains, including international brands, they tend to cater to foreigners, as Bulgarians prefer their fast food local style, which is tastier and usually better quality. Opt for the ever-popular spicy ground

WHITE OR YELLOW?

There are just two kinds of cheese in Bulgaria. Sirene is a white feta-type cheese made from sheep or cow's milk, and kashkaval, a hard, yellow cheese made with sheep's milk, often deep-fried in breadcrumbs. There is no word in Bulgarian for cheese: it is simply referred to by its colour – "white" or "yellow".

Milk and honey

It has to be said that Bulgarian food is not well known outside its borders. Even cosmopolitan cities that have their fair share of eateries from exotic destinations such as Ethiopia and Brazil have never seen a Bulgarian restaurant. However,

meat *kebapche* (kebab), a *krenvirshka* – rather like a hot-dog but with pastry instead of bread – or a *kyufte,* a flattened version of a *kebapche*. With chips and a *bira* (soft drink), all these can be bought very cheaply.

There are plenty of vegetarian fast-food options too, such as corn-on-the-cob and *zakusks*, pastries that come in a variety of guises: a *banitsa*, a savoury pastry with a cheese or spinach centre, a stick-shaped cheese pastry called a *piroshka,* or a *kifla*, a sweet croissant with jam or sprinkled with sugar.

LEFT: vegetables are always seasonal and often home-grown.
ABOVE: *kyufte*, simple but delicious.

elements of Bulgarian cuisine have caught on.

At the beginning of the 20th century, Iliya Mlechnikov, a French scholar of Bulgarian origin, was awarded the Nobel Prize for his research after he noticed that Bulgarian villagers eating a lot of yoghurt often lived to be more than 100 years old. Bulgarian yoghurt (normally made from cow's milk, but also sometimes from buffalo's milk) was found to contain *Lactobacterium bulgaricum*, a bacterium only found in Bulgaria.

Introduced to children from the age of about three months, yoghurt is eaten at almost every meal. It is not just eaten on its own, but used as an ingredient in dishes such as *tarator* – a cold soup made from cucumbers and yoghurt

– and in *airan*, a drink made of yoghurt and water. These days, the whole world knows about the health-giving properties of the live bacteria found in yoghurt, and around 200,000 tons of Bulgarian yoghurt are sold to Japan every year.

Honey has been made in Bulgaria for well over 3,000 years – from sunflower, acacia, pine, and even oak. Lone beekeepers dot the countryside, storing the honey in whatever comes to hand, until the local broker shows up. Whatever is not sold on the local market is exported to nearby countries, particularly Russia and Greece.

Delicious desserts

Before you ask you waiter for the *smetka* (bill) in Bulgaria, consider ordering a dessert, which is likely to be of either Central European or Middle Eastern origin. Viennese-style coffee shops do a roaring trade in the late afternoon, offering local versions of Austrian pastries and cakes, and *garash torta*, a Bulgarian kind of chocolate cake.

The French influence is evident in crème caramels, while Turkey and the Middle East are represented by *baklava* – flaky pastry stuffed with crushed pistachio nuts and coated in a sweet syrup.

Bread and butter

Hundreds of years ago, bread – sometimes served with salt or cheese – was the main diet for many Bulgarians. Even today, Bulgarians consume considerably more bread than their Balkan neighbours. *Khlyap* (bread) also has a symbolic role in society and plays an important part in many of the country's festivities and rituals. For example, loaves of bread are baked by the eldest woman in the family for saints' days as well as for Easter. Sometimes the loaf is marked with a sign representing a vineyard or a sheep pen in the hope that it will bring good crops and fertility. At meal times, the eldest son traditionally breaks (rather than slices) the bread to be shared among the family. ❑

LIQUID FOOD

A cheap and nutritious option on most menus, soups are eaten year-round, and sometimes for breakfast (indeed you will probably find other breakfast dishes under the soup section of the menu). There are many regional and seasonal varieties.

Bob Traditional bean soup with vinegar and chilli.

Chorba Any kind of thick broth.

Postna A thick vegetable soup.

Tarator Cold yoghurt and cucumber soup, cooked with garlic and salt.

Panada Combines two of Bulgaria's favourite dishes – bread and soup

Shkembe chorba Tripe soup.

Wine, Beers and Spirits

When Bulgarians have a drink, they start with the strongest (usually local brandy known as *rakia*) and work their way on to wine and then beer – the opposite of the usual Western approach – and alcohol is always drunk with food, so that *rakia* normally goes with an appetiser, such as a salad, and wine and beer are consumed with the main meal or with bar snacks.

Rakia and other fire water

At 40 percent ABV (alcohol by volume) or even higher, *rakia*, the national drink, is certainly not for the faint-hearted. Bulgarians drink their brandy neat, without ice and often as a shot. Grape versions are the most common form, although it is sometimes made from apricots and plums, with many families distilling the spirit themselves. *Mastika* is another popular aperitif, very similar to Greek ouzo. International spirits are widely available in Bulgaria, but because so-called imported brands may in fact be counterfeit, you should avoid purchasing them from smaller shops.

Top wines

A visitor to Bulgaria would be well advised to say *"Nazdrave!"* (Cheers!) with a glass of locally produced, full-bodied Cabernet Sauvignon or Melnik. Bulgarian wine – particularly red – is good quality and incredibly reasonably priced, with a decent bottle costing a a couple of euros in supermarkets. White varieties of grape were traditionally used in brandies, with the result that Bulgarian white wines are generally of lower quality than the reds.

The country boasts a long tradition of wine making – some say the longest in the world. For many years, the industry was hidden behind the Iron Curtain, with distribution restricted to Eastern Bloc countries. Standards were generally low and it was mostly light and over-oxidized wines for immediate consumption that were produced.

Things started to change in the 1980s, when producers started to make inroads on western and world markets. With the fall of Communism and the beginning of privatisation, it was hoped that Bulgarian wines would really take off. However, poor harvests at the beginning of the 1990s led to a slump from which the industry has not yet fully recovered, although the creation of boutique wineries and the introduction of branded wines have somewhat reversed its fortunes.

Best beers

Beer drinkers should raise a glass with the richly flavoured Zagorka, ordered *studena* (cold) for maximum enjoyment. Brewed in Stara Zagora by a subsidiary of the Dutch brewing giant, Heineken, it is probably the best lager in Bulgaria. There is also a good choice of quality, locally produced beer, usually continental in flavour, and much cheaper than their imported equivalents. Pleven, which comes from the city of the same name, Kamenitza (pro-

duced in Plovdiv), and Shumensko (made in Shumen) are three recommended brews.

Water and soft drinks

With several hundred springs around the country, Bulgarian mineral water is sold commercially both for domestic use and for export. Fresh, high-quality fruit juices are widely available, and the adventurous might like to try the very popular but very unusual tasting *boza*, a sweet drink made from roasted flour (typically millet, but sometimes oat, barley or corn). The thick brown beverage may look like it tastes of chocolate, but has a distinct sour flavour that is an acquired taste. *Ayrian* is another unique drink in the Balkans, a cooling mix of yoghurt and water. ❑

LEFT: yoghurt and *balnica* is similar to British bread and butter pudding. **RIGHT:** wines for sale in Melnik.

PLACES

A detailed guide to the country with
the principal sites clearly cross-referenced
by number to the accompanying maps

Bulgaria has long been visited for its Black Sea coast. Roman emperors, 19th-century aristocrats, Politburo members and package tourists have all holidayed there. But since the end of Communism much more has been revealed about this outstandingly beautiful country, in particular its huge variety of landscapes, from the high mountains of the Rila, Pirin and Rhodopes to the Danubian Plain and the borderlands with Turkey, where many villages still follow a way of life that has barely changed in a century.

With two to three weeks at your disposal, it is possible to devise a driving tour that links all of these places (using public transport would be more limiting). Roads are on the whole reasonable-to-good, and clean and comfortable guesthouses are springing up in even the remotest areas as the concept of rural tourism gains sail.

But if you want to experience the essence of Bulgaria, you should explore its cities and towns, the repositories of a rich and varied cultural heritage. Sofia, backed by the magnificent Vitosha mountain, is an exhilarating capital, but more fascinating perhaps are Plovdiv, an ancient city with Roman, Ottoman and National Revival buildings, and Veliko Tarnovo, an exquisite medieval city wrapped around the Yantra river that was capital of the Second Bulgarian Kingdom.

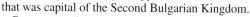

Be sure to leave some time to explore the coast. Between the package resorts are the fortified port of Sozopol and the picturesque island of Nessebar, a World Heritage Site, while midway along the coast is Varna, an elegant 19th-century resort that makes an excellent springboard for excursions north and south. If you simply want to relax at a beach hotel with a pool, the resorts in the northern part of the coast are a little more upmarket than those in the south. Golden Sands, for example, is smaller and quieter than Sunny Beach, its equivalent in the south. But to really escape the crowds, venture north of Balchik or south of Tsarevo, where long, blond beaches backed by forests have so far escaped much development. ❏

PRECEDING PAGES: sea taxi approaching Nessebar; wildflowers in the Pirin Mountains: village in the Rhodopes. **LEFT:** boats beside the Rusenski Lom River. **THIS PAGE FROM TOP:** Rila Monastery; yachts near Nessebar; ancient Pliska.

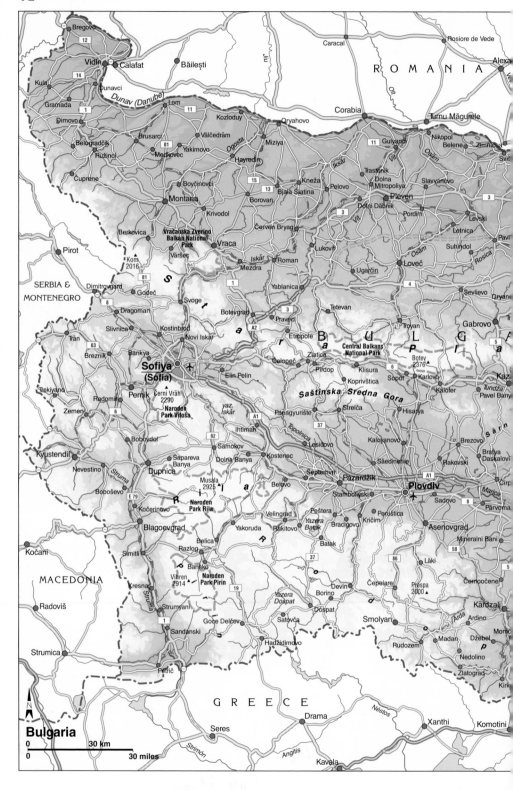

Bulgaria

0   30 km

0   30 miles

Sofia

300 m
300 yds

PARK OBORIŠTE

Vasil Aprilov

Oborište

Georgi

Šipka

Hristo Georgiev

Csar Osvobr

Veliko Tarnovo

Šipka

San Stefano

Oborište

Krakra

National Library

Mausoleum of Knyaz

Yanko Sakazov

Trakija

Trakija

Marin Drinov

Csar Stfan Ransilman

Knyaz Aleksander Dondukov

Malkara

Byalo more

Čataldža

Vasili Levski
Levski Monument **1**

Academy of Fine Arts **25**

National Gallery of Foreign Art **26**

Sofia University St Kliment Ohridski

Russian Cultural Centre

Vasili Levski

19-ti levski

Parliament Building **29**

Narodno Sabranie

Csar Ivan Šišman

Hadži Dimitar

Aksakov

Sv. Makedonski Music Theatre

Panayot Volov

Botanical Garden

Moskovska

pl. Al. Nevski

Sv. Aleksander Nevski (Cathedral) **23**

Dunav

Dunav

Vrabča

11-ti avgust

Parž

Flea Market **22**

Sv. Sofiya (St Sofia) **21**

Sv. Nikolai **19**

Central Military Club **20**

Csar Osvoboditel

Šipka

National Opera House **24**

Natural History Museum **18**

Dobrudža

Slavyanska

Ivan

6-ti september

Ivan Vazov Museum

Georgi S. Rakovski

Georgi Benkovski

Budapešta

Bačo Kiro

Knyaz Aleksander Dondukov

pl. Aleksander Batenberg

Ethnographic Museum **17**

Bulgarian National Art Gallery (Former Royal Palace) **16**

GRADSKATA GRADINA (CITY GARDEN)

National Museum of Archaeology **6**

Bulgaria Hall

Ivan Vazov National Theatre **30**

G. S. Rakovski

Budapešta

Bačo Kiro

Veslec

Serdika

Serdika

Tsentralnya Banya (Former Central Bathhouse)

Serdika

Banya Bashi Mosque **11**

TZUM Department Store **12**

Pl. Nezavisimost

Presidency Building **3**

Rotunda

Former Headquarters of the Communist Party **4**

Sofia Gallery of Art **31**

Stefan Karadža

Pl. Slavejkov

Knyaginya Mariya Luiza

Zhenski Pazar (Ladies Market) **15**

Sv. Kiril I Metodi

Sofiyska sinagoga (Sofia Synagogue) **14**

Halite **13**

Sv. Petka of the Saddlers **10**

Grand Hotel Balkan

Statue of Sofia

Sadebna palace (Palace of Justice)

Sv. Nedelya **8**

Pl. Sv. Nedelya

Bus & Train Station

Knyaginya Mariya Luiza

Bratya Miladinovi

Vladaiska reka

Sv. Kiril I Metodi

Ekzarh Yosif

Pirotska

Car Samuil

Car Samuil

Hristo Botev

Alabin

Alabin

Solunska

Bistrica

Car Asen

Vitoša

Solunska

Ivan Denkoglu

Ivan Vazov

Lavele

Aleksandrov

Stamboliyski

Hristo Botev

Todor Alexandar

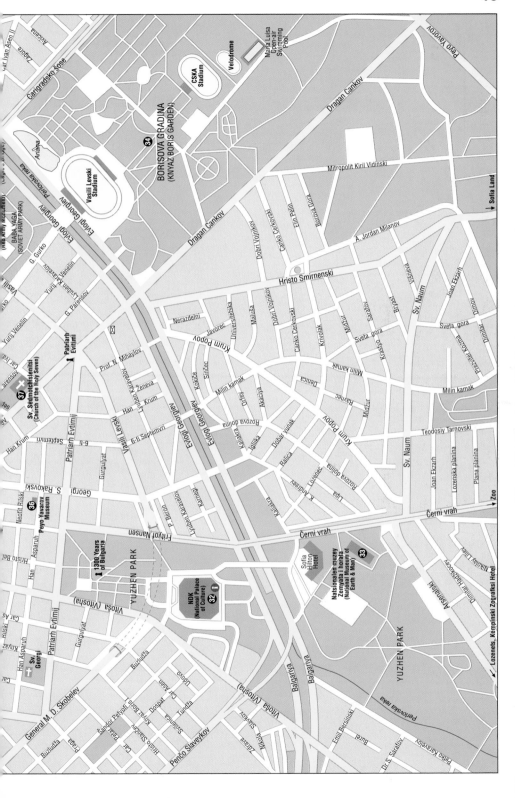

Zague
vul. Ivan Asen II
Aleksana
Mara Luisa Open-air Swimming Pool
Velodrome
CSKA Stadium
Pejo Yavorov
Dragan Cankov
Mitropolit Kiril Vidinski
BORISOVA GRADINA (KNYAZ BORIS GARDEN)
34
Ariana
Vasill Levski Stadium
Sofia Land
Dragan Cankov
Perlovska reka
Evlogi Georgiev
BABA VAGA (SOVIET ARMY PARK)
(Red Army Monument)
G. Gurko
Lyuben Karavelov
Yuri Venelin
G. Parensov
Dobri Vojnikov
Čanko Cerkovski
Elin Pelin
Borova Gora
A. Jordan Milanov
Hristo Smirnenski
Joan Ekzarh
Višneva
Sv. Naum
Bryast
Patriarh Evtimi
Nerazdelni
Universitaska
Maluša
Dobri Vojnikov
Čanko Cerkovski
Krivolak
Sveta gora
Krastyo
Mudžur
Sveta gora
Sveta gora
Prof. N. Mihaylov
Krum Popov
Javorec
Mirko
Joan Ekzarh
Dimitar
Krum
Han Karavelov
Ženeva
Milin kamak
Oreg
Akaciya
Milin kamak
Milin kamak
Ravnec
Denica
Mudžur
Teodosiy Tarnovski
Sv. Sedmotchislenitsi (Church of the Holy Seven)
37
Yuri Venelin
Patriarh Evtimi
Vasili Levski
Han Krum
6-ti Septemvri
Evlogi Georgiev
Evlogi Georgiev
Rozova dolina
Kalakra
Oreg
Dobar yunak
Krum Popov
Sv. Naum
Joan Ekzarh
Lozenska planina
Plana planina
Han Krum
Septemvri
Georgi
S. Rakovski
Gurgulyat
P. Beron
Kamaq
Ralica
Lipa
Lozanec
Rozova dolina
Zoo
Neofit Rilski
Peyo Yavorov Museum
36
Lyuben Karavelov
Frityof Nansen
Kalakra
K. Andreev
Černi vrah
Černi vrah
Hristo Bel
Asparuh
Han
1300 Years of Bulgaria
YUZHEN PARK
Sofia Hilton Hotel
Nacionalen muzey Zemyata i horata (National Museum of Earth & Man)
33
Nikolay Liliev
Dimitar Hadžikocov
Lozenets, Kempinski Zografski Hotel
Car As
Hristo Bel
Vitoša (Vitosha)
NDK National Palace of Culture
32
Asparuški
Knyaz
Han Asparuh
Patriarh Evtimi
Gurgulyat
Sv. Georgi
Burgudža
YUZHEN PARK
Balgariya
Balgariya
Perlovska reka
Car
Car As
Bžilski
General M. D. Skobelev
Buzludža
Draga
Petar Parčevič
Sándor Petyofi
Krivi Asen
Hristo Stančev
Dospat
Car Asen
Sulnica
Tundža
Ljovo
Zdrave
Nikola Stavkov
Vitoša (Vitosha)
Penčo Slaveykov
Emil Berzinski
Burel
Petko Karavelov
Dr. S. Saratov

SOFIA

Sofia may be Bulgaria's capital, but the city does not define the country. Expect a melange of cultures, styles and experiences and a modern city of extremes

Sofia

Maps:
City 74–5
Area 99

Even to the unfamiliar eye Sofia (София;Sofiya) is immediately a Balkan city. Commerce takes place on the streets and the minarets of mosques share the skyline with Orthodox cathedrals and modern skyscrapers; that this was once part of the Ottoman Empire is never in doubt. Yet modern Sofia is a fine European metropolis that looks west, not east. Spared many of the ravages of state socialism that all but extracted the soul from any number of Bulgarian towns and cities, Sofia city centre is a fascinating mix of cultures and ages. Walking its streets is a veritable history lesson.

A history of names

The first of those ages could well have been as long as 7,000 years ago. Recent archaeological finds suggest that the area around Sofia was inhabited by pre-Thracian tribes as early 5000 BC. If such finds are confirmed, Sofia will be recognised as one of the oldest cities in Europe.

Even as history stands today Sofia is a thoroughly ancient city. Settled by Thracians around 500 BC, and fortified by Romans after they annihilated the Thracians in AD 29, the original name of the city was Serdica, or sometimes Sardika. It became a *municipium*, or centre of an administrative region, during the reign of Emperor Trajan (r. 98–117), and among other things a large amphitheatre called Bouleutherion was built. When Emperor Diocletian divided the province of Dacia into two, Serdica became the capital of Dacia Mediterranea. The city expanded so much over the next century and a half that Emperor Constantine (r. 306–337) allegedly called it "my Rome".

Serdica continued to flourish after the split of the Roman Empire in the 4th century, when the city fell under the jurisdiction of Byzantium. It was temporarily conquered, and partially destroyed, by the Huns in 447, but rebuilt by Justinian I (r. 527–565), who

LEFT: café on Boulevard Vitosha with Mount Vitosha in the background. **BELOW:** Alexsander Nevski Cathedral.

*During Ottoman
times churches were
not allowed to be
higher than mosques.
The curious sunken
churches of central
Sofia are testament
to this peculiar law.*

BELOW LEFT: the
Rotunda, founded
in the 4th century,
is the oldest
complete building
in the city.
RIGHT: the Holy
Wisdom
Monument, also
known as the
Statue of Sofia.

is reported to have adored the city and subsequently spent much time here, funding major construction.

Slav tribes began settling in the Sofia plain from 600 onwards, calling the city Sredets, and Khan Krum had made it part of his First Bulgarian Empire by 809. It was not his capital, however; that was at Pliska. The city once again became part of Byzantium in 1018, before Tsar Ivan Asen I (r. 1189–96) made it part of his Second Bulgarian Kingdom. Over the next two centuries the city, like the kingdom, thrived, until Sofia was conquered by the Ottoman Empire during the reign of Murad I in 1382, becoming the capital of the Ottoman Protectorate of Rumelia. The name Sofia, from the Greek for wisdom, was first used in 1376, and almost certainly comes from the Church of Sv. Sofia. However, documents show that it was called both Sofia and Sredets until well into the 16th century.

Life under the Turks was generally tolerable, though a number of prohibitions made things difficult. Like much of the country Sofia was finally liber-ated from the Turks by Russian forces in 1878, during the denouement of the Russo–Turkish War of 1877–78.

Birth of the modern city

Twenty-first century Sofia is a joyful mix of Balkan chaos and modern efficiency. At times the city's straight, wide boulevards are strangely reminiscent of Paris, unsurprising given that much of the city was planned and laid out according to a grand design based on the French capital. Much of this city planning was carried out in the two decades that followed Bulgarian independence from Turkey in 1878. Inner and outer ring roads made access to the city centre easier, vast sums were invested in proper sewerage, and a number of showpiece buildings went up along the Largo, also known as the Yellow Brick Road (*see page 80*). The city's defining landmark, the Aleksander Nevski Cathedral, was built during this period.

Having survived the Balkan and Great Wars relatively unscathed, Sofia in the 1920s flourished. Terrorist attacks aside (such as the destruction of the Sv.

Nedelya Church, *see page 81*) Bulgaria's unstable political climate did not stop the city expanding, and becoming relatively wealthy. Smart town houses went up along Vitosha Boulevard, and the city expanded quickly as Bulgarians came here from the countryside to make their fortune.

Brief but heavy Allied bombing in the latter stages of World War II flattened much of central Sofia, and the Communist authorities that took control of Bulgaria after the war made the most of this opportunity to reshape the city in their own image. Though there are some choice pieces of architecture from the immediate post-war period (including the former Party House, the Presidency and the Sheraton Hotel), the most visible legacy of socialism are the thousands of decrepit high-rise blocks that make the inner suburbs of Sofia such a miserable place. No visitor to Sofia can ignore these blights whether arriving by air, by train or by car: their ubiquitous presence casts a dark and sinister shadow over the rest of the city. Fortunately, rising high above even the socialist blocks that house an estimated third of the city's population is Mount Vitosha, Sofia's saving grace. Whatever the architectural make-up of Sofia, whatever quarter of the city the visitor may be in, one glance upwards to the north, to Vitosha's majestic peaks, and the city suddenly appears to smile.

Ploschad Sveta Nedelya

What remains of Roman Sofia is confined to the area around **Ploschad Sv. Nedelya ❶** and the Sheraton Grand Hotel Balkan. In the rear courtyard of the hotel is St George Church (Св. Георги, Sv. Georgi), known to all as the **Rotunda ❷** (Ротонда, 2 Ploschad Sv. Nedelya; 8am–5pm; free admission charge but donations expected). This late-Roman church was built in the 4th-century AD and is considered to be the oldest complete building in the city. It has changed enormously since its original construction, however, and is indeed as celebrated for its

12th-century frescos of Jesus and the disciples on the central dome as for any of its original features. Incredibly, the frescos were rediscovered only in the 1920s, having been painted over by the Ottomans who used the building as a mosque. There are actually three layers of frescos, dating from the 12th–14th century, and finding even earlier paintings has not been discounted. Behind the church, in the shadow of the Presidency, are further – though far less well preserved – ruins of Roman Serdica.

Bulgaria's **Presidency Building ❸** (Президенство, 2 Bulevard Knyaz Dondulkov) was part of a large complex of outsized, even gargantuan constructions by the Communist regime in the late 1940s. The twin buildings opposite (home to various government ministries) and the **Former Headquarters of the Communist Party ❹** (Партийн дом; Partien Dom, Ploschad Nezavisimost) that stands between them went up at the same time. The Partien Dom – now a simple office building – is fascinating for the faded but clearly visible remnants of Communist iconogra-

Map on pages 74–5

Partien Dom or Party House, the Former Headquarters of the Communist Party.

BELOW: the Banya Basha Mosque.

TIP

The male choir of
Sv. Nedelya is
internationally
recognised. You can
hear the choir sing
Orthodox hymns and
chants by attending
the daily service at
8am and 5pm.

BELOW:
the Changing of
the Guard at the
Presidency, held
every even hour,
on the hour.

phy on the front of the building. There are more inside; you may wander in and look around. The Presidency, alas, is closed to the public, but the immaculately attired soldiers who protect the building's entrance have become a tourist attraction in summer. The elaborate Changing of the Guard Ceremony (every even hour, on the hour) attracts large crowds of perplexed onlookers. Civil servants coming and going from inside the building take it all in their stride.

The large square on which these buildings stand, **Ploschad Nezavisimost 5**, is famous for its mustard-yellow cobblestones. During much of the Communist period the area marked with the yellow stones (which quickly became known as the Yellow Brick Road) was off limits to all road traffic except vehicles belonging to the privileged elite.

Behind and to the right of the Presidency, the **National Museum of Archaeology 6** (Археологически Музеи, 2 ulitsa Suborna; Tues–Suna 10am–6pm; admission charge) is now one of Bulgaria's finest museums.

Most of its exhibits have recently been re-catalogued and rearranged, and the museum serves as a perfect primer on the city's and the country's historical legacy. The museum is housed in an eclectic, multi-domed former mosque, originally built in the late 15th century and fully restored (minus the minaret) in the 1920s. It offers outstanding collections of Thracian, Greek and Roman antiquities, including the celebrated gold burial mask of a 4th-century BC Thracian king, found near Shipka in 2004. Unfortunately, impressive as the museum's collections are, the best pieces have for the most part been brought here at the expense of other museums around the country.

Grand hotel

The last of the monumental buildings to go up in the 1940s was the **Grand Hotel Balkan 7** (Гранд Хотел Балкан). Adjacent to the Presidency but with its distinguished neoclassical facade on ploschad Sv. Nedelya, it was – until the construction of the Kempinski in 1979 – the only luxury hotel in the city. Its lobby, bars, nightclub and

Map on pages 74–5

casino were the scene of much spying and intrigue during the Cold War, and the building positively oozes mystery at every turn. Though it now has fierce competition, it is also still the finest hotel in the city.

Sv. Nedelya

In front of the hotel, on a peninsula that juts awkwardly into the traffic, is the church that gives the square its name, **Sv. Nedelya 8** (Св. Неделя; 8am–6pm). There has been a succession of churches on the site since around 980, and before that the Romans almost certainly used this spot as part of a Forum. Forming Sofia's heart ever since there has been a city, the square cries out to be cleaned up and pedestrianised. As it is, visitors and locals have to compete with trams, buses, cars, taxis and aggressive beggars for space.

The modern Sv. Nedelya church itself is not especially appealing from the outside. Dating from 1927, it is imposing, but it lacks the majesty of its 19th-century predecessor (destroyed in a terrorist attack in 1925, *see below*). It contains a real treasure, however.

The golden iconostasis is the 19th-century original (it survived the attack), while the colourful murals were added in the 1970s by a team of local artists led by Nikolai Rostovtsev. The church has 11 enormous bells in its belfry, eight of which date from 1879, a gift from the Russian Prince Dondukov-Korsakov. The others were donated by the Serb Orthodox Church. The 15th-century Serb king, Stefan Uro II, and Joseph I, first Archbishop of the Bulgarian Orthodox Church, are buried inside the church.

Two churches of Sv. Petka

There are two other churches in and around Ploschad Sv. Nedelya, each of which is worth closer inspection. The first is the **Church of Sv. Petka of the Saddlers 9** (Св. Петка Самарджийска, ploschad Nezavisimost; 8am–6pm; admission charge), a 14th-century place of worship – now defunct – submerged beneath the modern square in what is in fact the entrance to Sofia's central metro station, Serdica. A gorgeous neo-Byzantine creation, it houses fine frescoes that honour the

The saints Cyril and Methodius, creators of the Cyrillic alphabet, are honoured in the church of Sv. Petka of the Saddlers.

BELOW: Sv Nedelya.

Church of Terror

Sv. Nedelya is built on the site of an older church that was destroyed in 1925. In April of that year the outlawed Bulgarian Communist Party was conducting a terrorist campaign against the royal government. On 14 April the party's armed wing succeeded in killing General Konstantin Georgiev, a deputy of the ruling Democratic Accord, by shooting him on the steps of Sv. Nedelya church.

Just two days later, at Georgiev's funeral, held in the same church, communist terrorists waited for the church to fill with dignitaries and mourners before detonating a massive bomb. The church was almost entirely destroyed in the attack, and more than 150 members of the congregation were killed and a further 500 injured.

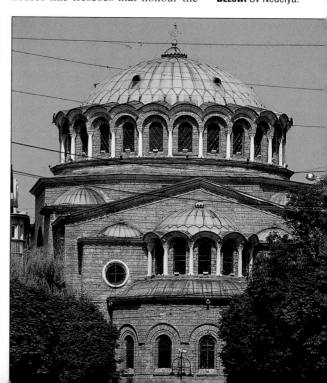

A reminder of Sofia's Ottoman past – the minaret of the Banya Basha Mosque.

BELOW: the facade of the Sofia Synagogue.

saints Cyril and Methodius (who created the Cyrillic alphabet).

Another Sv. Petka, **Sv. Petka Paraskeva** (Св. Петка Параскева, Ploschad Nezavisimost; 8am–5pm; admission charge), lends her name to a small, 13th-century chapel sunk into the ground behind Sv. Nedelya Church. Most of its original icons depict the 6th-century Sv. Petka Paraskeva herself, who spent years in the wilderness of the Jordan desert, eating and drinking only after sunset.

Shopping in TZUM

Even during the grim years of state socialism, TZUM **department store ⑩** (ЦУМ, 2 bulevard Mariya Luiza; www.tzum.bg; Mon–Sat 9am–8pm, Sun 11am–6pm) was an impressive sight. Though it sold very little that people wanted to buy (but plenty that they did not), TZUM was distinguished by its distinctive green roof, ornately galleried interiors and marble loggias. Built in the sober, Soviet version of neoclassicism from 1954–6, the building has twice undergone renovation, first in 1986, and then again in the late 1990s. Today it is a bright, spacious and impressive shopping centre full of brand-name stores and interesting food courts. Compared to the modern breed of shopping malls popping up in the rest of the country (including the glass-and-steel Mall of Sofia a few blocks west), it remains a gem of Soviet-era architecture worth visiting for its aesthetic value alone.

Mosque and bathhouse

To the right of TZUM, the late-16th century **Banya Bashi Mosque ⑪** (Джамия Баня Баши, Dzhamiya Banya Bashi, bulevard Mariya Luiza; open outside prayer times) is the last functioning mosque in Sofia, and one of the oldest surviving mosques in Europe. Closed for most of the Communist period, it is one of the greatest works of Koca Mimar Sinan Agha (1489– 1588), and possesses a sublimely slim minaret. Chief architect to sultans Selim I, Suleiman I, Selim II and Murad III, Sinan Agha is widely regarded as one of the world's first earthquake engineers.

The mosque derives its name from the phrase *banya bashi*, which means "many baths". By coincidence, Sofia's **Former Central Bathhouse ⑫** (Централня Баня, Tsentralnya Banya) is found immediately behind the mosque, on the opposite side of a well-kept park. Built in over-the-top Secessionist style and completed in 1911, the bathhouse is decorated in the most wonderful majolica ceramic tiles, and is currently the subject of careful, painstaking restoration that will continue until at least 2008, when it will become the home of the Museum of Sofia.

The Halite and around

Built contemporaneously and in much the same style was the **Halite ⑬**, Sofia's indoor market (6am–8pm). With its own renovation complete, it is now a superb indoor market selling fresh produce on the upper level and with a downstairs food court that

incorporates some well-preserved ruins of Serdica.

The tall column that towers above ploschad Sv. Nedelya is the controversial **Statue of Sofia Monument**. From 1950 to 1990 Lenin held sway here, before being toppled early in 1990. The plinth then stood empty for a decade, amid much wrangling as to what should and should not be placed atop it. The Statue of Sofia (officially the Holy Wisdom Monument; Паметник на Света София) was placed here in 1999, a 24-metre (80-ft) high bronze statue of Sofia holding a dove. Locals now complain that a dove does not symbolise wisdom, and that it should be removed.

Sofia Synagogue ⓮ (Софийска Синагога, Sofiyska sinagoga, 16 ulitsa Ezarkh Yosif; Mon–Fri 9am–5pm, Sat 9am–1pm, closed Sun) is the second largest synagogue in Europe (only Budapest's Great Synagogue is larger). It was built in 1909, when it served a thriving Jewish community which represented one-fifth of the city's population (Sofia's Jewish population is today thought to be no larger than 5,000 people).

The design was the work of the Viennese architect Friedrich Gruenanger (1856–1929), who combined Secession and Byzantine influences with rather daring results. The highlight is the oversized chandelier suspended from the enormous cupola. With a capacity for 1,200 worshippers, the main hall is rarely used these days; smaller rooms at the front are used for Sabbath services.

Around the corner, on ulitsa Knijaz Boris I, is an elaborate but neglected **Romanian Orthodox Church**, whose dusty, musty interior hosts a magnificent wooden iconostasis. Opening hours are notoriously fickle, and the church is often locked, but it is worth seeing if you can.

Shopping thoroughfare

Pirotska is a pedestrian shopping street that is a delight to stroll along, though the standard of the shops here is not as high as on Boulevard Vitosha. It has a couple of good, lively terraces and street cafés in summer, and at the northern end you will see shoppers coming and going from the enjoyable

Map on pages 74–5

The Former Central Bathhouse built in over-the-top Secessionist style.

BELOW: spices and dried fruits for sale in the Ladies' Market.

Spire of the Russian Church of Sv. Nikolai, topped with gilded onion-domes.

BELOW: detail on the Russian Church of Sv. Nikolai.

panoply of madness that is the **Zhenski Pazar**  (Ladies' Market, ulitsa Stefan Stambilov; 6am–2pm). This is Sofia's main market, where locals – who consider the prices at the Halite inflated – buy produce. You can buy almost anything here, and it is a wonderful place to watch real Bulgarians living real lives.

Along the Largo

East of ploschad Nezavisimost the Largo continues for a kilometre (½ mile) or so, passing some of the most impressive public squares and buildings in Bulgaria. What was known as the Third Kingdom of Bulgaria – or the Third Bulgarian Empire to a nationalist few – lasted little more than 50 years, from independence from Turkey in 1878 to the abdication of King Simeon II in 1946, but the lasting legacy of the imperial regime will endure, thanks to the massive building projects of the period. The Largo was not the least of these.

Built for Tsar Ferdinand from 1894–5, the **Former Royal Palace** , (today home to the Ethnographic and National Art museums) dominates the northern side of ploschad Alexander Battenberg, the first major public square east of Ploschad Nezavisimost. Designed by Friedrich Gruenanger – who would go on to design Sofia's synagogue, the palace is an accomplished piece of neo-baroque architecture, distinguished by its grand entrance and by a number of exquisite motifs on its facade.

Of the two museums in the palace, the **Ethnographic Museum** (Етногафски Музей, ploschad Aleksander Battenberg 1; Tues–Sun 10am–6pm; admission charge) – in the east wing – is the best, a vast collection of folk art from all of Bulgaria's regions.

Well laid out and with many polyglot captions, the museum successfully and succinctly explains the less than happy story of the Bulgarian peasant. Besides art there are also costumes and national dress, musical instruments and an increasing number of hands-on exhibits. It is one of the best museums in the country for children, and has an exemplary gift shop, a good place to buy interesting and well-made souvenirs.

The **Bulgarian National Art Gallery** (Национална художествена галерия, 1 ploschad Aleksander Battenberg; Tues–Sun 10am– 6pm; admission charge) is less impressive, as its collection is small for the country's national gallery. While most of Bulgaria's greatest painters are present in the permanent galleries, including the 20th-century masters Vladimir Dimitorv-Maistora (1882–1960) and Tsanko Lavrenov (1896–1978), much of the gallery's space is devoted to temporary exhibitions. The museum also boasts what could be the squeakiest wooden floors in the Balkans.

Ploschad Aleksander Battenberg

The Former Royal Palace looks out onto the impressive **Ploschad Aleksander Battenberg** , for decades known as Ploschad 9 September, to

Map on pages 74–5

commemorate the day in 1944 when Bulgarian politicians realised the Nazi goose had been cooked and staged a coup to topple the passively pro-German wartime government. In the middle of the square stood an enormous mausoleum housing the body of Georgi Dimitrov, the first Communist leader of Bulgaria who died in 1949 (see box below). Today nothing of the mausoleum remains, not even a plaque to mark where it once stood (though the outline of its vast footprint can – just – be made out).

The Natural History Museum

Further east along the Largo, the building situated next to the Former Royal Palace is the **Natural History Museum** ⑱ (Национален Природонаучен Музей, 1 Bulevard Tsar Osvoboditel; www.nmnh.bas.bg; 10am–6pm; admission charge). Expect a bizarre but supremely interesting collection of fossils, rocks, butterflies, insects, stuffed animals and a large display of live reptiles, from snakes and lizards to geckos and iguanas. It is a children's favourite.

Next on the left is the **Russian Church of Sv. Nikolai** ⑲ (Св Николаи, 3 Bulevard Tsar Osvoboditel; 7.30am–6pm), built over the winter of 1912–13 on the whim of a Russian diplomat who refused to worship in Bulgarian churches. It is arguably the most charming church in the city, with its charismatic onion domes covered in gold leaf donated by the Russian Orthodox Church.

The church's crypt contains the body of Bishop Serafin, a popular local religious leader who died in 1950. So revered was the bishop by the local population, and so profound the outpouring of grief at his death, that the recently installed Communist regime did not dare bury him in the anonymous grave they had planned. Though not a saint, Serafin has become the unofficial saint of the city's population, who throng to the crypt to offer prayers, which he is said to answer.

Across the busy Rakovski Boulevard is another fine building, the **Central Military Club** ⑳, built in 1876, almost immediately after Bulgaria's liberation from Turkey. A classic

The Military Club, an elegant venue for concerts, weddings and media events.

BELOW:
the Communist Martyrs Memorial.

Erasing the Communist Past

Built much in the mould of Lenin's Tomb in Red Square, Moscow, the mausoleum of Georgi Dimitrov, Bulgaria's first Communist leader, had a guard of honour and each year was visited by millions of Bulgarians who would shuffle through to pay their faux respects to the founder of the Peoples' Republic. Quite how the people genuinely felt was evident in 1990 when one of the first acts of Bulgaria's first non-Communist government was to close the mausoleum and remove Dimitrov's remains to a less public resting place in a cemetery on the city's outskirts.

Though considered by many to be an eyesore and a reminder of a tragic period in history, the mausoleum also had its supporters,: including, ironically, both hard-line Communists and historians who had served time in Communist prisons. This motley band successfully resisted attempts to destroy the mausoleum for nearly a decade. Only in 1999 was a decision finally made to remove it. Even then it did not go easily, as the thickness of the mausoleum's walls meant that the dynamite used for the job made no impression whatsoever. In the end the Bulgarian Army's special forces were called in to blow the mausoleum to pieces.

piece of neo-Renaissance architecture its facade is outdone by its elegant marble foyer and staircase. Once the sight of high-society and military balls the club today hosts various events, from the weddings of Sofia's nouveaux riches to exhibitions, from media launches to chamber music concerts. Under normal circumstances it should never be a problem to wander in and have a look at the sumptuous decoration.

Sv. Sofia

The exterior of the **Church of Sv. Sofia** ㉑ (Базиликата Св София, ploschad Aleksander Nevski; 8am–6pm) is modern-looking and disappointingly plain; it bears no resemblance to the original Roman church that once occupied this spot, the highest in downtown Sofia. The church is named after its founder, alleged by locals to be Sofia, the daughter of Emperor Constantine, the first Roman Emperor to allow his subjects to practise Christianity.

The church has been partly destroyed and rebuilt a number of times; the Turks used it as a mosque from the 16th century onwards, while the present structure dates from the late 19th century, and was built to replace the previous building, a more attractive neo-Byzantine construction complete with towering minaret, destroyed during Sofia's last great earthquake, in 1858.

Inside the church – renovated with funds from the city council in 1999 – is an exhibition charting its history, with illustrations and artists' impressions of how it looked or may have looked over the past 1,500 years. There are also some tantalising fragments of the past, including pieces of a fresco believed to be from the 12th century, and brickwork from the original 5th-century church. Less distinguished but no less important to Bulgarians is a lock of hair shorn from the head of the revolutionary hero Vasil Levski *(see page 31)*. Another revolutionary hero of the liberation, the poet Ivan Vazov is buried in the garden in front of the church: an apparently haphazard rock marks the spot. A far more pleasing memorial is the statue of Vazov in front of the grave.

The Church of Sv. Sofia still functions as a place of worship, and was, until the construction of the Aleksander Nevski Cathedral just up the road, the seat of the Orthodox Church in Bulgaria. The building of the Holy Synod stands opposite the church, a Secessionist building from 1906.

Bulgaria's **Unknown Soldier** is buried in the tomb set uncomfortably close to the southern wall of the church. A flame burns eternal while a bored young soldier keeps a less than keen-eyed vigil.

The Flea Market

The **Flea Market** ㉒ on the path that leads from Sv. Sofia up to the Alexander Nevski Cathedral is a stubborn remnant of the bandit days of capitalism that overtook Bulgaria and many parts of Eastern Europe in the immediate aftermath of the collapse of Communism. Though the city's authorities

BELOW: the Flea Market on the path between Sv. Sofia and Aleksander Nevski Cathedral.

make half-hearted attempts to close it down from time to time, it has become one of the city's main tourist attractions. You will find a variety of weird and wonderful goods on sale here, from genuine (and not-so-genuine) World War II memorabilia to Communist badges and flags. There is also a small area where young Bulgarian artists try to hawk their work, and another section where old ladies sell fine lace and reproduction national costumes at inflated prices.

Aleksander Nevski Cathedral

Of all Sofia's sights, the enormous **Aleksander Nevski Cathedral** ㉓ (Храм-Паметник Свети Александър Невски, Hram-Pametnik Sveti Aleksandar Nevski, ploschad Alexander Nevski; daily 6am–9pm) is the most immediately recognisable, serving as the city's defining landmark. It was built in honour of the Russian soldiers who died during the Russo-Turkish Wars of 1877–8, the war that led to Bulgarian independence. For all that, the name carried by the church,

Alexander Nevski, honours a medieval Russian prince of Novgorod who fought the Crusaders. Inside the cathedral is covered – from top to bottom – in the richest, most intricate frescoes and icons. The cathedral crypt (10am–6pm; admission charge) contains the finest exhibition of Orthodox iconography anywhere in the world.

The Opera House

A short but steep walk downhill north from the cathedral, along Rakovski Boulevard, is Bulgaria's **National Opera House** ㉔ (Национална Опера и балет, 1 ulitsa Vrabcha; tel: 02-987 13 66; www.sofiaopera.com), something of a hidden gem. Though it lies only 200 metres/yds off the beaten track, the building is sadly ignored by many visitors. Neoclassical in style both in and out, it boasts a wonderful, three tiered auditorium, topped with an inspiring cupola.

The statue in front of the building is of Alexander Stamboliski (1878–1923), a Renaissance man who founded the Bulgarian Agrarian Party in 1918, before serving as the country's prime minister

Map on pages 74–5

Russian dolls among the souvenirs and bric-a-brac on sale near the cathedral.

BELOW: the gleaming domes of Aleksander Nevski Cathedral.

By all accounts Grand Hotel Bulgaria, on ulitsa Tsar Osviboditei has seen better days but at one time it was one of the city's premier hotels.

BELOW:
buskers perform
in a city garden.

from 1919 to 1923. Bizarrely, a rear part of the opera house was for years used as the headquarters of the party.

Vasil Levski Monument and Boulevard

The simple **Vasil Levski Monument** commemorates the place where Bulgaria's legendary revolutionary Vasili Levski was hanged by the Turks in February 1873. Levski was a professional revolutionary who dedicated his life to Bulgarian independence, at first through negotiation, and later – after 1869 – through armed resistance *(see page 31)*. He was eventually arrested in 1872 for robbing a post office after his organisation had run out of funds.

The northern corner of the square is occupied by Sofia's **Academy of Fine Arts**, where many of the icons that form part of the Alexander Nevski Crypt Collection are painstakingly restored.

Opposite the Academy, and somewhat hidden, is Sofia's **Botanical Garden** ㉕ (49 ulitsa Moskovska; Tues–Sun 10am– 6pm), run by the city's university. Though small, it crams in a vast number of exotic plants, from

banana to coffee, and has a rose garden.

A neoclassical, late-19th century building designed by the Austrian Schwanberg contains the **National Gallery of Foreign Art** ㉖ (Национална Галерия за Чуждестранно Изкуство, 1 ploschad Aleksander Nevski; www.nga.icb.bg; Wed–Mon 11am–6pm; admission charge), renowned for its fine collection of Flemish art. Works on display include Anthony van Dyck's *Portrait of Jan van Monfort*, Adriaen van Utrecht's *Still Life with Game*, Frans Franckens's *The Marriage of Neptune* and Jan Braedel's *Landscape with Ruins*. Founded in 1985, the gallery mainly comprises works bequeathed by wealthy Bulgarian expatriates, whose personal collections were often gathered by their great grandfathers whilst exploring far continents in the 19th century.

Even the gallery building, once a printing house and the property of the St Cyril and Methodius Academic Foundation, was a donation. There is art from Africa, the Middle East, the Far East, Latin America and Europe, and in the basement a few remains of

Roman Serdica. The museum received a boost in the 1990s when the foreign art collection of the National Art Gallery was brought here, including the largest collection of *fin-de-siècle* French art in Eastern Europe. Courbet, Carrier, Rodin, Daumier and Renoir are all well represented.

Bulgaria's **National Library** (Народна Библиотека; Mon–Fri 8.30am–8.30pm) is the stark, neoclassical building that stands beyond the next crossroads. Completed in 1953, it betrays a Soviet influence, as does the superb, stylised statue and monument to Cyril and Methodius, creators of the Cyrillic alphabet *(see page 27)*, which rises in front of the building.

It is worth popping into the entrance hall of the **Russian Cultural Centre** ㉗ (34 ulitsa Shipka; Mon–Fri 9am–5pm) to take a look at the life-size replica of the Vostok-3 capsule that made cosmonaut Yuri Gagarin the first man in space in 1961.

A little further east is another of Sofia's hidden gems, the **Doctors' Park and Memorial**. The park is cared for by a group calling itself the "Friends of the Doctors' Garden" whose volunteers often walk around with a bucket for donations. The fruits of their labours are clear to see: immaculate flower-beds, well-equipped children's playgrounds, and a bizarre collection of random, uncatalogued archaeological finds in the northeastern corner.

Top university

Sofia University St Kliment Ohridski (Софийски Университет Св Климент Охррдски) was founded in 1888 and is easily the most prestigious in the country; there are usually three applicants for every undergraduate vacancy. The building that houses the main offices and lecture halls of the university was completed in 1920, with donations from the great and the good of the day. The two largest donors were the brothers Georgevi, Evlogi and Hristo, who are honoured with a seated statue each on either side of the main entrance of the neo-classical building. The university is named after St Clement of Ohrid, allegedy Bulgaria's first student, who studied under Cyril and Methodius in the 9th century.

Red Army Monument

Sofians appear to be at ease with the continued presence of the **Red Army Monument** (Pametnik na Suvetskata Armiya), which stands in a neat but plain square known as **Baba Yaga** (Soviet Army Park) that is located between Vasil Levski Bulevard and the River Perlovska. Though imposing (it stands 34 metres/110 ft tall), it is not close enough to the city centre to be threatening, and although most Bulgarians blame the Soviet Union at least in part for imposing Communism on them, they do not seem to feel the resentment that Romanians or Hungarians do on the subject. It is worth remembering that Bulgarians once viewed the Russians as liberators.

The monument itself is a masterclass in mediocrity. The socialist-realist statue that forms the centrepiece features a

Map on pages 74–5

BELOW: city newsstand.

Time for refreshment in City Garden, a good spot for outdoor cafés.

BELOW: sketching in City Garden, one of the finest public spaces in the city.

Bulgarian peasant woman and child thanking a Red Army soldier. It is more comic than inspiring.

Directly opposite the monument is the **Mausoleum of Knyaz Aleksander Battenberg** ㉘, Bulgaria's first post-liberation leader. Considering that the mausoleum was commissioned by Aleksander's successor, Prince Ferdinand (who allegedly couldn't abide the vulgar Aleksander), it is surprisingly grand, topped with a fine cupola. Inside, a marble sarcophagus holds the prince's body, alongside a few of his personal effects, including uniforms worn at the front during the First Balkan War of 1885.

The southeastern part of the park was once the home of Sofia Zoo, and it has recently been tidied up and enlivened with models of the animals that once lived here, as well as a decent children's playground.

National Assembly Square and City Garden

Bulgaria's **Parliament Building** ㉙ (Народно Събрание на Република България) on ploschad Naradno Sabranie, once stood in splendid isolation, fronted by the huge equestrian statue of the Tsar Liberator, Aleksander II that stands atop the Monument to the Liberators in the centre of the square. Built in 1884, and a fine example of neo-Renaissance architecture, the building is the work of Serb Konstantin Jovanovic, whose other works include the remarkably similar Parliament of Serbia building in Belgrade.

Today the building is faced by the Radisson Hotel, the most modern in the city, and home to a rooftop garden and terrace that affords fantastic views of all the sights in the immediate area.

The **City Garden** (Градската Градина, Gradskata Gradina) occupies the southern two-thirds of ploschad Aleksander Battenberg. Exceedingly well-kept, it explodes with colour when the flowerbeds bloom in spring. (It was not always so: in the years immediately after the fall off Communism the whole square and garden became an impromptu rubbish tip). Surrounded by cafés and terraces, it is delightful in summer.

Occupying the eastern side of the

square, facing the garden, is the **Ivan Vazov National Theatre** ㉚ (Народен Театър Иван Вазов, 5 ulitsa Dyakon Ignatil; www.nationaltheatre.bg), dedicated to Bulgaria's greatest playwright, Ivan Vazov. One of the many buildings funded by the generous Imperial Bulgarian state, construction began in 1904 to plans by the prominent Viennese architects, H. Helmer and F. Felner, who had also designed opera houses and theatres in Vienna, Prague and Budapest. The neoclassical building was officially opened in January 1907, but burnt down during a fire in 1923 (which broke out during celebrations to mark the 20th anniversary of the decision to build it). Immediately reconstructed, the facade was changed slightly to include a couple of cheeky baroque elements: look for the two towers that flank the neoclassical loggia.

Inside, the theatre is no less impressive, with rich decoration featuring specially commissioned paintings of scenes from Bulgarian history. The theatre is not officially open as a tourist attraction, but the box office is inside the main entrance and nobody appears to mind visitors having a look around. To view the sublime, ornate auditorium (with its wonderfully ostentatious royal box), you will have to see a play – which may be hard going if you don't understand Bulgarian.

The **Ivan Vazov Museum** (Музеи Иван Вазов; Tues, Sun 1–6pm, Thur–Sat 9am–5pm; closed Mon, Wed; admission charge) stands two blocks behind the theatre, in a house in which the great playwright lived from 1895 until 1920. The house has been splendidly preserved, and recreates in glorious detail the life and times of the writer. More than most museums of its type it contains a large display of personal effects. The man's entire life story is told in four languages.

The **Sofia Gallery of Art** ㉛, also known as City Gallery (Софийска Градска Художествева Галерия; Tues–Sun 10am–6pm; admission charge), stands at the foot of City Garden and hosts perhaps the finest collection of Bulgarian art in the country. Set up in 1923, the collection here features a large number of works devoted to the capital and its buildings.

Modern Sofia

The **National Palace of Culture** ㉜ (Национален Дворец на Културата, НДК, 1 ploschad Bulgariya; www.ndk.bg; 9am–7pm), or NDK, is unquestionably the ugliest building in Sofia. It is also the largest, and it cannot be missed. It stands prominently at the head of the scruffy northern part of **Yuzhen Park** (more concrete than greenery). The building was constructed in the early 1980s, at frightening cost, as a congress and conference centre. It serves much the same purpose today, though there is also a tacky shopping mall on the basement level, as well as cafés and a cinema.

There have been a number of attempts to renovate the building but it is too big a project for one developer. The sheer ghastliness of its design is matched only by the bizarre **1,300**

Map on pages 74–5

The star exhibit in the Sofia Gallery of Art is Tsanko Lavrenov's Bombing of Sofia, *regarded by many as Bulgaria's* Guernica. *The costly Allied bombing of the city at the end of World War II is today considered by all sides involved to have been entirely unnecessary.*

BELOW: pediment of the neoclassical Ivan Vazov National Theatre

The 1,300 Years of Bulgaria Monument in Yuzhen Park marks the arrival of Bulgar tribes in the region.

BELOW: the National Palace of Culture, a venue for conferences.

Years of Bulgaria Monument that stands forgotten, poking out from behind hoardings at the other end of the park. The monument was built at the same time as the NDK, and very loosely marks the arrival of Bulgar tribes in the region.

Behind the NDK is the glass-fronted **Sofia Hilton Hotel**, almost as ugly as the NDK itself, though far more sumptuous inside. Just to the south of that is the **National Museum of Earth and Man** ❸ (Национален музей Земята и хората, Natsionalen muzey Zemyata i horata, 4 bulevard Cerni Vrah; www.earthandman.org; Tues–Sun 10am– 6pm; admission charge). Housed in a superb former armoury, with most exhibitions arranged around an interior, galleried courtyard, the museum contains some 20,000 pieces of rock, and is considered a gem by geologists. Non-specialist visitors may find it rather dull, but the building – which has outstanding wall frescoes painted by Teofan Sokerov – is worth a look if you are in the area.

The southern section of Yuzhen Park, behind the Museum of Earth and Man, is a far more satisfactory place, which becomes more wild and overgrown the further you venture. A real urban jungle, it is reputedly home to birds rarely seen in a city, and is therefore popular with bird-watchers.

Beyond here lies the residential district of **Lozenets**, home to the expensive apartments of the city's elitem and the historically important **Kempinski Zografksi Hotel** (Хотел Кемпински Зографски, 100 bulevard James Bourchier; tel: 02-969 2230; www.kempinski.bg). Opened in 1979 and the product of Japanese investment, the modernist Kempinski was originally called the New Otani, and was designed by the celebrated Japanese architect Kisho Kurokawa. When built, it was the tallest building in the city. Its extensive Japanese garden is open to non-residents; it also has one of the best Japanese restaurant in Sofia, in the basement.

Knyaz Boris Garden

Knyaz Boris Garden ❸ (Княз-Борисова Градина) is the oldest and largest of Sofia's public parks. It is

reached by crossing **Orlov Most** (Eagles' Bridge), the beginning of the road to Plovdiv, and eventually Istanbul. The bridge takes its name from the four bronze eagles that stand atop 12-metre (40-ft) high poles on each corner. The bridge was where Bulgarian prisoners of war returning home from captivity after the wars of liberation were officially declared freemen.

Extended since being laid out in 1884, Knyaz Boris Garden today incorporates various sights and places of interest, including Bulgaria's enormous superbowl of a national stadium, the **Vasili Levski**, and its little brother, CSKA stadium, which hosts local football matches. There is also a large open-air swimming pool complex (open in summer 9am–9pm), tennis courts, an open-air theatre and a cycle track. The real pleasure of the garden, however, comes from wandering along its paths. The southern part of the park, away from the stadiums, is where the hand of the landscape artists is most evident, and there are pleasant walks along the tree-lined avenues.

The first of those landscape artists was Daniel Neff, a Swiss whose Cismigiu Gardens in Bucharest impressed Sofia's mayor when he visited the Romanian capital in 1883. Neff's original design, featuring exotic trees and shrubs not native to Bulgaria, was adapted and extended by the local landscape artist Georgi Duhtev in the 1940s. One of these later additions was the fetching **Monument to Freedom**, rising to over 40 metres (130 ft) and built to commemorate the fight against fascism and capitalism. With stylised statues at its base, it is a classic piece of socialist agitprop.

The gardens were declared a national monument in 1986, but this has not stopped a gentle creep of construction – this is highly valuable real estate – on its southern fringes.

Bulevard Vitosha

Bulevard Vitosha ㉟ remains the grandest and most commercially important thoroughfare in the city, and probably the country. Lined with shops, banks, cafés and restaurants, its wide pavements bustle day and night. Extending from Yuzhen Park and the

Map on pages 74–5

Bulevard Vitosha, Sofia's smartest thoroughfare.

BELOW: Bulevard Vitosha in early autumn.

*Sofia's metro system
is small but
expanding.*

BELOW:
frescos inside
Sv. Semotchislentsi
Church, one of the
highlights of Sofia.

NDK to Ploschad Sv. Nedelya, it is the perfect conduit between modern and historic Sofia.

The side streets that lead to and from Vitosha Boulevard are themselves lined with shops, and are well worth exploring. Many are home to attractive, if tired, houses from the turn of the 19th century. One of these contains the **Peyo Yavarov Museum** ㊱ (ulitsa Peyo Yavarov; Tues–Sat 1–5pm; admission charge), dedicated to the life and works of one of Bulgaria's best-loved romantic poets. The first Bulgarian to be nominated for a Nobel Prize (literature), Yavarov tragically killed himself at the age of 36 after being abandoned by his lover and muse. The museum building was one of Yavorov's last places of residence.

The **Palace of Justice** (completed 1908) is a neoclassical building at the head of Vitosha Boulevard, on the left just at it tips into ploschad Sv. Nedelya. Guarded by two menacing-looking lions, everything about the building is monumental, from the Corinthian columns that support its tympanum, to the entrance, apparently built for giants. With Communist disdain for the law the building was iconoclastically removed from the judicial circuit in 1947, and used as offices, as a government storage facility, and finally, from 1963–99, as the home of Bulgaria's National History Museum, now in Boyana. The refurbished building was returned to its original purpose in 2003.

Ulitsa Graf Ignatiev

Graf Ignatiev rivals Vitosha Boulevard for its sheer number of shops, and it is here that you will more than likely find real bargains. It is pedestrianised too, and can sometimes be a far nicer place to take a Saturday afternoon stroll. Just like Vitosha it has cafés aplenty, and Sofia's trendiest restaurants and bars are found in the streets that run off here.

Graf Ignatiev's main attraction, however, remains its unrivalled **book market** on ploschad Slaveikov. Established decades ago, it is renowned throughout the country. You will find second-hand books in every language known to man, vintage stamps and

first-day covers, second-hand vinyl records, and what should probably be assumed to be illegal copies of CDs, videos and DVDs. Fittingly, on a bench opposite the market is a statue of Petko and Pencho Slaveikov, the father and son publishing duo who did much to nurture Bulgarian as a literary language in the 19th century.

The tiny **Sv. Sedmotchislentsi Church** ❸❼ (Church of the Holy Seven, ulitsa Graf Ignatiev; 7am–7pm) is dedicated to the seven saints (Cyril and Methodius, and their five known disciples: Clement of Ohrid, Sava, Gorazd, Angelerius and Naum), who spread Christianity amongst the Slavs. It is one of Sofia's must-sees, though its rather unkempt exterior would try to convince you otherwise. The church dates from 1589, was designed by the Turk Siman, and was originally a mosque. Much of the exterior was rebuilt in the early 20th century, and the minaret removed.

Battle your way through the drunks and other undesirables who litter the small park in which the church stands, to make your way into a treasure

trove of frescos and iconography. In the immediate aftermath of the liberation it served as lockup for Turkish prisoners of war.

The statue at the far end of Graf Ignatiev is called **Popa** (Попа), a delightfully understated monument to Patriarch Evtimi, a 14th-century church leader who led a mini-Bulgarian cultural uprising before being tortured and killed by the Turks.

SOUTHERN SUBURBS

Legend has it that so underfunded was **Sofia Zoo** ❸❽ (Зоологическа Градина, Зоопарк; 9am–6pm; admission charge) in the early 1990s that when an advertising agency asked if they could use one of the zoo's lions in a commercial, they were told "of course, as long as you promise not to give it back to us." Urban myth aside, the story illustrates the problems that Bulgarian institutions suffered in the years that followed Communism's downfall. Today Sofia Zoo lacks for nothing, and it is once again the pride of the city; just as it was when it opened more than 100 years ago.

The zoo was founded by royal

Maps:
City 74–5
Area 99

BELOW:
the interior and exterior of Sv. Sedmotchislentsi Church.

Tourists take stock on Boulevard Vitosha.

decree in 1888, and is Bulgaria's oldest and largest zoological garden. It covers an area of around 230,000 sq. metres (57 acres) and houses more than 250 species of animal. The zoo was originally located in the gardens of the former royal palace, and its primary attraction was a black vulture caught in Bulgaria and exhibited in a cage. Later, pheasants, deer and bear were added to the collection.

Soon the menagerie grew far too big for even a king's garden. Tsar Ferdinand ordered the zoo to find a new home, which became the city's former Botanical Garden. In 1984 it moved to its present, purpose-built site here on the city's southern outskirts. Today's main attractions are the hippos, rhinos and elephants, but there is also an excellent display of native Bulgarian wildlife (including brown bears, wolves, foxes and vultures).

In a park close to the zoo is **Sofia Land ③** (София Ленд, 61 bulevard Nikolai Vapstarov; tel: 2-962 11 11; www.sofialand.bg; Mon–Fri 11am–8pm, Sat–Sun 10am–8pm; admission charge), opened in 2005 and Bulgaria's

BELOW: strolling along Vitosha Boulevard, with the slopes of the eponymous mountain in the background

first genuine, modern amusement park. Loosely medieval in theme – the main entrance is in the shape of a castle drawbridge, complete with moat, and the centrepiece is a mock-Renaissance castle – it covers 35,000 sq. metres (8.65 acres) and features roller coasters, merry-go-rounds, big wheels, go-karts and other funfair rides of varying sizes. There are also shows for children, and a number of relatively expensive places to eat and drink. Some of the attractions are under cover, but it is best to choose a sunny day to get the best out of the place.

Boyana's frescos

Boyana Church ④ (Боянската Тсюрква, 1–3 ulitsa Boyansk Ezero; www.boyanchurch.org; Tues–Sun 9am–5.30pm; admission charge) has been protected by UNESCO since 1979, and is the only such site in the Bulgarian capital. It is reached by a taxi from the city centre in around 20 minutes; public transport goes as far as the village of Boyana but the uphill walk from there is tough. Boyana consists of three churches. The first was built in the 10th century, and covered with frescos in the 11th and 12th centuries, of which fragments have been preserved in the lower parts of the apse and the north wall, and in the upper part of the west wall and the south vault. The church was enlarged at the beginning of the 13th century by Sebastocrator Kaloyan, who ordered a second, two-storey building to be erected next to it.

It is the frescoes in this second church, painted in 1259 by an unknown group of artists, that people come to see. The title Boyana Masters has been given to these anonymous painters, who almost certainly studied at the Turnovo School of Painting. Their work is among the finest medieval painting anywhere. It includes a magnificent representation of Christ the Almighty in the dome, while below a host of angels are depicted with the Four Evangelists – Matthew, Mark, Luke and John. Four images of Christ

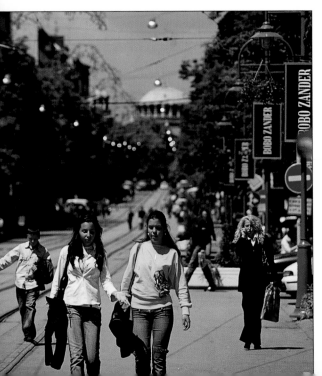

adorn the face of the arches. Given the fragile nature of the church and the frescoes, visitors are admitted in groups of four, and may only spend 10 minutes inside. If the church's warden feels that too many people have visited that day it is not beyond him to refuse entry. With that in mind it is best to visit the church in the morning.

The Boyana ensemble is completed by a third church, built at the beginning of the 19th century, which features representations of the two patron saints of Boyana, St Nicholas and St Panteleimon. They were painted in 1882.

Boyana waterfall

Above the village, at 1,260 metres (4,100 ft), and accessible by a well-marked but steep hiking track that begins from just behind the Boyana Church, is the **Boyana Waterfall** (Боянски Водотод), an impressive, 15-metre (50-ft) cascade which gushes violently and beautifully in spring with the melting snows of Vitosha.

National History Museum

In one of Sofia's finer Communist era buildings (once the private home of Todor Zhivkov), Bulgaria's **National History Museum** ❹ (Национален Исторически Музей; 16 ulitsa Vitosha Lale; www.historymuseum.org; 9.30am–5.30pm; admission charge) is a brilliant collection of artefacts and memorabilia from every era in Bulgaria's history up to 1944, when according to this museum the country's history came to an abrupt end.

Housed until 1999 in the Palace of Justice on Vitosha Bulevard, the decision to relocate the museum here was met with anger and much resistance by the city's academic community. They argued, not without reason, that the collection was being relocated to fill a void, and that a building so tarnished by the recent past was no place to house a history museum.

The new museum opened in 2000. Its superb quality laid all the arguments to rest: exhibits that had been cooped up and overlooked in the city centre now have room to breathe. Even at busy times the museum never feels crowded.

Of the thousands of exhibits on show at any one time, many make essential viewing. In the hall on the first floor, devoted to Bulgaria from 600 BC–AD 600, the **Panagyurishte Treasure** – believed to be part of the wedding dowry of a Thracian princess – is the most striking exhibit. A jug and six receptacles, all made of solid gold and weighing in total more than 6 kg (13 lb), found near Mramor, in the Rhodopes, in 1949. Though thought to date from around 400 BC, the objects may be older, as an inscription on the jug identifies it as originating in the Asia Minor town of Lampsak. More modern collections include documents of the National Revival, early Bulgarian photography and a superb collection of early Bulgarian stamps.

All of the museum's exhibits are displayed chronologically, with a number of maps and diagrams explaining the political context of the times (only some of these are in English, however).

Map
on page
99

TIP

Turn to page 27 of the history section of this book to see the portrait of Sebastocrator Kaloyan and his wife, one of the frescos in the second church in the Boyana complex.

BELOW:
carved doorway of the 10th-century Boyana Church.

TIP

Mount Vitosha can be reached by taking bus No. 6 from Sofia. It leads directly to Zlatni Mostove, one of the best viewpoints on the mountain.

BELOW: a church among the forests of Vitosha.

In the garden at the rear of the museum – where Todor Zhivkov once discussed the finer points of implementing Leninism with Leonid Brezhnev – is a good playground for small children bored with artefacts and history. The museum hosts interesting temporary exhibitions, which have recently ranged from Bulgarian Christian Art of the 13th–15th century, Embroidery of the Paleologue Renaissance, and Early Thracian Treasure.

Mount Vitosha

Sofia's single greatest asset as a visitor destination is its proximity to the stunning national park that is the Vitosha mountain. Though universally known as **Mount Vitosha** (Витоша), the granite mountain that towers like an enormous dome over Sofia is, in fact, a range of crags and peaks, none of which is actually called Vitosha. The highest is **Cerni Vrah** ❷ (Черни Връх, Black Peak), which rises to 2,290 metres (7,500 ft). The whole of the Mount Vitosha area – around 720 sq. km (278 sq. miles) – was declared a national park in 1934, and is the most visited mountain range in the country. It was here, legend has it, on 27 August 1894, that mountain tourism in Bulgaria was born, when the writer Aleko Konstantinov led a group of men and women from central Sofia on a hike to the top of Cerni Vrah. They called themselves the Shtaslivetsa (the Happy Men), today the name of the mountain's biggest hotel. Aleko Konstantinov gave his name to the area's main resort, Aleko, a popular base for hiking and skiing.

In ancient times the mountain was known as Skopios (from the Greek word for steep), a name preserved in that of Vitosha's third highest peak, **Skoparnik** (2,227 metres/7,300 ft) Among Vitosha's 10 other peaks that top 2,000 metres (6,500 ft) are **Golyam Rezen** (2,277 metres/7,470 ft) and **Karachair** (2,109 metres/6,920 ft).

The name Vitosha is first recorded in an 11th-century document, and is thought to be the name of an obscure, hermit-like early-Christian monk, Vitosh, who was believed to live somewhere on the mountain. Vitosha can look a little bare in places, the result

Wild at Heart

Though on the doorstep of the busy capital, and a popular ski area in winter, the Vitosha massif is an important national park with a wide range of flora and fauna. Most of the forests of the mountain are formed of juniper, dwarf pines, and beech, and there are more than 1,500 species of flora, which attract specialist botany tours in spring when the area is covered in alpine flowers. Many of these plants are found in the nature reserve of Bistrishko Branishte, on the eastern slopes of the mountain, close to Aleko (see page 100).

Vitosha's forests are also a habitat for a variety of large mammals, including wolves, bears and even wild cats, alongside more common species such as badger and deer.

of trees being chopped down and replaced with grassland for grazing livestock in the Middle Ages.

Dragalevtsi, Simeonovo and Bistritsa

The most visited, eastern face of Mount Vitosah, which is the one looking out over Sofia, is prefaced by two villages, Dragalevtsi and Simeonovo. **Dragalevtsi** (Драгалевци) makes a worthwhile excursion to see **Dragalevtsi Monaster**y ❹ (Драгалевци Манастир; Tues–Sat 9am–4.30pm; admission charge). The monastery – which lies 3 km (2 miles) above the village in a wonderful wooded glade of beech – was founded during the reign of Tsar Ivan Alexander in the latter part of the 14th century.

The monastery was part of a wider complex of 14 monasteries, known as the Mala Sveta Gori (Little Mount Athos), spread around the foothills of Vitosha. Some of these, including Dragalevtsi, were fortified. Unlike many Bulgarian monasteries, Dragalevsti, which is sometimes called the Virgin Mary of Vitosha, escaped destruction

by the Ottomans. Although the Turks demanded the evacuation of the monks, it was operational again by 1476 thanks to the efforts of a local merchant, Radoslav Mavar, who traded with and was trusted by the Turks. Mavar funded the beautiful frescoes in the monastery's church. Much admired today, they depict Mavar, his wife and two sons.

During the later centuries of the Ottoman occupation the monasteries of Vitosha became a centre of dissent and ultimately resistance. The national hero and revolutionary Vasili Levski hid from the Turks in the monastic cells of Dragalevtsi in the 19th century, and founded an armed unit here.

The monastery continues to operate, and much of it is off limits to visitors, as the Patriarch of the Bulgarian Orthodox Church keeps his summer residence here. You can, however, visit the 14th-century **Church of the Virgin Mary** (Св. Богородица) in the central courtyard – the only part of the original monastery to survive – and the newer **St Mina Church** next door (built in 1932). The Church of the Vir-

Map on page 99

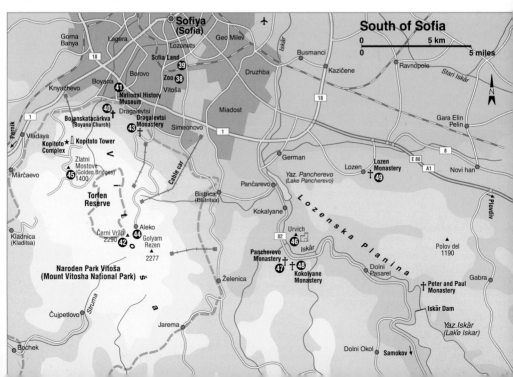

High meadow on the top of the Vitosha massif.

gin Mary has two glorious recesses behind the altar, a simple but striking effect common in late Romanesque churches in the Balkans, and colourful exterior brickwork. The more modern buildings, where the monastery's monks continue to live, date from the early 19th century and display Italianesque, neo-Renaissance features, not least the sublime loggias and balconies.

Simeonovo (Симеоново) has few charms. Its fast, modern gondola lift up to Aleko is the main attraction, though there are a couple of good hotels, the Montana and the Georgi, in the woods above the village.

Bistritsa (бистрица) is the third of the villages that surround the northeastern flank of the mountain. Sv. Georgi Church, a run-down 19th-century building with a newly added belfry stands on the site of the once-magnificent Mala Sveta Gora Monastery.

Skiing on Vitosha

Aleko ㊹ (Алеко) is less a resort per se and more a small collection of hotels, ski-hire shacks and snack bars. Perched on a ledge two-thirds of the way up the Vitosha range, at 1,800 metres (5,900 ft), views down over Sofia from here are stunning, spoilt only by the smog, fog or low cloud that can often settle above the city while Vitosha remains bathed in glorious sunshine.

The main activity on Vitosha is skiing, though the resort does not yet feature in any western holiday brochures; despite the fact that the resort boasts far better (and challenging) ski terrain than either Pamporovo or Borovets. Access to the skiing is the same as for the mountain itself: by car or No. 66 to Aleko, or by gondola from Simeonovo or chairlift from Dragalevtsi. Snow can usually be guaranteed from December to the beginning of April, and often longer. When the snow is very good there is a piste which leads all the way down to Dragalevtsi.

Weekends on the slopes can be very busy, though the on-going development of Bansko in the Pirin Mountains *(see page 142)* has taken some of the pressure off Vitosha. It is still best to come here during the week, when you may even find yourself alone on the slopes. In good weather the skiing here

Map on page 99

can be blissful. One common problem, however, is wind: Vitosha is prone to high winds, and as the upper chair lifts and slopes on Cerni Vrah are exposed to the elements, they are often closed on safety grounds.

Rock formations

Zlatni Mostove ㊺ (Златни Мостове, Golden Bridges) is a less populated and visited part of Mount Vitosha, on the northeastern flank of the mountain, above Boyana, at an altitude of 1,400 metres (4,600 ft). Besides offering some limited skiing it is worth visiting for its exquisite rock formations, called *moreni*, which look much like rivers of rock cascading down the mountain (they are in fact piles of huge granite stones, the remnants of ancient glacial movement). Though there are *moreni* all over Vitosha, those at Zlatni Mostove are the most impressive, being 2 km (1¼ miles) in length, and in places as much as 50 metres (164 ft) wide.

Due north of Zlatni Mostove is a television tower (Kopitoto), rendered useless by modern broadcast technology but impressively tall nevertheless. The terrace of the newly renovated five-star hotel next door, the Kopitoto Complex, offers one of Vitosha's most outstanding views.

Hiking on Vitosha

In summer, hiking replaces skiing as the main activity on the mountain, and there are well-marked routes leading up all the way from Sofia, criss-crossing the entire Vitosha range. These vary from the strenuous, multi-day hikes that cover the full breadth of the park, to day, half-day or even shorter hikes covering the most spectacular parts of the mountain. Most of the winter ski transport system operates for hikers in summer.

The shortest hikes are those that begin at Aleko. There is a route from here up to the weather station on the **Cerni Vrah** summit which takes around an hour, and is a sensational walk through a landscape of high pasture, stunted conifers and some impressive *moreni*. The less energetic can take the chairlift from Aleko to **Maluk Rezen**, from where it is a 30-minute

TIP

There is an excellent 1:40,000 topographical map of the mountain, and all of its tracks, trails, hotels, cabins and mountain huts published by Domino. It is available at most Sofia newsstands and bookshops, or online at www.domino.bg. It is essential for those who want to explore the park in full.

BELOW:
Vitosha rooftops.

walk up to the summit. A good half-day route runs from Aleko via Cerni Vrah to **Zlatni Mostove**, and will bring walkers in to close contact with the longest stretch of *moreni*. You will also brush past the peat bog that covers most of the Cerni Vrah plateau, a protected area (the Torfen Reserve; Торфен Резерват) to which access is limited. Walking the other way, from Zlatni Mostove to Cerni Vrah, takes around three hours.

The best routes, however, are those on the western side of the mountain, beginning at the village of **Kladitsa** (bus No. 22 runs here from the centre of Sofia). A five-hour walk takes in the stunning **Lake Studena**, and ends at the village of **Bochek** on the southern slopes of Vitosha.

The monasteries of the Lozenska Massif

The southern valley of the Iskar river, known as the **Lozenska Planina** (Massif), can make a pleasant alternative to Vitosha. In recent times its spectacular scenery has been rediscovered by Sofians who now take day trips to its two lakes, Pancherevo and Iskar. The massifs are also home to three spectacular but remote monasteries.

Lake Pancherevo is approximately 10 km (6 miles) from Sofia and served by bus Nos 1 and 3 from the capital's bus station. Just past the lake (you will need a car to proceed), where the Iskar darts west and south in quick succession, is the hill of **Urvich** ⓰, on the top of which are the spectacular ruins of a legendary fortress. Allegedly Tsar Ivan Shishman (r. 1371–93) held out against the Turks here for seven years in the 14th century. When the fortress eventually fell, it is said, so did Bulgaria.

The recently restored ruins can be seen from the road but are best viewed close up. There is a church hollowed into the rocky hill side, next to a similarly hollowed-out cavern that was probably a private home. During renovation work in 2002 coins depicting Ivan Shishman were found on the site; these are now in the National History Museum in Boyana. A circular route around the Urvich Hill that takes in the fortress on the way will take a good walker about 90 minutes to navigate. The route is not well marked and a map is essential.

On the opposite bank of the river are two monasteries, the Pancherevo and Kokolyane. **Pancherevo Monastery** ⓱ is the most accessible, at the end of a dirt track about 20 minutes' walk from the main road. It is not certain when the monastery was founded, but it may date from as early as the 12th century. It was destroyed by the conquering Turks in the 14th century, and not rebuilt until 1938, when it was dedicated to Sv. Nikolai Letni (St Nicholas the Miracleworker). More building work and restoration was carried out in 1996, including the construction of a new, Italianesque church and belfry, making it one of the newest monasteries in Bulgaria. Indeed, work continues to the present day on a new residential building.

Kokolyane Monsatery ㊽ is dedicated to the archangels Gabriel and Michael, and sometimes simply called the Urvich Monastery. It dates from the 11th century, but was destroyed twice: first by the Turks and secondly in the earthquake of 1858. A simple but superb church in neo-Romanesque style was built in 1898, and residential buildings shortly afterwards. A wooden belfry was added in 2000. The entire complex is now surrounded by a 2-metre (7-ft) high wall.

The monastery is very remote, and to access it you need to follow a track that begins a long way back in the village of Kokalyane, and takes in the monastery (after a 90-minute walk) before crossing the Plana Planina.

Iskar Dam and Loven Monastery

The village of **Pasarel** is the starting point for a well-marked and relatively easy 2½-hour hike that cuts through the Lozenska Planina and ends in Lozen (from where bus No. 5 runs back to Sofia). Six km (4 miles) further on, past the Peter and Paul Monastery of Loven, is **Iskar Dam** and its by-product, **Lake Iskar**, a 16-km (10-mile) long man-made lagoon often referred to as the Sea of Sofia. It is popular with water-sports enthusiasts. The hiking route from Pasarel to the dam, which follows the tight bends of the river, is steep in places but worthwhile. It can be walked in around 1 hour 45 minutes.

Loven Monastery (around 40 minutes from Lozen on foot), was built in the 11th century but destroyed during the Ottoman invasion. It was rebuilt in the 17th century, while the present-day monastery church was built in 1821 to a design by Tsvyatko Todorov.

The frescos for which the church is famous were added in 1868 by a team from the Samokov School *(see page 133)* led by Nikola Obrazopisov and Hristaki Zahgariev. They feature Cyril and Methodius, the inventors of the Cyrillic sript *(see page 27)* as well as John of Rila and Patriarch Evtimi. The monastery (populated entirely by nuns) offers accommodation in its simple residential quarters, and monastic meals. ❏

Map on page 99

BELOW:
Mount Vitosha is an excellent and easily accessible area for walking.

RESTAURANTS & BARS

Restaurants

Bai Gencho
15 ul. Dondulkov
Tel. (02) 986 65 50
www.baigencho.com
A well-known wine bar and restaurant, whose cellar is one of the best-stocked in Sofia. Bai Gencho serves traditional Bulgarian food at decent prices, and five shops of the same name sell a great range of wines at various locations around Sofia. €€€

Beyond the Alley, behind the Cupboard
31 ul. Bupapeshta
Tel: (02) 983 5581
You will find adventurous fusion cuisine alongside some better-known dishes in this legend of a restaurant. The decor is enjoyably unkempt, with delightful knick-knacks standing on every spare inch of shelf space. The excellent service is a rare treat. The place can be tough to find in the dark. €€€€

Bravo
12 ul. Aksakov
Tel: (02) 981 4916
Cheap and cheerful pizzeria in a central location. The terrace is one of the most popular in the city, and getting an outside table on a summer weekend can be tough. €€

Café Lavazza
13 bul. Vitosha
Tel: (02) 987 3433

At the expensive end of Vitosha Boulevard this trendy café and Italian restaurant is full from dawn to midnight with people who want to see and be seen. €€€€

Da Vidi
36 ul. Khan Asparuh
Tel: (02) 980 6746
Vaguely Italian food given a wider Mediterranean flavour, including some outstanding seafood dishes, a rarity in Sofia. The décor is classy and chic, and though prices are a little high it is worth every penny for the food and atmosphere. €€€€

Egur Egur
10 ul. Dobrudzha
Tel: (02) 989 3383
Convincingly authentic Armenian restaurant that offers a variety of mainly meat dishes, which range in taste from the slightly tangy to the very spicy. Your waiter will warn you before ordering anything too hot. €€€

Enoteca Uno
Bul. Vail Levski
Tel: (02) 981 4372
Though too flashy and sophisticated to be a genuine *enoteca* the wine list is worthy of anywhere in Europe, and the food – while straying from *enoteca* chop-house basics – is a good mix of trattoria

Italian and international favourites. Cheaper than you would think from the lavish decor. €€€€

Flanagans
4 pl. Narodno Sobranie
Radisson SAS Sofia
Tel: (02) 933 4740
Though in many respects a typical Irish pub abroad with Guinness and pies, this place is actually a little bit more besides: the menu is far more adventurous than you would expect and it is popular with locals as well as the expat crowd.€€€€€

Fox & Hound
34 ul. Angel Kanchev
Tel: (02) 980 7427
As the name implies, this is a very English pub and restaurant in the middle of Sofia. The food is tasty but unfussy, and generous portions are served by happy, smiling staff. It is on a side street just behind bul. Vitosha. €€

Greenville
36 ul. Atanas Dukov
Tel: (02) 819 1918
Set in residential Lozenets, it is a taxi ride from the city centre, but worth it. You can find traditional Bulgarian dishes here alongside plenty for vegetarians. In summer, take one of the tables in the lovely garden. €€€

Kashtata

4 ul. Verila
Tel: (02) 952 0830
Kashtata (which means the Little House) has been around for ever, and is almost always full. The reason is the well-priced, non-touristy Bulgarian menu. You will need to make a reservation. €€

Krim

17 ul. Slavyanska
Tel: (02) 981 0666
The very finest Bulgarian and Russian dishes have been served to the rich and famous at Krim for as long as anyone can remember. Though prices can be a tad high and service surly, it is nevertheless recommended. €€€

Onda

8a bul. Tsar Osvoboditei
Tel: (02) 986 5643
Great little café where a wide range of coffees, exotic teas, cakes, pastries and huge, filling sandwiches make it one of the city's preferred lunch spots. €€

Panorama

Bul. James Bouchier
(Kempinksi Hotel Zografski)
Tel: (02) 969 2440
As the name suggests, the best views in Sofia can be had from this restaurant – on the top floor of the Kempinski – which while expensive is worth every penny. Food here carries the personal stamp of the Kempinski's top chef, who oversees everything that goes on in the kitchen. Expect new flavour combinations and a wonderful wine list. €€€€

Panorama BBQ

Pl. Narodno Subranie
(Radisson SAS Sofia)
Tel: (02) 933 4334
The Radisson SAS's top-floor terrace offers a barbecue serving slightly overpriced but always great tasting steaks, ribs, *kyufte*, accompanied by terrific views of the Nevski cathedral. €€€€

Preslav

5 pl. Sveta Nedelya (Sheraton Sofia Hotel Balkan)
Tel: (02) 937 80 61
Another five-star hotel restaurant, and in Sofia that usually means quality. This restaurant is no exception: the best French food in Bulgaria is served here for high prices to high flyers. For a gastronomic binge there is nowhere better in the city to go. €€€€

Pri Yafata

40 ul. Raiko Alexiev
This is a wonderful little Bulgarian place serving only the most simple but tasty Bulgarian dishes: the sour soups are meals in themselves. Its prices are incredibly low. €€

Seasons

1 Bul. Bulgaria
(Hilton Sofia)
Tel (02) 933 5000
There can be few Hilton's in the world that can boast a restaurant to match Seasons, rightly regarded as one of the best in Sofia. The Sunday brunch here is the city's best, and the main menu changes weekly.
€€€€

Tambuktu

10 ul. Aksakov
Tel: (02) 988 1234
The African decor may be misleading: this is in fact a very good seafood restaurant, the only decent one in Sofia for that matter. Tuck into a vast range of imported treats cooked as well as you would hope for, but expect high to very high prices. €€€

Upstairs

18 Bul. Vitosha
Tel: (02) 989 9696
This place is, indeed, upstairs, though the best tables (those overlooking the street below) are on a cramped terrace: to enjoy your meal of East-Asian inspired cuisine you are better off leaving the terrace to the posers and sitting inside in the elegant dining room. €€€€

PRICE CATEGORIES
Price categories are per person for thee courses: € = under 10 leva €€ = 10–25 leva €€€ = 25–50 leva €€€€ = over 50 leva

LEFT: café on Bulevard Vitosha.
RIGHT: hanging out in a Sofia bar.

AROUND SOFIA AND THE NORTHWEST

There are monasteries, castles and natural beauty aplenty within easy reach of Sofia. The far northwest, between Berkovitsa and Vidin, is remote but rewarding, a forested highland assoicated with many legends

The town of **Novi Iskar** ❶ (Нови Искър) – now little more than a suburb of the capital – is all expensive villas in secluded places built by and for the Sofia rich. It marks the beginning of the Iskar Gorge, the most spectacular and magnificent of Bulgaria's many canyons. Carving a route of 156 km (97 miles) from the plain around Sofia, at an altitude of 550 metres (1,800 ft), down to the town of Cherven Bryag, 450 metres (1,480 ft) below, the gorge is at its most jaw-dropping between Novi Iskar and Cherepish, but is never less than impressive along its entire length.

An hour and a half's walk (or 20 minutes' drive) from the Kurilo district of Novi Iskar (the road is well marked) are the so-called **Katinski Pyramids** (Катинскн Пирамите), natural rock formations about 10 metres (30 ft) high that are impressive from afar, but less so close up. Accelerated erosion over the past century has recently prompted the local administration to take action to protect the pyramids. This may include limiting access to visitors – who have been known to chip off pieces of rock for souvenirs – in the near future.

Passing through the successive villages of **Trichkov** (Трчков), **Rebrovo** (Реброво), **Lukovo** (Люково) and the strangely named **Thompson** (Томсьн), the gorge becomes narrower and steeper before widening slightly at the beautifully set town of **Svoge** ❷

(Своге), which, like Novi Iskar, has become a popular place for weekend and holiday villas. Once popular as a hunting base, the town is today a popular health spa, along with the village of **Iskrets** (Искрец), a short drive west along the Iskretska Valley, which is the largest sanatorium in Bulgaria and renowned for its treatment of pulmonary illnesses. Svoge itself has a decent Archaeological Museum (Аркеологически Музеи; ulitsa Tsar Simeon; Mon–Fri 1–5pm), with finds from Svoge and the surrounding

Map on page 110

PRECEDING PAGES: landscape around Belogradchik.
LEFT: a train travels through Cerevo.
BELOW: the Iskar Gorge.

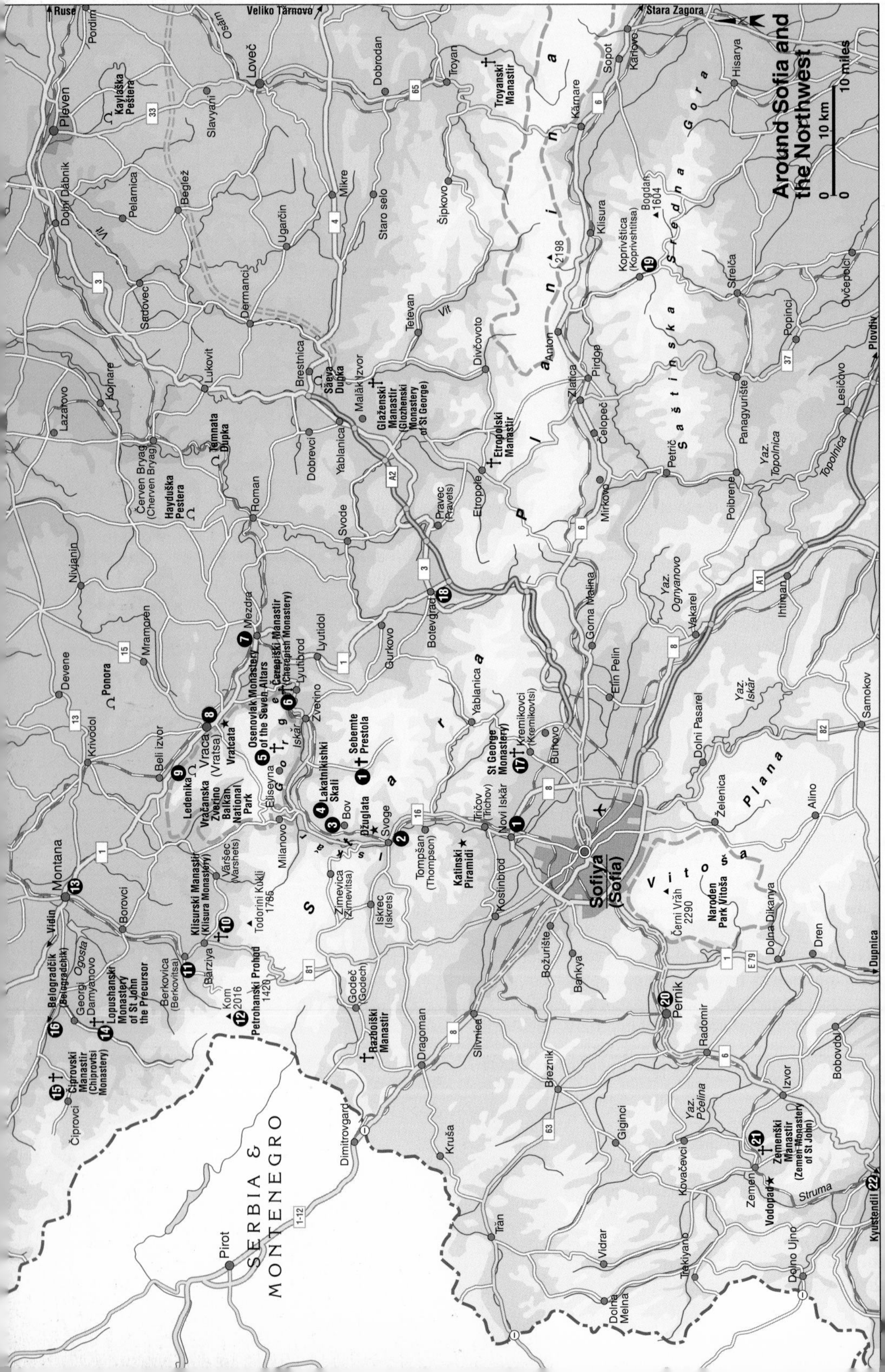

Around Sofia and the Northwest

0 — 10 km
0 — 10 miles

Ruse
Pordim
Pleven
Kaylâška Pestera 33
Dolni Dâbnik
Pelarnica
Lazâtovo
Beglež
Setovec 3
Slavjani
Ošam
Loveč
Veliko Tárnovo
Dobrodan
Troyan
65
Kámare
Troyanski Manastir
Sopot
Karlovo
Hisarya
Stara Zagora
Nikre
Ugârčin
Staro selo
Šipkovo
Šipkovo
Bogdan 1604
Koprivštica (Koprivshtitsa) 19
Srelda

Devene 13
Mrámoren
Ponora
Beli Izvor
Krivodol
Borovci
Montana
Nivjanin
Červen Bryag (Cherven Bryag)
Hayduška Pestera
Lukovit
Temnata Dupka
Dobrevci
Roman
Brestnica
Sáeva Dupka
Malák Izvor
Glažanski Manastir
(Glozhenski Monastery of St George)
Tetevan
Vit
Divčovoto
Yablanica
A2
Svode
Pravec (Ravets)
Etropole
Etropolski Manastir
Mirkovo
Yablanica
Gurkovo
Lyutidol
Lyutibrod
Zverino
Mezdra
Osenovlak Monastery of the Seven Altars 5
Čerepiš Manastir (Cherepish Monastery) 6
Iskár
7
Z1198
Pirdop
Zlatica
Klisura
Petrič Manor
Panagyurište
Celopeč
Zlatica
Pirdop
37
Popinci
Plovdiv
Lesičovo
Ovčepolci
Strelča

Vraca (Vratsa) 8
Vrácata
Zverino
Ledenika 9
Vračanska Zlatno Balkan National Park
Lakatnikishki Skali
Sebemte Prestola 1
Elisejna
Eliseyna
Bov
Žuglata
Milanovo
Svoge
Zimevica (Zimevitsa)
Todorini Kukli 1785
Iskár
Kalinski Piramidi
Tompšan (Thompson)
Novi Iskár
Botevgrad
Yablanica
Elin Pelin
Gorna Malina
Kremikovci (Kremikovtsi)
St George Monastery 17
Bunovo
Dolni Pasarel
Yaz. Ogryanovo
Vakarel
E79
Ihtiman
K1
Sofiya (Sofía)
Vitoša
Naroden Park Vitoša
Čerli Vráh 2290
Dolna Dikanya
Alino
Samokov
B2
Plana
Železnica
Dren
Dolna

Kilisurski Manastir (Kilisura Monastery) 10
Varšec (Varshets)
Berkovica (Berkovitsa)
Bârziya
Kom 2016
Petrohanski Prohod 1420
Godeč (Godech)
Razbojiški Manastir
Iskrec (Iskrets)
Kostinbrod
Tričovci (Trichovi)
Novi Iskár 1
Bożurište
Bânkja
Radomir
Izvor
Yaz. Pčelina
Kovačevci
Zemen
Zemenski Manastir (Zemen Monastery of St John) 21
Vodopad
Struma
Dupnica

Belogradčik (Belogradchik) 14
Georgi Oposta Damjanovo
Lopushanski Monastery of St John the Precursor 11
Ciprovski Manastir (Chiprovtsi Monastery) 15
Čiprovci (Chiprovtsi)
16
13
Vidin
Dimitrovgrad
Dragoman
Silvmed
Breznik
Kruša
Trán
Giginci
Vidrar
Kjustendil 22
Tikvjano
Dolno Ujno
Dolno Melna

Pirot
SERBIA & MONTENEGRO
1-12
63
1-12

Pernik 20

villages, including both Thracian and Roman jewellery and pottery.

The gorge narrows again shortly after Svoge, and its sides rear up increasingly steeply, until sheer walls of rock line both sides of the road. Access to this part of the gorge was for centuries all but impossible, and it has provided sanctuary to many a brigand. Indeed, the revolutionary outlaw Vasili Levski *(see page 31)* hid here from the Turks in the 19th century. When the railway arrived here in 1889, it was regarded as an engineering miracle.

Bulgaria's highest waterfall

At the village of **Bov ❸** (Бов), a well-marked route (one of only a few trails in what should be a superb region for walking) leads to the **Skaklya Waterfall** (Водопадът Скакля) in about an hour. The highest waterfall in Bulgaria with a drop of 130 metres (426 ft), the wild and deafening spring torrent turns to a mere trickle in high summer, allowing the limestone rock to glisten in the sun. It is no wonder that the poet Ivan Vazov chose the area as a retreat. One of the paths leading north, past the villages of Zesela and Zimevitsa, is called the Vazov Path: it ends at the Proboinitsa Cabin, where Vazov often spent the night.

At **Lakatnik** (Лакатник), there are more unique rocks: the **Lakatnikishki Skali ❹** (Лакатнишки Скали) – almost sheer cliffs 250 metres (820 ft) in height, dotted with natural caves and leading up to a wonderful, grassy clearing. The Skali is most popular as a mountaineering venue but a walking route zigzags its way up the cliffs, passing the Dark Cave (Темната Дупка), 3 km (2 miles) long and home to an underground river.

At the foot of Izmarets Peak, the **Osenovlak Monastery of the Seven Altars ❺** (Осеновлашкият Манастир Седемте Престола) is reached by taking a right turn off the main Iskar road just past the village of Eliseyna, heading for the village of Osenovlak. For those without their own transport, the

monastery can be reached in three hours on foot from the railway station at **Eliseyna**.

Built in the 14th century close to the site of a Roman fortress (whose less than impressive ruins can be viewed by following a well-signposted path), the monastery was razed to the ground by the Turks in 1737, only to be rebuilt in 1769. The seven altars of the monastery's name can be seen inside the small monastery church (built in 1815), and are believed to represent the seven elders of the seven villages in the surrounding area: Osenovlak, Ogoya, Ogradishte, Bukovets, Leskov Dol, Zhelen and Lakatnik. Look out for the church's carved wooden chandelier, covered in stunning 19th-century icons by an unknown artist. The monastery is popular with day-tripping Sofians, and is well catered to visitors: it has its own pub, restaurant and terrace, and guests can stay in the monastery's simple rooms.

As the gorge continues, passing the village of **Zverino** (Цверино), it narrows abruptly, forcing the road and the railway into tunnels.

Map on page 110

ABOVE AND BELOW: Inside detail and exterior of Osenovlak Monastery of the Seven Altars.

A tiny village in the Iskar Gorge is named after Major Frank Thompson, sent to Bulgaria to evaluate the fighting potential of the local partisans during World War II. Like many such emissaries Thompson, a committed Marxist, quickly went native, and was killed fighting alongside the partisans in 1944.

Cherepish Monastery

Ten km (6 miles) beyond Zverino is a turn-off for the **Cherepish Monastery** ❻ (Черепишки Манастир Успение Богородично, founded during the rule of Tsar Ivan Shishman (1371–93). Legend has it that Shishman executed a group of would-be conspirators on the site, before crushing their skulls to mark the spot on which the monastery should stand. Cherepish can indeed be loosely translated as "Place of Skulls". During the Turkish occupation the monastery was burnt down time and time again, only to be rebuilt: each time more spectacularly than before.

At the end of the 16th century the artist Pimen of Sofia made the monastery his home, and set about constructing and decorating much of what remains today. The tiny, stone monastery church – which looks ready to fall down at any moment – contains one of Pimen's original frescos, alongside better preserved, 19th-century works by Yonko Popvitanov of the Tryvana Painting School on the ceiling. The belfry was also added in the 19th century.

A small monastery museum in a former library exhibits colourfully illustrated gold-bound gospels from 1512. The monastery is at its liveliest at the Festival of the Assumption on 15 August, when it is swamped by pious day-trippers from Sofia.

Back on the main road the Iskar Gorge has one more twist in store, just – the so-called **Ritlite** (Ритлите), three sets of parallel stone walls ranging from 50 metres (165 ft) high on the left bank to 200 metres (656 ft) on the right, all around 2.5 metres (8 ft ft) thick and more than 200 metres/yds long. The Romans used the Ritlite to block entry (and exit) from the gorge, by building a fortress at their base. The Ritlite are today popular with rock climbers and mountaineers.

Also on the outskirts of Lyutibrod are the ruins of one of the earliest Christian monuments in Bulgaria: the foundations of a huge basilica, probably built as early as 450. There is not much to see, but some of the original paving of the basilica floor is clearly visible through the undergrowth, and you can make out the location of the

BELOW: Cherepish Monastery nestling in the Iskar Gorge.

colonnades. A little further on are the remains of a medieval church, built in the 12th century and with its interior frescoes just visible.

Mezdra to Vratsa

Mezdra ❼ (Мездра) means empty or deserted place in Bulgarian, and after the Turks destroyed the village of Torbaritsa – which had stood here since Roman times – in 1398, the site was indeed empty and deserted until the late 19th century, when shepherds settled here. It was, though, hardly a boom town: the first Bulgarian census (1881) put the population as 86. After the railway from Sofia opened in 1893, however, the pleasant climate and fine air made it a popular holiday spot. It was especially popular with writers, who came here for peace and inspiration. Aleko Kostadinov adored Mezdra and eulogised it in his work. Since then it has become the most important railway junction in the country, but has little else to keep you from moving on to Vratsa.

On a plain presaging the western Stara Planina, few Bulgarian cities have as dramatic a backdrop as **Vratsa ❽** (Враца). While the high- rise blocks and reeking factories of the modern industrial city reduce the charm of the view, Vratsa is a pleasant enough place of around 80,000 people, with two good museums, historic buildings, and an appealing, pedestrianised city centre around ploschad Hristo Botev and ulitsa Nikola Voivodov, which are lined with terrace cafés and bars in summer. The town is a good base for exploring the Vratsa hills and gorge, and in winter there is good but limited skiing close by at Parshevitsa.

The unusual **Meschii Tower** (Кула на Меските) is the city's main attraction, just north of ploschad Hristo Botev. It dates from the 16th century, stands 13 metres (43 ft) high and is almost as wide as it is tall. It was used as highly-fortified apartments for local noblemen, before being converted into a clock tower in the 19th century. A similar tower, the **Kurtpashova Tower** (Кула на Курт Пашовци), built at roughly the same time, served a similar purpose as the fortified home of an ostentatious nobleman. Neither tower is currently open to the public.

Map on page 110

Statue of the poet and revolutionary Hristo Botev, on Vratsa's square of the same name.

BELOW LEFT AND RIGHT: inside Cherepish Monastery.

One of many superb items of Thracian silver from the hoard known as the Rogozen Treasure in Vratsa's History Museum.

BELOW: strolling through Vratsa's pedestrianised city centre.

Close to the Kurtpashova Tower is the **History Museum** (Исторически Музей, Pl. Hristo Botev 1; Tues–Sun 9am–noon, 2–5pm; admission charge), housed in an ugly but spacious and airy museum completed in 1976. It contains a number of outstanding artifacts, from the Thracian, Roman, Byzantine and medieval eras, with clear explanations and good maps of the Vratsa region showing where everything was found.

The highlight of the collection is the **Rogozen Treasure**, a substantial stash of 5th-century BC silver found at the nearby village of Rogozen. Buried simply for preservation (no sign of a burial chamber has ever been found at the site), it comprises 165 jugs, plates, cups and other vessels, all skilfully decorated with animals, flora and scenes from Thracian legend. Most remarkable of all is the immaculate condition of most of the treasure.

On the same ticket as the History Museum is the **Ethnographic and National Revival Complex** (Етнографско-възрожденският Комплекс Софроний Врачански; ulitsa Leonov; Tues–Sun 9am–noon, 2–5pm; admission charge), a collection of National Revival-era houses around the tiny 18th-century Ascension Church, which once gave refuge to Vasil Levski (*see page 31*). Though much renovated, the buildings retain their original essence.

The oldest building in the complex is the **Hadjitoshe House** (1812), once home of Dimitri Hadjitoshe, a leading revolutionary figure in northwest Bulgaria. The **Ivan Zambin House** next door pays homage to the Vratsa tradition of silkworm breeding and silk weaving, while the Ascension School (built in 1832) is a superb collection of folk costumes on the first floor, and another of horse-drawn coaches in the courtyard. The **Ascension Church** contains a collection of religious art assembled from churches in the Vratsa area.

The Vratsa Gorge

The most spectacular part of the **Vratsa Gorge** (Вратсата Планина) is just 2 km (1 mile) southwest of the city centre and is an easy walk; follow the signs for Milanovo (Миланово) and Zgorigrad (Згориград). The sheer ragged cliffs that line either side of the Leva river are 350 metres (1,150 ft) high in places – the tallest in the country – and are popular with climbers: this is the most challenging terrain in the country. There are 120 different routes for all categories of climber, ranging from one to 13 rope lengths.

The road through the gorge is not the best, and can be very busy on summer weekends, when Vratsa's residents desert their dreary apartment blocks and turn the valley floor into one enormous barbecue area, parking their cars wherever the mood takes them.

Another 10 km (6 miles) further on is **Ledenika Cave** ➒ (Леденичката Пещера; 9am–noon, 2–4pm; admission charge), which, with its range of karst stalactites and stalagmites, and in winter icicles (from which the cave gets its name: *ledena* means icicle) is one of Bulgaria's most spectacular caves. Concerts are sometimes held here.

TOWARDS THE NORTHWEST

Kostinbrod (Костинброд) is an old-fashioned spa town 15 km (9 miles) northwest of Sofia, and the thermal waters of the town have been harnessed for healing purposes since Roman times. From here a scenic drive of 40 km (25 miles) passes through undulating, sparsely populated territory that steadily climbs up to 900 metres (2,950 ft), before the startling, hair-raising hairpins of the final assault to the **Petrohan Pass**.

At 1,420 metres (4,600 ft) the pass is one the highest in Bulgaria to remain open throughout the year, and its northern side, leading down towards Berkovitsa, is more dramatic still, cutting through the forest and descending alarmingly quickly. There is a mountain chalet close to the top of the pass, from where there is a good two and half hour hiking route up to the summit of Todorini Kukli, at 1,785 metres (5,856 ft), and another, six-hour walk over to the Proboinitsa Chalet close to the Skalkya Waterfall.

Some 10 km (6 miles) over the top of the pass, just after the village of Burziya (Бурзия), a minor road to the spa resort of **Varshets** (Варшец) passes by the **Klisura Monastery of Svs Cyril and Methodius** (Клисурски манастир Св. Св. Кирил и Методий). Founded in 1240 and repeatedly destroyed and rebuilt during the Ottoman occupation, it was burnt to the ground once and for all by the Turks in 1862, allegedly as punishment for the monks' concealment of Vasili Levski here. All of the monks were subsequently killed, on the orders of the brutal pasha of Berkovitsa, Yousuf Bei.

The monastery was rebuilt following Bulgarian independence, and officially consecrated in 1891. The handsome Svs Cyril and Methodius church sports twin belfries, and fabulous interior frescoes and iconography, all painted in 1937 by Gospodin Zhelyazkov and Georgi Bogdanov, two renowned Bulgarian artists. A smaller church, dedicated to **Sv. Nikola**, was added to the monastery complex in 1999.

The monastery offers excellent accommodation, in 80 rooms all with en-suite facilities, and the monks make

Map on page 110

TIP

For information on hiking, mountaineering and caving in and around the Vratsa and Iskar gorges, contact the Iskarski Prolom Tourist Association, at 3 ulitsa Aleksandar Stamboliski, Svoge, tel: 0726-23 95. Whether you are after maps and guides, or weather information and reservations at mountain chalets, the staff here are delighted to help.

BELOW: the Vratsa Gorge.

Berkovitsa was once renowned centre of pottery and you will still find plenty of it for sale. But the town is reinventing itself as a modern ski resort.

BELOW: carrying it all back home.

a decent living offering visitors horse-riding lessons and guided walks around the surrounding countryside.

Berkovitsa

Sitting at a cooling altitude of 405 metres (1,328 ft), **Berkovitsa** ⑪ (Берковица), a former health spa and one-time home of Bulgaria's finest pottery, is currently undergoing a massive revamp as a modern ski resort. There is currently some limited skiing on Kom, one of the highest peaks in the northwest (2,016 metres/6,079 ft), but there are advanced plans to construct a modern ski-lift system – including a cable car to the top of Kom from Berkovitsa itself. This should put the resort on a par with Bankso, Borovets and Pamporovo.

The town was first settled by the Romans, who built a fortress here in the 2nd century. The Byzantines added a Christian church in the 5th century (one of the first in Bulgaria, of which some scant remains can be seen in the Kaleto suburb of Berkovitsa), and the town thrived during Turkish times, when it was an important trading post

(Berkovitsa sits on the shortest route from the Danube to the Aegean). The Romans had also built baths here, a legacy taken up in the 19th century when the town was developed as a health resort. Its climate was considered beneficial for sufferers of tuberculosis and it became a fashionable resort. The now-defunct bathhouse – built by the Turks in 1665 – is a short walk south of ploschad Slaveikov.

Berkovitsa remains a pleasant town, with much to see. Its symbol is the superbly simple **Clock Tower** in ploschad Slaveikov, the central square. Built in 1762 and still with is original copper bell (said to be the biggest in the region), it is in perfect working order. North of here, down by the Berkovska river, is the **Church of the Holy Godmother** (Църквата Рождество Богородично), built in 1843 in neo-baroque style and boasting a fine belfry, as well as interior icons painted by Dimitri and Zohari Zograf.

A short walk east, the **Ivan Vazov Memorial Museum** (Къща Музей Иван Вазов; 2 ulitsa Ivan Vazov; Mon–Fri 9am–noon, 2–4.30pm;

admission charge) is set in a house once owned and occupied by the great writer during his tour of duty as a regional lay magistrate from 1879–80. The house was built in 1815 in National Revival style and retains both its original interior decoration, complete with frescoed ceilings painted by unnamed members of the Tryvana School and central heating, said by proud staff to be fully operational. The small exhibition of Vazov memorabilia is a bit of a disappointment.

Nearby is the **Berkovitsa Ethnographic Museum** (Етногафски Музей Сърбиската Къща; 1 ulitsa Poruchnik Grozhdanov; Mon–Fri 9am–noon, 2–4.30pm; admission charge), set in a single-floor house typical of the early National Revival era. Opened as a museum in 1992, it contains a fine exhibition of the simple, colourful pottery for which Berkovitsa is famous, though that at the Ethnographic Museum in Montana is superior.

If time allows, it is worth going a little further east, past the bus station on ulitsa Brezi, to take a look at the 19th-century **St Nicholas Church**, which has

a fine fresco by an unknown artist in the central apse and a sublime neo-Renaissance belfry (added in 1898). On 4 and 5 June each year, the town hosts Bulgaria's Strawberry Festival.

Soon to be a serious ski resort, **Mount Kom** ⓬ is currently a popular spot for nature lovers and walkers. The walk from Berkovitsa up to the summit – which is only a couple of kilometres from the Serb border – takes around 10 hours but can be split over two days by staying at one of the mountain huts halfway up. There are routes of similar length down the other side to the simple, modern monasteries at Golesh and Godech.

Montana's monasteries

Called Hristo Mihailov during the Communist period – in honour of a local Communist killed during a skirmish between rival resistance groups in 1944 – **Montana** ⓭ (Монтана) stands on the site of *Montanensium*, a Roman city founded here in AD 160. Strategically important at the foot of the Stara Planina, it was later reinforced by a fortress (Kaleto, Калето)

Map on page 110

Mount Kom is a popular destination for hikers.

BELOW: carts are as common as cars on some country lanes.

TIP

The pretty location of the Gradeshnitsa Monastery of St John makes it a popular wedding venue. Come here on any Saturday in summer and you are almost guaranteed to see at least one colourful Bulgarian Orthodox wedding in full flow.

BELOW LEFT AND RIGHT: visiting the fortress at Belogradchik.

on Gradishteto Hill to the northeast of the city, and many of its recently excavated remains can be explored. After the Roman withdrawal, the fortress helped the city withstand the Barbarian invasions of the Middle Ages, and Montana went on to become a wealthy trading town under the Turks.

Today Montana is a neat and tidy but rather dull place, home to 50,000 people, but it does have a very good **History Museum** (Исторически Музей Монтана, 3 ulitsa Graf Ignatiev) featuring a fine collection of Berkovitsa pottery, Chiprovtsi carpets and a room full of flags, emblems and other iconography from the Communist era. The main building of the museum is currently undergoing complete reconstruction and is not due to reopen until 2008.

Head instead for the **Michailov House** (Михайловата Къща; ulitsa Cherkovna; 8am–5pm; admission charge), currently the only fully renovated National Revival house in town, built in 1852 and once the property of Father Michail Variklechkov, a popular local priest. Ruins from Roman Mon-

tanensium can be seen in a small lapidary in the park behind the house.

The **Gradeshnitsa Monastery of St John** (Градешки Манастир Св Йоан) northeast of the city (just past the ruins of the Kaleto) was founded in the 14th century, but destroyed by the Turks in 1595. Rebuilt by local villagers from 1861–5, it is modest, with a tiny, single-nave church, but in a beautiful setting.

West of Montana are two other monasteries worth visiting. The first is the **Lopushanski Monastery of St John the Precursor ⓮** (Лопушански Манастир Св. Йоан Предтеча), founded in the 12th century, destroyed in the 14th, and rebuilt in 1850. It is famed for its enormous church, a five-dome affair with no interior wall paintings, but with a magnificent wooden iconostasis, carved and painted in 1863 by Nikolai Dospevski of the Samokov School.

The **Chiprovtsi Monastery of St John of Rila ⓯** (Чипровски Манастир Св. Иван Рилски), in the valley of the Chiprovska Ogosta river, was built in the 10th century, one of the original 30 monasteries founded

Map on page 110

during the First Bulgarian Kingdom to strengthen Christianity's hold over the Slavs. During the 17th century, outlaws launched raids against the Ottomans from here, including the Chiripovski Uprising of 1688, which eventually led to its destruction by the Turks and the massacre of its monks. The monastery was rebuilt in 1800, and was sent a gold-plated gospel by the Russian Tsar, Paul I, as a symbol of Slavonic fraternity. The ossuary of the charming stone monastery church holds the remains of many of the rebels of the 1688 uprising.

Belogradchik

The town of **Belogradchik** ⓰ (Белоградчик) has several well-preserved National Revival-era houses, but visitors come here from all over the world to see the **Belogradchik Rocks** (Белоградчишки Скали) These remarkable rocks were formed over one million years ago when the Balkan mountains folded and were preserved by a prehistoric sea before being infused with iron ore during the Jurassic period, when the Balkans were dry. The rocks, with their red and yellow shading, spread over an area 30 km (18 miles) long and 3 km (2 miles) wide. Each rock has a name, usually based on what it resembles: Adam and Eve, the Schoolgirl, the Bear, the Shepherd, the Camel, the Mushrooms …the list is long.

Among the town's National Revival houses is the 1810 **Panov House** (Исторически Музей, 1 ulitsa Tsolo Todorov; Mon–Fri 9am–12.30pm, 2–5.30pm; admission charge), today home to a good exhibition devoted to the Bulgarian resistance during the Ottoman period.

Between the city and the rocks is the city's **Fortress** (Белоградчишка Крепост; 9am–6pm; admission charge), which looks far more impressive than it is thanks to the dramatic backdrop the rocks – which are over 200 metres (650 ft) high – provide. A fortress was first built here by the Romans, but strengthened by Ivan Stratsimir in the 14th century, before falling into the hands of the Turks in 1395. Most of the fortress that remains today is the result of Turkish reconstruction in the early 19th century.

Prehistoric art

The **Magura Cave** (Пещерата Магура), close to the village of Rabisha (Рабиша), is one of the largest caves in Bulgaria; some of its galleries are 200 metres (650 ft) long and over 50 metres (164 ft) high. Its stalagmites and stalactites are immense, but the cave is best known for its paintings, produced using bat droppings by prehistoric humans at various times; the earliest date from the late Paleolithic era, 10–11,000 years ago.

The even temperature and low humidity of the cave make it a perfect wine cellar, and a part of it is indeed used to make sparkling wine.

EAST OF SOFIA

One of the most beautiful examples of Orthodox ecclesiastical architecture in Bulgaria, **St George Monastery at**

Prehistoric art in Magura Cave. The cave can only be visited as part of a tour. These can be arranged through the travel agency at the Avramov Hotel in Vidin.

BELOW: Belogradchik's distinctive rocks.

BELOW:
Koprivshtitsa's National Revival architecture.

Kremikovtsi ⑰ (Кремиковски Манастир Св. Георги Победоносец) is also one of the most overlooked. Situated around 30 km (18 miles) northeast of Sofia, the fine early-16th century monastery is overshadowed by a neo-baroque church of 1902. The interior of the earlier church is covered with beautifully preserved frescoes, whose rich, deep colours were considered revolutionary when they were executed in 1611.

The monastery's treasury includes a priceless gospel handwritten in the most intricate calligraphy from 1497. Given that so few people make the trip here, it is not unusual for visitors to have the place to themselves. One day they will not, however, is St George's Day (6 May in the Orthodox calendar), when locals flock here in large numbers. It is impossible to reach without a car.

Botevgrad ⑱ (Ботевград) is a quiet town with a slender medieval tower in its otherwise dull, concreted central square. The nearby village of Pravets (Правец) is infamous throughout the country as being the birthplace of the brutal Communist dictator Todor Zhivkov. Neither place really has anything to offer the visitor but they are en route to the **Glozhenski Monastery of St George** (Гложенски Манастир Св Георги Победоносец), 70 km (43 miles) northwest of Sofia, close to the village of Malak Izvor. Founded in the 13th century by a Ukrainian prince, Glozh, the monastery sits atop a small hill, looking more like a castle than a monastery. The original monastery church – which contained 14th-century frescoes – was destroyed in an earthquake in 1913, and the present, rather utilitarian church dates from 1951.

In 1893–4, the writer Vasili Drumev, at loggerheads with the Ivan Stamboliski government over foreign policy, was imprisoned here for 18 months. His former cell is open to the public. Though spartan, it is clearly far more comfortable than a standard 19th-century Bulgarian prison would have been.

Koprivshtitsa

Known to all Bulgarians as the cradle of their modern state, **Koprivshtitsa** ⑲ (Копривщица), 75 km (47 miles)

east of Sofia, is reached by taking a right turn shortly before the top of the spectacular Klisura Pass, which marks the entrance to the heart of the Balkan Mountain range.

Today a living museum, Koprivshtitsa was the site of the ill-fated April Rising of 1876, when a rudimentary force of Bulgarian nationalists sought to spark a nationwide revolt that would free Bulgaria of the Turks once and for all. Though the Rising was quickly and brutally suppressed, it did at least raise international awareness at the brutality of the Turkish regime in Bulgaria.

Nestled at an latitude of 1,016 metres (3,333 ft), Koprivshtitsa drips National Revival, and six of its finest period houses (the Karavelov, Oslekova, Debelyanov, Kableshkov, Lyutova and Benkovshki) are open to the public. A combined ticket for all of the houses, as well as an English-language guidebook, can be bought from the Museum Administration Centre (ploschad 20 April; open Mon–Sat 10.30am–6.30pm; the houses keep the same hours) on Koprivshtitsa's central square.

The closest house to the square, and the finest in the village, is the **Oslekova House**, a glorious three-level house with an unusual exterior staircase, built in 1856. Also built in 1810, the **Kableshkov House** was later owned by Todor Kableshkov, a merchant turned revolutionary who, according to legend, fired the first shot of the April Rising. Weapons used in the revolt are displayed in the house, a simple but delightful two-storey building with an overhanging upper floor. Behind the house and to the right is a small statue of Kableshkov, allegedly placed on the site from where he fired that first shot.

A memorial to the dead of the April Rising (Мавзолей на Априлци) dominates the square. In the cemetery behind here is the blue and white **Church of Sveta Bogoroditsa** (Църква Успение Богородично; ulitsa Garanilo), built in 1817 in a blend of the neo-baroque and National Revival styles. It was decorated by a veritable who's who of Bulgarian religious artists: Zahari Zograf, Ivan Nikolov and Hristo Enchev all contributed to the interior.

 Map on page 110

The statue of Todor Kableshkov, who fired the first shot in the April Rising.

BELOW: the Oslekova House, Koprivshtitsa.

National Revival

The spark for the April Rising of 1876, Koprivshtitsa was at the centre of the National Revival movement, a renaissance of Bulgarian culture and identity that got underway between the late 18th and early 19th centuries. It was part of an independence struggle against the Ottoman Empire that had many manifestations from political and military to religious and artistic, with a great surge in literature, architecture, arts and crafts.

For today's visitor to Bulgaria the movement is most evident in the architecture of places such as Koprivshtitsa, Arbanasi, Plovdiv and Bansko, where wealthy merchants celebrated the rebirth of traditional culture, and the new freedom they found to trade during this period, by building large and extravagant houses. Using wood and stone, the architects married the robust materials locally available to create sturdy but elegant architecture. Domestic buildings were often fronted by delicate colonnades and adorned with frescoes of classical scenes or extravagant swag work and other decorative embellishments.

Though the buildings are recognisably Bulgarian in character, traditional Ottoman influences are often apparent, though rarely recognised by the nationalistic Bulgarians.

Map
on page
110

*Besides Pernik, there
are Kukeri festivals
in Shiroka Luka (see
page 180), Kopriv-
shtitsa (see pages
120–1), Separeva
Banya and Rakovski.
The festivals are held
to mark the New Year,
early spring or
harvest time too.
See Festivals,
pages 48–9)*

BELOW: Zemen's
11th-century
church.

WEST OF SOFIA

A centre of the coal-mining industry, **Pernik ⓴** (Перник), named for the pagan god of thunder, Perun, is, at just 25 km (16 miles) west of Sofia, one of the best places in Bulgaria to witness the bizarre kukeri *(кукери)* festivals for which the country is famous. Over the last weekend of January thousands of men dress in costumes made of dead animals (including the heads), which are designed to evoke fear and scare off evil spirits. They spend long hours in a semi-trance, dancing and chanting through the town. The traditions of Kukeri are vague, but are thought to have derived from the religion of the Thracians. The participants are always male.

Note that older Bulgarians sometimes call Pernik Dimitrovo, its name during Communist times, in honour of Bulgaria's first Communist leader, Georgi Dimitrov.

Past Pernik, following the road to Kyustendil, the **Zemen Monastery of St John ㉑** (Земенски Манастир Св. Йоан Богослов) is situated just outside the town of **Zemen**, about 15 km (9 miles) off the main road. The monastery's 11th-century church contains Bulgaria's best collection of 14th-century frescoes, all of which were painstakingly restored in the 1970s. The church is considered to be one of the best-preserved examples of Bulgarian medieval art and architecture. One fresco, of St Ann, is as old as the church itself. Deconsecrated, the church is preserved as a national monument and entrance is limited to individuals and very small groups. Queues to get inside the church can be long at weekends in the summer.

Gorges and waterfalls

Back on the main road, the **Zemenski Gorge** is a miniature version of the Iskar Gorge, and yet every bit as spectacular, with caves and springs, culminating in the 50-metre (165-ft) high **Polsko-Skakavishki Waterfall** at the village of Polsko-Skakavitsa. Note that no road follows the full length of the gorge: the only way to see it is on foot (there are marked trails from Zemen to Polsko-Skakavitsa and on to Kyustendil), or by train, a lovely ride through the gorge. The railway, on the Sofia-Skopje line, was cut through the gorge in 1909, and there are regular local trains from Pernik to Kyustendil.

Known as Paulitia in Roman times, **Kyustendil ㉒** (Кюстендил) has some impressive Roman ruins. But it is also one of the poorest towns in Bulgaria and lacks anywhere decent to stay or eat. Aside from the ruins, the city's other attraction is the **Vladimir Dimitrov Museum** (Художествена галерия Владимир Димитров – Майстора, ul. Patriarch Eftimii 20; Tues–Sun 9am–noon, 2–5pm; admission charge). Its collection of some 200 works by Dimitrov (1882–1960), the Bulgarian master of socialist-realist painting, is not to many people's taste, and will probably convince you to head back to Pernik or Sofia on the next train. ❏

RESTAURANTS

Iskar Gorge

Cherepish Monastery
The best and most picturesque place to stop for lunch while exploring the Iskar Gorge is the Cherepish Monastery. The bread is made on the premises and goes well with the soups that are a meal in themselves. Prices are astonishingly cheap: a lunch for two will cost no more than 10 leva. €

Vratsa

Hushove Hotel
Tel: (092) 661 349
This gorgeous hotel and restaurant is about 3 km (2 miles) from the centre of Vratsa, on the road to Mezdra. Its garden and terrace offer outstanding views of the surrounding area. The food is also good, which is rare in this area. €€

Klisura Monastery
Tel: (0886) 6560612
A good option for lunch or dinner. The food (not cooked and served by the monks) is terrific, and great value. Expect simple grilled meats with large portions of fresh vegetables and good salads. €€

Berkovitsa

Adashite
3 ul. Zdrazhchenitse
Tel: 0886 741909
An old house close to the centre of the village,

this lovely restaurant serves cheap, simple food. The soups are meals in themselves and make a good lunch time choice.€

Krustevata Kashta
5 ul. Shenovo 5
Tel: (0953) 88099
Restaurant and music venue with live bands, and occasionally a folk show on weekend evenings. Food is good if a little overpriced. Expect international dishes alongside Bulgarian classics.€€€

Belogradchik

Madona Tavern
26 ul. Hristo Botev
Bulgarian bagpipes adorn almost every wall of this little restaurant. Food is cooked and often served by the lady who owns the place (also a small hotel). She takes great care of her customers. €€

Koprivshtitsa

Bulgaria
Bul. Hadzhi Nencho
31 Palaveev
Tel: (01784) 2183
Just north of the village's main square, this cheap and cheerful place possesses a great terrace – perfect in summer – and a cosy inside dining room for winter. Choose from a modest menu featuring all the Bulgarian favourites.

Pod Staata Krushta
Bul. Hadzhi Nencho
56 Palaveev
Tel: (01784) 2163
Bistro-type restaurant serving a wide selection of snacks, meals and beer. Unfussy and unpretentious, it is popular with backpackers on a budget.€

Dyado Liben
Blvd. Hadzhi Nencho
47 Palaveev
Tel: (01784) 21 09
This is the best restaurant in Koprivshtitsa. The charming house in which it is located is half the attraction, but the food plays its part too: a more refined menu than elsewhere in the village, and a great wine list.€€

Pernik

Free Style
8 ul. Naicho Tsanov
Tel: (0898) 548944
About as close to sophistication as Pernik gets. This is an unusually trendy place for the provinces, with great decor and a terrace. The food is simple but tasty, and there is a great range of coffees and aperitifs: locals use it more as a bar. €€€€

PRICE CATEGORIES
Price categories are per person for thee courses:
€ = under 10 leva
€€ = 10–25 leva
€€€ = 25–50 leva
€€€€ = over 50 leva

RIGHT: a hearty and tasty *gyuvech*.

THE SOUTHWEST AND RILA MOUNTAINS

The highest mountains in the Balkans are topped with dramatic peaks and scattered with thousands of tiny lakes and springs. To make the most of this spectacular landscape you will need good walking boots

The Rila is the sixth-highest mountain range in Europe, and the Moussala Peak, at 2,925 metres (9,596 ft), is the highest mountain in the Balkans. Nowhere in Bulgaria – indeed, few places in Europe – can match the majesty of the Rila. Its peaks are dramatic, and so steep that just one mountain pass – the Klisura Pass linking Dupnitsa with Kostenets via Samokov – traverses the range. Elsewhere, brutal, dead-end climbs up battered roads lead to hidden villages. The area has long been associated with the lawless – who came for refuge – and the faithful – who came in search of serenity in its many monasteries.

Inaccessible as much of the Rila may be to man, it is a veritable paradise for wildlife. The Rila is home to three nature reserves: Central Rila, Parangalitsa and Ibar. They are home to more than 2,900 species of animal and insect, from the peculiar short-horned chamois to the Bulgarian *souslik*, a delightful little ground squirrel. Scotch, spruce and ddwarf pines characterise much of the landcape, while the glorious purple spring crocus steals the show. But amongst naturalists the Rila is best known for its moss; more than 242 different species grow here, of which more than 40 are unique and endangered.

The bird life is also amazing. Even casual twitchers can expect to see more than 50 species in the Rila, while anyone on a specialised organised tour can expect to see more than 150 species, including European rarities such as hazel grouse, wall creeper, three-toed woodpecker, rock thrush, rock partidge, alpine accentor and shore lark.

Along the Struma Valley

There are two ways of heading into the **Rila Mountains**. The first is to follow the E79, the main road linking Sofia and Athens, following the Struma valley and passing the Rila and Pirin mountains along the way. This is the best route for visitors who want to see

Map on page 126

LEFT: ceiling frescos in Rila Monastery.
BELOW: a roadside picnic in the Rila.

The martagon lily is one of the loveliest high-altitude flowers that blossoms in the Rila. It is heavily scented and can be seen on many of Rila's trails, most spectacularly in groups of several dozen.

the Rila Monastery and little else. The second, and far more scenic route, is along the mountain road that follows the southern part of the Iskar Valley, passing the Iskar lake and heading into the mountains at Samokov.

Dupnitsa area

Know as Stanke Dimitrov throughout the communist period, **Dupnitsa ❶** (Дупница) is the first town of any size on the Struma river south of Sofia. It was thought until recently to have existed only since the end of the 15th century, but discoveries of a Thracian burial mound, and of a Roman fortress suggest otherwise.

Situated at an altitude of around 500 metres (1,600 ft), Dupnitsa made its fortune in the 18th century as one of Bulgaria's first centres of iron-ore mining, before tobacco farming became the area's main source of income. Today it is the largest tobacco-producing town in the country. Around the modern city centre, centring on the concrete extravaganza that is **Ploschad Svoboda**, a well-preserved 16th-century mosque is an oasis of elegance,

while the town clock-tower, built in 1782, is the town's pride and joy. Of three churches around the town centre, the best is the 17th-century Church of St Constantin and Elena, restored in 1902 and given a National Revival twist. Visitors can also scramble over the ruins of both a medieval and Roman fortress (Kulata) on a hill on the north bank of the Bitritsa river.

Due southeast of Dupnitsa, along a road that will soon be entirely lined with expensive villas, the village of **Bistritsa ❷** (Бистрица) is the first gateway to the Rila Heights. There are two routes up into the high mountains, one via the chalet at **Byal Kladentes**, and another via **Otovitsa**, from where a network of hiking routes and mountain cabins crisscross their way across the entire Rila range.

The hottest mineral spring in Europe (with a mean temperature of 103.8°C/ 218°F), and the Balkan Peninsula's only active geyser, is found at **Sapareva Banya ❸** (Сапарева баня), 14 km (8½ miles) east of Dupnitsa on the road to Samokov. The geyser spurts into the air every 20 seconds, and is

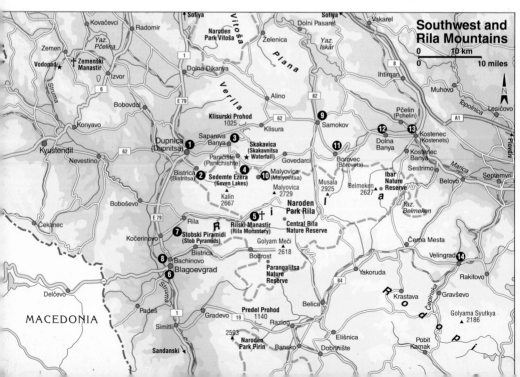

Southwest and Rila Mountains

Map
on page
126

spectacular at night, when it is superbly lit. The resort – originally known as Germania – was the birthplace of the the Byzantine general Flavius Belisarius (505–565), the favourite general of Emperor Justinian I until he was found guilty of corruption and poor leadership during a campaign against the Ostrogoths. Justinian ordered his eyes to be gouged out, and Belisarius died a beggar on the streets of Constantinople.

The resort is popular today as a health spa, and the recently restored mineral baths (Половин Век в Санаториума на Сапарева баня; 7am–7pm; admission charge) harness the water of the hot spring to feed three indoor baths (one for men, one for women and one for families) and one outdoor pool. The baths also offer mud treatments, said to work wonders for sufferers of skin complaints. Ruins of Byzantine Germania can be seen in the sanatorium grounds.

Also close by is the simple Romanesque **Church of St Nikola** (Св. Ннкола), dating from the 13th century. There are *kukeri* festivals in the resort on New Year's Day, while on Shrove Tuesday (known as Todorov Day in Bulgaria), young men from Sepereva Banya and surrounding villages take part in long-distance horse races.

Hiking possibilities

A further 8 km (5 miles) into the mountains **Panichishte** (Паничисте), at 1,300 metres (4,250 ft), is a minor ski resort and major hiking centre. A relatively easy route of around two hours leads up to the **Skakavnitsa Waterfall** (Скакавишки Водопад), the highest in the Rila at 1,750 metres (5,700 ft), with a drop of 70 metres (230 ft). Another easy route of about two hours leads to the incredible **Seven Lakes ❹** (Седемте Езра), an other-worldly sequence of seven glacial lakes, all at different altitudes, with the highest of the lakes, **Salzata** (Салзата, the Tear), lying at 2,535 metres (8,317 ft). None of the lakes is more than 4.5 metres (15 ft) deep, and if you can brave the near-freezing water temperature (even in high summer), swimming is blissful, though at this altitude also very strenuous.

A steep, mainly downhill and very

BELOW: of all the natural wonders of the Rila, the Seven Lakes (Sedemte Ezera) are the most fascinating and popular. They can be accessed by relatively easy hikes from Bistritsa, Sapareva Banya and Malyovitsa.

TIP

The Rila Monastery is visited by most people on day trips from Sofia, but for many the only way to visit Bulgaria's best-known sight is to hike there. There are routes from Blagoevgrad, Bistritsa and Malyovitsa.

BELOW: a visiting patriarch at Rila Monastery.

awkward route from the Seven Lakes mountain cabin takes experienced walkers over to the Rila Monastery in about five hours.

Rila Monastery

The UNESCO-listed **Rila Monastery ❺** (Рилски Манастир Свети Иван Рилски; summer 7am–8pm, winter 8am–5pm; admission charge for the monastery's museum), an outstanding example of Bulgarian National Revival-period architecture, can be seen on a very rushed day trip from Sofia, though a far more leisurely visit is recommended, with tours departing from Borovets, Bansko and Blagoevgrad almost every day of the year.

There is a regular bus service to the monastery from Blagoevgrad, Dupnitsa and the small village of Rila. Independent travellers with cars can drive to the monastery from Blagoevgrad in about an hour. The fit can hike over from Panichiste or Malyovitsa in five hours.

Despite its fame, size and importance, the origins of the monastery – which sits at an altitude of 1,147 metres (3,763 ft) – are unclear. St John of Rila – to whom the monastery is now dedicated, and whose relics are the monastery's most important sacred exhibits – is widely thought to have founded Rila in the 10th century. However, John actually lived in a cave about an hour's walk from the site, and it is more likely that his disciples founded the monastery after his death. For the next three centuries it was expanded and enriched by generous donations from all of Bulgaria's rulers, until being all but destroyed by the Turks in the mid-15th century, on the orders of Sultan Murad II.

Almost immediately however, Murad appeared to have realised that the monastery's destruction was ill-judged, and he set about facilitating its reconstruction. Though it is doubtful that he funded any of the new building, he did not prevent the Russian Orthodox church from doing so. Indeed, the Russians paid for almost everything, donating gospels, icons and vestments to the new monastery, besides sending experts to restore what

remained of the previous building. Despite the goodwill of Sultan Murad, subsequent Ottoman rulers were not so kind. The monks of Rila were harassed, sometimes attacked, and in 1833 a fire (possibly arson) destroyed much of the monastery.

The present-day complex is considered by many to be the country's national treasure, and symbol. Most of it dates from 1833–47, when generous donations from Bulgaria's newly confident families, in the full flush of the National Revival, funded its repair after the 1833 fire.

The sheer size of the complex – from the exterior the monastery looks like a medieval fortress – is impressive, but it is the interior that makes this monastery so outstanding. The only clues to the brilliance within are the painted arcade that serves as the main entrance and the rather awkward, afterthought of a belfry that appears to be breaking through the roof of the main building.

Once inside the eye is drawn immediately to the most spectacular of the monastery buildings, the **Church of the Virgin Birth** (Света Богородица), with its distinctive neo-Byzantine stripes, five brightly-coloured domes, sublime porticos and high colonnades. The murals on the outside depict apocalyptic scenes, from the fall of Constantinople to the fate of people who commit any of the seven deadly sins. The church was designed by architect Pavel Ivanovich, and built between 1834 and 1837.

The **frescoes** inside were added in 1847 by Zahari Zograf, who – most unusually for both him and for sacred art – signed his work. The **iconostasis** is a mass of elaborate gold leaf, and contains many original icons salvaged from the church of the medieval monastery. The hand of St John of Rila (his left hand; the right was lost while his body was touring Russia in the 17th century) is kept inside the church, though it is rarely placed on display. It is said that it has healing powers *(see box, page 130).*

Equally revered is the **grave of Tsar Boris III**, which now contains little more than the former king's heart. Boris died under mysterious circum-

Map on page 126

Detail of a fresco inside Rila's Church of the Virgin Birth.

BELOW:
Rila's extravagantly adorned interior.

BELOW RIGHT: depiction of St John of Rila.

stances in August 1943, after refusing Hitler's request to declare war on the Soviet Union. He was buried here in September 1943, only for his body to be exhumed by the Bulgarian Government in 1944 and moved to Vrana Palace near Sofia. In 1993 an attempt was made to exhume the body again and rebury it at Rila, but only the heart was found.

Less gruesome exhibits in the church include the 12th-century **icon of the Virgin**, paraded around the monastery on Assumption Day (15 August) but usually kept under lock and key and opened only for large tour groups.

The elegant **Tower of Hreylo** looms large beside the church, and is the only part of the original monastery that survives. The **Preobrazhenie Chapel** on the top floor houses a fine museum of 14th-century murals.

Most of the original treasures are now housed in the East Wing Museum. The newest part of the monastery, it was added in 1961. Its outstanding exhibits include the original doors of the Hrelyo Church, countless icons and the Rafail Cross, an amazing work of art that took Rafail – a local priest – 12 years (1790–1802) to complete, and left him all but blind. One piece of wood, the cross contains 104 religious scenes and 650 small figures.

Something resembling an entire village has now grown up around the monastery to serve the tourists and pilgrims who visit it year round, including two hotels, the Tsarev Vruh and the Rilets, of which the latter is easily preferable. The monastery also offers the most basic of accommodation in its dormitories.

There are several excellent hikes in the immediate vicinity, including one to the **Cave of St John of Rila**, where St John lived for most of his life. The cave is northeast of the monastery, and can be reached in about an hour. Access into the cave is via a long, narrow hole through which, it is said, only the penitent may pass. On the way to the cave is the small, 18th-century **St Lucas Chapel** (Свети Лука), with fine but rapidly fading frescoes by Toma Vishanov, a founder of the Bansko school of iconography

The Exorcist

The son of a Serdica (Sofia) merchant, St John of Rila (*circa* 876–946) became a priest at the age of 25 before abandoning civilisation on the death of his parents to take up residence in a dark, damp cave in the Rila Mountains. But he was foiled in his attempt to live a solitary life by great numbers of followers and pilgrims who besieged his cave seeking his help, for he was said to be an outstanding exorcist.

On his death some disciples founded Rila Monastery, which they dedicated to him, preserving him an eternal place in the Bulgarian Orthodox canon. His remains – said to have the same miraculous powers as John himself – were taken to Serdica on the orders of Tsar Peter I. After the Magyar King Béla III conquered Serdica in 1183, they were sent to the Hungarian capital of Esztergom and remained there for four years before being returned to Sofia in 1187. In 1194, Bulgarian Tsar Ivan Asen I ordered them to be moved to Veliko Tarnovo, his capital. They survived the Turkish conquest of the city in 1393, before being returned to Rila Monastery in 1469 on the orders of Sultan Murad II, partly in repentance for having destroyed the original monastery 10 years earlier. Since then parts of John's body have been stolen, destroyed or simply lost, and only the left hand remains.

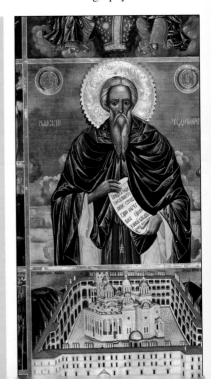

Blagoevgrad

Often called Bulgaria's Cambridge, **Blagoevgrad ⑥** (Благоевград) is the largest city in the southwest of Bulgaria, with a population of around 75,000. Associated with culture and learning, it sits on a wide shelf, between the Rila Heights and the Macedonian border, dissected by the Struma river. It was known as Gorna Dzumaya until 1950, when it was renamed in honour of Dimitar Blagoev, the founder of the Bulgarian Communist Party. Unlike other place names changed in Communist times, this one has stuck.

Traditionally a centre of industry, including the tobacco industry, it is also a cultural hub. A centre of erudition since the Rila monks set up a university here in the 17th century, it has four universities and thousands of students who swell the population during term time. It has a fine history museum, extensive parks, and in Varosha *(see below)*, one of the best-preserved quarters of National Revival houses in the country. It is also a major and long-established spa resort with more than 30 hot springs,

some of which reach temperatures of 55°C (130°F).

Varosha (Вароша), which sits at the foot of the Loven Dom, the hill above Blagoevgrad, is a beautifully preserved district dotted with often outrageously designed but soberly decorated National Revival-era houses. Described by steep and often narrow cobbled streets, the district is home of the rather dotty **Church of the Assumption of the Virgin Mary** (Вуведение Богородично, ulitsa Bistritsa; 9am–6pm), topped with fantastic Byzantine squiggles and a high, elegant belfry. Built in the 18th century, the church was much renovated in the 1990s.

Close to the church is Blagoevgrad's excellent **History Museum** (Исторически Музей Благоевград, ulitsa Rila 1, tel: 73-235 57; Mon–Sat 9am–noon, 1–5.30pm; admission charge), with exhibits from every period of Bulgaria's history, from the Thracian to the Communist periods. It has a good collection of icons, and a recently opened department devoted to the natural history of the Rila Mountains.

Map on page 126

Blagoevgrad Kukeri festival, held on Christmas Day, is one of the largest in Bulgaria.

BELOW: Blagoevgrad's pedestrianised city centre.

Exploring the exhibits in Blagoevgrad's excellent History Museum.

Crossing the river, smart, pedestrianised streets lead to **Ploschad Makedoniya**, the city centre, dominated by the Nikola Vaptsarov Theatre on one side, and the former city Communist party HQ on the other. Ironically, the latter is today the American University in Bulgaria.

Given its annual influx of bright young things, it is no surprise that Blagoevgrad is one of the major cultural centres of Bulgaria, with a varied programme of concerts, exhibitions and plays. It has a chamber opera noted throughout the country, and also plays host to the Pirin folk ensemble, the most popular folk music combo in Bulgaria (when not away touring they perform at the American University, whose website, www. aubg.bg, posts its programme of events).

The city is also a busy nightlife scene, with more bars, clubs and discos per capita than any other city in the provinces. This centres on ploschad Makedoniya, which is lined with cafés, restaurants and bars, whose smart and relatively expensive terraces spill out on to the square in summer.

The Stob Pyramids

A short drive north of Bagoevgrad at **Stob** (Стоб), on the route to Rila Monastery, are the spectacular **Stob Pyramids** ❼ (Стоб Пирамите) – natural red rock formations of varying shapes (though none like pyramids), some as high as 18 metres (60 ft). The best time to visit is at sunset, when the late sun bathes the rocks in a glorious deep-red light. Access to the rocks – currently a tricky and energetic 45-minute walk up a rocky path from the village – is set to improve with the construction of a proper trail, complete with information centre at the base.

Hiking options

Bachinovo ❽ (Бачиново), 3.5 km (2 miles) north of Blagoevgrad, is the starting point for hikes across the mountains. Routes lead to the Seven Lakes *(seee page 127)*, and to Dupnitsa *(see page 126)* via the Ivan Vazov mountain cabin. Further along the same valley is the resort of **Bistritsa** (Бистрица), another hiking base and the best point of access to the

(seee page 127) ... *(see page 126)*

BELOW:
architectural detail, Blagoevgrad.

Parangalitsa Nature Reserve (Парангалица Резерват), the second oldest in Bulgaria, having been set up in 1933 and listed on the UNESCO List of Biospheric Reserves under the Man and Biosphere Program since 1977. Its name is derived from the Greek *parangalos*, meaning "forbidden" or "off limits".

Occupying part of the southwestern slopes of the Rila Mountain, the reserve contains some of the oldest spruce forests in Europe, with many of the trees more than 200 years old and one particular tree that is said to be 63 metres (206 ft) high. These forests provide ideal habitats for bears, wolves, foxes and deer.

Samokov and the High Rila

The most direct route into the Rila Mountains from Sofia is along the Iskar Valley. It is a good road whose rise is gradual, though there are a few switchback hairpins just before it reaches **Samokov ❾** (Самоков), the commercial centre of the region, and long a byword for crafts and art. The town is home to 30,000 people, and famous for its potatoes.

During the 19th century Samokov School of Art was the leading producer of woodcarvings and frescos for monasteries and churches throughout the country. Fine examples of the school's work can be seen at the town's Church of the Assumption of the Holy Virgin *(see below)*, and in the lavish murals at Rila Monastery *(see page 128)*.

Today Samokov is really little more than a gateway to the ski resorts of the Rila range, in particular Borovets, which is just 11 km (7 miles) away *(see page135)*. It has also become a popular place for Sofia's wealthy middle class – and many foreigners – to purchase second homes.

Samokov's **History Museum** (Исторически Музей Самоков; 4 ulitsa Liubtcho Baramov; Mon–Fri 9am–5pm; admission charge) tells the story of the town's evolution from becoming

the hub of the local mining and smelting industries in the 14th century to a centre of craftwork.

Other buildings worth seeking out are the late-Ottoman **Bairakli Dzhamiya Mosque** (Ploschad Dzhamiya, Mon–Fri 8am–5pm) on the main square, dating from 1840, and the **Church of the Assumption of the Holy Virgin**, a short walk south of the mosque. The church is exquisite, having been built from 1790–93 by a collective of the finest builders, architects, painters and woodcarvers that the Samokov School had to offer.

Malyovitsa ❿ (Мальовица) – which sits underneath a dramatic peak of the same name – is a small ski resort 27 km (17 miles) southwest of Samokov. While Vitosha is regarded as the birthplace of Bulgarian hiking, so Malyovitsa is considered the cradle of Bulgarian mountaineering. It is easy to see why: the Malyovitsa peak simply begs to be climbed, and will give the most jaded of climbers itchy feet. There is a mountain cabin at the top, from where there is a trail descending to Rila Monastery.

Map on page 126

TIP

From the village of Yavorova Polyana near Govedartsi, 13 km (8 miles) southwest of Samokov, a three-hour botanical trail to Urdin Cirque showcases the best in Rila's flora. The signposted hike takes in caves, natural rock formations, and nine viewing points from where walkers can see more than 60 species of alpine flower.

BELOW: the Stob Pyramids.

Hiking in the Rila

If you only go hiking in one region of Bulgaria, make it the Rila. There are more than 2,000 km (1,240 miles) of marked trails, spectacular scenery, challenging but accessible peaks, lakes – both natural and man-made – flora, fauna and superb mountain cabins. The entire range is crisscrossed by superb well-marked hiking routes, sustained by a vast network of excellent mountain cabins.

Preparation is all

Hiking trails in Bulgaria use the four-colour marking system common throughout Europe: red, blue, green and yellow, with red usually signifying the most precipitous route. In winter a fifth symbol is used: yellow and black stakes, which denote the safest route to shelter in thick snow.

It is essential that hikers take the weather forecast into consideration before setting out. The majority of Rila's trails take in terrain over 2,000 metres (6,500 ft) high, and the weather up here can quite literally change from one moment to the next. Always carry a warm layer of clothes (even if setting out for a hike in hot sunshine in the middle of summer) and waterproofs.

Hikers will also need to get hold of a good map, with all routes and cabins clearly marked.

The best – of many – is the 1:55,000 map published by Kartografiya Eood. It can be bought in most Bulgarian bookshops, and is stocked by most hotel receptions in and around the Rila range. The same publishing house produces similarly good maps of the Balkan and Rhodope mountain ranges.

The mountain cabins of the Rila range offer food, shelter, first aid and camaraderie for the legions of tourists who walk the mountains every year. There are currently 21 cabins offering a total of more than 1,500 beds. The chalets range from the basic to the semi-luxurious, but all offer simple food and accommodation for very little money. Almost all of the cabins are operated by the Rilski Tourist Association, which has its headquarters in Samokov (2 ul. Iskar, tel: 0722-22 205). They can arrange accommodation in their cabins and help hikers plan routes best suited to their ability, experience, and prevailing weather conditions.

If things go wrong, the Bulgarian Mountain Rescue Service – part of the country's Red Cross – is on hand, with volunteers patrolling most of the country's busiest trails. In emergencies – if you have a mobile telephone – they can be contacted on 088-18 43. Another option is the Rila National Park Hotline, tel: 073-805 37.

Hiking areas

The Rila can be roughly split into three sub-ranges. The first, the **Eastern Rila**, around the Moussala peak, is the highest and offers the most challenging terrain for hikers. The route from Malka Moussala to the Moussala cabin, along a startling ridge, passing eight lakes, including the Ledonoto Lake (at 2,709 metres/8,887 ft the highest in the Rila) is not for the faint hearted.

The **Middle Rila**, around the Central Nature Reserve, is rich in glacial lakes, and extremely remote. It is a day's hike just to get up here, and can only really be seen as part of a multi-day hike. There are cabins with beds for the night at Ribnite Ezera (Fish Lakes) and more above Smradlivoto Lake.

The **Western Rila**, around the Rila Monastery, offers the easiest and most accessible terrain in the range, and is best suited for hikers wanting to get up and down the mountain in a day. The Seven Lakes, the monastery itself and the Dodov Vrah peak can all be reached on long one-day hikes to and from Bistritsa or Malyovitsa. ❏

LEFT: be prepared for changing weather conditions.

Skiing and hot baths

The largest and best-known of Bulgaria's ski resorts, **Borovets** (Боровец) has been playing host to visitors since the mayor of Samokov built a chalet here in the 1890s for his wife to stay in in order to alleviate her tuberculosis; other wealthy families quickly followed suit, including the tsar, who built a hunting lodge known as the Tsarska Bistritsa (Царска Бистрица) in a glade above the resort (the beginners' ski route down from the top of the Sitnyakovo chairlift passes by the lodge).

The resort, then known as Chamkoriya, remained an exclusive hideaway of the rich until the early 1950s, when the Communist authorities made the decision to develop the resort primarily for the use of party members. The idea of investing heavily in hotels and ski lifts to attract foreign cash was a 1960s afterthought, but an inspired one.

Since then the resort has seen massive development, and is today dominated by two enormous hotels, the Rila and the Samokov, in many ways self-contained resorts themselves. From the Hotel Rila a network of chairlifts and drag lifts branch out to form one of the ski areas, known as the Sitnyakovo, while a fast gondola lift whisks skiers up to the second and far more challenging ski area, the Yastrabets, from its terminus just beside the Hotel Samokov.

In all there are 58 km (36 miles) of piste in Borovets, some of it quite challenging. Snow is usually reliable from late December to the end of March, and the pistes at the top of the Yastrabets gondola, in the Markudjik bowl, are often skiable well into May. The vertical drop at Borovets is over 1,300 metres (4,270 ft), by far the longest in the country.

Hiking around Borovets

Once the snow has gone, skiers give way to hikers, walkers, mountain bikers and lovers of the mountain air. The gondola and chairlifts remain open throughout the year, and in recent times the resort has become as busy in summer as in winter. The most interesting and challenging – for

Map on page 126

TIP

Wherever you stay in Borovets, be it the luxurious Samokov or the simple Malina chalets, prices are always cheaper as part of a package tour. Turning up on spec can be expensive, and at weekends during the high season (February and Easter) risky, as the resort is usually full.

BELOW: a sleigh ride in Borovets.

Map on page 126

the fit – is the walk up to Yastrabets (which takes a good five hours) and from there onwards to the peak of Moussala itself (another 90 minutes). A less strenuous way to enjoy the same route is to take the gondola lift up, and then walk down.

Spas of the Maritsa Valley

Just past Borovets the mountain road joins up with the Maritsa Valley, home to several spa resorts that make the most of their often meagre thermal waters. The largest resort is at **Dolna Banya** ⑫ (Долна Баня), whose decent public-bath complex offers infusions of healing waters by every imaginable means.

Neighbouring **Gornovasilishki** and **Pchelin** also have public spas but are less accessible and far less used to foreign visitors.

A bit further on is probably the most satisfactory resort in the area, **Kostenets Banya** (Костенец Баня), a somewhat exclusive place 7 km (4 miles) south of the small town of **Kostenets** ⑬ (Костенец). It is worth visiting for its incredible waterfall, which, while not

the highest in Bulgaria, is certainly one of the most dramatic. You will find it immediately south of the resort, on the path that leads up to the Belmeken (Белмекен) cabin and peak at 2,627 metres (8,618 ft).

From here marked trails lead over to **Lake Belmeken**, an artificial but supremely picturesque and eerily quiet lake formed by the construction of the Belmeken hydro-electric complex.

Velingrad

From Kostenets the mountain road skirts around the edge of the Rila Mountains to Bulgaria's leading spa resort, **Velingrad** ⑭ (Велинград). On the site of more than 70 springs, some of which reach 86°C (187°F), the resort's waters have been used to heal arthritis, varicose veins and pulmonary illnesses since Roman times. The main bath complex in the resort is the Velyova Banya, built by the Turks in the 16th century, while in the summer the outdoor complex of Kamenitsa is more popular. The choice of hotels in Velingrad is the best in the Rila range outside Borovets.   ❑

BELOW: Borovets as dusk falls.

RESTAURANTS

Dupnitsa

Starata Vorba

3 ul. Vardar

Tel: 0899 250025

A short walk from the town centre this little *mehana* serves a wide variety of Bulgarian food in extraordinary surroundings: check out the local take on *The Last Supper* that fills one of the walls. Full of nooks and crannies, and with live music at weekends. €€

Blagoevgrad

Dream

7 ul. Arseni Kostentsev

Sharing a building with the popular Underground pub (which is in the basement) this classy restaurant serves a good range of international dishes alongside some Bulgarian favourites. Service is slick if a bit too ceremonious.€€€

Mehana Kristo Hotel

ul. Komitrov

Tel: (073) 88 04 44

For traditional Bulgarian food in Blagoevgrad this great little *mehana* on the first-floor of the Kristo hotel is the only place to come. Decorated in a superbly over-the-top traditional style, it serves food that is hearty and homely, and simple but tasty. €€

RIGHT: soup and salad in a *mehana*.

Tuborg

ul. Bratia Kitanovi

One of the best places in the city. Expect good pub food and a friendly student crowd that gets a little loud later on in the evening. €€

Govedartsi

Govedartsi

53 ul. Iskar

Close to the ski resort of Malyovitsa, this small hotel and restaurant possesses one of the loveliest settings in the country. Come in summer when you can sit outside and enjoy the wonderful air and great mountain cuisine. €€€

Borovets

Hungry Horse

Opposite Hotel Rila

Live English football coverage brings in rowdy groups of Brits when a match is taking place, but if you can avoid them then this cosy place is the best choice in the resort. Sunday roasts and English breakfasts, plus huge and tender steaks. Plenty for vegetarians too. €€€€

Mamacita's

Opposite Hotel Rila

Tel: (0889) 591 234

Food is simple but good, and slanted towards the Brits who flock here (English breakfast a speciality). €€€

White Magic

Opposite Hotel Samokov

Tel: (07128) 27 53

You'll find good steaks, Bulgarian classics and huge salads in this pub and restaurant run by a former Bulgarian ski champion and his wife. More popular as a bar than a restaurant, it gets very crowded during the peak ski season. Make a reservation. €€€

Velingrad

Dvoretsa Hotel

8 ul. Tosho Staikov

Tel: (0359) 56200

Perhaps the only place in the resort where a real chef actually creates food as opposed to merely preparing it. Expect high standards of modern European cuisine, at correspondingly high prices. €€€

Omar Tavern

Hotel Rich

500 Bul. Svedinenie

Tel: (0359) 57803

Holds a kitsch floorshow on Friday and Saturday nights featuring belly dancers alongside traditional Bulgarian folk musicians. Go for the fixed menu: a long procession of Bulgarian favourites. €€€

PRICE CATEGORIES

Price categories are per person for 3 courses:

€ = under 10 leva

€€ = 10–25 leva

€€€ = 25–50 leva

€€€€ = over 50 leva

MONASTERIES – THE NATION'S TREASURE HOUSES

Centres of religion, art, learning and national consciousness, Bulgaria's monasteries tell the story of the country's history

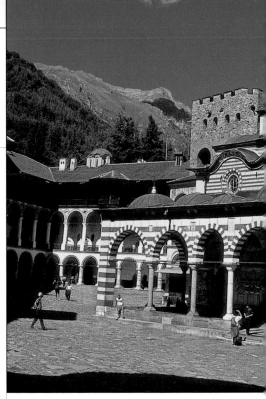

It is a tale that began in 865 AD when the country converted to Christianity under Boris I. While much of European architecture was, well, monastic, Bulgarian monasteries were often fanciful, with dramatic outlines and colourful facades, the free and elaborate expression of the first Bulgarian Kingdom.

In 972, Bulgaria was annexed by the Byzantine Empire, and the monasteries were all but demolished. They flourished again during the renaissance of the Second Bulgarian Kingdom (1185–1396) and were rebuilt with fortifications, houses and even farms within their control.

Under Ottoman rule (1396–1876), the clergy was forced to lie low, but Christian Bulgar culture lived on in the monasteries, and many of them came to be citadels in the struggle for liberation.

When the Communists came to power in 1944, it was a mixed blessing. The monasteries were painstakingly restored, but they were stripped of any religious significance, and turned into lifeless museums. Now back in the hands of the Church, the more popular monasteries, replete with hotels, shops and restaurants, have become national treasures, and magnets for Bulgarian and international visitors alike.

ABOVE: Rila Monastery is an outstanding example of National Revival architecture. A UNESCO World Heritage Site on account of its stunning interior frescos, it is considered the country's most important monument.

ABOVE: in the 13th and 14th centuries a number of churches and chapels were dug deep into the rock face of remote gorges. Here at the Ivanovo Rock Monastery, founded near Rousse in the 13th century, exquisite medieval frescos by artists from Velika Tarnovo survive to this day.

TOP: Christ Pantocrator ("Christ, Ruler of All") was one of the earliest Christian icons.

LEFT: a Bulgarian Orthodox priest visiting Rila Monastery.

ICONS AND MURALS

"Idols are seductive and temptations unrelenting"
Pope John Paul II, at Rila Monastery, 2002

The late pope, on his visit to Bulgaria, was echoing the sentiments that led the Orthodox Church to resist three-dimensional religious depictions, such as statues of their saints. In ancient Rome, pagans prayed to their statues for riches, fertility and courage in battle. Orthodox icons on the other hand were "windows to the kingdom of Heaven", and the saints depicted were only to be venerated – they could intercede with God on behalf of the faithful, but they were not to be prayed to.

Religious icons are found in homes all over Bulgaria, and churches are bursting at the seams with them. The largest is the iconostasis, an icon-covered wall between nave and sanctuary, symbolising the border between Heaven and Earth. The iconographic style (the palette, the forms, the composition) is carried over into the large scale wall and ceiling murals that grace many Bulgarian churches, the most famous of which is at Rila.

BELOW: the wall paintings at Bachkovo Monastery, one of the largest and most celebrated monasteries of all, are among the most treasured Orthodox art works of the 14th–19th centuries.

BELOW: in this St George icon from the Cherepish Monastery, the church bells toll the dragon's demise as the warrior arrives on his mount.

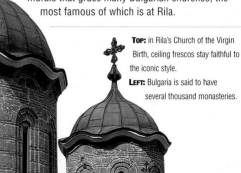

TOP: in Rila's Church of the Virgin Birth, ceiling frescos stay faithful to the iconic style.
LEFT: Bulgaria is said to have several thousand monasteries.

THE PIRIN MOUNTAINS

The smallest of the Bulgarian ranges, the remote Pirin was seldom visited by outsiders until recently. However, the development of Bansko as an international ski resort has put the entire region on the map

I f you believe the local legends the men of the Pirin Mountains were the most feared in all of Thrace, and later provided the backbone of the Macedonian Army that swept all before it on its journey to the ends of the earth. One legend even has it that Spartacus, the famous gladiator who became leader of the Third Roman Slave Revolt of 73–1 BC, was born in Sandanski.

Given the rugged terrain that distinguishes the Pirin, it is easy to see why legends of supermen have been nurtured here. The Bulgarian Pirin range can roughly be described by the Gradevska and Elovitsa rivers to the north, the Mesta river to the east, the Greek border to the south, and the Struma river to the west. **Mount Vihren** (Вихрен) is the Pirin's highest peak, and at 2,914 metres (9,560 ft) is the second highest in Bulgaria, after Moussala.

Bansko makes a good base for most people, and with its handsome architecture and lively town centre it certainly offers more than other town, in the region. But if you want to push on into the remote and deeply traditional Pirin, Gotse Delchev or Melnik may be slightly better choices.

In 1979 the bulk of the Pirin range was declared a national park, and since 1983 much of it has been on UNESCO's World Heritage List, mainly to protect the hundreds of rare and endemic species of Balkan Pleistocene flora.

Along the Gradevska Valley

At **Simitli** ❶ (Симитли), a small, attractive but dull town, the E79 from Sofia to Athens splits in two, with one fork continuing along the Struma Valley to the Greek border, and the other heading off into the deep Pirin. Passing through the villages of **Gradevo** (Градево), **Sarandachka** (Сарандачка) and **Baba Sveta** (Баба Света), this mountain road climbs steadily but spectacularly up to the **Predel Pass** at 1,142 metres (3,746 ft), which according to tradition marks the border

Map on page 142

LEFT: a village in the Pirin.
BELOW: meeting and greeting in Bansko.

The Thracians knew
the Pirin as the
Orbelus (Snowy)
Mountains, the Slavs
knew them as
Judenitsa (Land of
Legend), and the
Turks Berid
(Remote). Though the
modern-day name,
Pirin, has been in
common use for less
than 200 years, it has
its origins in the
Thracian word for
rock, Perinto.

between the Rila and the Pirin ranges. The top of the pass has become a little spoilt in recent years by the construction of some tacky snack bars and fast-food outlets. A more satisfactory mountain cabin just above the top of the pass is the starting point for a long but superb two-day hike up to the summit of the almost perfect natural pyramid that is **Mount Vihren** ❷ (stopping overnight at the Yavarov chalet). On the other side of the pass is **Razlog** (Разлог), a pleasant enough place whose main attraction is its narrow-gauge railway which runs up to Dobrinishte via Bansko. It also has a good number of National Revival era houses, situated around ploschad Makedoniya, the central square of the old town.

Paradise lost and found

Nowhere in Bulgaria illustrates better the mixed blessings and conflicts of unfettered capitalism than the town of **Bansko** ❸ (Банско), 60 km (37 miles) from Blagoevgrad, and 120 km (75 miles) from Sofia. While conservationists scream that the recent devel-

opment of the ski area and hotel building – since 2003 more than 100 hotels and holiday apartment complexes have been built – have seen paradise lost, for skiers and the many locals who have made fortunes on the back of mass tourism, the place is paradise found. Our opinion is that everyone will find something enchanting about Bansko, whether it is the skiing (*see page 144*) or the cobbled streets and *mehanas* of the Old Town.

Local legend has it that the town was founded in the 11th century by the blinded army of Tsar Samuil, who had recently lost a battle at Blagoevgrad to the Byzantine Emperor Basil II. Instead of taking prisoners, Basil blinded 14,000 of Samuil's soldiers, leaving just one man in a hundred with the sight in one eye, to lead the others home. Samuil blamed himself for the defeat and committed suicide when the army reached Bansko; his soldiers then refused to go any further and stayed, founding the town.

Like many legends in Bulgaria, however, the facts do not support the myth. The first documented evidence of

Pirin Mountains

a settlement here dates from as recently as the 16th century, after which the town quickly became an important trading post on the alternative route from the Aegean to central Europe. It developed into a centre of arts and crafts in the early 18th century, and was at the forefront of the National Revival movement in the late 18th and 19th centuries. Much of the town's architecture dates from this time.

Banskso's town centre

With the majority of its new buildings confined to the outskirts around the gondola lift station, downtown Bansko is an architectural theme park, with more than 130 houses, churches, inns and other buildings which have been declared national monuments. Its cultural credentials are impressive too: it is the home town of Paisius of Hilendar, whose *History of the Slav-Bulgarians* (1792) marked the birth of the National Revival movement; Neofit Rilski (1783–1881), author of the first Bulgarian Grammar (*Bulgarska Gramatika*, 1835); Toma Vishanov (1750–1819), founder of the Bansko

School of Arts, who painted many of the frescos in the Church of the Assumption at Rila Monastery; and Nikola Vaptsarov (1909–43), widely considered Bulgaria's greatest 20th-century poet.

Unsurprisingly, most of the town's main sights all have a connection to these three sons of Bansko. Pride of place is given to the **Nikola Vaptsarov Museum** (Къща-музей Никола Вапцаров, 3 ploschad Nikola Vaptsarov; 9am–noon, 2–6pm; admission charge) on the city's modern square, **ploschad Nikola Vaptsarov**, which also features a comically socialist-realist statue of the great poet. Having been shot as a revolutionary by Bulgarian fascists, Vaptsarov had the necessary recommendations for a museum in Communist Valhalla, and the house is a recreation of the poet's childhood home. Besides the requisite Vaptsarov exhibition (which for no apparent reason features his mother prominently), there is also an art and craft gallery, where many items are for sale.

The cobbled centre of Old Bansko

Map on page 142

BELOW: Bansko's monument to Paisius of Hilendar. Bansko.

Bulgaria's Ski Resorts

Skiing in Bulgaria is fast becoming as important to the tourist industry as the Black Sea resorts. Facilities are improving all the time and prices are extremely competitive. The three main centres – Pamporovo, Borovets and Bansko – are experiencing a massive boom, with money pouring into resort infrastructure.

All three of the main ski resorts have decent lifts, runs and après ski, and for the more adventurous there is night- and cross-country skiing, the best of which is the picturesque lantern-lit run in Bansko. Snowboard and ski-rental rates are among the cheapest in Europe, and there are ski schools in all the resorts, with English-speaking instructors catering to all levels of experience. Off-piste skiing is possible although a guide is recommended.

Bulgaria's bid for the Winter Olympics in 2014 was unsuccessful, but it signalled just how seriously the country is taking its winter sports. It was not the country's first bid – it tried twice in the 1990s – and it will not be the last.

Bansko

Bansko is establishing itself as the country's ski resort of choice, mainly because it combines an historic town centre with good facilities, both on and off-piste. It also has the best snow record and the longest ski season, invariably beginning in mid-December and lasting until the end of April and sometimes into May. Traditional wooden buildings sit alongside smart apartments with state-of-the-art spas, luxury hotels and log-fire heated *mehanas*.

The town sits just below the 1,000-metre (3,280 ft) mark, but the runs which tower above are usually well-covered. The slopes of Todorin Vruh are the best spot for novices, but the more adventurous can take the triple chair lift to the top of the peak and try the new "Alberto Tomba" black run,

Vitosha

The small resort of Vitosha, just 10 km (6 miles) outside Sofia, gets crowded with Bulgarian skiers during weekends, but is unlikely to interest most foreign travellers, unless as a day trip during the week *(see page 100)*.

Borovets

Although this is Bulgaria's oldest resort, dating back over a century, its buildings are almost exclusively modern (don't expect chocolate-box scenes). Over a hundred years ago, Prince Ferdinand came to Borovets and built a handful of villas and a hunting lodge here in the middle of the scenic pine forest. The Communist Party commandeered it for its members soon after gaining power, and today it forms a centre for package holidays and regularly hosts winter-sports competitions. Expect a fairly young crowd, attracted by the specially designed snowboarding run, with a vertical drop of 320 metres (1,049 ft), a man-made "Rotata" half-pipe and plenty of natural hits and rollers. The skiing here is perhaps the most challenging in Bulgaria *(see page 135)*.

Pamporovo

This purpose-built resort in the middle of the Rhodope Mountains is the most southerly ski resort in eastern Europe; this means visitors often get sun with their snow, which lasts more than 100 days on average. There is a wide range of runs, most biased towards beginners, making it a good choice for families. Novice snowboardes will appreciate the high teacher-to-student ratios. Like Borovets, it has plenty of boisterous clubs and bars, but families are better catered for here. *(See page 175.)* ❑

LEFT: let it snow, from December to May.

is a sharp walk up **ul. Nikola Vapt-sarov** – there is no escaping the poet here – which tips out at **Ploschad Vazrazhdane** (Пл. Възраждане), a glorious showcase of National Revival architecture. The sights come thick and fast as you walk around this part of Bansko – a pleasure in itself given the richness of the stone architecture – but look out for the **Icon Exhibition** (Постоянна Иконна Изложба, 3 ulitsa Yane Sandanski; 9am–noon, 2–6pm; admission charge), a jaw dropping collection of icons painted by the top boys of the Bansko School, including its founder Toma Visharov, and his son Dimitar.

Ploschad Vazrazhdane – with a monument to the historian and monk Paisius of Hillendar at its centre – is overlooked by the enormous tower of the **Church of the Holy Trinity** (Цирка Света Троица), the largest church in Bulgaria when built in 1850 (and still second only to the Alexander Nevski Cathedral in Sofia). It is rather plain on the outside, and most of its treasures are within, although even here the straight lines and flat ceilings are in marked contrast to the extravagant interiors of most Bulgarian Orthodox churches. The undoubted highlight is the wooden iconostasis, carved by local maestro Velyan Ognev and packed with icons by local – though unidentified – painters.

Just behind the church the **Neofit Rilski House Museum** (Къща-музей Неофит Рилски, 17 ulitsa Pirin, 9am–noon, 2–6pm; admission charge) was founded in 1981 and commemorates Rilski, the founder of the Bulgarian secular educational movement. The house is a jewel, dating from the late 18th century and built for the Benina family. It is far larger than most of the National Revival era, with big rooms and enormous bay windows. Most are simply furnished in the contemporary style, but a couple of rooms on the upper floor are given over to the life and work of Rilski (with a special fuss made of an original copy of his groundbreaking *Bulgarska Gramatika*).

Fans of National Revival interiors should also head for the 18th-century **Velyanova House** (Велянова Къща; 5 ulitsa Velyan Ognev; 9am–noon,

Map on page 142

TIP

To help generate year-round interest in the Bansko area, there are plans to create an Ian Woosnam- signature 18-hole (par 72) golf course in the area, linked to a sports complex and horse-riding centre.

BELOW: local textiles for sale in Bansko's market.

The counter of a typically rustic mehana.

BELOW: the idyllic village of Delchevo.

2–6pm; admission charge) distinguished by its carved wooden ceilings, the work of its original owner, Volyan Ognev.

Skiing at Bansko

Bansko's main attraction though is its skiing. Until very recently would-be skiers had to take a treacherous and rather unpleasant 45-minute coach ride up to the ski centre at **Shiligarnika** (Шилигарника), as a result of which most foreign visitors went skiing elsewhere. Everything changed when a high-speed, two-stage gondola lift was built for the 2003–4 ski season, linking the town directly to the ski area. At the same time, the ski area itself was modernised, with new lifts and ski runs constructed, and a massive international promotional campaign launched to attract skiers. It worked.

Bansko today offers 66 km (40 miles) of ski runs. In good snow it is possible to ski from the top station at Mount Todorka (2,560 metres/8,400 ft) all the way down to Bansko itself, a route of 22 km (14 miles), one of the longest ski runs in Europe. Most of the skiing on Mount Todorov is almost snow-sure from early December to mid-April, and almost all is suitable for beginners and intermediate skiers. Until the neighbouring Kutelo Mountain is further developed, there is little for advanced skiers in Bansko.

Lift queues are rare, though it is wise to get the gondola lift up the mountain as early as possible on weekends in high season, as the mid-station can become a mid-morning bottleneck. Unlike the other Bulgarian resorts, pistes in Bansko are kept immaculately groomed; artificial snow-making machines cover half of the ski area.

Around Bansko

The terminus of the Pirin narrow-gauge railway, **Dobrinishte** ➍ (Добринище), 6 km (4 miles) from Bansko, is another ski resort in the making, with a recently constructed chairlift up to the Bezbog chalet at 2,259 metres (7,411ft) attracting skiers looking for a more challenging experience than Bansko provides. For now though Dobrinishte is a charming little village with a large outdoor ther-

Map on page 142

mal-bath complex fed by hot springs, open all year round, allowing you to take a steaming hot bath while surrounded by snow.

The village is a great starting point for hikes, and it offers probably the easiest route up into the high Pirin, a 4½-hour walk up to Bezbog via the Gotse Delchev chalet. Halfway up this route is the **Tall Fir** (Високата Ела, Visokata Ela), at 45 metres (148 ft) the tallest tree in the Pirin Mountains.

From the Bezbog chalet innumerable hikes cross the Pirin, including assaults up the peaks of **Polezhan** (2,850 metres/9,350 ft), **Kamenitsa** (2,816 metres/9,238 ft) and **Samodivski** (2,730 metres/8,956 ft). The area is punctured with many small lakes, but the steep ridges of the high Pirin make them less accessible than those in the Rila. Another route takes in the Pirin cabin on the way down to Gotse Delchev, a superb two-day hike.

Along a scenic mountain road **Gotse Delchev ❺** (Гоце Делчев) is 48 km (30 miles) past Bansko, and is the modern successor to the Roman town of Nikopolis ad Nestum, founded close by in the 2nd century. A Greek version of the Roman name, Nevrokop, survived until 1959 when the town was renamed for Bulgaria's greatest revolutionary, Gotse Delchev.

It is a wonderful town to explore, not just for its sights but for its relaxed air and good choice of hotels. The **Town History Museum** (Исторически Музей Гоце Делчев; ulitsa Hristo Botev; Mon–Fri 9am–noon, 2–5.30pm; admission charge) offers a sizeable exhibition of costumes, handicrafts and photographs documenting the town's history, all housed in the **Prokopovata Kashta**, a stunning three-storey house dating from 1879, and far more Secession or Art Nouveaux than traditional National Revival in style.

For National Revival architecture, take a good long walk around the ensemble of houses along ulitsa Hristo Botev, ulitsa Targovska and ulitsa Ivan Vazov in the old city centre.

Just north of here, on the modern town's main square, **Ploschad Soloun**, is the 1838 **Church of the Assumption**, with a wide range of frescos painted by artists from the Bansko

Roman artefacts in the Town History Museum in Gotse Delchev, the modern successor to the Roman town of Nikopolis ad Nestum.

BELOW:
preparing tobacco leaves for drying in Gotse Delchev.

A trusty horse sports a festive pompom. Sandanski hosts the Pirin Folk Festival, held in September.

BELOW: rainbow over a valley floor.

school. The earlier **Church of the Archangel Michael**, built in 1811, is notable for its iconostasis, added in 1881 and incorporating the church's original gates, besides 70 icons painted by local artist Sergi Georgiev. It is in the south of the town, on ulitsa Evarkh Antim on the other side of the river.

Outside of town – to the east – there is a modern and rather dull monastery at **Gotsedelchevski**, while at the end of the same twisting road is the sweet village of **Delchevo** ❻ (Делчево), a gorgeous place at an altitude of 1,300 metres (4,265 ft), from where a superb two-day hike over to Petrovo begins.

East of Gotse Delchev are the ruins of **Nikopolis ad Nestum** (Никополис ад Нестум), just past the modern spa complex at **Ognyanova** (Огняновски Минерални бани; daily 7am–7pm; admission charge). Nikopolis was founded by Emperor Trajan to celebrate his victory over the Dacians, and served as a staging post on the route from Constantinople to the Adriatic. The site is constantly being excavated and yields new finds all the time. So far the bases of fortifications and towers, the site of

the forum and remnants of an early Christian basilica have been uncovered.

Twenty-five km (15 miles) northeast of Gotse Delchev (take the left fork at Ognyanova) is the unique architectural and historical reserve of **Kovachevitsa** ❼ (Ковачевица), a living village though only just, with fewer than 50 inhabitants, and declared a national monument in 1977. Founded in the late 17th century as something of a quasi-commune, all of the houses are built of stone and wood, and all are very similar. Tradition held that when a new house had to be built, all the men of the village would drop everything and chip in with their labour until it was completed. Many of the houses are now sadly derelict, but potential buyers – who want the fortress-like houses as exclusive, get-away-from-it-all weekend retreats – are put off by crippling legislation that forbids a single brick being moved without authorisation.

One of the country's finest poets, Ludmil Stoyanov, was born and raised here, and writers still come here for inspiration.

A couple of entrepreneurs have

managed to wade or bribe their way through the bureaucracy and convert their houses into small hotels offering bed and board, but walking around the cobbled and mud streets, you get the feeling that the whole village could end up suspended in limbo unless the laws are loosened slightly.

THE SOUTHERN PIRIN

Locals insist that the climate of **Sandanski** ❽ (Сандански), the last town of any size before the Greek border, is ideal for asthmatics, as it is officially both the warmest and sunniest place in Bulgaria. Named for Yane Sandanski, a Macedonian rebel who fought against the Turks, it occupies the site of an old Thracian settlement. The Romans built a huge public bath complex here, the *Askelpion*, and the town flourished until the 6th century when it was destroyed by the Goths and fell into decay, becoming little more than a village. At the time of Bulgaria's liberation from Turkey in 1912, the town had a population of just 500. Today's population is around 25,000.

Sandanski's revival came courtesy of the huge park and thermal-bath complex (daily 7am–8pm; admission charge) built in the 1920s. It is found behind the Hotel Sandanski – which looks like an enormous cruise ship shipwrecked on the mountain side – and is famous throughout Bulgaria as the country's largest spa. Besides the indoor and outdoor pools, medical treatments and hydrotherapy on offer, the park has more than 100 types of tree and 150 species of flowers. There are guided walks, children's play areas and a boating lake.

The town's **Museum of Archaeology** (Археологически Музей Сандански, 12 bul. Georgi Dimitrov; Mon–Fri 9.30am–noon, 2–5.30pm, Sat–Sun 10am–noon, 2–7pm; admission charge) was built over a Roman villa in 1970, and features an original mosaic in the main foyer. Visitors will also find exhibits from every era of Bulgarian history, and, in the grounds, the remains of an early Christian basilica, baptistry and atrium, complete with decorated stumps of Corinthian columns. East of the town a good mountain road (at 18 km/11 miles it

Map on page 142

Wine has been produced in Melnik for hundreds of years.

BELOW: locally produced wine and honey for sale in Melnik.

A convenient perch for a nesting stork, a common sight in rural Bulgaria.

BELOW: the "Pyramids" around Melnik.

can be walked in a day) leads up to **Popina Luka** (Попина Лъка), a splendid mountain retreat made up of four cabins and a restaurant, at 1,230 metres (over 4,000 ft). At the dead centre of the Pirin range, the place is a haven for hikers, and five major routes across the mountains meet here.

Wine town

Melnik ❾ (Мелник) is the smallest town in Bulgaria. Its present population hovers around the 300 mark, but its classification as a town betrays its eventful and glorious past. Melnik was founded by the Thracians around 600 BC, and 700 years later the Romans built a bridge over the Melnishka river here – this survives in part, but has been consolidated and rebuilt many times. The name Melnik appears to have been around since the Slavs passed by, and comes from the Slav word for chalk – *mel*. It is a serious misnomer: the natural rock formations that make the town a magnet for geologists are formed of eroded sandstone, not chalk.

Melnik blossomed in the 12th century when it was the capital of the independent kingdom of Alexius Slav, a renegade baron and descendent of the Assen tsars who ruled the southern Pirin as a personal fiefdom. Slav built a great fortress here, of which much remains to this day. His fiefdom did not last long, however: he was defeated and killed in 1230 by the forces of Tsar Ivan Asen II, who reincorporated Melnik into Bulgaria.

The town continued to flourish, only for the Ottoman invasion and conquest of 1395 to ruin things. The fortress was partially destroyed, and the town's influence waned.

A century or two later the locally produced wine revived Melnik's forturnes, spreading the town's name far and wide once more. Melnik is still a renowned name in viniculture circles, the broad-leaved vines of the Struma Valley being among the oldest in Bulgaria. The Melnik grape is grown only in Melnik and the nearby villages of Hursovo, Kromidovo, Marikostinovo, Vinogradi, Lozenitsa and Hotovo. Locals insist that the grape was brought here by the Thracians more than 2,500 years ago. In any

event it made the town one of the wealthiest in Bulgaria for much of the 17th and 18th centuries.

During the Second Balkan War (1913) much of Melnik was destroyed and native Greeks (the vast bulk of the 20,000 population) then moved 25 km (15 miles) south, into Greece proper. The vineyards were bought by large landowners who operated them from afar, and only a handful of people remained; it is their descendants who form the bulk of the present population.

Melnik's sights

Melnik lies in a valley to the east of the Melniska river, and is all but hidden behind the cliffs and crags of the valley. Most of the more impressive sights sit atop these crags, such as the remains of a Slav **fortress** (Крепаст) – whose ramparts can be explored freely by anyone who can manage the steep climb up – and the **St Nikola Church** (Църква Свети Никола) next to the fortress, built in the 18th century with bright frescoes added by artists of the Bansko School a century later.

At the far end of the town – and also crowning a commanding crag, is the **Kordopulov House** (Кордопулова Къща; Mon–Fri 9am–noon, 2–5pm; admission charge), one of the largest National Revival houses in the country. Built in 1754 for the wine grower Manolis Kordopoulos, it remains in private ownership, but is open to the public as a *mehana* and small museum. The real pull, however, are the views from the upper windows.

In the centre of town, around the smart central square, is the **Pasha House** (Пашовата Къща; Mon–Fri 9am–noon, 2–5pm; admission charge) a neo-Byzantine construction built in 1815 as the residence of the pasha, the Turkish governor of the village. On the other side of the stream – across the Roman bridge – is **St Nicholas Church** (Църква Свети Николаи Чудотворец), built in 1756 and one of the few in the village that continues to serve the faithful.

Rozhen Monastery

To get to Rozhen Monastery from Melnik, visitors pass the **Pyramids of Melnik** (Мелниски Пирамите),

Map on page 142

A typical rural church in the Pirin.

BELOW: homes in Rozhen.

Map on page 142

The village of Rozhen gets its name from the monastery's Church of the Birth of the Holy Virgin. Rozhen comes from Rozhdenie, the Bulgarian word for nativity.

BELOW: frescos in the refectory of Rozhen Monastery.

impressive sandstone cliffs in the vague shape of pyramids. Spread over 17 sq. km (6½ sq. miles), and 80 metres (260 ft) high in places, the pyramids are the result of years of erosion, and their red hue gives them an unearthly look.

Rozhen Monastery ❿ (Роженски Манастир Свето Рождество Богор-одично) is situated 6 km (4 miles) further along the valley, and accessible by bus from Sandanski. Many visitors prefer to walk there, however, either along the road or by two mountain routes (one taking about two hours, the other three – both are well signposted from Melnik).

Tucked away in this remote corner of the land, it is unsurprising that Rozhen should be the least visited of all the great Bulgarian monasteries. It is hardly welcoming: from the exterior it looks like a maximum-security prison. The original monastery was founded in 1217 by Alexius Slav. It suffered repeated attack and was burned to the ground a number of times. The current structure dates from 1732, though murals on display in the monastery's museum survive from the earlier buildings. Most impressive are the two-tiered living quarters, the sober dining room and the peculiar ossuary, with its skeleton-like belfry.

The main monastery church, the Church of the Birth of the Holy Virgin, built in 1733 over the remains of the 13th-century original, has less than perfectly preserved frescoes on its walls, as well as the oldest stained-glass windows in Bulgaria.

Scramble down the path behind the monastery to take a look at the grave of revolutionary Yane Sandanski (1872–1915), a nationalist and proto-communist who expropriated much of the monastery's land for his cause, greatly reducing its power.

The monastery celebrates its feast day on 8 September, when its Icon of the Virgin is paraded around the monastery grounds. According to legend, this icon was originally owned by a widow of Nikea in Greece, but thrown into the sea to escape the wrath of Emperor Theophilus. Apparently it did not sink, as expected, but set sail and eventually turned up at Iviron Monastery on Mount Athos. ❏

RESTAURANTS

Bansko

Baryakova Mehana
ul. Velyan Ognev
Well known, some might say legendary *mehana* in the heart of Bansko's charming old town. In winter its open fires are warm and welcoming, yet the food brings people here in high summer too (there is no garden). Music accompanies your meal all year round. €€

Dedo Pene
ul. Bujnov
Tel: (07443) 5071
Housed in a building dating from 1820, this is one of the best little restaurants in the town, and offers a genuinely enjoyable, boisterous Bankso experience to the tour groups who flock here. Getting a table usually requires a reservation. €€€

Kapiziina Mehana
77 ul. Pirin
Tel: (07443) 3603
Nice little tavern with one of the best and most atmospheric court-yards in Bankso, this is the perfect place to try the local favourite, *Banska kaparna*, beef in pastry oozing with red wine. €€

Kasapinova Kashta
4 ul. Yane Sandanski
Tel: (07443) 51 76
Superb mehana boasting an enormous open fire and friendly, helpful staff keen to make everyone welcome. Though the building is not one of the finest in the town, the food and choice of wine are more than satisfying. €€€

Milush
ul. Yulen
Tel: (07443) 2510
Serves local specialities. In winter there are lively folklore shows most nights. Has only a few tables so make sure you reserve in advance. Evenings only. €€

Sirlestevo Kashta
ul. Yane Sandanski
Tel: (07443) 46 68
There are two hooks that keep people coming back to this place: firstly the traditional wooden pots that most dishes are served in, and secondly the fine courtyard that gets enjoyably packed out during the spring and summer. €€

Sharkova Kashta
ul. Peti Oktomvri
Tel: (07443) 50 24
What makes this place different to the many similar restaurants in Bansko is the decent selection of seafood dishes that are served alongside the traditional Bansko fare. Prices are very reasonable. €€€

Dobrinishte

Pavlevic
8 ul. Vaniusha Valchuk
Tel: (0887) 329 215
A real Bulgarian *mehana* where everything from the tablecloths to the stone floors reek of tradition. Great food and often a lively band. €€

Melnik

Despot Slav Hotel
Tel: (07437) 248
The excellent restaurant of the Despot Slav hotel serves a wide range of local specialities, with the house ensuring only local ingredients are used in all dishes. A great selection of wines matured in the cellars below the hotel is also on offer. €€€€

Sandanski

Mehana Sandanski
Interhotel Sandanski
Tel: (0885) 828 209
Not only is the Sandanski the best hotel in this spa town, but its mehana is the best too: delicious, homely food, and a lively floor show at weekends. €€€€

Pizzeria Sandu
ul. Makedonia 65
Thin and crispy pizzas cooked on a wood-fired oven are lavishly topped with anything you ask for. An unfussy, cheap and cheerful place. €€

PRICE CATEGORIES

Price categories are per person for thee courses:

€ = under 10 leva
€€ = 10–25 leva
€€€ = 25–50 leva
€€€€ = over 50 leva

RIGHT: rustic detail in a typical *mehana*.

PLOVDIV

Spread over three hill tops, Old Plovdiv is an architectural gem, and one of the best reasons there is to visit Bulgaria. In addition, its vibrant modern quarter is dotted with the remains of Greek Philipopolis and Roman Trimontsium

Approaching **Plovdiv**❶ (Пловдив) by train or car it is difficult to distinguish this city of around 340,000 people from many of the other dusty settlements that dot the Plain of Thrace. The regulation grey socialist era-blocks are present in the suburbs, streets are potholed and dangerous, and the city's public transport is crowded and decrepit. The old city centre, however, is one of finest in Bulgaria, a thrilling mix of Roman, Orthodox and National Revival architecture, and to many foreign visitors more vibrant than Sofia.

Even the planners of the Communist era acted with some mercy; the suburban blocks aside, modern Plovdiv is radiant. Wide, pedestrianised streets and larger-than-life public squares are exploited to the full by the city's well-dressed residents, who like to boast that they live in one of the greatest cities on earth.

That has not stopped many from migrating, however. Though the haemorrhage has now stopped, Plovdiv is one of many Bulgarian cities to have seen its population fall since 1990. Many citizens went abroad to seek their fortune, Muslims to Turkey, others to Greece and Italy. Slowly they are returning home, and with cash to invest. The garish and in many cases half-finished villas that dot the hills around the city are testament to this influx of new money, as are the many new businesses, cafés, shops and restaurants. Whether it is these pots of new money or the sunny climate, the place has a spring in its step the like of which is not found anywhere else in the country.

Some history

Philip of Macedonia was not a modest ruler, and had a habit of naming the towns and garrisons he founded or conquered after himself. Plovdiv was one such town, christened Philipopolis when overrun by Philip's forces in 342 BC. The city is situated on the western

Maps:
City 156
Area 174

LEFT:
the cobbled centre of Old Plovdiv.
BELOW: the modern city is also thriving.

Enjoying a peaceful snooze in Plovdiv.

BELOW:
National Revival
balconies in
Plovdiv's Old Town.

flank of the Upper Thracian Lowlands, straddling six small hills, called *tepe*, on either side of the Maritsa, Bulgaria's longest river. The southern bank of the Maritsa has been inhabited since the Stone Age, but the first real settlement in the area was Eumolpias, a fortified Thracian village which stood on Nebet Tepe, the highest of Plovdiv's hills.

After Philip conquered the settlement he created the most feared fortress in Thrace. The Celts tried and failed many times to take the city, but the town which they called Poulpoudelva would next be appropriated by the Romans, in the 1st century AD. In their literal way of doing things the Romans renamed the town Trimontsium (Three Hills), for the town had by then grown to cover three of Plovdiv's hills).

That the Romans made an impact bigger than anyone before or since is witnessed in the rich legacy that they bequeathed. Nowhere in Bulgaria are there so many well-preserved examples of Roman ingenuity and design (this despite a Gothic attempt to raze the city in the 3rd century). The amphitheatre for example still hosts performances of theatre and music to this day. It is one of the city's most visited sights.

After the ultimately futile division of the Roman Empire in 395, Plovdiv fell into the realm of Constantinople and Byzantium. The Slavs settled here in the 6th century, and the city's name changed again, this time for good: Plovdiv. For the next 600 years the city was destroyed a number of times, as the Bulgarian and Byzantine empires – and their successors – fought over it.

Plovdiv first became part of the Bulgarian state around 815, but was soon reconquered by Byzantium. Bulgarian rule was restored during the reign of Ivan Asen II, in 1225, only for the restored Byzantine Empire to regain it in 1263. It remained in Byzantine hands until it was taken by George Terter II of Bulgaria in 1322, only for Byzantium to strike back and recapture the city a year later. In 1344 the city was surrendered to Bulgaria as the price for Ivan Alexander of Bulgaria's support for John V Palaiologos in the Byzantine civil war.

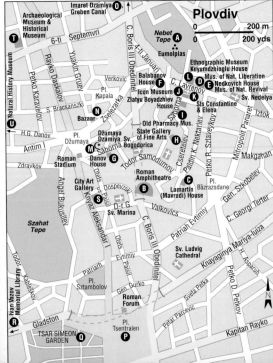

Map on page 156

Plovdiv then remained Bulgarian until it was taken by the Ottoman Empire in 1369.

Under Ottoman rule, Plovdiv became a distinctly Muslim city, at one stage home to more than 500 mosques. Nevertheless, the city was one of the first centres of the National Revival, and many of its finest structures – the National Revival houses of welathy merchants in the old town – were built before the liberation of the city during the Battle of Plovdiv in 1878. After liberation the city was not yet part of the newly established Principality of Bulgaria; instead it was chosen as the capital of the quasi-independent Protectorate of Eastern Rumelia, an artificial creation of the Treaty of Berlin in 1878 *(see page 32)*. Eastern Rumelia – and Plovdiv with it – only joined Bulgaria in 1885.

Thracian citadel

The whole of **Old Plovdiv** is a protected architectural reserve, and with good reason. However, at the top of **Nebet Tepe Ⓐ**, the site of the original Thracian settlement, it is difficult to see much protection in action. The remains of Philip's first citadel, whose walls are clearly visible amongst the undergrowth, are given no context and cry out for explanation, preservation and better presentation. The most agreeable remnant of the old citadel is the Hisar Kapiya, or **Fortress Gate**, once the entrance to Philip's citadel and in theory more than 2,000 years old. In reality, however, it has been destroyed and reconstructed at least twice since it was built, the last time by the Turks in the 15th century. Indeed, so neglected is the whole area that even experienced archaeologists are unsure as to the provenance of many of Nebet Tepe's ruins.

Despite Nebet Tepe's faults, it is still worth the climb up here, if only for the chance to stand and look out over the river to picture just how fearful any fortress on this site must once have looked to the would-be conqueror.

The Roman Amphitheatre

A far more aesthetically satisfactory reminder of the city's ancient history is the extraordinary **Roman Ampitheatre**

BELOW: though poorly documented, Nebet Tepe, the site of Plovdiv's Thracian settlement, is well worth the climb.

B (daily 9am–5pm; admission charge) that sits at the foot of the hill. First built in the 2nd century and not rediscovered until 1972, little remains of the original. Almost all of what is visible today is a reconstruction, though it remains impressive. The stage and backdrops contain original elements, and the rows of seating are convincingly ancient-looking; their white stone radiates in the summer sunlight.

Other Roman remains include a small part of a **stadium** sunk into Ploschad Dzhumaya *(see page 163)*, which at its peak in the early 3rd century would have held 25,000 spectators. By that stage Trimontium had become a regional capital of some importance, and the chariot races, gladiatorial duels and athletic competitions held here would have been of the highest calibre. There are also sunken remains of the original **Roman Forum** on the southern side of Ploschad Tsentralen, just in front of the Trimontrium Princess Hotel.

Old Plovdiv

The area that is known as Old Plovdiv is roughly described by ulitsa Mitropolit Parnet to the east, Boulevard Tsar Boris III to the west, Nebet Tepe to the north and ulitsa 20 April to the south. Most of the buildings here date from the National Revival period of the late 18th and 19th centuries, and are fine examples of a uniquely Balkan style: white, pink or deep-blue stucco, with dark-wood frames, gracefully curving buttresses and trademark slender columns. They represented the avant garde of increasingly daring Bulgarian architecture.

Nowhere more so is this in evidence than at the **House of Lamartin C**, or Mavrudi House (19 ulitsa Tseretleev; Mon–Wed 9am–noon; admission charge). It served as a holiday home in 1833 of the French poet Alfonse de Lamartin, though the property of local nobleman Georgi Mavrudi. Today it houses the Bulgarian Writer's Union, and a small exhibition dedicated to De Lamartin.

Built from 1828–9 and one of the earliest National Revival houses, its two upper levels extend further out into the street than the lower floor, and the building looks set to topple over at any

Map on page 156

moment. Though later houses of the genre were more intricately decorated, none match the sheer audaciousness of this construction.

Close by is the walled, early-19th century neo-Romanesque **St Marina Church** (Св. Марина; ulitsa Dospevski; 7am–7pm), worth visiting for its superb wooden iconostasis carved by Kosti Pasiko and painted by Nikolai Odrikanina and Stefan Dospevski (1823–78), the eldest son of Dimitar Zograf, who took over his father's role as the leader of the Samokov School. Dospevksi died in prison in Constantinople after being arrested for his role in the 1877 uprising against the Turks. The church also boasts an unusual belfry, added in 1890.

Back upon Nebet Tepe is the **Georgiadi House**, a bright-yellow mansion that is today home to the **Museum of National Liberation** ❶ (1a ulitsa Tsanko Lavrenov; Mon–Fri 9am–noon, 2–5pm; admission charge). The house was built in 1848 by Hadji George, and is the largest National Revival mansion in Plovdiv. The museum inside is a good introduction to the Bulgarian liberation struggle, as well as the roots of the National Revival movement.

The bell which was tolled to signal the beginning of the 1876 April Rising is displayed alongside a cannon used by the Bulgarian rebels in that ultimately futile attempt to oust the Turks.

The **Nikola Nedkovich House** ❶ next door (3 ulitsa Tsanko Lavrenov) dates from 1863 and boasts a suberb symmetrical facade with a peculiar high loggia.

Recently restored after possession returned to the city authorities, it hosts the **Museum of the National Revival** (Mon–Fri 9am– noon, 1.30–4.30pm; admission charge), and visitors can admire the wooden decoration and fine 19th-century furniture. There are also displays of National Revival-era jewellery and ornaments.

The **Balabanov House** ❶ (1 ulitsa Stailov; Mon–Fri 9am–5.30pm; admission charge) is one of the few Plovdiv National Revival houses to boast a large courtyard and garden. The house was originally built at the beginning of the

A balloon seller in downtown Plovdiv, a vibrant modern city with an elegant old town.

BELOW:
the Roman
Amphitheatre.

A modern statue of Philip II, who founded Plovdiv in the 4th century BC, stands over the Roman Forum.

BELOW: Ploschad Dzhumaya.

19th century for Hadji Panayot Lampsha, but it bears the name of a later proprietor – Louka Balabanov. It was destroyed by fire in 1979, but rebuilt a year later under the supervision of local Plovdiv architect Hristo Peyev. It is furnished with copies of original 19th-century furniture, and some of its rooms can be visited when not being used by the local council for receptions.

At the foot of a steep flight of steps the **Hindlian House** (4 ulitsa Artin Gidikov; Mon–Fri 9am–5pm; admission charge) was built from 1835–40 and its interior is decorated with impressive frescoes. Its original owner, Stepan Hindlian, was a widely travelled trader and the niches of the walls are painted with street scenes of some of the cities he visited.

Other National Revival houses closed to the public but worth passing by for their facades are the **Hadzhi Dragan House**, built in 1854, at 32 ulitsa Slaveikov, the **Hadzhikalchov House** (1831) at ulitsa Mitropolit Paissil 6, and the stunning **Gidikov House** (1848) at 4 ulitsa 15 January.

A walk along ulitsa Saborna

Ulitsa Saborna begins its path at Ploschad Dzhumaya, just behind the Dzhumaya Mosque *(see page 163)*. The first building of importance on the stret is the **Danov House** ⊙ (Експозиция Българско Книгоиздаване; 2 ulitsa Mitropolit Paissiy; daily 9am–6pm; admission charge), more mansion than house, set back from the street and the former home of Hristo Gruev Danov, a pioneer of the Bulgarian publishing industry who lived here from 1866 to his death in 1911. Fronted by skeletal Corinthian columns, the house is today a memorial not just to Danov but to the printing press in general, and in particular to its role in making Bulgarian a recognised literary language. Danov did more than print books, however: he was a genuine revolutionary who conrtibuted to the cause, and risked his liberty, by distributing illicit literature. *Maritsa*, the city's first newspaper, was published by Danov.

On the other side of the road look out for the **Birdas House**, built in 1856 and today the office of Plovdiv's mayor.

Just past here, and up a short flight of stairs opposite well-preserved remnants of Plovdiv's old city walls, is the early 19th-century **Church of the Virgin Mary** (Св. Богородица, Sveta Bogodoritsa). Its vaguely baroque exterior is distinguished by a sublime bell tower, all pink and blue, and its interior by frescoes portraying various Orthodox saints. The gold and silver iconostasis behind the altar includes paintings by local legend Dimitar Zograf (1796–1860), the founder of the Samokov School of Iconography. The church comes alive on 15 August, when a vast pilgrimage ends here in honour of the assumption of the Virgin Mary.

A little further along a now fiercely steepening street is the neoclassical **State Gallery of Fine Arts** ⊕ (Mon–Sat 9am–5.30pm; admission charge), devoted to Bulgarian art from the 17th–20th century, including icons and portraits by Stanislav Dospevksi.

Beyond the gallery on the same side of the street is the **Old Pharmacy Museum** ① (ulitsa Saborna; 10am–5pm; admission charge), whose National Revival-era exterior, complete with overhanging upper level, is not matched by the dull exhibition of old medicine bottles and phials inside.

Two doors along is the former house of the revolutionary Stoyan Chomakov, completed in 1860 (18 ulitsa Saborna; 9am–5pm; admission charge). Once the home of Prince Ferdinand, much of whose rich interior decoration remains, it displays 76 paintings by Zlatyu Boyadzhiev (1903–76). Known as "The Painter from Bresovo" (Bresovo being a village close to Plovdiv), Boyadzhiev spent most of his career depicting the lives and trials of the villagers who lived in places just like Bresovo. His brutal and realistic style pre-empted socialist realism and assured him state patronage for most of his career. The charming seated bronze sculpture of the painter in front of the house was completed for the museum's opening in 1984.

The **Museum of Icons** ① (Градска Художествена Галерия Пловдив – Иконна Сбирка; 22 ulitsa Saborna; 9am–12.30pm, 1.30–5pm; admission charge) is part of the City Art Gallery,

Map on page 156

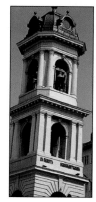

The distinctive pink bell tower of Plovdiv's Church of the Virgin Mary.

BELOW: newlyweds leaving the Church of the Virgin Mary.

The slender minaret of the Friday Mosque.

BELOW: frescos in the Church of Sts Constantine and Elena.

and is home to a fine collection of icons gathered from churches in and around Plovdiv. Most date from the 16th–17th century, but there are later icons from exponents of the Samokov School, almost all of which are dedicated to the Virgin Mary. The most resonant portrays Mary as the source of all life, as she sits atop a mountain, water flowing from her body.

The **Church of Sts Constantine and Elena** Ⓚ (ulitsa Saborna; daily 8am–5pm) that stands to the rear of a walled courtyard next door is the oldest church in Plovdiv, originally founded in 337 by Emperor Constantine. The present National Revival construction was completed in 1832, and is elaborately painted inside and out. Among its many fine features is an outstanding gilded iconostasis, with frescoes by Zahari Zograf – the elder brother of Dimitar Zograf – and a gloriously colourful and intricately decorated ceiling. The finest fresco, however, is in the simple wooden porch. It depicts Constantine asleep, dressed as a medieval Bulgarian monarch, as Christ emerges from a cloud above him.

Though considered the best preserved part of the Nebet Tepe fortress, the Hisar Kapiya (literally *Fortress Gate*) that stands at the head of Saborna Street, guarding the entrance to the plateau where the fortress once stood, has changed beyond all recognition since it was first constructed by Philip of Macedonia. It has been continually reinforced and one wonders if anything of the original remains. That does not make it any less impressive. Indeed, half hidden by trees it can appear unworldly.

The Kuyumdzhioglu House

Beyond the gate Saborna goes even steeper uphill and becomes **Dr Chumakov**, home of Plovdiv's renowned Ethnographic Museum. Several fine National Revival houses line this street, prefacing the fortress, but few have been restored: a couple lie empty and some are occupied by elderly residents who have lived here for many years.

The building of the **Ethnographic Museum** Ⓛ (2 ulitsa Dr. Chmakov; Mon, Fri 2–5pm, Tues–Thur, Sat–Sun

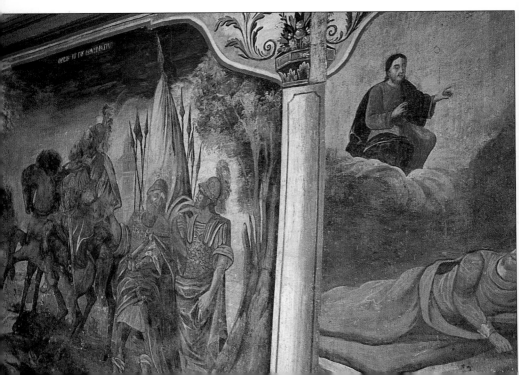

9am–noon, 2–5pm; admission charge), known as the Kuyumdzhioglu House, is one of the high-water marks of National Revival architecture, and perhaps the point where elegance was replaced with ostentation. Named after its first owner, Argir Kuyumdzhioglu, a wealthy Greek merchant, and built over two years from 1846–8, the house is a beautifully restored riot of deep blue and gold leaf, with motifs, squiggles and arabesques at every turn. The elegant loggia, supported by slender columns, is topped with an undulating roof.

The museum contains a fascinating collection of local artefacts, detailing the elaborate culture and civilisations of the Plovdiv region. Costumes, fabrics, jewellery, embroidery and musical instruments show the diversity of folk culture. Every year, in late June or early July, the museum hosts classical music concerts as part of the Plovdiv International Chamber Music Festival.

The Ottoman legacy

Plovdiv, like most of Bulgaria, was ruled by the Ottoman Empire from 1369 to 1878, and this is still very evident in the cityscape. Probably the most visible landmark in the city is the minaret of the **Dzhumaya dzamiya** (Friday Mosque) on ploschad Dzhumaya. The immense nine-domed mosque was built at the end of the 14th century, during the reign of Sultan Murat I, and is one of more than an incredible 500 mosques built in Plovdiv during the Ottoman era. Indeed, 19th-century photographs of Plovdiv show a forest of minarets.

As famous for its splendid sundial as for its minaret, the Dzhumaya mosque continues to function, and is closed on Fridays when Plovdiv's Muslim faithful pray. Admission is free but donations are expected. The highlights are the 19th-century murals by Nakshi Mustafa Zelebi.

The gaggle of streets north of the mosque is the heart of the former Ottoman quarter, or **Bazaar** , and its streets still carry the names of the tradesmen who used to congregate here. The area is popular today with artists, who hawk their wares to visitors while working on new master-

Map on page 156

BELOW:
National Revival houses and the Ethnographic Museum.

Plovdiv has a long history of organising trade fairs, dating back to 1892 when it proudly hosted "The First Bulgarian Agricultural and Industry Fair." It remains the most important trade fair venue in the Balkans, and events are now held at a modern facility on the north bank of the Maritsa (an area called Fair City). The biggest events are held at the beginning of May and in September, when accommodation can be expensive and hard to come by.

BELOW: art for sale around ploschad Dzhumaya.

pieces. Antiques shops and peculiar little places found only in Bulgaria – such as one shop selling fine porcelain alongside children's toys – make this an engaging area to explore at random. There are cafés, bars and Turkish food outlets at every twist.

Plovdiv's Muslim community, which dwindled during the latter years of communism but which has now stabilised at around 10,000, has renovated and reopened the city's second-largest mosque, the **Imaret Dzamiya**  on Han Krubat, after it had been closed for decades by the communist government. Built in 1444 on the orders of Sultan Murat II, it is distinguished by its wonderful minaret, from which imams announce the call to prayer far less conspicuously than in centuries past.

Close by, on ploschad Hebros, are the ruins of Plovdiv's former central **bathhouse**, here since Roman times. Currently being renovated, they are set to reopen as a leisure facility in spring 2008 – with modern additions and attractions such as water slides and – in spring 2008.

Jewish Plovdiv

Jews have been a presence in Plovdiv since Roman times. As artisans and merchants, they contributed to the urban bustle of the city for centuries. About 5,000 Jews lived in Plovdiv before World War II, but the exodus to Israel that followed immediately after the war left a community about one-tenth that size. Members of Shalom, Bulgaria's Jewish organisation, have worked hard to preserve Plovdiv's historic Sephardic synagogue and continue to hold periodic services there.

Visitors will find the 19th-century **synagogue** (Синагога) at 13 ulitsa Tsar Kaloyan, in what was once the heart of the Jewish quarter. As one of the finest example of Ottoman-style Balkan synagogue architecture, decorated with intricate Moorish-style details, it is the recent beneficiary of a substantial restoration grant from the US Commission for the Preservation of Heritage Abroad (USCPHA).

Modern Plovdiv

Ploschad Tsentralen (Пл. Централен) is unquestionably the largest

public square in Bulgaria, and is charming despite its immense size, kept immaculately clean by an orange-vested cleaning staff of what appears to be hundreds. Its benches are popular with courting couples, who meet here before disappearing into the Tsar Simeon Garden next door.

The square is dominated by the monolithic **Trimontium Princess Hotel and Casino** which spreads along the whole of the southern side, and the post office building opposite.

The hotel was built in the early 1950s and its facade – the ghastly faux-golden entrance aside – is an almost exact replica of the TZUM department store in Sofia. It has recently been restored to luxury status, after decades of state-run neglect, and is the best in the city. The top-floor restaurant offers panoramic views over modern Plovdiv.

The ugly high-rise next door houses the **Plovdiv Philharmonic Orchestra and Opera** (Оперно-Филхармонично Дружество; 1 ploschad Tsentralen; tel: 032-62 55 33) in a concert hall on the ground floor.

The **Tsar Simeon Garden** ❼ (Цар Симеоновата Градина) or simply City Garden, is one of the finest in the country, and extends over several hundred square metres from the east side of ploschad Tsentralen. Shaded entirely by trees, the garden site was for a long period home to Plovdiv's legendary trade fairs. Indeed, it was laid out in 1891 by the Swiss landscape gardener Lucienne Schevalas with trade fairs very much in mind. Its highlight today is its bizarre, kitsch but delightful singing fountain, which is best viewed at night when lit in bright colours by 90 projector-bulbs.

The small square in which the fountain stands is lined with small cafés, terraces and ice-cream vendor stalls. In summer it throngs with locals, especially teenagers too young to go to the city's trendier cafés, pubs and discos. Note that the garden did once suffer a stray-dog problem, and though this has largely been resolved by the local council you should be careful of lone dogs, as they have been known to bite, especially late at night.

At the southern end of the park is the

Map on page 156

National and European flags on Bulevard Knynaz Aleksandar I Battenberg.

BELOW: a roaring trade in takeaway burgers.

Prince Aleksandar I of Battenberg was the first prince (knyaz) of liberated Bulgaria. He reigned from 1879–1886.

hideous **Ivan Vazov Memorial Library** Ⓡ (17 ulitsa Avksentii Veleshki; Mon–Sat 8am–8pm, Nov–Mar until 7pm), built in 1974 and an utter abomination of a building. The collection inside, however, at 1,350,000 volumes, is the second largest in Bulgaria, and includes a number of precious works, including some of the earliest Bulgarian manuscripts in existence, and illustrated bibles written in Old Church Slavonic. The library was founded in 1879 by Yoakim Gruev, a polymath teacher and important figure of the Bulgarian National Revival.

Bulevard Knyaz Aleksandar I Battenberg

If ulitsa Saborna is the primary course of Old Plovdiv, the brilliant white paving stones of **Bulevard Kynaz Aleksandar I Battenberg** (Княз Александър Батенберг) is modern Plovdiv's principal artery and favourite place to promenade. The boulevard is lined with expensive shops, cafés, bars and restaurants, almost all of which have outside terrace in summer, and it can feel positively Mediterranean on warm summer evenings.

Beginning at ploschad Tsentralen the boulevard – closed to traffic all the way up to ploschad Silovnitsa on the other side of the river Maritsa – is lined with fine houses, either from the National Revival era or from the period immediately following independence, though the post-World War II buildings and fountains of ploschad Ivan Stambolov provide a starkly modernist contrast.

Plovdiv's City Art Gallery Ⓢ (Градска Художествена Галерия Пловдив; 15 ulitsa Knyaz Aleksandar I Battenberg; Tues–Sat 9.30am–12.30pm, 2–5pm; admission charge) is superb. Built in 1846 for the National Revival figure Dr Stoyan Chomakov, the ground floor is given over to exhibitions of young Bulgarian artists – one to keep an eye out for is Neli Gocheva, executor of striking, moody landscapes – while upstairs there are fine displays of 18th-, 19th- and 20th-century Bulgarian paintings, including works by Tsanko Lavrenov (look for the apocalyptical depiction of Treskavets Monastery in

BELOW: the main artery of modern Plovdiv, Bulevard Knyaz Aleksandar I Battenberg, is a great place for a stroll.

Macedonia) and Zlatu Boyazdhiev (1903–76), famous for his colourful, semi-cubist renderings of Old Plovdiv.

Main museums

Further north, close to the Maritsa river, is Plovdiv's **Archaeological Museum** ❶ (Археологическият Музей Пловдив, 1ulitsa Saedinenie; www.archaeologicalmuseumplovdiv.org; Tues–Sun 10am– 5.30pm; admission charge). This was one of the first genuinely Bulgarian institutions created after independence, opening its doors in 1882.

The museum's extensive collection, featues pieces from all eras of the city and region's history, from prehistoric times through the Thracians, Romans and Ottomans, and it has an unsurpassed collection of Bulgarian National Revival art. The jewellery, porcelain, pottery and statuettes of that era are proof that the National Revival was not limited merely to fine architecture. The museum is also home to a coin collection (there are more than 60,000 in the museum's vaults, though only a selection are on display

at any one time). The most valuable are 2nd-century gold coins found in the village of Gornoslav, minted under the rule of Alexius I Comnenus.

The other half of the same building is home to Plovdiv's less impressive **Historical Museum** (История Музей Пловдив, 1 ulitsa Saedinenie; Tues–Sun 10am–12.30pm, 2–5 .30pm; admission charge). The museum has recently been given a makeover but remains more full of space than exhibits. It does have a good exhibition devoted to the liberation and the short-lived Ottoman protectorate of Eastern Rumelia, but the monolingual captions make it inaccessible to all but Bulgarians.

A stone's throw from the museum, on ulitsa Khan Kubrat, is **Imaret dzhamiya**, an 15th-century mosque, which after many years of increasing dilapidation has been restored and is again in use for prayer.

A short walk south of ploschad Saedinenie is the **Natural History Museum** ⓤ (Приподонаучен Музей; 34 ulitsa Hristo Danov; Tues–Fri 9.30am–12.30pm, 1.30–4pm), housed

Map on page 156

BELOW: enjoying some refreshments on Knyaz Aleksandar I Battenberg.

Map on page 156

in Plovdiv's former Town Hall, a fine neoclassical building dating from 1880 and designed by the architect Iosif Shniter. The museum is one of the finest of its kind in Bulgaria, with notable collections of rocks, fossils and botanical species. The basement contains the largest freshwater aquarium in Bulgaria, with more than 40 species of exotic fish.

Plovdiv's other hills

Besides Taxim, Nebet and Jambaz – the three hills of Old Plovdiv – there are three other hills around the city centre: Sahat, Bunarjik and Jendem. Like Rome, Plovdiv originally had seven, though the seventh, Markovo Tepe, is today indistinguishable, having subsided under the development of the modern city.

Sahat Tepe (Сахат Тепе; 212 metres/695 ft) is the closest hill to the city centre, looming large over Kynaz Aleksandar I Battenberg. An easy path up to the top from ulitsa Zdravkov can be climbed by the fit in around 20 minutes, and is well worth it for the superb views. The clock tower on the summit is reputedly the oldest in Europe, first built in the 16th century, though the current one dates from 1809. The enormous television and radio mast on the other side of the hill is far less charming.

East of Sahat Tepe is **Bunarjik Tepe**, or Hill of Liberators (238 metres/928 ft), topped by two very different monuments. The first, the Soviet Army Memorial, is capped by a bizarre granite statue of a mythical, cloaked Soviet soldier, Alyosha (Алеша), who, rifle in hand, may or may not have taken part in the Soviet invasion of Bulgaria and liberation of Plovdiv in late 1944. The base of the monument – constructed from 1955–6 – affords terrific views over the city.

Slightly lower down is a more conventional-looking memorialto Alexander the Great and the Imperial Russian Army, which gives thanks for their role in an earlier liberation of Plovdiv, in 1878.

The tallest of Plovdiv's hills is **Jendem Tepe** (283 metres/928 ft), meaning "Hell's Hill" in Turkish but better known by its Communist-era name of Hill of Youth. Its summit is reached by a long path that circum-navigates the hill twice.

Greben Canal

Plovdiv has long been a centre for international rowing competitions (including the 2006 World Rowing Championships) on its purpose-built rowing canal, the **Greben Canal** (Гребен Канал) in the northwest of the city. Part of a larger recreation complex, when not being used for competition the canal is a popular summer escape for Plovdiv's locals.

Besides rowing, the canal offers canoeing and swimming at a large pool. There is also a good restaurant with a terrace overlooking the canal, cycle tracks and a small zoo housing deer, bison, horses, foxes and various farm animals. The canal is bridged by a startlingly cambered walkway that is not for the faint-hearted. ❏

BELOW: girls go by in Plovdiv.

RESTAURANTS

Alafrangite
17 ul. Kiril Nektariev
Tel. (032) 26 95 95
This charming and now legendary restaurant is set in a beautiful National Revival-period house in Old Plovdiv. The traditional Bulgarian meals are served by great staff, and chamber music is played in the lovely courtyard most evenings during the summer. €€

Bulborg Pub House
4 Bul. Vasil Aprilov
Close to the train station this simple, cheap pub serves hearty portions of local food in a great atmosphere. Live music most evenings and if you just want to sit and have a beer nobody seems to mind. €

Chevermeto
4 ul. Dondukov
Tel: (032) 628 605
Great little *mehana* serving some less common Bulgarian dishes, including lamb's liver with fresh herbs, and *drob*, a kind of lamb or pork paté made with various parts of those animals that might not otherwise be eaten. €€

Chuchura
12a ul. Otets Paisii
Tel: (032) 623 409
The charming little courtyard tempts in passersby, who are never disappointed by the good local cuisine

served with a smile by terrific staff. It can get full on warm summer evenings so reserve if you can. €€

Dreams
1 Bul. Knyaz Aleksandar 1
Tel: (032) 627 142
For a good burger, sandwich, snack or just coffee as opposed to a heavy meal, this upmarket fast-food joint on Plovdiv's main pedestrian street is just the trick. Views of the street below from the upper level are fantastic. €€

Gusto
26 ul. Otetz Paisii
Tel: (032) 623 711
An Art Deco interior gives a clue as to the nature of the menu: adventurous and avant garde, and now really what you expect from Plovdiv. Try some fusion cuisine with French and Asian influences and leave happy, if a little lighter in the wallet. €€€

K2
6 ul. Tsaribrod 6
Tel: (032) 626 907
Bright, breezy, laid-back and modern, this is a great place to enjoy some very non-Bulgarian food if the local meats fest has got to you. Great salads and a good wine list. €€€

Loven Park
ul. Yasna Polyana 10
Tel: (032) 442 090

Tremendously popular with locals during the summer, although they tend to use it more as a bar than restaurant. It is a decent place serving international dishes in a great spot away from the centre of the city. You will find it near the zoo. €€

Pri Lino
135 Bul. September 6
Tel: (032) 63 17 51
The best Italian in Plovdiv comes with its own Italian chef who avoids the usual trattoria staples and prepares regional cuisine. €€€

Puldin
3 ul. Knjaz Tsereletev
Tel: (032) 631 720
This is the oldest

restaurant in the city. The Puldin salad, a showcase platter featuring a variety of Bulgarian salads, is what this place is famous for, but there is so much more on offer too. There are many Bulgarian specialities, including the best *kiuftete* in the country. The garden is the nicest place in Plovdiv to eat during the summer. €€€

PRICE CATEGORIES
Price categories are per person for thee courses:
€ = under 10 leva
€€ = 10–25 leva
€€€ = 25–50 leva
€€€€ = over 50 leva

RIGHT: a popular and tasty standby.

THE RHODOPES

Southern Bulgaria is dominated by the Rhodopes mountain chain, which sweeps across the country from Sofia to the Black Sea. Dotted with caves, lakes and waterfalls, it forms an enchanting natural theme park

Legend lurks at every turn in the Rhodopes (Родопи, Rodopi). According to Greek mythology the mountains were formed when the gods Zeus and Hera turned Rhodopa, wife of Thracian King Haimos, to stone after growing angry at her conceit. It was in the wilderness of the Rhopodes that the legend of Orpheus and the cult of Orphism gained a hold; it was here that the mythical poet fell for his muse Eurydice, and where, after turning his back on the female sex, he was brutally killed by drunken, sword-wielding lesbians known as maenads.

Drunken, sword-wielding lesbians are few and far between in the Rhodopes these days, and the locals are by and large friendly. Yet the overcrowded ski resort of Pamporovo aside, this remains a remote and neglected part of Bulgaria, awaiting discovery by mass tourism.

The Rhodopes neatly divide into two distinct parts: the western and eastern ranges, split by the relatively well-populated Chepelarska Valley. The highest peak, Golyam Perelik (2,091 metres/6,860 ft) is in the more dramatic, western part of the range.

Assenovgrad

Around 20 km (12 miles) south of Plovdiv, just before the Smolyan highway shoots fiercely upwards, the fortress town of **Assenovgrad** ❷ (Асеновград) stands guard, as it has done for centuries, at the foot of the

Rhodopes. At a gently cooling altitude of 180 metres (600 ft) control of this town – whose present inhabitants number around 55,000 – was essential to any would-be conqueror of Thrace or Bulgaria.

Assenovgrad dates back to Thracian times, though the first written mention of it is from a document found at Bachkovo Monastery, dating from 1038, when the town was known as Stanimahos (meaning "a defensive place" in Greek). It changed hands a number of times over the following two centuries, found as it

Map on page 174

PRECEDING PAGES: sunflowers fill the view. **LEFT:** one of the three Roman bridges in Shiroka Luka, the western Rhodopes. **BELOW:** Rhodopes rooftops.

was on the road to the Holy Land. The Crusaders called it variously Stanimako, Estanimak, and Stanimaka, a name which persisted even after Tsar Assen II took the town and fortress in 1230. Assen renamed the fortress in his own honour – Assen Krepost – but the town below retained the name Stanimaka until 1934, when it became Assenovgrad, or Town of Assen.

Tsar Assen enlarged the fortress and made the town a military base of some significance, but this did not prevent the town suffering the fate of so much of Bulgaria. Dominion passed from the Bulgarian kings to Byzantium and back with some regularity until the Turks made it their own in 1371.

During Ottoman times Assenovgrad's importance as a garrison then diminished, and the town and fortress fell into decline, the population dwindling to just a few hundred people by the end of the 18th century. Salvation came in the form of tobacco and wine, both of which have been produced here since the late 18th century onwards. The red wines made from the cabernet grapes that grow around Assenovgrad, called Mavrud, are among the best in the country and most celebrated internationally.

Now a quiet, leafy town, Assenovgrad is popular with Plovdiv's rich set, who keep second homes here. It has more than 50 churches, of which a number are of exceptional architectural interest. The 1785 **St Mary of the Assumption Church** – situated close to the town centre – is perhaps the finest, a brilliantly preserved example of Byzantine ostentation with its separate, painted bell and clock tower. The **Holy Trinity Church** close by is less impressive from outside, but notable for its interior icons painted by local artist George Ksaff. Likewise the **St Dimitar of Solun Church** (built only with special permission from the Turks in 1866) possesses an ordinary neo-Romanesque exterior that houses stunning frescos added in 1930, including a famous depiction of Noah's Ark by Dimitar Shterev.

Two churches in Assenovgrad are dedicated to St George. The first, which is known as **St George Metoshki**, is an 18th-century recon-

struction of a 12th-century original, and is decorated with frescos by Zohari Zograf. The second, **St George Ambelino**, is a charming Bulgarian National Revival rendition of the baroque, designed by Vasil Dimov and completed in 1848. Its rich exterior – note the attractive belfry – is not matched by a somewhat plain interior.

The oldest church in Assenovgrad is **St John Predtecha**, found a short walk to the east of the city centre. It dates from the 13th century, though the cupola was added much later, in the 1830s, when the **Church of the Holy Virgin of the Annunciation** was added next door. Both churches house fine iconography.

Of Assenovgrad's various museums the two worthy of time are the **History Museum** (1 ploschad Trakia; Mon–Fri 9am–noon, 2–5pm; admission charge), on the main square and divided into three separate exhibitions: archaeology, National Revival and ethnography. A better exhibition of the National Revival, however, is found at the **National Revival Museum**, situated in a large period building in Old Assenovgrad (31 ulitsa Stanimaka). It has a lively collection of art, clothing, and other personal items from the National Revival era.

Map on page 174

The Assen Fortress

Two km (1¼ miles) from Assenovgrad, the **Assen Fortress** (Асен Крепаст) is reached via a tough climb up a well-marked but poorly surfaced track whose latter stages can be climbed only by the most agile. Like the town below it, the fortress almost certainly dates back to Thracian times, though all of what we see today was built by Tsar Assen II or his successors. Set over two crags, an inscription on one of the rocks at the fortress's scarily steep entrance leaves no doubt as to its provenance: "In the year 739 (1231), Ivan Assen, by God's will, raised Tsar of Bulgarians and Greeks, and also of other lands, built this fortress."

Careful excavation of one outcrop has revealed three fortress walls and two water-storage tanks, though the site is dominated by the superb remains of the three-level **Petrich Church of the Virgin Mary** (Св. Богородица

Pausing on the tough climb up to the Assen Fortress.

BELOW:
the Assen Fortress, built by the heroic Tsar Assen II.

Assenovgrad has many monasteries, chapels and churches perched above the gorge.

BELOW: Church of the Virgin Mary in Assenovgrad Monastery.

Петрих, Sv. Bogoroditsa Petrich; Wed–Sun 8am–5pm; admission charge; guides available) that stands on the lower peak. A late-Romanesque construction of some achievement, the church was built in the late 13th century. Extensive restoration in the 1930s and 1980s has kept the exterior of the church in impeccable condition, while inside there are small fragments of original 14th-century frescos. Recent archaeological excavations have revealed that the lower level of the church was originally used as a burial chamber.

Assenovgrad's monasteries

So numerous are the monasteries, chapels and churches of the area around Assenovgrad that since medieval times it has been known as Little Jerusalem. The largest monastery – though no longer used as such – is the **Sts Kirik and Yulita Monastery at Gornovoden** (Свети Кирик и Юлита; 9am–5pm; admission charge, free for hotel guests), 3 km (2 miles) north of Assenovgrad, on the road back to Plovdiv. Founded in the 13th century, the monastery has burned down twice: in 1605 and 1810,

but was fully restored in 1838, when its wonderful **St Paraskeva Church** (Св. Параскева) was built, complete with icons by Zahari Zograf contained in a glorious wooden iconostasis by an unknown artist. Frescoes were added in 1847–50 by Alexi Atanassov, a local artists of some renown.

After the Communist takeover, the monastery was abandoned by its monks, who, fearing persecution, sought refuge at nearby Bachkovo. After lying derelict for decades it was converted into a luxury hotel and conference centre by the Bulgarian Architectural Society in the 1980s.

A couple of kilometres further north, above the village of Kuklen, is the **Vrach Monastery of Sts Kozma and Damian** (Св. Козма и Дамиан; open irregularly), famous for a sacred spring, which is said to have healing powers. It was first constructed in the 13th century, during the Second Bulgarian Kingdom, almost certainly on the site of an earlier, Thracian holy place. It rapidly became one of the leading centres of learning in Bulgaria, and its most famous exhibit, the Kuklen Psalm Book, was written here in 1337. There are well-preserved 17th-century frescoes in the monastery church, including a wonderful depiction of the Archangel Gabriel in the southern recess. The scenes of the Apocalypse in the old vestibule were added in the 19th century by Greek monks resident at the monastery at the time. Look out for the life-size paintings of Kozma and Damian on one of the monastery's many fountains.

Belashtitsa Monastery of St George the Victorious (Св. Георги Победоносец) was first built in 1014 by a Byzantine military commander, Nikifor Skifi, who defeated a Bulgarian army close to the current monastery site. Most of the current monastery dates from the 19th century, including the tall, imposing bell tower. The monastery's church dates from the 17th century, and like the entire

monastery comes alive on 6 May (St George's Day, according to the Julian calendar).

Arapovo Monastery (Арапово Манастир), 8 km (5 miles) west of Assenovgrad, is unique as it is the only Bulgarian monastery built on a plain instead of hidden in a forest or enclosed in mountains. Founded in 1854, its construction was a direct challenge to the Turkish authorities. Dominating the monastery is its superb neo-Byzantine church, which has a high and attractive cupola. Inside are celebrated frescoes painted in the 1860s by Georgi Danchov-Zografina. Like so many of the monasteries of the Rhodopes, it has an allegedly healing spring nearby.

Seven km (4 miles) southeast of Assenovgrad is **Mouldava Monastery of St Petka** (Св. Петка), founded at the end of the 14th century and celebrated for its icons by Zahari Zograf and Petar Miniov, added in 1836. The monastery served as one of Vasil Levski's preferred hide-outs, and for much of the latter part of the 19th century was a hotbed of revolution and Bulgarian nationalism. Levski is com-memorated with an almost life-size bas relief on a monastery wall.

Bachkovo Monastery

Beyond the Assen Fortress the tight and spectacular **Chepelarska Gorge** is a stunning entrance to the winding valley carved out by the Chepelarska river. The Romans built a road along here in the 2nd century AD, linking Trimontsium (Plovdiv) with the Aegean, and the charming little village of Bachkovo dates back just as far.

The town is famous for its monastery, founded in 1083 by two Byzantine statesman of Georgian origin, Grigorij Bakuriani and his brother Abbasij. The **Bachkovo Monastery** ❸ (Бачковски Манастир; daily 7am–9pm, English-language guides available 10am–4pm; admission charge) is second only to Rila Monastery in terms of importance and size.

Like Rila it is a UNESCO World Heritage Site, and is a fine collection of well-preserved historic buildings from various eras. Split over two leafy courtyards the undoubted highlight is the refectory, with its frescoed outer

Map on page 174

A fresco on the lavishly decorated wall of the refectory at Bachkovo.

BELOW:
Bachkovo Monastery.

Ski school at Pamporovo, an ideal resort for beginners and families.

BELOW:
a boy selling plants near Bachkovo Monastery.

walls presenting the monastery's history – most of these paintings were executed in the 19th century by a team of artists led by the National Revival artist Zahari Zograf – and its stunning interior featuring Jesus, Mary and St John the Baptist, painted from 1622–43 by an unknown artist.

There are two monastery churches. The **St Nikolai** is the newest, built in 1834 in simple, neo-Romanesque style and featuring more paintings by Zograf, while the **Church of the Virgin Mary** is the oldest building in the monastery, dating from 1604. Its golden iconostasis and frescoes depicting the Assumption are in outstanding condition. The church also houses an icon of the Virgin Mary – allegedly brought from Georgia in 1310 – which is said to have magical healing powers. Every year on 15 August (St Mary's Day in the Orthodox Calendar) it is paraded by thousands of pilgrims in a ritual procession around the monastery.

During the 14th and 15th centuries successive Bulgarian patriarchs were exiled to the monastery from Turnovo, and an important school of medieval teaching and philosophy was created here. The monastery's library preserves many precious manuscripts dating from these dangerous times.

Outside the monastery's walls is the **Ossuary**, a Romanesque church from the 11th century containing reasonably well-preserved portraits of the monastery's founders, alongside Tsar Ivan Alexander. The sepulchre is kept in the crypt.

A short walk further on, through some fantastic scenery, and passing the so-called **Rock Church** – a small chapel built into the mountain to which the monastery's miraculous icon is carried in pilgrimage every Easter – is the **Kluviata**, a holy spring also reputed to have miraculous powers of healing.

Miraculous Bridges

The spa resort of **Narcahenski Bani** ❹ is one of the largest in Bulgaria, and besides drinking, bathing and massage cures the active can try a number of hikes from here, including one route that leads up to the top of **Cerni Vrah**,

at 1,534 metres (5,032 ft). At the point where the Chepelarska Pass is breached and the road once again goes downhill, a poor road that quickly becomes little more than a dirt track (you will need a good car to get here) branches off to the natural wonder known as the **Miraculous Bridges ❺** (Чудните Мостове). Formed millions of years ago by an earthquake, two almost perfect bridges of rock cross the Aidarsko Dere river 200 metres (650 ft) apart in a sensational setting below the Chernatitsa Ridge. The upstream bridge is the largest, almost 100 metres (320 ft) long and up to 45 metres (1,478 ft) high in places, and can be crossed on foot; the downstream bridge is too dangerous to traverse.

Back on the main road the small town of **Chepelare** is slowly emerging from the shadow of its bigger neighbour, and rival, Pamporovo, 10 km (6 miles) southwest. A new chairlift a short bus ride south of the town has improved the skiing in Chepalare immeasurably, and locals are proud of the fact that the top station is actually (at 1,850 metres/6,000 ft) a metre or two higher than at Pamporovo. It offers a quieter and more relaxed skiing experience, and in summer serves as the base for long but relatively gentle hikes. It is also home to Bulgaria's only **Museum of Speleology** (9a ulitsa Shina Andreeva; Tues–Sun 9am–noon, 1.30– 5.30pm; admission charge), reflecting the large number of caves in the Rhodopes region.

Skiing in the Rhodopes

Famous for its rocket-style television mast, **Pamporovo ❻** (Пампорово) has been a staple of budget skiers from all over Europe for almost 30 years. At an altitude of 1,620 metres (5,315 ft), is a gorgeous place, with a far better choice of hotels than Borovets, almost all of which have the most wonderful views of the enclosing forests. It is not all good news, however. The resort is overcrowded and needs serious investment; queues are infamously long, especially at weekends when

locals from Assenovgrad and Smolyan come skiing here. Weekdays, however, are significantly less busy, and foreign skiers may find they have the slopes almost to themselves.

The resort is best suited to beginners and families. Except for one extremely short black run, most of its pistes – all of which cut delightfully through tall conifer trees – quickly become accessible to all but the most hapless of novices. In summer there is some fine (if rather tame) hiking.

Cathedral city

There has been a settlement in or around **Smolyan ❼** (Смолян), the main town of the southern Rhodopes, since the 2nd millennium BC. The modern town, however, dates only from 1960, when three villages: Ustovo, Raikovo and Ezerovo were merged. The name was taken from the Slavic Smolyani tribe, who settled in the region in the 7th century before helping to overthrow the Byzantine rulers of Bulgaria and contributing to the creation of the First Bulgarian Kingdom in 837.

Map on page 174

Pamporovo's distinctive television mast.

BELOW: view over the Miraculous Bridges.

Flowers brighten a ramshackle wooden cottage in the Rhodopes.

Unlike most of Bulgaria, the Smolyan region (along with much of the southern and eastern Rhodopes) was not liberated in 1878: it remained under Turkish control until the end of the First Balkan War, in 1912.

Home to a number of fine National Revival-era houses (the best can be seen in Old Raikovo and around the churches of Ustovo), Smolyan is spoilt by its 1960s suburbs of crumbling apartment blocks, which are home to the majority of the town's 35,000 inhabitants.

It is worth making a special trip to see Smolyan's astonishing new cathedral, the **Cathedral of St Vissarion of Smolyan** (Катедрален Храм Свети Висарион Смолянски), not yet fully completed but already the city's primary attraction. Second in Bulgaria only to Sofia's Aleksander Nevsky Cathedral in size, it is a kitsch, modernist construction, all curves and arches, topped with a 32 metre- (102 ft-) high dome and a 50-metre (160-ft) belfry containing 11 enormous bells, made to order in Russia, and reputedly the loudest in the Balkans.

BELOW: the picturesque village of Shiroka Luka.

THE WESTERN RHODOPES

West of Pamporovo the villages are populated almost entirely by Pomaks, the name given to Slavs and Bulgarians who converted to Islam in the 17th century, either forcibly or voluntarily. Though the occasional Christian village is dotted here and there (it is not difficult to tell the two types of village apart) mosques – many brand-new – dominate the landscape.

Shiroka Luka ❽, a short distance from Pamporovo, is a village museum made up of five separate villages and populated by a mix of Christians and Pomaks, happy to band together in the interests of tourism. The place is often full of day-trippers from Pamporovo, trying to get a feel of the real Bulgaria, and though the whole thing is just a little too postcard-perfect, there are worse places to do so.

First stop on any itinerary is the **Church of the Assumption**, famously built in 38 days in 1834 by locals, and adorned with frescoes painted by both Zahari and Dimitar Zograf. Also worth admiring are the three bridges across the river, all of which survive (with

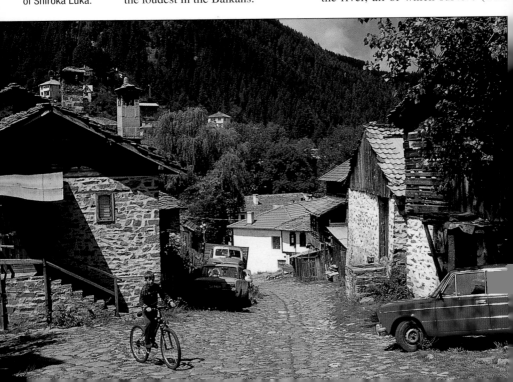

much repair) from Roman times. Otherwise the village's attractions are limited to wandering around the many houses typical of the region (walled, two storey stone buildings with thick exterior walls, high chimneys and deep cellars), many of which are open to the public.

On the first Sunday of March Shiroka Luka plays host to one of Bulgaria's biggest Kukeri festivals (*see pages 48–9*), when the village men don frightening costumes to ward off winter for another summer. At other times of the year you will come across musicians wandering through the streets playing a Bulgarian version of the bagpipes (*gaidi* or sometimes *cimpoi*).

At the end of a dirt track (take the right spur when the track forks), the village of **Gela** (Гела) is said to be the birthplace of the legendary Orpheus, and home to an annual and fiercely contested *gaidi* festival held at the beginning of August.

The small spa town of **Devin ❾** (Девин) lends its name to Bulgaria's most popular mineral water, which is taken from a spring close to the town

and bottled nearby; it is also the best base for serious hikers in the western Rhodopes. There are trails from here to the Orpheus chalet above Teshel, and a two-day hike over to Lake Batak, taking in the highest peak in this part of the Rhodopes, **Batakshki Snezhnik** (2,082 metres/6,830 ft). The lake is man-made, formed by the construction of the Batak Dam in the 1950s (one of five that make up the Batak Hydroelectric Complex).

The resort of **Tsigov Chark** (Цигов Чарк) has recently been developed for water sports on the lake, and skilifts have also been installed to make it a year-round resort. The town of **Batak** (Батак) is notorious as the site of a massacre of Bulgarians by Pomaks – acting on the orders of the Turks – during the April Rising of 1876: a small museum and memorial commemorate the event.

Along the Trigrad Gorge

From Batak a decent road through some spectacular scenery leads through **Dospat** back towards Devin. The primary attraction of the area is

Map on page 174

Playing the gaidi, *a Bulgarian version of the bagpipes.*

BELOW LEFT AND RIGHT: one of Shiroka Luka's ancient bridges and the Church of the Assumption.

Ripe raspberries, a speciality of the Rhodopes.

the 7-km (4-mile) long Trigrad Gorge (Триградско Ждрело), a steep, narrow chasm cut by the lively Trogradska river that flows below the surface for much of its course. At their highest points both sides of the gorge reach over 300 metres (1,000 ft) above the valley floor (which is itself 1,450 metres/4,750 ft above sea level). The road here is narrow and extremely bumpy, though the fact that one exists at all should be considered a miracle of engineering.

At the apex of the gorge the river plunges down into a cave known as the **Dyavolskoto Gurlo ❿** (Дяаволското Гурло, Devil's Throat; Wed–Sun, guided tours only; admission charge), one of the most spectacular natural sights in the country. A viewing platform has been positioned over the point where the river disappears underground, while the tour of the cave itself – though memorable for its sheer size and the deafening echo of the gushing water – is for not for the faint-hearted.

The village of **Trigrad** (Триград) has little to recommend it, but a couple of comfortable hotels make it a good base for hiking and especially caving .

Trigrad is in fact just one of three spurs off the Dospat–Devin road. The first (head right as the road bends sharply shortly after the village of Borino) leads to the village of **Yagodina ⓫** (Ягодина), a major centre of Bulgarian caving, and at the end of the third spur (turning right shortly before the gorge), along an even worse road, is the village of **Mugla** (Мугла), which would not figure in any tourist guide were it not for the annual *gaidi* festival that takes place here in August.

THE EASTERN RHODOPES

Though somewhat lower on average than the western Rhodopes, the eastern range is far more remote in character, and the hundreds of tiny villages that dot the area around the Kurdzhali lakes are among the most timeless places in Europe.

Socialist city

The gateway to the eastern Rhodopes is **Dimitrovgrad ⓬**. The city was created in 1947 – as part of the forced

BELOW: a typical Pomak village in the western Rhodopes.

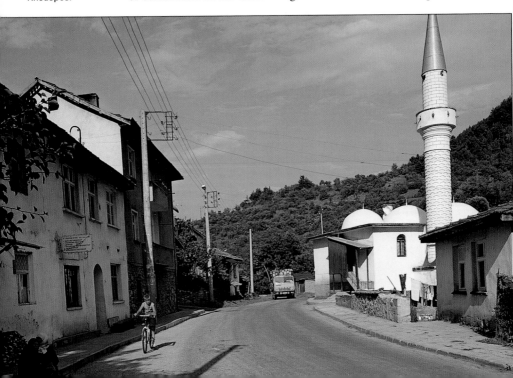

industrialisation of the Bulgarian economy – by moving the residents of three villages – Rakovski, Mariyno and Chernokonyovo – lock, stock and barrel into a planned, industrial city built entirely in socialist-realist architecture. It was given the name Dimitrovgrad in honour of Georgi Dimitrov, the former Comintern leader who became the first communist prime minister of Bulgaria in 1946. Unusually, the name has survived the fall of Communism (all other mention of Dimitrov in Bulgaria has been erased including his mausoleum in Sofia). This is possibly not so surprising in a city whose main hotel is still called The Moscow.

The bulk of the modern city centre, around **Bulevard Bulgaria** and **Ploschad Tsar Simeon**, was built over three years from 1947–50 by "volunteer" brigades of some 50,000 young Bulgarians, called Mlada Gvardia (Young Guards), brought from all over Bulgaria to construct the perfect socialist city. Their slogan was "We are building a city, the city is building us." They built apartment blocks, factories, railways, parks and artificial lakes. The results are not altogether dislikeable, and though there is little to actually see, an afternoon wandering around provides an interesting insight into the kind of world Bulgaria's Communists wanted to create: soulless wide avenues lined with monolithic apartment blocks interspersed with giant industrial complexes placed close to people's homes so that they did not have to "waste" time travelling.

Also worth an excursion is the **Penio Penev Park** to the south of the city centre. It is dedicated to the socialist-realist poet Penio Penev, who eulogised Dimitrovgrad and the socialists who were born and moulded here. Stones engraved with Penev's poems litter the park; Bulgaria's first **Planetarium** (opened in 1962) is in the park opposite. Dimitrovgrad is twinned with Nowa Huta in Poland, near Krakow, Europe's only other entirely planned socialist city.

Architectural hotchpotch

The chaos of **Haskovo** ⑬ (Хасково), a 1,000-year old city at the foot of the

Map on page 174

Pointing the way to sights and tourist facilities in the Trigrad Gorge.

BELOW: fishing near Dospat.

Locals will not allow you to leave Haskovo without visiting the Monument to the Virgin Mary (Статуята на Богородица), a 32 metre- (105 ft-) high statue of Mary and Jesus standing on a hill south of the city centre. Unveiled in 2003, it is allegedly the largest statue of the Virgin Mary in the world – a fact the city rams down visitors' throats at every opportunity.

mountains whose centre is a joyful amalgamation of the Byzantine, the Ottoman, the National Revival and the neoclassical, can come as a pleasant surprise after the utilitarian straight lines and utter sombreness of Dimitrovgrad.

A fortress (of which nothing remains) was constructed here in the 9th century during the reign of Tsar Boris I, but by the end of the 14th century the town, known as Marsa, was populated almost entirely by Turks. Bulgarians did not return until the middle of the 19th century when the town grew, becoming a centre of the tobacco industry. Its current population hovers around 100,000.

Boasting one of the most extensive pedestrianised centres in Bulgaria, Haskovo is a good place to shop, eat, drink and generally relax before heading off into the Rhodopes. The **Eski Mosque** (Ески Старата Джами, ulitsa Otets Paicii; dawn–dusk daily except Friday; admission charge) dates back to 1395, and was the first purpose-built mosque in the Balkans (until then the conquering Ottomans

had converted churches for prayer); look out for its leaning minaret. Just west of the mosque is the bright-red, neoclassical **Ivan Dimov Theatre** (Драматичен Театър Иван Димов), built in 1921 and recently restored to full splendour, complete with tympanium and slender columns that evoke – ever so slightly – the Bulgarian National Revival.

Further west, across the river in Old Haskovo, is a collection of fine National Revival-era houses, none more lovely than the so-called **Kirkov** or **Blue House** (Кирковата Къща, Синята Къща; Mon–Fri 10am–5pm; admission charge) on ulitsa Tsar Osvobodi Tel: At the end of the same street is the **Church of the Archangels Michael and Gabriel** (Църквата Св. Архангели Михаил и Гавраил), built in 1861 by Greek Orthodox worshippers.

It is worthwhile comparing the style of the Greek iconography inside the church with that of the city's main Bulgarian Orthodox church, the **Church of the Virgin Mary** (Църквата Св. Богородица) – built in 1837 – on the other side of the river.

BELOW: local crafts for sale.

Rock formations

Heading south from Haskovo, the pink **Kurdzhali Pyramids** signal Kurdzhali town. Just one of many weird rock formations in what was once an actively volcanic area, the pyramids (Кърджалийски Пирамиди; also known as the **Stone Wedding**, Каменна Сватба) are said by locals to be a wedding party turned to stone by the gods to punish the bridegroom's mother for envying the bride's beauty.

There are other strange rock formations in the area, including giant mushrooms (Каменни Гъби) at Beli Plast (Бели Пласт), and the **Rock Window** (Скален Прозорец) at **Kostino** (Костино), both to the north of Kurdzhali. The most amazing rock in the area, however, is the **Rock Womb** (Храмът-Утроба) at Nenkovo (Ненково), 15 km (9 miles) northwest of Kardzahli. Discovered in 2001, it is believed by locals to be the infamous "Thracian Wanton Place" described by Herodutus in his *Histories*. The hollowed-out rock resembles an enormous vagina, and was said to have been used for debauched Thracian practices; it is also thought to have been a sacred place to the followers of the Orpheus cult. A car and sturdy footwear are necessary to properly explore any of these sites.

Kardzahli

Sitting on a land bridge between two enormous artificial lakes created by the construction of the Kardzahli Dam, **Kardzahli ⓮** (Кърджали) itself is a nice enough town. The town has some good places to stay, and its **Museum of History** (Историческият Музей; 14 ulitsa Republikanska; Mon–Fri 9am–5pm; admission charge) displays a range of jewellery, pottery and other artefacts found up at Perperikon *(see page 186)*, the ruins of an ancient city 15 km (9 miles) northeast of town.

West of the city centre, on the road to Ardino, the **Monastery of St John Prodromus** (Манастирът Св. Йоан Продром) is a 1990s reconstruction of an 11th-century monastery which was destroyed by the Knights of the Fourth Crusade in the 13th century. A few fragments of original frescoes have been saved and restored.

Map on page 174

A minaret peeps above the rooftops.

BELOW: tobacco fields near Kardzahli.

Map on page 174

TIP

A large and well-attended arts festival featuring music, dancing and theatre takes place at Perperikon in June.

BELOW:
Perperikon perches on a rock above the high plain.

Ancient Perperikon

Perperikon ⑮ (Перперикон; open site; www.perperikon.bg) stands on a wide, flat outcrop of rock high above the present-day village of Perperek (Перперек). Thracians built the first settlement on this spot, but it was the Romans who fortified it, constructing a palace and castle over the original Thracian settlement. The Byzantines built a Christian palace in the 6th century, and most of the remains that have so far been unearthed date from these periods, including the bath-house, an altar and the walls of the main palace.

Perperikon thrived until the Turks invaded Bulgaria in the 14th century, and the town was abandoned around 1393, after being all but destroyed by the invaders. Large-scale archaeological work on the site did not get underway until 2000, and access to Perperikon is currently free, though there are plans afoot to begin charging fan entrance fee. Finds from the site have included everyday domestic vessels and coins, in particular silver coins of Tsar Ivan Alexander.

Fishing and twitching

East of Kardzhali the River Arda (Арда) – the longest in the Rhodopes – wends its way towards Turkey, providing the best fishing in the mountains: it is full of large trout and red mullet, which can be fished all year round.

Along the 9-km (5-mile) length of the spectacular **Arda Gorge**, the volcanic cliffs attract bird-watchers who at various times of year can view black storks, vultures, long-legged buzzards, honey buzzards, eagles, peregrine falcons and goshawks. The whole area surrounding the gorge, including the former mining town of **Madzehrovo** (Маджарово), has been declared a nature reserve.

West of Kardzhali the river passes through the spa resort of **Ardino ⑯** (Ардино), which has an unusual mosque with twin minarets, before passing under the so-called **Devil's Bridge** (Дяволски Мост), 10 km (6 miles) from Ardino. The bridge was built by the Turks (hence the less than flattering name) in the 16th century, and has been well-preserved, remaining open to pedestrians. ❑

RESTAURANTS

Assenovgrad

Ogi
3 ul. Raina Knyaginya
Tel: (0331) 34058
Game is a speciality at this split-level restaurant with a summer garden, so try the grilled rabbit, the pheasant (if they have it) or the fresh foie gras. Prices are astonishingly low. €€

Salasha
Tel: (0887) 420 869
A kilometre outside Assenovgrad on the road to the fortress, this huge restaurant offers Rhodope specialities, such as *patatnik* (potato pastry) in a splendid setting. There are indoor and outdoor seating areas, a playground for children and live music on Wednesday evenings.€€€

Stanimaka
13 ul. Tsar Ivan Assen
Tel: (0331) 679 32
With its odd decor, this place can feel strange at first. Once the food is served (try the Stanimaka stuffed-cabbage rolls) and the floor show starts, however, you'll be glad you came.€€€

Devin

Bulgarian Village
2 ul. Dryzhba
(Devin Spa Hotel)
Tel: (03041) 24 98
While the décor is a little bit of a letdown, the food is sensational.

Enjoy Rhodope specialities, from locally made cheese to sour soups and grilled lamb, and wash it down with a good local wine.€€€

Haskovo

Gourkova Kashta
6 ul. Gourko 6
Set in a lovely National Revival era house this superb restaurant serves local treats and classical Bulgarian dishes at excellent value prices. The staff will patiently help you choose from the Bulgarian-only menu. €€€

Pamporovo

Bialata Kashata (White House)
Resort centre
This is a large white house in the centre of the resort. Its interiors suggest the usual Bulgarian tourist trap but are, in fact, mercifully deceiving: the menu is varied and includes fish dishes, which are rare in this area. €€€

Chanove
Opposite Hotel Perelik
Tel: (03021) 82 12
Though built for and catering to package tourists, there is nevertheless a charm about this place. Recommended are the lamb dishes, the huge salads and excellent selection of local wines. €€€€

Chevermeto
Next to bus station
Tel: (03021) 83 38
Watch entire lambs get thrown on the fire or pigs being roasted on spits while eyeing up the vast array of furs and hunting trophies that cover the walls. Getting a table is often difficult in high season as package companies often book the whole place. €€€

White Hart Pub
Adjacent to the Hotel Mourgavets
This is a pub, restaurant and karaoke bar that specialises in providing comfort food such as bacon and egg and steak- and-kidney pie. Lively and nois,y it is the most popular place in the resort.€€€€

Shiroka Luka

Shiroka Luka
In the centre of this tiny village, where the streets have no name, this touristy restaurant is as kitsch as they come but serves some good Rhodopean food, including locally made delicious feta cheese.€€€€

PRICE CATEGORIES

Price categories are per person for thee courses:
€ = under 10 leva
€€ = 10–25 leva
€€€ = 25–50 leva
€€€€ = over 50 leva

RIGHT: succulent kebabs with potato salad.

BIRD-WATCHING IN BULGARIA

Bulgaria's position at the crossroads of Europe and its great variety of landscapes make it wonderful bird-watching territory

The combination of high mountain ranges, flat plains, coast and river estuaries, and its location on the Balkan peninsula, mean that Bulgaria, home to over 400 bird species, is an increasingly popular destination for ornithologists. The various wild habitats give shelter to numerous endangered species, while millions of birds use the Via Pontica – one of two major migratory routes in Europe – which passes through the country. Bird-watchers may see tens of thousands of red-breasted geese, thousands of pygmy cormorants, Dalmatian pelicans, ferruginous ducks and rarities such as black vultures, imperial eagles and slender-billed curlews. The main periods for sightings are spring, with migration and breeding taking place from April to June, and in August and September during the autumn migration. Over-wintering birds can be spotted from November through to February.

Sources of Information

The Bulgarian Society for the Protection of Birds (www.bspb.org/index.php) is a useful source of information and runs conservation programmes – success stories include the white-tailed eagles which are nesting and breeding after years of absence along the Danube River.

Two useful books (although they are out of print, they can be found on the internet or in libraries) are: Where to Watch Birds in Bulgaria by Petar Iankov (Pensoft Publishers, 1996) and Finding Birds in Bulgaria by Dave Gosney (Gostours, 1994). The following websites are helpful: www.birdwatchingbulgaria.com or www.birdwatchingbulgaria.net.

BELOW: male and female penduline tits, with their extraordinary hanging nests, can be found near lakes and river estuaries, especially near Bourgas on the Black Sea coast

LEFT: armed with the right equipment you will not be disappointed.

LEFT: mountain rock thrush *(Monticola saxatalis)*, the Rhodopes.
RIGHT: a pair of European bee eaters *(Merops apiaster)*, the Strandzha Natural Park.
BELOW: common/European roller *(Coracias gamulus)*, Rusenski Lom.

BEST BIRD-WATCHING AREAS

Danube and Maritsa Rivers
Plains and marshes around the Danube and Maritsa rivers and the Black Sea coast attract European herons, glossy ibis, spoonbills and little bittern. The Srebarna UNESCO Reserve in northern Bulgaria Dalmatian pelicans, as well as red-necked and black-necked grebes, great and pygmy cormorants, egrets and other species.

Shabla Lake
This area is known as the wintering site for the vast majority of the world's red-breasted goose population. Greylag and ferruginous ducks, whooper swans and red-throated and black-throated divers can also be seen.

Black Sea coast
In the north, the Kaliakra coastal headland is a breeding place of the Mediterranean shag, long-legged buzzard, and black-eared, pied and isabelline wheatears. Near Bourgas, four lakes with extensive reed beds attract a range of birds year-round, while in winter whooper swans and various ducks can be seen.

Trigrad Gorge, Western Rhodopes
This is known for raptors, sparrow hawks, golden and short-toed eagles and peregrine falcon which are attracted to its high cliffs. The forests are home to the black woodpecker while kingfisher, grey wagtail and dipper flit around the streams. The gorge is also known for its population of wallcreepers and attracts specialist wallcreeper tours.

Rila
The Ibar reserve is the preferred habitat of the Alpine accentor and shore lark, both unique to the Balkans.

ABOVE: little egret *(Egretta garzetta)* feeding her chicks in the nest. Egrets (little and great) can be seen in many locations but especially in the lakes along the Black Sea coast – Poda lagoon, Shabla Lake and Priomorsko, south of the Ropotomo river.

BELOW: great crested grebes *(Podiceps cristatus)*. Grebes of various varieties are common along the Black Sea coast.

THE BALKAN RANGE

This mountain region is both the spiritual and physical heart of Bulgaria. The lush countryside is generously sprinkled with scenic monasteries and historic towns

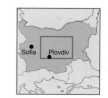

The Balkan mountain range forms the 550 km- (340 mile-) long backbone of Bulgaria, running from the border with Serbia to the west, all the way to the Black Sea and its eastern coastline. Known to natives as Stara Planina, meaning "Old Mountains", this spine of granite peaks has been central to the country's history, the birthplace of the nation-state in the 7th and 8th centuries and is the keeper of ancient traditions.

Much of this area can be explored in an easy week's driving tour from either the capital or the coast. Cars and foreign tourists are a rarity and the endless, empty swathes of thick forest a constant delight. Alternatively, take the train – either on the Sofia–Bourgas line, which skirts the southern side of the range, passing through the Valley of the Roses, or the Sofia–Varna route following the mountains' northern edge.

Ideally, make time to stop off and hike along the way. Trails have been established through areas thick with wildflowers in summer, and characterful accommodation can be found in homes in local villages. The area is also good for caving and climbing.

Lovech

One of Bulgaria's oldest towns, **Lovech ❶** (Ловесч) has a rollercoaster history. First inhabited by Thracians in around the 4th century BC, it was later made into a military post by the Romans, who appreciated its strategic location. By the 12the century it was a thriving trade centre, and in 1187, its fortress held against the Byzantines, resulting in the Lovech Peace Treaty and the restoration of the Bulgarian Empire.

The Turks successfully captured the fortress in 1446, but had to quash several rebellions in subsequent years and in 1784 almost destroyed the town. A century later, in 1872, Lovech became the headquarters of the Internal Revolutionary Organisation of Vasil Levski, the leader of the armed revolution

Map on page 192

LEFT: the Shipka Pass Monument.
BELOW: view over Lovech.

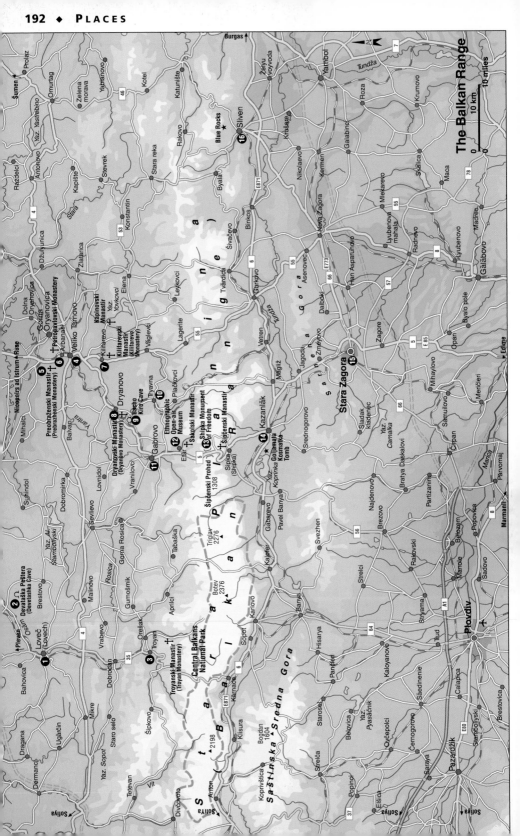

The Balkan Range

0   10 km
0   10 miles

against Ottoman rule *(see page 31)*. After several bloody raids on Lovech, he was captured and hanged in Sofia.

Ancient and modern

Today, Lovech lies peacefully on either side of the Osam river. Its main area of interest for visitors is the old quarter, or Varosha, which is linked to the modern town by a pretty covered bridge, the only one of its kind in Bulgaria. Originally built in 1874, but twice rebuilt, the bridge is lined with modern gift shops.

Attractive National Revival buildings, mainly from the 19th century, line Varosha's steep and cobbled streets. The **Ethnographic Museum** (Mon–Sat 8am–noon, 2–5pm; admission charge) comprises two historic houses. The first, and most interesting, shows the evolution of domestic architecture and furnishings during the 19th century, beginning in simple rooms with low furniture and a bed that was slept in by three generations. As visitors move through the house, they can see how interiors became more sophisticated over time, with an English bed, a French

mirror and Viennese chairs. Porcelain plates on the wall come from Romania, China and Germany, and there is a trunk that belonged to pilgrims bound for Jerusalem. The second house is furnished according to domestic fashions in the 1930s.

Up the hill from the museum is the **Vasil Levski Museum and Monument**, commemorating the local revolutionary hero. The museum contains photographs, maps and personal effects, but all explanations are in Bulgarian.

On a hill on the east side of the town, **Stratesh Park** has a zoo and lily pond, flanked by fine National Revival homes.

Twenty km (12 miles) northeast of Lovech, just north of the village of Devetaki, the **Devetashka Cave ②**, featuring 11 underground lakes and beautiful cave formations. Inhabited since paleolithic times, it has yielded many archaeological finds, including tools and votive tablets.

Troyan

About 35 km (22 miles) south of Lovech, on the banks for the Beli Osum River, **Troyan ③** (Троян) is

Map on page 192

The pedestrianised covered bridge linking old Lovech and the new town.

BELOW:
the interior of Lovech's covered bridge is lined with boutique-style shops.

You will find no shortage of flags flying in Bulgaria, especially in Veliko Tarnovo, a focus for Bulgarian pride in the country's history and culture.

BELOW RIGHT: the Assen Monument, erected in the 1980s to mark the 1,300th anniversary of the Bulgarian state.

an attractive town that serves as the main market centre for the villages of the Central Balkan region. The **tourist office** (Mon–Fri 10am–6pm; tel: 0670-60964; mobile 0889 719941) at 113 ulitsa Vasil Levski, a 10-minute walk from the main square, can make reservations in hotels and local houses for a small fee. It also stocks a wealth of information about everything from spa breaks to hiking, horse riding and bicycle rental (it can also sell a map detailing local cycle routes).

The **Museum of Folk Art and Applied Crafts**, on the main square, (summer daily 9am–5pm, winter Mon–Fri 9am–5pm; admission charge) is probably the best of its kind in Bulgaria, reflecting the town's strong arts and crafts tradition, especially in ceramics. The information panels include English translations and there is also an English-language audio tour.

Medieval capital

For more than 200 years from 1185, **Veliko Tarnovo ❹** (Велико Търново) was not only the capital of the Bulgarian Second Kingdom, but a major European commercial and political centre, rivalling Rome and Constantinople.

Spectacularly set on the steep banks of the looping Yantra river, it is crowned by the enormous hill fortress of **Tsarevets** (daily 8am–7pm summer; 9am–5pm winter; admission charge), meaning Tsar's Place, which sits on top of the highest of the three hills on which the city is set. With its superb defensive location, this spot has been fortified since Thracian times, but the fortress you see today, with its dramatic ramparts, was begun by the Slavs in the 10th century. It contains the restored royal palace, around 400 houses, and churches and monasteries.

A visit to the fortress takes in the gates, towers and remains of the palace, including the throne room, and, at the top, the **Patriarchal Church**, reconstructed in the 1980s to celebrate the 1,300th anniversary of the Bulgarian state, but its interior is disappointingly modern.

A sound and light show, a dramatic recreation of the history of the Second Kingdom, takes place on some summer evenings (call for further information,

The Rise and Fall of Veliko Tarnovo

After the overthrow of the Byzantines by the Assen brothers in 1185–87 the new Bulgarian state and its capital Veliko Tarnovo entered a golden age of prosperity and power in Europe, even rivalling Constantinople in terms of influence. Many splendid monasteries and churches were built during this period, and arts, crafts and literature flourished, including the esteemed Tarnovo School of Art, which was patronised by the royal court. Work by the Tarnovo School can be seen in the Forty Martyrs Church in Veliko Tarnovo and in the rock monastery of Ivanovo *(see page 214).*

After the deaths of the Assen brothers, the Second Bulgarian Kingdom declined, but it revived again under Ivan Alexander (1331–1371), and the Tarnovo Literary School developed, producing works such as the *Tetraevangelia of Ivan Alexander* (The Four Gospels of Ivan Alexander, 1356), an illustrated manuscript (now in the British Museum) containing more that 350 exquisite miniatures..

The seemingly impregnable position of Veliko Tarnovo, wrapped in the bends of the Yantra river, made it an ideal capital, but it was also vulnerable to siege. In 1393, almost 200 years after it was founded, the city capitulated to the Turks, a far superior force that had laid siege to the fortress for three months.

tel: 062-636 828). Even if you do not buy tickets for the show there are vantage points around town where you can see, if not hear, the spectacle.

Below Tsarevets, at the eastern end of ulitsa Mitropolsla, is the **Church of the Forty Holy Martyrs**, which has recently undergone massive restoration. Built on the orders of Assen II to mark his victory over the Byzantines at Klokonitsa in 1230, it was later turned into a mosque. It was here, in 1393, following the city's fall to the Turks, that 110 prominent citizens were massacred.

Among the church's interesting features are two inscribed columns, one detailing Assen II's military success at Klokonitsa, and another, Khan Omurtag's Column, describing his building achievements and signed "Omurtag, the Sublime Khan". Several tsars are buried in the church , including Tsar Kaloyan, whose gold cygnet ring was discovered during excavations here several decades ago.

Opposite the river here is the **Church of St Dimiter** where tsars Assen, Peter and Kaloyan were crowned.

Veliko Tarnovo town

The river west of the fortress is flanked by the attractive old town. Wander around the cobbled streets, taking in the **Samovodende Marketplace**, or bazaar, where workshops and houses have been restored. Although most of these are now souvenir and antiques shops, it remains an atmospheric place, and is a good spot to buy quality pottery.

The **Museum of the National Revival and the Constituent Assembly** on ulitsa Ivan Vazov (Tues–Sun 8am–6pm; admission charge) is a well laid-out museum, but few of the explanations are in English. The ground floor displays books, medals, paintings and other items relating to Bulgarian rebellions against the Turks. Upstairs, the room that held the first Bulgarian parliament in 1879 is being renovated.

Next door, at the bottom of some steps, the **Archaeological Museum** (daily 9am–6pm; admission charge) has finds from the area, many of them from the nearby Roman town of Nikopolis ad Istrum, including the statues in the courtyard, but few have full explanations in English. On the first floor,

Map on page 192

Visiting Veliko Tarnovo's Tsarevets Fortress.

BELOW: Tsarevets' Patriarchal Church and the impressive fortress walls.

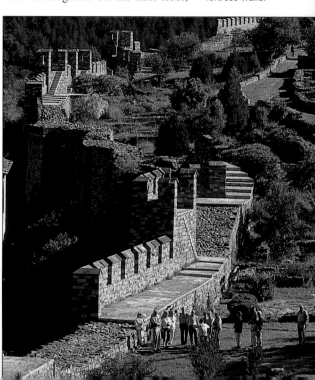

Window detail in the handsome village of Arbanasi.

there is a skeleton, thought to be of a medieval aristocrat. At the back of the building, the **Bulgarian Contemporary History Museum** and a small **Prison Museum** are of minor interest.

Sarafkina House at 88 ulitsa General Gurko (Sun–Fri 9am–noon, 1–6pm; admission charge) may be, as it claims, the most majestic house in Veliko Tarnovo. Built in 1861 for a wealthy banker, the house appears, from the street, to have just two floors, but actually has five, as can be seen from the riverside. Inside, an exhibition shows regional town life in the 19th century.

Mountain monasteries

Around 6 km (4 miles) north of Veliko Tarnovo is **Prebrazhenski Monastery** ❺ (Приображенски Манастир; normally open in daylight hours; admission charge for the church), the Monastery of the Transfiguration. One of Bulgaria's largest monasteries, it commands sweeping views across the valley and to the much more modern-looking Petropavlovski Monastery (with which it is easily confused), 5 km (3 miles) from Arbanasi. Prebrazhenski's Church of the

BELOW LEFT AND RIGHT: door and ceiling frescos in the Church of Archangels, Arbanasi.

Transfiguration, begun by master builder Dimiter Sofialiyata, who was later executed for rebel activities, is covered in murals inside and out. On the southern section of the exterior wall look out for the *Circle of Life*, by Zahary Zograf, showing the passage of the seasons. Although it was originally built in the 14th century, the monastery was rebuilt in the 19th century after being demolished by the Turks and later damaged by landslides.

Arbanasi

Four km (2½ miles) northeast of Veliko Tarnovo is **Arbanasi** ❻ (Арбанаси), a gorgeous village set high on a plateau and overlooking the hills below. It was a wealthy centre for trades and crafts way back in the 17th century, and a good number of its stone merchant-houses date from this period. Declared a historical village of national importance, it is popular both with tourists and wealthy Bulgarians.

Five churches and nearly 100 historical houses (of which only a few are open to the public, and even then from only Apr–Sep, though this is liable to change,

tel: 062-349 460 for up-to-date information) comprise an open-air museum. Typically, the houses have high walls and large wooden gates leading to courtyards, and fine interior details, a testament to the skills of the craftsmen and the wealth of the owners.

Konstantzaliev's House (summer 9am–6pm; admission charge), built in the 17th century with later additions, is a wonderful example, with fine living quarters, a servants' quarter, cellar, stables, sentry and warehouse. Colourful fabrics and intricate woodcarving and plasterwork enrich the interior. Opposite the house, the **Kokon Fountain** (1786) displays the Islamic blessing: "Light will come in the eyes and soul of those who look at it and drink."

Arbanasi's churches are all decorated with wall paintings. The frescos in the **Church of the Nativity** (summer 9am–6pm; admission charge) have put it on the UNESCO World Heritage list. Built in the 16th and 17th centuries, it is the oldest church in the village. Inside, the stunning frescos depict familiar biblical scenes such as *The Nativity* and *The Last Judgement*, as well as the more unusual *Circle of Life* portraying the signs of the zodiac. The elaborately carved main iconostasis is one of the oldest wood-carvings in Bulgaria, executed by Tryvana craftsmen *(see page 199)*.

The village's other outstanding monument is the **Church of Archangels Michael and Gabriel** (summer 9am–6pm; admission charge), covered in 17th -century murals.

A little further afield (18 km/11 miles) north of Veliko Tarnovo, but worth a stop if you are driving around the area, are the peaceful ruins of ancient **Nicopolis ad Istrum** ❼, founded by Emperor Trajan in the 2nd century. The foundations of temples, baths and a forum and other public buildings can be discerned.

SOUTH OF VELIKO TARNOVO

From Veliko Tarnovo two main routes head south, the road to Stara Zagora via Kiliferevo Monastery, and the road to Gabrovo via Dryanovo, running close to the railway for some of the way. **Kilifarevo** ❼ (Килифарево), 16 km (10 miles) south of Veliko Turnovo, was both a much-loved retreat for the tsars of the Second Kingdom and the "second university" of medieval Bulgaria. Founded in 1350 by the enlightened ecclesiast Theodossius of Turnovo, with donations from Tsar Ivan Alexander, the monastery educated hundreds of monks from Bulgaria and beyond.

Its chapel contains intricate decoration, including a fine iconostasis featuring mythical beasts made by craftsmen from Tyravna, but the monastery's thick fortified walls and multi-storey tower hint at its turbulent history. It was repeatedly attacked and reconstructed during the Ottoman occupation; today it is a nunnery, peacefully located in thick forests near the Belitsa River.

Dryanovo Monastery

Nestling among limestone cliffs and dense forest, **Dryanovo Monastery** ❽ (Дряновки Манастир; daily 7am–

Map on page 192

Harvesting the summer lavender.

BELOW: the courtyard of Dryanovo.

Statue of rebel hero Vasil Levski in the courtyard of Dryanovo Monastery.

BELOW: typical Tryavna building with barrel entrance. Even many ordinary homes have defensive features.

10pm; free admission) is 35 km (21 miles) south of Veliko Turnovo. It was a centre for rebellion against the Turks, where famous rebel leaders such as Vasil Levski organised secretly, and it was the site of a number of bloody battles fought by monks during the 1876 April Uprising. It was burned to the ground twice. Renovation of the monastery and construction of residential buildings took place in the 19th century.

The peaceful central courtyard, which has a café, leads to a small museum (Mon–Fri 8.45am–noon, 12.30–4.45pm, Sat– Sun 9.45am–noon, 12.30–3.45pm; admission charge) commemorating the April Uprising. It includes a gruesome pile of skulls, as well as artefacts belonging to the rebels, but no information is in English.

Bacho Kiro Cave

A 300-metre/yd walk from Dryanovo Monastery, **Bacho Kiro Cave** ❾ (daily Apr–Oct 9am–5pm, Nov–Mar 10am–4pm; admission charge) forms a spectacular four-level labyrinth of chambers and galleries. Wonderful for-

mations, with fairytale names such as "The Dwarfs", "The Bear Slide" and "The Sleeping Princess", have been carved out of the limestone cliffs by underground rivers.

Excavations in the 1970s revealed the earliest traces of man on the Balkan Peninsula in the form of flint and bone tools dating back 40–70,000 years. Electrically lit since 1938, the cave has long been a popular destination for Bulgarian tourists, and it is even a venue for concerts, which take advantage of its excellent acoustics. The entire cave system stretches for 3,600 metres/yds, with a visitor area of 700 metres/yds. An "eco-trail" runs from the cave for 3 km (2 miles) through forest along the river gorge, with picnic spots and possible bird sightings.

Living museum

The quaint whitewashed town of **Tryavna** ❿ (Трявна), 17 km (10 miles fom Dryanovo, features on many a Bulgarian postcard, for this living museum of the National Revival School is an architectural gem. It is mainly visited by Bulgarian day-trippers, but the

occasional tour bus with international visitors also roars through.

Historically, it was an important centre for a community of about 40 craftspeople, including goldsmiths, weavers, silkworm breeders and rose oil producers, whose products were widely exported. Over time the town's icon painting, woodcarving and masonry developed their own style, which became known as the Tryavna School. The guild of Tryavna masons was involved in decorating not only Bulgarian buildings, but also those in neighbouring countries; the woodcarving school established in 1920 still trains wood carvers today.

Pause at the **Old Square** at night, when it is prettily lit, or when there are few tourists, to appreciate its architectural harmony. The distinctive **clock tower** (1814), the quaint **Kivgiren vaulted bridge** (1845), and **Archangel Michael Church** (1819), which has a large collection of ornate icons, form a pleasing ensemble.

On the square, the **Old School** (1846–39; daily 9am–6pm; admission charge) was one of Bulgaria's first sec-ular schools. One room shows an original schoolroom; another displays a collection of clocks and watches. A large part is devoted to the Kazakov brothers, one a woodcarver, the other a painter, who produced unusual pieces using mud on sacks, as well as portraits and landscapes.

To the north, **Kanchev Angel House** (Tues–Sun 9.30am–1.30pm, 2–6pm; admission charge), on the street of the same name, was home of the revolutionary Angel Kanchev (1850–1872), a compatriot of Vasil Levski. His father crafted the wooden panels and cupboards in the house.

South of the main square, at 27 ulitsa P.R. Slaveikov, the **Daskalov House**, a splendid house with a walled garden, includes the **Museum of Woodcarving and Icon Painting** (8am–5pm; admission charge) and a woodworker's bench. Don't miss the spectacular wooden suns in the upstairs ceilings, displaying Islamic influences in the interlocking geometric motifs.

At No. 50, on the same street, the **Slaveikov House Museum** (daily 9am–7pm; admission charge) was the

Map on page 192

TIP

Many of the museums in this part of Bulgaria may look closed outside of the peak season, even during official opening hours. Just knock loudly on the door and an attendant will usually let you in.

BELOW: Tryavna's distinctive clock tower and bridge.

A stone fountain in Gabrovo displaying a lion, the ubiquitous symbol of Bulgaria.

home of the father and son poets, Petko and Pencho Slaveikov during the National Revival period. Almost opposite, **Kalinchev's House** (1830s), displays a broad range of Bulgarian art from the turn of the 19th century to the present day. The house was being restored at the time of writing.

Gabrovo

The longest town in Bulgaria, **Gabrovo** (Габрово) ⓫, 46 km (28 miles) southwest of Veliko Tarnovo, stretches for 25 km (13 miles) either side of the Yantra River. On a rocky island in the middle of the river stands a monument to the blacksmith Racho Kovacho, the mythical founder of the city.

Gabrovo is essentially a dull administrative centre, and its inhabitants are the butt of numerous Bulgarian jokes, mainly for their supposed meanness. That said, some attractive National Revival buildings, including houses, churches and a clock tower, date from the days when the town was a significant crafts centre.

The Gabrovnians embrace their comical reputation in the quirky **House of**

Humour and Satire (64 ulitsa Bryanska (daily 9am–6pm; closed Sun in winter; admission charge; guided tours in English; www.humorhouse.bg). Ten halls display cartoons, humorous art, photographs and sculpture from around the world, as well as local jokes, including the most repeated (at least in Bulgaria) one of all – that the people of Gabrovo cut off their cats' tails so their doors shut more quickly and less heat is wasted. Not everything translates well, but the museum is well worth a look.

The **Historical Museum** (Tues–Sat 9am–5pm; admission charge), on cobbled ulitsa Opulchenska, is housed in a restored 19th-century town house, with a handsome interior and changing exhibitions. Once the property of a successful local businessman, Hadzhi Detchko, it is sometimes known simply as Detchko House.

One of Bulgaria's first secular schools, the Aprilov secondary school, founded in 1835, educated a number of famous Bulgarians. Its courtyard leads to the small **Museum of Education** at 13 ulitsa Aprilovska, which has irregular opening times.

Open-air museum

The **Ethnographic Open-air Museum** ⓬ (daily, 9am–6pm summer; 9am–4.40pm winter; admission charge; www.etar.org) at **Etar** (Етъра) is set beside a stream 8km (5 miles) south of Gabrovo. Fun for visitors of all ages, and educational too, it recreates life in the region during the National Revival period when it was famous for its highly skilled craftsmen, who decorated houses and churches all over Bulgaria. The museum is well geared up to tourism, with full explanations in English as well as excellent guided tours.

Water-driven equipment works a sawmill, and there are craftsmen's houses and workshops, a tannery, and an olde-worlde sweet shop with an upstairs café (9am–6pm). Traditional cowbell (*hlopki*) making, goat-hair weaving and shoemaking can all be seen on site, while a full programme of events and festivals showcases the best in local folk music and culture. Make sure to stop at the **Renaissance Tavern** at the southern entrance (there are two entrances) and enjoy traditional fare such as spicy flat sausage and *parlen-itza* (traditional flat bread) with *lyutenitza* (fresh pepper relish) under the trees, with maybe a buffalo yoghurt with honey for dessert.

The Shipka Pass

The dramatic mountain pass between Gabrovo and Kazanlak forms the main route between the River Danube and Turkey. It is often shrouded in dense fog, but on a clear day there are sweeping views over a dramatic landscape.

The area was the site of four fierce battles in the Russo-Turkish War of 1877–8. At the top of Mount Stoletov, overlooking the pass, 894 steep steps lead up to the **Shipka Monument of Freedom** ⓭. Its tower houses a small museum containing weapons and paintings in honour of the 7,000 Russian soldiers and Bulgarian volunteers who died defending the pass against Turkish soldiers, who outnumbered them almost four to one.

Another monument to those who died is the lovely **Shipka Memorial Church** (or Church of the Nativity) in Shipka village, off the main road. Its elaborate arches, splendid pink and

Map on page 192

A water-driven exhibit at the Ethnographic Open-air Museum at Etar.

BELOW: posing for pictures at the Shipka Monument of Freedom.

The Memorial to Freedom, the Shipka Pass, attracts many Bulgarians, who come to pay their respects to the dead.

BELOW: the rose fields near Kazanlak.

green facade, and gleaming onion-shaped gold domes were inspired by 17th-century Russian church architecture. The bells in the 53-metre (170-ft) bell tower were made from cartridges used in the battle for the Shipka Pass; one of the bells weighs 11 kg 12 tons. The interior is beautifully decorated with folk-inspired murals depicting important figures in Russian history.

Rose capital

Kazanlak ⓮ (Казанлък), 48 km (30 miles) south of Gabrovo, is both the "capital" of the rose-growing region, the much-vaunted Valley of the Roses, and of the so-called Valley of the Thracian Kings.

Apart from the first weekend in June, when the Festival of Roses takes place, there is little opportunity for the visitor to experience the rose industry at first hand. But the town has a small **museum** (summer 9am–6pm) where you can learn about the 350-year-old history of rose production in Bulgaria. The special rose, introduced from India, is picked only between 5am and 10am, before the sun can cause the oil to evap-orate, from 20 May until 20 June. The oil, which is distilled twice, is considered the best in the world. Exhibits include paraphernalia relating to the industry and there opportunities to buy rose products.

Valley of the Thracian Kings

The Valley of the Roses is also known as the **Valley of the Thracian Kings**, as it is dotted with around 1,500 Thracian burial mounds. These have been the source of extraordinary finds, including gold masks, armour, horse tackle, jewellery and drinking vessels. One of the first tombs to be excavated was the **Kazanlak Tomb**, dating from around the late 4th century BC, on the outskirts of town. A replica of the tomb can be visited next to the original site (Apr–Oct 9am–5pm; more limited hours in winter; admission charge). Murals on the tomb depict the chieftain's life, battles and burial feast.

Nearby, the **Kulata Ethnographical Complex** includes a typical house of a wealthy 19th-century rose merchant.

In the last few years, as archaeology has recovered from the collapse in fund-

ing that followed the fall of Communism, the valley has yielded several important finds. In 2004 the Bulgarian archaeologist Georgi Kito found a spectacular solid-gold mask, almost certainly belonging to a king, in a mid-5th century BC tomb. Another tomb, known as the Goljamata Kosmatka Tomb, dating from the 5th century BC, was discovered just 2 km (1¼ miles) away. One of the biggest tombs so far found in Bulgaria, it was later identified as belonging to King Seutus III. The following year a huge hoard of gold discovered further east was found to include some 15,000 gold rings.

The **Iskra Museum** (Mon–Fri 9am–noon, 2–5pm; admission charge), on plochtad Sevtopolis, Kazanlak's main square, is filled with archaeological finds from the area. The museum can arrange tours to a small number of tombs that are open to the public.

Behind the mountains

Stara Zagora ⓕ (Стара Загора), 35 km (22 miles) southeast of Kazanlak, means "Old Town behind the Mountains", a fitting description for the 7,000-year-old settlement that is dominated by the Sredna Gora. Today, Bulgaria's sixth largest city, it is best known for producing the leading Bulgarian beer, Zagorka, a crisp pilsner. Its wide, tree-lined streets create the impression of a pleasant city. Although it is mostly modern, with few sights, it is worth stopping here for an hour or two if you are passing through.

At the crossroads of two important trade routes and surrounded by richly fertile lands, Stara Zagora has been of strategic importance since antiquity. In the 4th century BC, the Thracians settled here, in the place they called Beroe. The Romans, who arrived around AD 100, founded their own town here, Augusta Traiana, that minted its own coins and was second ony to Philipopolis (Plovdiv). The Turks destroyed the city on many occasions, most dramatically during the Russo-Turkish war in 1877. Completely rebuilt, today the city boasts an easy-to-follow grid system of streets.

The **Neolithic Dwellings** (Tues–Sat 10am–noon, 2–5pm; admission charge) are the top sight in Stara

Map on page 192

On the first Sunday in June the Valley of the Roses hosts it annual Festival of Roses, with folk singing and dancing and a search to find the year's rose queen.

BELOW: rose-oil products for sale.

Rose Oil

Each May at dawn in the Valley of the Roses, women and children come together to pick the delicate, pink petals of damask rose (*R. damascena*), gathering them into large cloth bags that hang from their necks. The precious petals must be collected early and quickly, before the morning dew evaporates, taking the fragrance with it.

It is a method of harvesting that has changed little since the 17th century when the Ottomans first realised that the area's sandy soil, mild temperatures and healthy rainfall were ideal for the cultivation of this variety of rose. The damask rose's petals have a penetrating and long-lasting scent that makes it particularly suitable for oil production. It is an essential ingredient in many perfumes and aromatherapists claim it is a balancer of emotions.

Local villagers may collect as many as 30 kg (66 lbs) of petals, a yield that will earn them just a few euros. No less than 3,000 tonnes of petals are required to produce one kilogram of oil, which will then sell for several thousand euros. After collection, the valuable consignment of petals is taken to the nearest distillery, where they are steamed and the rose oil collected from the resulting condensation. Finally, the essence will be exported to countries such as France, the US and Saudi Arabia.

Zagora and one of the most important Neolithic sites in Europe. It is an inexpensive taxi ride or a 30-minute walk west of the town centre (go down ulitsa General Stoletov), near the District Hospital. The museum is not obvious, so look for a grey and brown building with a sign on the door (if it appears to be closed during opening hours, just knock on the door).

On the first floor, the remains of two Neolithic houses dating from the 6th century BC, appear at first sight to be simply a pile of rubble. But with the help of the information leaflet in English included in the admission charge you can make out features, such as rubbish holes and furnaces, and get a sense of how closely these New Stone Age families lived. There are the remains of an earth "couch", and at one time shelves held the many earthenware vessels on display downstairs.

The downstairs exhibition includes the usual delicately crafted bone and flint tools, but also boldly patterned ceramic pots, vases and mugs, attractive Henry Moore-like sculptured objects and jewellery made out of shells and bone. These objects, both aesthetic and practical, and all found in the vicinity of Stara Zagora, are testament to the sophistication of Stone Age society.

Local life

The tree-filled **City Garden** in the pedestrianised centre is both the heart and lungs of the city, and always full of people of all ages chatting on benches, and old men playing with giant chess pieces. Join locals strolling up and down the main artery of **Tsar Simeon Veliki**, running along the garden's edge, stopping to have a coffee or a Zagorka beer at one of the many pavement cafés. Look out for the 15th-century **Eski Mosque**, disused but picturesque, just east of the garden.

A few blocks further east along this road is the colourful **Central Market**. It's worth a look, even if you don't shop – its stalls sell mostly fresh produce, including locally made honey, alongside clothes and shoes – to get a taste of local life. Close by, on Sv. Knyaz Boris I, is the post office, where at the eastern entrance you can see the badly lit remains of a Roman floor mosaic.

It is sometimes possible to hire small boats at **Ezeroto Lake** just south of the centre (by the hotel of the same name). Alternatively, visit **Ayazmo Park**, with 400 hectares (nearly 1,000 acres) of trees and parkland, carved out of the slopes of the Sredna Gora Mountains, which flanks the city's northern side.

City of culture

Stara Zagora's **State Opera Theatre**, founded in 1928, was the first provincial opera house in Bulgaria and is still one of the country's most prestigious venues, staging world-class performances as well as an opera festival in May and June. Behind the Opera House, on the northwestern corner of the City Garden, is the restored section of the **Roman Theatre**, built in the 3rd century. Wander around, admire it from the terrace café, or try and take in one of the evening concerts held there. Other Roman remains are dotted nearby, including the forum.

There are one or two rather dusty museums in the town. The **State Gallery** (above the tourist office to the northeast of the City Garden) has eclectic, changing exhibitions of works by local artists, while north of the gardens is the **Museum of 19th-century Town Life**, a distinctive blue and sepia building, open by appointment only (tel: 042 239 31). The **Historic Museum**, opened in 1907, has been closed for some years, but is due to reopen in the near future.

Geo Milev House-Museum (Tues–Sat 10am–noon, 2–5pm; admission charge), one block north of the City Garden, houses the simple living quarters of the poet, Geo Milev (1895–1925). Milev was a political poet, famous for his poem *September,* which criticised the bloody suppression of the 1923 Agrarian Uprising. It resulted in his violent murder, along with that of other prominent intellectuals. The poet's house, accessed by a pretty courtyard, contains graffiti and other writings and drawings relating to the revolution. Among the photographs is one of a mass grave of the victims of the revolution and another of Milev with his hair over his missing eye, lost in World War I. None of the information panels is in English.

Map on page 192

TIP

Stara Zagora's tourist office (northeast of City Garden) can arrange village tours in the surrounding countryside, staying in a traditional farmhouse and experiencing local life.

BELOW: mind games in the open air.

Sliven

Around 75km (46 miles) east of Kazanlak, **Sliven** ⑯ (Сливен) sprawls at the foot of the Eastern Balkan Ranges. It is a mix of traditional red-roofed buildings and modern concrete blocks. The name Sliven comes from the Bulgarian word for "merge", a reference to its position at the confluence of three rivers.

In the early years of the Ottoman empire, Sliven was a centre for breeding army falcons and was a checkpoint on the mountain passes. By the beginning of the 19th century, successful textile and craft industries had evolved, while the nearby mountains formed a refuge for hundreds of anti-Turkish bandits known as *haiduti*.

The **Hadzhi Dimitar House-Museum** on ulitsa Asenova (Mon–Fri 9am–noon and 2–5pm; admission charge) was once an inn and home to Hadzhi Dimitar, one of the leaders of rebel attacks against the Turks. The museum shows living conditions from different periods, although there are few explanations in English. A monument to Dimitar, who was eventually hanged in Ruse, stands in a leafy square in the centre of town. At his feet are busts of important people living in Sliven during the National Revival period.

The town's **History Museum** (18 ulitsa Tsar Osvoboditel (Mon–Sat 9am– noon and 2–5pm; admission charge) has archaeological and ethnographical displays on three floors, as well as changing exhibitions.

Blue Rocks

From Sliven a chairlift (4 km (3 miles) off the Kotel road) whisks passengers up 600 metres (2,000 ft) to the **Blue Rocks** (so called because of their misty blue hue at the end of the day) northeast of Sliven. Clusters of rocks have been given names such as "The Camel", "Baby Frog" and "The Dolls" on account of their suggestive shapes. Look out for the *Halkata*, or "Ring", an impressive arch that is associated with many legends. Further up the slopes is the Karandila Hotel, which offers refreshment facilities and is the starting point for marked walking trails around the area. ❑

Map on page 192

BELOW: summer café in Stara Zagora.

RESTAURANTS & BARS

Restaurants

Arbanasi

Restaurant Arbat
Lovely and atmospheric restaurant on the main square. Sit by the real fire in winter, or on the terrace in summer. Menu in Bulgarian and German only, but helpful service. €€

Gabrovo

Strannopriemnitsa
Ul. Opalchenska
This a typical *mehana* in the old part of town, with an attractive court-yard. Somewhat touristy; live music on some evenings. €€

Kazanlak

Hotel Palas Peko
ul. Stainov
Tel: (0431) 62311
Classic restaurant offering traditional food, usually with live music at during the evening. Garden barbecues in summer. €€

Lovech

Varosha Mehana
Ul. Popukanov
Perennial favourite in the old town, with a pleasant outside eating area. It is popular with tour groups, so it is best to avoid peak times to be sure of a table. Typical Bulgarian fare on the menu and live music some evenings. €€

Stara Zagora

Forum
94 ul. H. D. Asenov
Tel: (042) 623 221
Chic, cellar restaurant with good service and an enormous selection of food from mussels, foie gras and caviar to carpaccio and tiger prawns. €€€

Happy Bar and Grill
100 Bul. Tsar Simeon Veliki
Tel: (042) 600 621
www.happy.bg
This large, loud chain restaurant serves burgers, chicken pasta and the like, making it popular with families. €

Uniquato
36 ul. Sava Silov
Tel: (042) 661 155
www.uniquato.com
Modern, upmarket restaurant with outside terrace, in the hotel of the same name. Emphasis on Italian cuisine. Long wine list. €€€

Tryavna

Domino Pizza
Tel: (0677) 2322
The upstairs of this smart town house serves giant pizzas, salads and a good value children's menu. Downstairs is a small bar, which often plays loud popular music. €€

Veliko Tarnovo

Ego Pizza and Grill
Ul. 17 Nezavisimost
Tel: (062) 601804

Modern and airy with lovely views from terrace. More than just pizzas and grills; Mexican and Chinese dishes too. €€

Mustang
Pl. Maika Bulgaria
This chain offers a huge menu with something to suit everyone. Popular with Bulgarians, although it isn't great on atmosphere. €€

Gurko
ul. 33 Gurko
Tel: (062) 627 838
www.hotel-gurko.com
It's a good idea to book at this established, family-run hotel restaurant. Enjoy a leisurely, traditional meal, washed down with a choice from the decent wine list. €€

Bars

For a provincial city Stara Zagora has a lively bar scene. Among the best places to go are **Caribi** (105A Bul. Tsar Simeon Veliki), which has six bowling alleys and a pool table plus a good bar. **Bacchus**, near the main post office (58 Tsar Ivan Shishman) combines Balkan jazz with Western pop music.

PRICE CATEGORIES

Price categories are per person for thee courses:
€ = under 10 leva
€€ = 10–25 leva
€€€ = 25–50 leva
€€€€ = over 50 leva

RIGHT: one option in Stara Zagora.

THE DANUBIAN PLAIN

The River Danube forms Bulgaria's border with Romania, a frontier land that has prospered and languished according to fluctuating fortunes in warfare and trade

Map on pages 210–11

The most northerly region of Bulgaria, the Danubian Plain is characterised by rich agricultural land and gently rolling hills. Its sights are mostly low-key, though there are interesting, well-preserved fortifications in Vidin, Cherven, and Pliska; an impressive rock monastery at Ivanovo; and the Rusenski Lom National Park. There are few major cities, as flooding is a constant problem, but there are several modern river ports with late-19th century origins, which evolved after the Danube opened up to shipping in 1836. Those looking for scenic riverside views or boat trips will be mostly disappointed, although some lovely glimpses of the once-blue (now sadly polluted) Danube can be had.

Beginning in Vidin, this route, which is best done by car to allow for diversions and stops, moves west to east. Avoiding the industrial and unattractive stretch of the Danube immediately east of Vidin, it hops south to Pleven, before regaining the Danube at Nikopol.

Remote outpost

Situated on the cusp of the Danube's final bend, **Vidin** ❶ (Видин), 200 km (125 miles) northwest of Bulgaria, is unique in being the only town in Bulgaria that stands on the north of the Danube, with Romania due south. The Romans were here first, calling the place Bononia, but the immaculately preserved **Baba Vida Fortress** (Крепост Баба Вида; Tues–Sat

9.30am–5pm; admission charge), which makes a visit to this remote city worthwhile, was constructed in the 10th century, when the First Bulgarian Kingdom was at its zenith. All of the subsequent invaders who held the town (the Byzantines, Turks, Habsburgs, Turks again and Bulgarians) added to and improved the fortress, which guarded important central European trade routes.

What has been rather hopefully called a "triangle of tolerance" is formed by three very different centres of worship within 100 metres/yds of

LEFT: statue at the entrance to Pliska.
BELOW: downtown Pleven.

Coat of arms, Pleven.

one another: the Eastern Orthodox **St Nicholas Church**; the **Osman Pazvantoglu Mosque**, named after an 18th-century Ottoman governor who rebelled against the distant sultan; and the second-largest Jewish **synagogue** in Bulgaria.

The **Historical Museum** (13 ulitsa Tsar Simeon Veliki; Tues–Sat 9am–noon, 2–5pm; admission charge), occupying a former *konak*, or police station and barracks, has exhibits dating mainly from the Roman and National Revival periods.

In June 2006, the long-awaited go-ahead was given for the construction of a bridge over the Danube, which will link Vidin in Bulgaria with Romania's Calafat, both economically depressed communities. It has taken 12 years to finalise the project and €230 million. The bridge will be only the second crossing of the 482 km (300 mile) stretch of river that forms the border between the two countries and, it is hoped, a concrete symbol of the neighbours' joint intention to end their mutual isolation. The other crossing, the "Friendship Bridge", also known as the Danube Bridge, built in 1954, links Ruse and Giurgiu in Romania.

Pleven

Some 50 km (30 miles) south the river, in the foothills of the Balkan Range, **Pleven** ❷ (Плевен) is primarily an administrative and agricultural centre. It has a smattering of attractions and pleasant, tree-lined streets. Several points of interest in the city relate to the famous siege of Pleven in 1877, an event that led to the liberation of northern Bulgaria from Ottoman rule. The town has Thracian origins, and was one in a sequence of Roman strongholds along the Danube, but it wasn't until the 19th century that it developed into a major market town, particularly for livestock.

A **mausoleum** (daily 9am–noon, 1–6pm; admission free) stands in the main square of ploschad Vuzrazhdane as a magnificent Russo-Byzantine memorial to the Russian soldiers who died in Pleven. Just west of here, the **Svetlin Rusev Gallery** (Mon–Fri 10.30am–6.30pm; admission charge) in the old public baths shows Pleven-born

Rusev's paintings and work by other Bulgarian and foreign artists.

North of here, the tiny **Museum of Liberation**, on ulitsa Vasil Levski, contains items relating to the surrender of the Turks. A little further north, the 14th-century **Church of St Nicholas** houses a collection of icons and a portrait of Sv Nikolai himself.

The **Regional Historical Museum** on 3 ulitsa Stoyan Zaimov (Tues–Sat 9am–noon, 12.30–5pm; admission charge, free Thur) was once an old barracks. Its 24 halls are well laid-out and divided into areas of interest: archaeology; Ottoman Oppression and Bulgarian Revival; Ethnography; New and Contemporary History; Nature; and an enormous coin collection. Highlights include a 6,000-year-old Neolithic dwelling and Roman artefacts.

A short walk south of the museum, past the city art gallery, is **Skovelev Park**. Here, the **Panorama** (Tues–Sat; 9am–noon, 12.30–5pm) was built on the 100th anniversary of the liberation of Pleven. Standing on the battlefield itself, large-scale canvases depict battle scenes during the War of Liberation.

Historic port

Nikopol ❸ (Никопол), 54 km (33 miles) north of Pleven, is a small port and agricultural centre, and was an important trade and cultural centre in the Second Bulgarian Kingdom. When, in 1396, the Ottomans successfully defeated an army of Hungarian crusaders led by King Sigismund, it strengthened Turkish hopes to move in on Christian Europe. Nikopol benefited from Turkish fortifications and later, in the 18th and 19th centuries played a role in the Russo-Turkish wars.

Remnants of Nikopol's past can be found in the form of a 2nd-century drinking fountain, built in memory of a local man's wife, with a touching stone inscription describing his grief. There are the remains of **Shishman's Fortress**, named for Tsar Ivan Shisham, the last tsar before the Turkish invasion, and on a hill, a monument to the Russian soliders who died in the War of Liberation.

Svishtov

Just over 50 km (30 miles) east of Nikopol, **Svishtov ❹** (Свищов) began

Map on page 210–11

The Svetlin Rusev Gallery in Pleven.

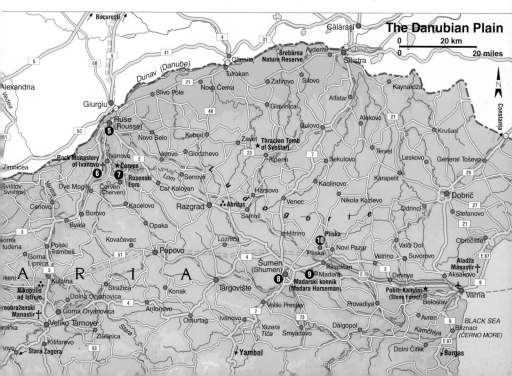

Window detail on a civic building in Rousse.

BELOW:
riverside Rousse

life as the Roman settlement of Novae, a few kilometres away from the present-day city. Commanding a strategic position on high ground, in 1810 the town was burnt to the ground by Russians. Under the Ottomans, Svishtov became a centre for commerce and culture and was one of the first towns to be liberated in 1877. It overlooks what was once a popular river crossing, which saw heavy steam traffic from 1835 until the bridge at Rousse was built.

Today the city is a busy Danubian port and the hub of a wine-producing area notable for the production of a fine cabernet sauvignon. All of Svishtov's sights are within easy walking distance of the main square. On ulitsa Tsar Osvoboditel, the **Holy Trinity Church** (1867) is a wonderful example of National Revival church architecture. Architect Kolyu Ficheto created an open layout topped by a large dome surrounded by three smaller ones and a dramatic octagonal bell tower. Inside are painted and silver icons.

Aleko Konstantinov was a much-loved late-19th-century satirist who was so controversial that he was even-tually gunned down (albeit acciden-tally) by his political opponents in 1897. His heart, complete with bullet hole, is on display in a glass jar in the **Aleko Konstantinov House-Museum** (daily 9am–noon, 1–5pm; admission charge). The house, which belonged to his wealthy merchant father, is an example of one of the first Western style houses in the region.

Rousse

"All that I experienced later had already happened in Ruse," wrote Nobel prize-winning author Elias Canetti, who was born in Rousse.

Fortified **Rousse** ❺ (Pyce), 97 km (60 km) miles northeast of Svishtov, was built in the 13th and 14th centuries on the remains of a Roman fortress and naval centre. One of the country's wealthiest medieval settlements, it was conquered by the Ottomans in 1388 and flourished both under Turkish rule and post-liberation. The city, whose Roman name meant "Port of the Sixty Ships", became the cradle for Bulgarian shipbuilding, and in 1881 the first iron ship in Bulgaria was built here.

A number of other significant "firsts" occurred in Rousse – the first Bulgarian newspaper was published here, and it had the first Bulgarian railway line (to Varna), which quickly became a symbol of cultural and economic growth.

The largest Bulgarian settlement on the Danube, it has many fine examples of 19th- and 20th-century baroque and rococo architecture which would not be out of place in central Europe. Indeed, many rich merchants from Venice and Dubrovnik came to live here and the city became known as "Little Vienna".

Today the city is primarily an industrial port. Until the proposed new bridge is completed at Vidin the Giurgiu-Ruse Friendship Bridge is the only bridge crossing the Bulgarian-Romanian section of the Danube. Proud of its cultural institutions – Rousse is home to the Rousse Philharmonic Orchestra (1948) and the Rousse State Opera (1949) – the city also hosts a number of cultural festivals, focusing on jazz, folk and theatre.

Filled with flowers and outdoor cafés, **Battenberg Square** was the original city centre and is the site of several splendid buildings, including the **Regional Library** (1911) and the **Secondary School** (1898). Also here, the **Rousse Historical Museum** (Mon–Fri 9am–noon, 2–5pm; admission charge) tells the story of Rousse from its Thracian roots through to liberation and the Bulgarian Renaissance. Housed in the underground **Battenberg Palace** (1882) in which Russian officers were interrogated, it is linked by a tunnel to the chief of police's house. Exhibits from the surrounding area include Thracian silver, medieval ceramics from Cherven and wall paintings from the Ivanovo Rock Monastery. A coin collection, early printed books and old photographs of families who lived in Rousse are also of interest.

Spacious **Freedom Square** is home to the Court of Justice and presided over by the **Monument to Freedom**

(1908), a woman with a raised sword in her right hand. The grand Revenues Building (Dohodno Zdanie), from 1902, has a statue of Mercury, known as the winged God of Trade. More commonly called the "theatre building", on account of its theatre, where most of Bulgaria's famous actors have performed, it is a wonderful mixture of architectural styles.

A short walk south of here is **Sveta Troista Church** (1638), a fine example of the difficulties of working with Ottoman restrictions on religious buildings. Originally only a tiny 2 metres by 9 metres (6 ft by10 ft), it was extended below ground level. A bell tower was added in 1878.

The **Pantheon of the Enlighteners** (1978) honours the 100th anniversary of Bulgarian liberation from Ottoman rule. The enormous marble hall contains the graves of 39 Bulgarian revolutionaries, many of them writers and educators. After much debate, the Pantheon was Christianised in 2001. A cross was placed on the dome and a chapel inaugurated in the building.

Rousse's riverfront has certainly seen

Map on page 210–11

A ponichki-*maker in downtown Rousse. You will see such doughnut makers on street corners all over Bulgaria.*

BELOW: pausing for a chat in downtown Rousse.

The Rusenski Lom National Park, 20 km (12 miles) from Rousse, has some lovely gorges that are attractive to walkers and climbers.

BELOW: murals in St Borogditsa Church at Ivanovo Rock Monastery.

better days, but most visitors will find themselves there, if only to take in its museums. **Zahari Stoyanov House Museum**, 15 ulitsa Stamboliski (Mon–Fri 9am–noon, 2–5pm; admission charge) is dedicated to Baba Tonka, a key figure in Bulgarian liberation, and her family. Nearby, **Kaliopa House** (1866; Mon–Fri 9am–noon, 2–5pm; admission charge) forms a museum of daily life in 19th-century Rousse. Once the property of Maria Kalish, wife of the Prussian consular, whose nickname was Kaliopa after the Greek demigoddess, it has a wonderfully over-the-top neoclassical interior.

The **National Museum of Transport and Communications** (Mon–Fri 9am–noon and 2–5pm; admission charge) on 5 ulitsa Bratia Obretenovi, is housed in Bulgaria's oldest railway station. It traces the history of rail and river transport and displays some of the first carriages used.

Ivanovo and its monastery

Four km (2½ miles) west of the village of Ivanovo and 20 km (12 miles) from Rousse is the **Rock Monastery of Ivanovo ⑥** (Иваово) listed as a World Heritage site by UNESCO. Consisting of a number of churches, it is carved out of vertical rocks, spectacularly located either side of the Rusenski Lom River. Monks began the monastery's construction in the 13th century, and lived here in solitude until the 17th century, living off roots and fruit growing in the forest. Originally as many as 40 churches and 300 cells were found here, although only a few of these are still standing.

The main church, St Borogditsa, is covered in exceptionally fine 14th-century murals. Other churches contain further murals, but these are less accessible. The so-called **Buried-Under Church** includes a portrait of Tsar Ivan Assen, under whose patronage the monastery was built.

Cliff-face citadel

Eager to escape persistent Slavic attacks, the people of Rousse moved inland in the 6th century and built a citadel high on a gorge. **Cherven ⑦** (Червен; usually Wed–Sun 9am–1pm, 2–6pm; admission charge) became one of the most important settlements in Bulgaria in the 13th and 14th centuries, a bishop's seat and the site of 12 churches – some of them the biggest in the Balkans during that time.

Today, medieval Cherven lies a few kilometres from the modern village. Its name means "red shore" and refers to the colour of the clay in the riverbank. Clinging to the cliff face, high on a hill in the River Cherni Lom canyon, it forms a kind of Machu Picchu in miniature, with sections of the fortified walls and gates and foundations of churches and palaces remaining.

Finds ranging from arrowheads to pagan paintings testify to the varied life of the inhabitants, who in the town's heyday numbered 10,000. They were skilled craftsmen and soldiers, and also expert builders, who constructed an underground water system, 12 metre- (40 ft-) high fortified walls

and a castle second only to Tsarevets, Veliko Tarnovo, in size.

Shumen

Situated halfway between Veliko Tarnovo and Varna, **Shumen** ❽ (Шумен) is an obvious stopping-off point for those travelling this route by car. Protected by a horseshoe of hills, the town has long held a strategic military position, as the extensive remains of fortifications show. Its history stretches back over 3,000 years.

Partly reconstructed, the medieval **Shumen Fortress** (summer Mon–Fri 9am–8pm; winter Mon–Fri 9am–5pm; admission charge) stands 2 km (1¼ miles) out of town. A path from here leads for several kilometres to the **Creators of the Bulgarian State Monument** (daily 9am–7pm; admission charge; lectures in English). This concrete monstrosity, on which every aspect of Bulgarian history is represented, was built in 1981 in honour of the establishment of the Bulgarian state.

In town, the enormous domes of **Tombul Mosque** (1744; daily 9am–6pm; admission charge) on ulitsa Pakovski shine out from Shumen's Muslim quarter. The largest operational mosque in Bulgaria, it welcomes worshippers from neighbouring Balkan states. The exquisitely decorated complex includes a courtyard with an ablutions fountain and Moorish arches, a theological college and an enormous prayer hall.

The red-brick **Regional History Museum** (Mon–Fri 9am–5pm, Sat 9am–4pm; admission charge; foreign language tours) on bulevard Slavyanski, holds an amazing 150,000 exhibits in eight halls. Most of the more significant finds are from the surrounding area, such as Pliska and Madara, but some relate to Shumen itself.

Shumen has four house-museums (all open Mon–Fri 9am–5pm), all of which are interesting for their National Revival architecture as well as for their fascinating past occupants. **Pancho Vladigerov House** also incorporates a concert hall, commemorating the Shumen-born composer. **Panaiot Volov House** commemorates one of the leaders of the April Uprising; **Dobri Voynikov House** remembers the 19th-

Map on page 210–11

The dome of a church and a slim minaret side by side in Shumen.

BELOW: the Creators of the Bulgarian State Monument.

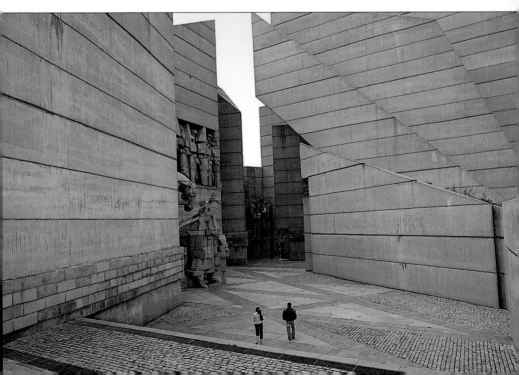

Map on page 210–11

The Madara Rocks lie 2 km (1¼ miles) from the small village of Madara, which has a railway station on the Sofia–Varna route. There is also a bus service to Shumen.

BELOW: the ruined city of Pliska.

century playwright; while on three-levels around a courtyard, **Layosh Kossuth House** is a monument to the Hungarian revolutionary.

Madara Horseman

Declared a World Heritage site by UNESCO, the **Madara Horseman** ❾ lies 7 km (4 miles) from Shumen. The 3rd century BC relief is carved high into a sheer rock face 23 metres (75 ft) above ground level. Sadly fading and visible only in sunlight it shows the life-size figure of a victorious man on horseback who has stabbed a lion lying at its feet, with his faithful dog running behind. The scene represents the power of the young Bulgarian state; three Greek inscriptions record events in Bulgarian-Byzantine relations.

The area surrounding the horseman has been named an historical and archaeological reserve (daily 9am–5pm; admission charge). Archaeological monuments dating from 4,000 BC to the 15th century have been found here, including prehistoric caves, Roman settlements and medieval churches. Cut into a terrace north of the horseman is a

significant, although barely discernable, collection, of 8th- and 9th-century monks' cells and churches. It is worth climbing the 400 steps to the Madara plateau and its fortress, carved out of white stone in the 5th or 6th century BC, where there are sweeping views.

Ancient capital

The ruins of **Pliska** ❿ (Плиска) one of the capitals of the First Bulgarian Kingdom (681–893), lie 2 km (1¼ miles) from the village of Pliska. The settlement had a highly advanced system of fortifications – covering 23 sq. km (9 sq. miles), and was almost completely surrounded by a defensive wall and moat. Inside was a rectangular "town" of walls, with cylindrical towers at each corner.

Although Pliska was sacked by the Byzantine army in 811, the invaders were driven out. It then evolved as a cultural centre, from where the Cyrillic alphabet was spread. But in 892, with the crushing of a pagan revolt, Boris I moved the capital to nearby Preslav, and the old city crumbled to its present state. ❑

RESTAURANTS

Pleven

Restaurant Dom
(Hotel Rostov)
2 ul. Tsar Boris III
Tel: (064) 805 005
This modern hotel has three restaurants, including Restaurant Dom, where well-cooked Bulgarian specialities and international fare are served in a spacious and elegant dining room. Good meat and game, and attentive service. A good option if you want somewhere smart. €€

Panorama
(Hotel Balkan)
85 Bul. Ruse
Tel: (064) 803 700
Situated on the 14th floor of the Hotel Balkan, this restaurant serves a wide range of international cuisine and offers splendid views over the town. €€

Rousse

Anna Palace
4 ul. Kniazjesta
Tel: (082) 825005
www.annapalace.com
This is the smartest hotel in town. Its restaurant is rather formal and old-fashioned but the food is decent.

Leventa
Tel: (082) 662 880
www.leventa-bg.net
Food and wine complex in the Tabia Fort, Ottoman fortifications on the south side of town. Attractively renovated in 2005, it comprises several dining rooms with high vaulted ceilings and frescos on the walls. It serves Bulgarian haute cuisine and has an excellent wine list offering the best of the regional wines. There are also opportunities to buy wine. €€€

Plaza
Pl Svoboda
Tel: (082) 822950
This hotel has several restaurants but in summer its popular garden restaurant with its large vine-covered terrace has the most atmosphere. It specialises in barbecued meat, but also offers some Bulgarian dishes. There is music most evenings.

Regal Restaurant
ul. Asparoukh
Tel: (082) 823 344
Part of the Bistra and Galina Hotel, with a pleasant summer garden. Good wine list; French and healthy options. €€

Strandjata
5 ul. Konstantin Irichek
www.strandjata.com
This is an unpretentious mehana with a cosy, barrel-shaped dining room and a small terrace. A good range of well-cooked Bulgarians specialities at inexpensive prices. €

Shumen

Panorama Restaurant
Shumen Hotel
1 pl. Oborishte
Tel: (054) 591141
Has sweeping views of the city and a grand piano. A safe if rather dull choice, it is often used by organised tour groups. €€€

Hotel Rimini Club
2 ul Haralan Angelov
Tel: (054) 890 202
This comfortable hotel also has a good restaurnt serving Italian and French food. Garden dining in summer. €€

National Revival-style Houses
At the eastern end of ulitsa Tsar Osvoboditel
This row of attractive 19th-century wooden buildings house several little mehanas. They all have outdoor seating and offer good, traditional Bulgarian food. €

Vidin

Bononia Hotel
ul. Baba Vida
Tel: (094) 606 031
The Bononia is one of the few places to get a reasonable meal in Vidin. It also has a coffee shop and bar. €€

PRICE CATEGORIES

Price categories are per person for thee courses:
€ = under xx leva
€€ = xxx leva
€€€ = xxx leva
€€€€ = xxxx leva£200

RIGHT: Rousse has a lively café scene.

VARNA

Bulgaria's third-largest city, Varna is the main hub on the Black Sea coast, a gateway for international visitors but also an important cultural centre with museums, arts festivals and an opera house

When the railway that links **Varna** (Варна) to the interior (first to Rousse, and then to Sofia) was built at the end of the 19th century, it transformed Varna's fortunes forever. The city blossomed and became a fashionable destination for the country's elite, with western European-style architecture and entertainment. In 1921 the city was declared a resort.

Today, **Varna** ❶ has a quiet grandeur, sprawling along the bay of the same name. It has a generous sprinkling of museums and the splendid Sea Gardens (becoming Primorski Park at its southern end) forming a wide green belt along its coast. Travel only a few kilometres out of the city and you will find a verdant landscape of gardens, vineyards and forests, as well as a palace (not open to the public) where Bulgaria's Politburo used to come for rest and relaxation.

Orientation

The wide streets, many of them pedestrianised, are good for wandering. The centre is dissected by long straight boulevards and part of it is laid out on a grid system, making navigation easy. Most of the key places of interest mentioned in this chapter can be reached on foot.

Varna is the best place to shop outside of Sofia, with modern boutiques selling designer clothes and plenty of stalls offering souvenirs and locally made crafts.

A brief history

The small fishing and farming community of Varna became an important centre for commerce way back in the 6th century BC, when the Greeks established a trading colony known as Odessos, meaning "town upon water". Under the Romans, it was an independent city-state and minted its own coins. The poet Ovid passed through the town on his way to Romania, where he was exiled.

By the time Varna was given its present name at the end of the 7th century,

Maps:
City 222
Area 232

PRECEDING PAGES:
Black Sea beach.
LEFT: Varna's
cathedral.
BELOW: Slivnitsa

The city's crest.

it had been ruled by Persians, Thracians, Romans and Slavs. In the latter part of the 8th century, it was incorporated into the Bulgarian Kingdom and developed as both a sea port and a fortress, with a defence system made up of three strongholds – at Cape Galata, Cape St Dimitar and Petrich, near lake Beloslav.

During the Middle Ages, control of the city changed from Byzantine to Bulgarian hands numerous times, before succumbing to Ottoman rule in 1386. This inevitably resulted in oriental influences gaining ground, with new mosques, *konaks* (government buildings) and Turkish baths being built while the construction of churches was forbidden. For many years, Varna guarded the northeastern borders of the Ottoman Empire, during which time it developed as a centre for commerce as well as for crafts. A protracted siege in 1829 ended with the Russian Army taking the city for a short time. In 1878 Varna was finally liberated from Ottoman rule.

Strangely, Varna was renamed Stalin in 1949 to commemorate the 70th birthday of the Russian leader. In 1956 the decision was reversed, but a monument to the man still stands at the entrance to the Sea Garden. The only other visible reminders of this time are manhole covers in the street bearing the old name.

Although not without its economic problems, Varna is a busy industrial centre, with shipbuilding, manufacturing and transport at its core. It forms an industrial complex with the town of Devnya to the west, where large manufacturing and chemical plants are found.

Heart of the city

Ploschad Nezavisimost Ⓐ is the principal square of the city, where locals linger over coffee and pass through on their evening promenade. Just north of here is the **Cathedral of the Assumption** Ⓑ (daily 6am–10pm; free admission), the second biggest religious building in Bulgaria; its six golden domes form the official symbol of Varna. Although work began in 1866, using St Petersburg's cathedral as a model, the building was not sanctified until 1910. The central wall painting

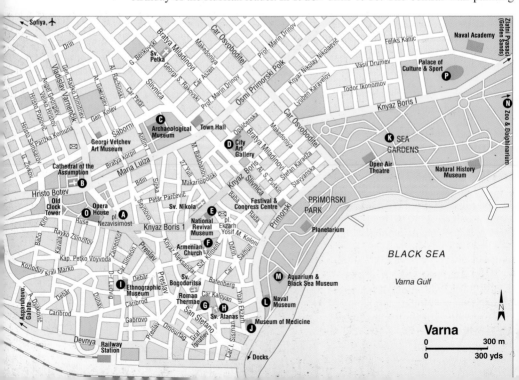

was completed even later, in 1950. South of ploschad Nezavisimost, a **clock tower** built in 1880 dominates the skyline.

The **Archaeological Museum** (Tues–Sun 10am–5pm; admission charge), housed in an old National Revival school on the corner of Mariya Luiza and Slivnitsa, is one of the best in the country, with some 100,000 objects and detailed explanatory notes in English. Despite its name, it actually has two sections – archaeology and art. The highlight in the archaeologoy section is a collection of 6,000-year-old gold objects found in a Chalcolithic necropolis near Varna in 1972. Some 3,000 items in total, they are thought to be the oldest examples of processed gold in the world.

The art section of the museum has a spectacular hall dedicated to antique art and religious icons from northeast Bulgaria, mostly dating from the 14th century.

Just east of the Archaeological Museum, on Lyuben Karavelov, is the **City Art Gallery** ❶ (Tues–Sun 10am–6pm; admission charge), opened in 1950 to showcase the work of local and international artists. It hosts permanent and temporary collections as well as winning entries to the biennial Varna Graphics competition. Forming part of the gallery is the **Georgi Velchev Art Museum**, at 8 ulitsa Radko Dimitriev.

Towards the port

The **National Revival Museum** ❶ (Mon–Fri 10am–5pm; admission charge), at 27 ulitsa Yuli, is housed in a building dating from 1861, the ground floor of which forms the original layout of Sv Archangel Mihail Church. There is also a well-preserved schoolroom where displays tells the story of the local struggle for religious enlightenment, the national fight for independence and scenes from the battles of the Russo–Turkish War of Liberation.

Just south of the museum is the **Armenian church** ❶ on the corner of Koloni and Kilment streets. This tiny 19th-century church still serves the local Armenian community, which numbers around 2,000 members. Some 1½ million Armenians living across the Ottoman Empire were killed by the Turks during World War I, an act of genocide commemorated by a small plaque outside the church.

The 2nd-century **Roman Thermae** ❶ (Apr–Oct Tues–Sun 10am–5pm; Nov–Mar weekdays only; admission charge) forms the remains of the largest Roman public building in Bulgaria, originally over 7,000 sq. metres (75,000 sq. ft), with a height of 20 metres (65 ft). Its existence is evidence of the wealth and importance of the town at that time. Sadly only part of the large, red-brick wall complex remains, including the remnants of mosaics. The baths were designed to be symmetrical, with each room performing a specific function. Bathers passed between the cold waters of the *frigidarium*, the lukewarm *tepidarium* and the scalding heat of the *caldarium*, after which they made use of the gymnasium or *palaestra* (athletics field). A

Map on page 222

Copies of icons are sold outside the cathedral, along with lace tablecloths and other souvenirs.

BELOW: the Cathedral of the Assumption by night.

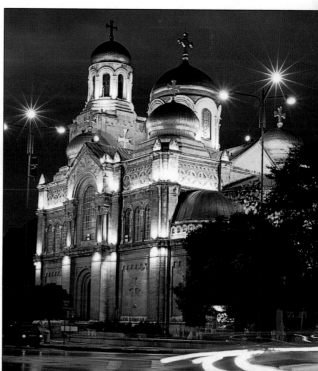

A Place in the Sun

When Bulgaria was given the green light for EU accession at the beginning of 2007, its property market for overseas buyers was already booming, especially on the Black Sea and in the ski resorts. Investors were mainly from the UK and Ireland, but there was German, US and Russian interest too.

Until January 2007 foreigners were not allowed to own land or take out a mortgage on a Bulgarian property. Developers got around this problem by also fulfilling the role of lenders. The buyer entered into a contract to buy a new-build apartment "off plan" (ie from architect drawings) and then made staged lump-sum payments to the developer. In January 2007, this rule was axed, as all EU citizens became entitled to buy Bulgarian land.

Many of the coastal and ski resorts currently resemble building sites, with the scale and pace of new developments continuing at such a frantic pace that many wonder if this section of the market has reached saturation point. Fears that Bulgaria was going to be turned into an eastern European version of the Costa del Sol were allayed when the the country's government finally acted, introducing new zoning regulations and a ban on high-rise buildings. By and large, developers have moved away from the concrete-block constructions that characterised Communist times, and moved towards traditional styles, using local stone and high-quality fixtures and fittings.

At one time Bulgaria was simply seen as a cheaper market for buy-to-let properties than Spain, a popular option for those who couldn't afford anything else. But more and more overseas buyers are choosing it because they have a genuine appreciation of the country, and an increasing number of individuals are looking to move here for good.

Language barriers and a very different culture can make the process of purchasing property in Bulgaria a daunting prospect, but most buyers report that it is much less stressful than in the UK and other European countries. All agencies aiming at foreigners have English-speaking staff and many also provide additional services, such as employing builders and cleaners and furnishing apartments. The locals are friendly and the cost of employing such personnel is significantly cheaper than, say, on the Costa del Sol.

The European Tourism Commission called Bulgaria "the fastest-growing country on the Old Continent". With labour, property and building costs all set to rise in the years after EU accession, there is something of a "gold rush" about the current market. Many investors plan to rent for a few years and then cash in on the rise in value. Properties on the Black Sea can be rented from May through to September, and those in ski resorts between December and March (and perhaps in summer too if rural tourism continues its upward trend). The average property increases in value by around 20 percent annually. More budget flights are added every year to serve the growing market, and the deregulation of Bulgarian aviation that must eventually follow EU membership will make getting to Bulgaria even cheaper.

There are concerns that locals are being priced out of the market. A house for £30,000 may seem like a bargain to foreigners, but for the average Bulgarian earning just £1,000 a year, it is a fortune – the equivalent of a UK office worker buying a £3.75 million property in Britain. However, most people agree that foreign investment can only be a good thing for Bulgaria. The standard of life for local people will improve as a result of EU accession, allowing Bulgarians as well as foreigners to benefit from the property boom. ❑

LEFT: European interest in Bulgarian properties continues to boom.

Map on page 222

large courtyard in the middle even had shops. (The thermae should not be confused with the Roman Baths on bulevard Primorski, a 4th-century construction closed to the public.)

Next door to the thermae is the **Church of Sv Atanas** , built in the National Revival style, with a lovely porch and a gilt and carved interior. It contains a good exhibition of icon-paintings.

The **Ethnographic Museum** (Tues–Sun 10am–5pm summer, Mon–Fri winter; admission charge) occupies a restored house dating from the National Revival period, rebuilt around 1860. It illustrates local life from the late 19th to the beginning of the 20th century through costume, crafts and industry. The first floor focuses on exhibits relating to farming, fishing and wine producing. National costumes on the second floor include some highly decorative items worn for festivals and special holidays, and on the third floor, the interior of a well-to-do home is shown.

The unusual **Museum of Medicine** (Mon–Fri 10am–5pm; admission charge) at 7 ulitsa Paraskeva Nikolau, claims to be the only one on the Balkan Peninsula. It began life as a private hospital in 1869 and today displays common medicinal plants and herbs, as well as surgical instruments and 10th-century skulls that appear to have undergone trepanation.

The Sea Gardens

The flowerbeds and pathways of the **Sea Gardens** were laid out at the end of the 19th century. They form a delightful and elegant park, in which there is an amphitheatre, an observatory, planetarium and zoo, although the chief pleasure is to stroll along the paths. There is also an open-air theatre which hosts festivals such as the Varna Days of Music and Varna Summer.

Below the Sea Gardens are the Central Sea Baths, built at the beginning of the 20th century to serve the town's developing tourist industry. At the garden's southern reaches, in **Primorski Park**, a **Russian monument** was erected in honour of the Russian soldiers who died in Varna during the War of Liberation.

TIP

A booklet in English is available from the Roman Thermae. Although there are some explanations in English posted alongside exhibits, they are limited and the booklet is informative.

BELOW: Varna's Sea Gardens.

The Russian Monument commemorating soldiers who died in the War of Liberation.

BELOW: exhibit in the Naval Museum.

Once the base of the Bulgarian Navy, today the Sea Gardens is the site of the **Naval Museum** Ⓛ (Mon–Fri 10am–5pm; admission charge), established by a group of local enthusiasts in the 1920s. The museum was moved to its present home in Villa Diana, a charming house built in 1890 for an Italian consul, in 1956. A series of 12 halls takes visitors through the city's history from its origins to the present day; in the gardens are old anchors, marine guns and the country's first mine sweeper. Look out for the Drazki torpedo boat, which sank a Turkish cruiser in the 1912 Balkan War.

Next to the Naval Museum is the **Aquarium and Black Sea Museum** Ⓜ (Tues–Sun 9am–7pm; admission charge), of minor interest, with a few displays of fresh- and seawater animals not labelled in English. Built on the instruction of Tsar Ferdinand in 1912, it has bas-reliefs of giant oysters and other Black Sea creatures on its outside wall.

Further east is the **Dolphinarium** Ⓝ (Tues–Sun; admission charge), a pop-ular attraction with regular 45-minute shows (at 10.30am, noon and 3.30pm; tel: 052-302 199), sometimes with supporting actors and clowns. Visitors can occasionally feed the dolphins.

Cultural events

Varna's role as a cultural city extends to its lively programme of festivals throughout the summer, beginning with the International Choir Gathering competition at the end of May. The festivals are well organised and most have websites in English, so it is easy to check details of performances and exact dates in a particular year.

Varna Summer (www.varnasummer-fest.org), the biggest of all the city's festivals, has been going for more than 80 years. Held in June, it is essentially a classical-music festival with performances and master classes, but folk (August), film (August) and puppet (October) festivals as well as an international graphic biennial also fall under its umbrella. The Progressive Jazz Festival in August welcomes musicians from all over the world, while August in Art (www.augustinart.com), which spreads

into early September, shows the works of significant Bulgarian artists, plus some international exhibits.

The **Opera House** on plochtad Nezavisimost hosts major musical performances through the year. Other cultural venues include the atmospheric open-air theatre and the modern Festival Complex, a striking building of aluminum and glass, which hosts exhibitions and festivals as well as ballet and theatre, near the entrance of the Sea Gardens. Most of the theatres are closed in high summer, but at the beginning and the end of the season it is possible to see international performances.

At 115 bulevard Knyaz Boris I, just outside Varna on the way to the resort of Golden Sands, is the **Palace of Culture and Sport** ❷, holding sporting events, rock- and classical-music concerts, exhibitions, festivals, competitions and business conferences. The design of the palace is a copy of the Palace of Culture in Lagos, Nigeria.

On the outskirts

Northeast of the city, close to the main crossroads to Sofia, the Park of Fighting Friendship is really a war memorial, sometimes called the **Vladislav Varnenchik Park-Museum**, commemorating the Battle of Varna, which took place here on 10 November 1444. A crusading army of mostly Hungarian and Polish men, bolstered by some Bulgarians and other nationalities, sought to repel the Ottoman Army as it pushed its way further into Europe. But the crusaders numbered only 3,000 compared to some 12,000 Turks, and promised reinforcements did not materialise. In the end, half of the men died, among them King Wladyslaw III of Hungary and Poland, who was beheaded. As a mark of respect, the Bulgarian people gave the king the name Vladislav Varnenchik, after the city in which he died.

The defeat marked the end of any hopes to halt the Turkish domination of eastern Europe, paving the way for the fall of Constantinople in 1453. A mausoleum (daily 9am–5pm; admission charge) to Vladislav Varnenchik was built on the top of a Thracian burial mound. It contains weapons and memorials to the different races who died in the battle.

Evksinograd Palace (not open to the public), to the north of Varna, is a splendid building, built as a royal summer residence in 1882 and later used as a holiday home for members of the Bulgarian Politburo. Designed by Viennese architect, Ruppelmeyer, to resemble a French chateau, its name means "hospitable town". The beautiful gardens with elegant palm trees and bridges are made up of well-kept woodland bordering a sandy beach where Politburo members had cottages. Work began on the garden in 1890, when plants from South America and Asia were introduced.

Today the palace is used as a government residence and to hold meetings with visiting heads of state.

The residential areas to the northeast of Varna are a popular place for locals to relax, walk and picnic. **Vinitsa** is

Map on page 222

Varna's Opera House is an important part of the city's rich cultural life.

BELOW: Varna Summer is a high-profile arts festival held in June.

Map on page 222

home to a minority group called Gagaouzi – Christians who speak Turkish and have distinct traditions.

Varna Necropolis

South of Varna is **Lake Varna**, a deep, elongated lake separated from the sea by a 2 km- (1¼ mile-) wide strip of sand with two canals linking the two bodies of water. The lake shores were the site of successive settlements in prehistoric times, as evidenced by the discovery of flint tools, ceramics, etc. On the northern shores of the lake, in the western, industrial part of the city, is the **Varna Necropolis** (closed to the public), an ancient burial site discovered by chance in 1972. Study of the necropolis changed the way historians looked at ancient civilisations in southeastern Europe, proving that they were significantly more sophisticated than was originally thought.

The graves here date from around 3000 BC, making them older than those in Ancient Egypt. Nearly 300 graves were uncovered; some contained bodies while others, serving a symbolic purpose, were empty of human remains but contained grave goods and gold artefacts. Around 2,000 pure-gold objects, including necklaces, breast decorations and ceremonial vessels were unearthed, along with many bronze and clay objects.

Stone forest

A fasincating **Stone Forest** (Побити Камъни) of fossil-laden limestone formations lies 18 km (11 miles) west of the city, next to the old road to Devnya. Its Bulgarian name, Pobitite Kamani, meaning "stones beaten into the ground", accurately describes the numerous limestone cylindrical pillars. Some are as high as 10 metres (30 ft), forming both hollow and solid cylinders with a diameter of about 2 metres (6 ft). The stones are positioned in seven large groups forming a total area of more than 7 sq. km (2½ sq. miles). Over the years, nature has sculpted the stones into weird and wonderful shapes, giving rise to names such as "the Camel" and "the Throne". The surrounding area is sandy with little vegetation, giving the site an eerie, desert-like appearance. ❑

BELOW: plunging off Asparouh Bridge.

Bunjee Jumping

The 2 km- (1¼ mile-) long Asparouh Bridge links the city centre with the suburbs of Asparouhovo and Galata. It boasts the longest span of any bridge in Bulgaria and, at 52 metres (170 ft) high, is a popular place for bungee jumping, with jumpers regularly skimming the water below.

Although bungee jumping is relatively new to Bulgaria, the "sport" is practised in several other locations – the Bebresh Viaduct at Vitnia, 60 km (37 miles) south of Sofia, which at 120 metres (390 ft) is one of the highest bridges in the Balkans; the Klisura Viaduct, 100 km (62 miles) from Sofia, with five high bridges; the 50-metre- (164 ft-) high Viaduct Kovacha over the Veleka River; pretty Stambolov Bridge in Veliko Turnovo, and the 42 metre- (137 ft-) high bridge in Rousse.

RESTAURANTS & BARS

Restaurants

Café Vienna
74 Bul. Knyas Boris I
Come here for the great cakes and ice creams, rather than a meal, although salads and sandwiches are on offer too at this Viennese-style café. €€

Happy Bar and Grill
Pl. Nezavisimost and Slivnica Boulevard.
www.happy.bg
This popular chain with international menu and lively atmosphere has several locations around the city (just two are listed above). Come for fast food rather than authentic local cuisine. €

Hashove
(Odessos Hotel)
1 bul. Slivnitsa
Tel: (052) 630 401
This hotel restaurant serves passable local dishes and seafood. Seafront location. €€€

Kashtata
7 bul. Osmi Primorski Polk
Tel (052) 602 879
Good choice of Bulgarian cuisine, including a fine selection of charcoal grilled meats, barbecued outside in the huge garden. €€

Maestro
4 ul. Shipka
Tel: (052) 614 514
Bistro-type food and Varna's best pizzas are served in a large, open and spacious restaurant. The upper level is about the best dining spot in the city. €€

Morska Sirena
47 bul. Primorski
Tel: (052) 692 096
This famous seafood restaurant is considered to be one of the best on the Black Sea Coast. Good food and excellent service. €€

Paraklissa
Paraskeva Nickolau and bul. Primorsko
Widely said to be one of Varna's best restaurants, the Paraklissa is in the courtyard of the Museum of Medical History. It serves excellent Bulgarian food, often with a modern twist. Try St George's lamb, Bulgaria's national dish. €€€

Shanghai
25 ul. Tsar Osvoboditel
Tel: (052) 225 275
Chinese food, with some European options are on offer at this large, mid-range restaurant. Chinese piped music. €€

Sherehadze
4 ul. Petko Karavelov
Tel; (052) 642 294
Fine Middle Eastern food in the heart of the city. There are a large number of Turkish and Middle Eastern restaurants in Varna, but this one is the best. €€

Bars

Most of the larger hotels, such as the **Musala Palace Hotel** have pleasant if rather staid bars. For more excitement, the **Mix Club Alexander** in the Cherno More Hotel, part of the Cascade Complex; www.alexander-mix-club.com) caters to a raunchier crowd. In the same hotel and complex is **O'Neills**, a popular Irish pub and restaurant, which is open until 3am. Catering to a similar crowd is the **Three Lions Pub** opposite the railway station. It is a pretty good imitation of an English pub, with a wide choice of beers and football on screen. If gambling is your scene, the **Grand Casino** is actually in St Konstantin Resort but serves Varna too (Mon–Fri 8pm–4am, weekends 4pm–6am. A string of discos by the coast below the sea gardens are open during summer. Venues and names change frequently, but leaflets are regularly handed out.

PRICE CATEGORIES

Price categories are per person for thee courses:
€ = under 10 leva
€€ = 10–25 leva
€€€ = 25–50 leva
€€€€ = over 50 leva

NORTHERN BLACK SEA COAST

North of Varna, the Black Sea Coast is fringed
with golden sands. The key sights
include a queen's retreat, an ancient
monastery and Kaliakra Cape

The Black Sea coast winds its way from Bulgaria's northern border with Romania all the way down to Turkey in the south, forming a large number of deep sandy bays along the way. The vast majority of international travellers will arrive at one of the two airports serving the coast – Varna in the north and Bourgas in the south. The Balkan Range provides a physical divide almost halfway along the coast – conveniently dividing the area in two.

Much of the northern section *(the southern section is covered on pages 245–262)* is backed by towering limestone cliffs and blanketed with huge swathes of the Baltata Forest. After Varna, between Albena and Balchik, the coast veers sharply east, tailing off into the sharp finger of land that is Kaliakra Cape. As it snakes gently up to the border it becomes wilder and emptier, but with development and golf courses under construction.

The Dobrudzha plain forms a large area of the northeastern corner of Bulgaria, which for much of the summer is turned a vibrant yellow by fields of corn and sunflowers. Dobrudzha is an unofficial region between the River Danube and the Black Sea that is shared by Bulgaria and Romania. Dobrich, the "capital" of the Bulgarian section, is a largely uninspiring administrative town, although it does have some interesting archaeological finds in its museum.

Most visitors to this section of coast will fly into Varna's airport. Just north

of the city is a trio of resorts (Riviera, Golden Sands and Albena) attracting large numbers of international package tourists. Further up the coast, Balchik tends to appeal more to independent travellers, and still further north small coastal settlements see few tourists, except ones passing through on day trips, or, increasingly, those attracted to the area's wildlife and golf courses.

Getting around

Regular bus services ply the coast between the main resorts from Varna

**Map
on page
232**

PRECEDING PAGES:
the beaches are
packed in summer.
LEFT: strolling
through the surf at
Albena.
BELOW: the wild
and lovely
Drobudzha region.

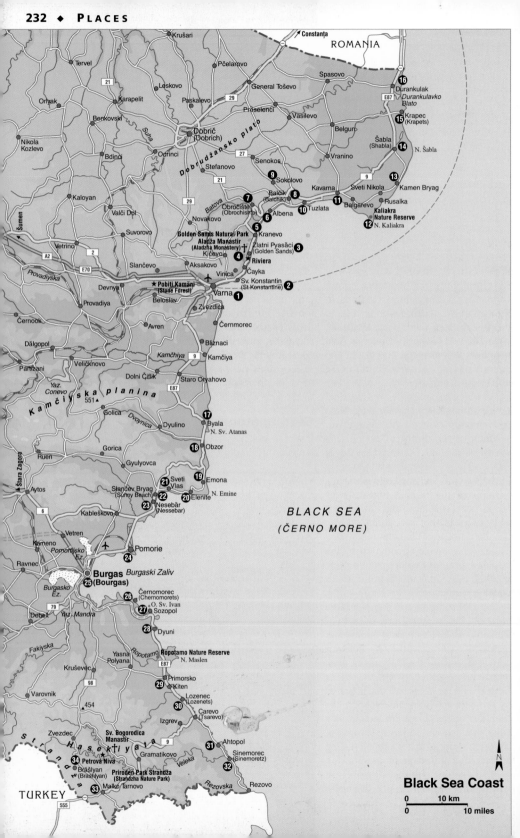

Black Sea Coast

to Balchik, making it relatively easy to explore the coast this way. There are also plenty of organised coach tours to Aladzha Monastery, Balchik and Kaliakra Cape. For those wanting to visit the smaller villages along the way, or the area north of Kavarna, a car is pretty well essential.

Sedate spa resort

Just 10 km (6 miles) from Varna, **St Konstantine ❷** (Sv. Konstantin; Свети Константин) is really a suburb of the city. Once called Konstantin and Elena after its monastery, this is the oldest resort on the coast. It was set up as a spa centre in the 19th century, and its combination of natural springs and clear mountain and sea air attracted a wealthy clientele.

Quieter now, St Konstantine has certainly seen better days. International visitors tend to be elderly holidaymakers on package tours, while Bulgarian visitors are mainly attracted by the rather medicinal spa facilities. The beaches, consisting of small bays backed by cliffs, are uninspiring, but the resort is filled with cypress and fig trees

and it makes a more sedate alternative to resorts up the coast.

The only attraction is the small **Monastery of St Konstantine and Elena** (sunrise–sunset; donations appreciated), which was built below street level at the beginning of the 18th century to meet Ottoman restrictions on church building and then rebuilt at the start of the 20th century. A stone slab in front of the altar of the small church covers a spring reputed to have miraculous powers. Services are still held here, and it is possible to stay overnight.

The Riviera

A 10-minute drive north from Sv Konstatin leads to The Riviera Holiday Club, often considered part of Golden Sands, but very different from its larger, brasher neighbour up the coast. Before 1989 the complex was a plush government residence, but was privatised following the fall of Communism and upgraded to include six hotels (3–5-star).

The Riviera is a stylish and serene resort on a lovely stretch of private beach surrounded by trees. Only visitors

Map on page 232

TIP

Independent travellers will be charged much more to stay in one of the hotels in Golden Sands than those on a package holiday.

BELOW LEFT AND RIGHT: cocktail time in Sv Konstantin.

Beach balls and toys for sale in Golden Sands, the largest resort on the northern stretch of the Black Sea coast.

BELOW: Aladzha Monastery, hewn out of the limestone cliffs.

staying or eating at one of the hotels can enter the gated complex. Facilities include two outdoor and two indoor pools, tennis courts and water sports, plus spa facilities in two of the grand old hotels.

Golden Sands

Just half an hour's drive north of Varna and its airport is the popular resort of **Golden Sands ❸** (Златни Пясъци), known in Bulgarian as Zlatni Pyasatsi, and by the occupying Turks as Quzounkoum, meaning "long sands". This is the northern Black Sea coast's largest resort, boasting 4 km (2½ miles) of golden sand, up to 100 metres/yds wide in place, and yet it is much less brash than Sunny Beach, its equivalent on the south coast.

Golden Sands began life in 1957, and today is the archetypal package resort with over 100 hotels, most of which perch on the tree-covered limestone bluff that backs the beach. The main promenade along the sands is lined with souvenir stands, restaurants and bars, and there are lots of amusements such as a big wheel, quad bikes

for rent, mini golf, horse carriages and a casino. Very few people actually live in Golden Sands; most come just to work here for the season. In the winter, the resort shuts down completely and the place resembles a ghost town.

The area behind Golden Sands was declared a natural park in 1943. Its southern section is mainly swampland, while the rest of the park is studded with trees such as the Turkey oak and the Oriental hornbeam. A 200-year-old sycamore with a circumference of 4 metres (13 ft) is one of the park's best known landmarks. Some 500 species of plants are found here, including orchid and lily of the valley, along with many varieties of birds and butterflies, and mammals such as deer, wild boar and hare. There are walking trails of varying degrees of difficulty and length.

Rock monastery

Within Golden Sands natural park is **Aladzha Monastery ❹** (Аладжа Манастир; Tues–Sun 9am–5pm; admission charge), a few kilometres south of the Riviera Holiday Club and Golden Sands resort, and a pop-

Map on page 232

ular excursion, either as part of an organised tour, or by private taxi. It lies in the heart of the Hanchuka Forest. Its name, which means "colourful" in Turkish, is thought to be an allusion to the medieval wall paintings inside, once brightly coloured but now sadly faded. Hewn out of the limestone cliffs about 40 metres (130 ft) above ground level are monks' living quarters and a small church on a lower floor, with an upstairs chapel.

The monastery is a popular local attraction, partly because of its scenic setting, but surprisingly little is known about its history. Its orgins are thought to date from the 4th century BC, but the present complex was constructed in the 12th century and probably modified during Ottoman times. From then until around the middle of the 18th century, the cave was inhabited by Hesychast monks – ascetics who tried to get closer to God by remaining silent and immobile, a mystical movement based on self-annihilation that evolved among the monks of Athos in the 14th century. A small museum shows how the monastery looked when it was fully operational. A kilometre or so away to the west are the **Katakombite**, or catacombs, a group of caves on three levels with a similar history to the monastery.

Kranevo

Idyllically situated on a sheltered, curving beach, the once-sleepy village of **Kranevo** ❺ (Кранево), 25 km (15 miles) north of Varna, is now a bustling resort sandwiched between Golden Sands and Albena and easily bypassed for the larger resorts. Its accommodation is low-key, with private rooms, family-run hotels and guesthouses, all very keenly priced. Although it has no obvious attractions of its own, Albena is a short walk away and Aladzha Monastery is close by.

Gated resort

The road from Golden Sands winds through thick forest to **Albena** ❻ (Албена), a gated purpose-built resort, where private vehicles are charged an entrance fee. Albena was constructed in the 1960s to a uniform architectural design and the whole complex feels

Albena is the main centre for water sports on the Black Sea coast, but prices here tend to be higher than elsewhere.

BELOW:
paragliding on Albena's beach.

TIP

In theory the entrance fee for vehicles entering Albena includes parking, but it is often difficult to get a place, with many drivers resorting to parking on the pavement.

BELOW:
aristocratic
Balchik.

rather sanitised. The majority of the 40-odd hotels are two- and three-star ; four-storey buildings set back anonymously in the trees with views of either the forest or the sea. The self-contained resort is sheltered by shrub-covered cliffs. Everything here costs significantly more than elsewhere in the country.

The resort was named after the eponymous and exceptionally beautiful female protagonist of a novel by the famous Bulgarian writer Yordan Yovkov. Albena's centre is made up of attractive squares and mainly pedestrianised streets, divided into two areas – upper and lower. The upper section contains the majority of the hotels, while the lower part, alongside the beach, is lined with bars and restaurants. A mini train transports holidaymakers between their hotels and the impressive 5 km-/3 mile-) long broad beach.

In summer, various water sports and amusements are on offer, from para-sailing to bumper boats. Windsurfing, boating and jetsking is offered by the yacht clubs. Landlubbers can opt for football, horse riding and tennis (equipment and tuition available), and there are bouncy castles, playgrounds and minigolf for children. The spa facilities built around natural springs welcome (mostly Bulgarian) visitors year-round.

Muslim shrine and monastery

The small settlement of **Obrochishte** ❼ (Оброчище) lies on the left bank of the Batova River, 7 km (4 miles) west of Albena. It is a typical Bulgarian village, with increasing investment in holiday and expat homes. On its outskirts is a 16th-century *tekke* (Dervish monastery), where archaeologists have unearthed the well-preserved tomb of a Turkish saint, Yazula Baba. Visitors can see the saint's domed mausoleum, decorated with frescos and geometric figures, and an inn where visiting dervishes and pilgrims could stay, both made of stone blocks. Obrochishte remains a place of pilgrimage for Christians and Muslims to this day. Pilgrims tie strips of fabric to nearby trees to bind their contract

with the saint and receive his blessing. The monastery and Orthodox Church are currently being restored.

Aristocratic retreat

Intimate, atmospheric **Balchik** ❽ (Балчик), 30 km (18 miles) north of Varna, is a charming alternative to the large resorts further down the coast. An inspiration to artists since antiquity, it prompted Ovid to exclaim, "O white stone town, I salute thee for thy inimitable beauty!"

The old section of the town has terraced, cobbled streets and is attractively set in a limestone bowl, with the new development set on a plateau behind. The port is the third most important in Bulgaria, after Bourgas and Varna; its rocky man-made beach is overlooked by working harbour cranes and used mostly by locals. A long promenade skirts the harbour where sleek yachts share space with weathered fishing boats.

In 1913, at the end of the Balkan War, Balchik was annexed to Romania. Queen Marie of Romania fell in love with the town and built a summer residence here in 1924, fondly naming it "Quiet Nest", 2 km (1½ miles) west of the town centre. Designed by Italian architects using a combination of Bulgarian National Revival and Ottoman design, it comprises a collection of simple stone buildings and follies, with a distinctive minaret. It includes a chapel that once contained the Queen's heart.

The Romanian aristocrats who followed Queen Marie here were the first of Balchik's tourists. Today, the **Summer Palace of Queen Marie and the Botanical Gardens** (daily 8am–6pm in summer; winter hours erratic; admission charge) is overrun with tourists in peak season. Rather than let the crowds affect the enjoyment of this tranquil location, try to arrive before 9.30am or after 4.30pm.

Only a few of the rooms are open, but the gardens are worth a visit in themselves. The formal terraces overlooking the sea are dotted with small waterfalls and bridges, such as the Venetian-style "Bridge of Sighs". Some 3,000 or more rare and exotic plants grow here, including several

A balcony view of the passing scene, Balchik.

Map on page 232

BELOW LEFT: Queen Marie's Summer Palace today.

Queen Marie

Queen Marie of Romania was born in Kent in England in 1875, the granddaughter of Queen Victoria. A free spirit, "Missy", as she was fondly known, cared deeply for people on the edge of society and was adored by her public. She went on to marry a shy cold man, and experienced poignant tragedy, in a life that was not unlike that of the late Princess Diana.

During a peasant revolt in Romania in 1907, Marie supported Britain against the Germans, causing her Russian mother to all but disown her. World War I photographs show her in a Red Cross uniform nursing the wounded in horrific scenes. During a visit to Paris in 1916 she described how "everybody is enthusiastic because of me. They treat me like some kind of narcotic... Reporters from all over the world are around me." When Romania was annexed by Germany in 1918, she bravely refused British protection.

Carol, Marie's first-born son, had a series of affairs, eventually renouncing his right to the crown and running off with one of his mistresses. He later returned to Romania to seize the throne, effectively exiling his mother, fearing that her popularity would affect his own. Marie sought solace in the villa that had become compensation for her troubled personal and public life.

BELOW: take your own shade to the more remote beaches.

hundred species of trees and cacti and a significant palm tree collection.

The palace and gardens are undoubtedly Balchik's star attraction, but the town also has a a few museums and an art gallery. Heading uphill from the port, turn right off the main street of Cherno More to visit the **Art Gallery** (10am–noon and 2–5.30pm; admission charge) containing two floors of work, mostly by local artists but with a few international additions.

In the town's central square, ploschad Nezavisimost, the **Historical Museum** Mon–Fri 9.30am–noon, 12.30pm–5.30pm; admission charge) plots Balchik's history from the 6th century BC to the mid-20th century with a wide collection of objects from Thracian times right up to the fight against Romanian occupation.

Opposite, an ethnographic museum (3 ulitsa Vitosha; Mon–Fri 9.30am–noon, 12.30–5.30pm; admission charge), occupying an old corn-merchant's house shows aspects of village and town life in the 19th century.

Further along Cherno More, at 4 Hristo Botev, is the **Ethnographical** Complex (9.30am–noon and 2–5pm; admission charge). Sometimes called the Bulgarian National Revival Complex, it includes the National Revival Sv Nikola Church built in 1845 and a reconstructed schoolhouse from the same period.

East of Balchik

East of Balchik, the **Lighthouse Golf Resort** is a vast new development with luxury villas and apartments being marketed at foreign investors. The resort will eventually also offer horse riding and a spa centre, but the focus will be on an 18-hole golf course designed by Ian Woosnam. Along with a sports complex, including tennis courts and mini football pitch, a marina with sailing and water sports is also planned. Restaurants, shops and play areas will be dotted around the landscaped gardens.

English village

Five kilometres (3 miles) inland from Balchik, **Sokolovo** ❾ (Соколово) should not be confused with the village of the same name near Gabrovo. This traditional community is developing fast, with plots of land and small houses being sold as retirement homes to overseas buyers. Some 50 new villas bought by British holiday-makers have led Sokolovo to being dubbed the "English village".

Tuzlata

Between Balchik and Tuzlata, a 6-km (4-mile) minor road hugs the coast, passing between towering cliffs and low scrub-covered hills. At **Tuzlata** ❿, two salt lakes contain mineral-rich black mud which is used to treat medical ailments, such as joint pain and nervous disorders. A health complex including a sanatorium, bungalows and camp site has been built around the lake and there is a mineral spring nearby.

Kavarna

A 20-minute drive east of Balchik, **Kavarna** ⓫ (Каварна) is a small,

quiet town that relies on agriculture and the trade of its small port, which handles fishing boats and medium-sized passenger and cargo vessels. It is not an obvious tourist destination, although a small artificial beach called Gore Chirakman has been built at the bottom of its high limestone cliffs. The main reason for a visit is to use it as a base for exploring the wildlife around Kaliakra Cape and to visit the lovely beaches to the north.

The town is full of history. Founded by the Greeks in the 5th century, it developed into a cultural centre in the Middle Ages, from which time churches and a necropolis remain. Conquered and almost completely destroyed by the Ottomans at the end of the 14th century, it became important for the export of grain between the 15th and 19th centuries. In 1913, following the Second Balkan War, it fell under Romanian rule, and after a long period of fierce local resistance was finally returned to Bulgaria in 1940.

A small **Museum of the Sea** (open irregular hours; free admission) occupies a 15th-century Turkish bathhouse just north of the town centre, and sign-posted from there. On display are stone anchors and coins and ceramics found during underwater expeditions along the nearby coast. The local library (Mon–Fri 9am–5pm; free admission) includes a small exhibition on local life from prehistoric times through to the War of Liberation.

An interesting twist in Kavarna's recent history has seen it become an unofficial centre for rock music. The energetic mayor, Tzonko Tzonev, a heavy-metal fan, has put on a series of rock concerts since 2004, with international bands such as Nazareth and Deep Purple performing at the small coastal town.

Thracian Cliffs

North of Kavarna, an 18-hole championship golf course, designed by Gary Player, is under construction, together with new roads, a four-star hotel and a five-star hotel complex complete with spa and villas. An "old village centre" and marina, including shops, restaurants, bars and apartments, has been designed to look like someone's idea of a tradi-

Map on page 232

BELOW: boats at Balchik.

Storks are just one of the many kinds of birds you will see in the Black Sea coast region.

BELOW: sunflowers and fruit in the fertile Drobudzha region.

tional Thracian village. Work on "Thracian Cliffs" (www.thraciancliffs.com) began in 2006, and is scheduled for completion in 2010.

Scenic cape

A minor road southeast from Kavarna leads to the unspoilt cape of **Kaliakra** ⑫ (Какнакра). This 2-km (1¼-mile) finger of land jutting into the sea is the most easterly point in Bulgaria. It ends with dramatic, 70 metre- (230 ft-) high cliffs, their wonderful red colour due to oxides in the rock. Kaliakra means "beautiful cape" and the name of this wild, untouched area is fitting. The land and sea around Kaliakra form a nature reserve rich in fauna and flora. In spring and summer the ground is bright with corn and sunflowers, the cliffs are home to nesting hooded commorants and rock blackbirds, and dolphins (both common and bottlenose) and seals can sometimes be spotted in the sea below.

The cape's inaccessibility made it an obvious place to build a fortress, and successive communities, including Thracians, Romans and Byzantines,

guarded it fiercely. A monument known as the **Gate of the Forty Maidens** stands at the cape entrance, in tribute to 40 girls who are said to have tied their long plaits together, held hands and jumped into the sea to escape marauding Ottomans.

St Nicholas, the patron of seamen, is the subject of another legend associated with the cape. It is said that when he was running towards the sea, away from the Turkish invaders, God extended the earth beneath his feet, to allow him to escape, and so the cape was formed. However, the saint was eventually captured and a chapel built in 1993 today symbolises his grave.

There is a fee to enter the car park at the entrance of the cape (most visitors will come by private vehicle or as part of a bus tour). From here, it is a good 15-minute walk past souvenir stalls to the cliff-side cave and small museum (daily 10am–6pm; admission included in car park charge). A model shows the long finger of land on which a citadel, village and mosque was built, all of which were destroyed in the 7th century. Coins, decorated plates and

jewellery are clues to domestic scenes once lived out here. Descriptions are provide in English, although they are rather academic in content. A restaurant next to the museum has a pleasant terrace with good views out to sea. Nearby are a weather station and lighthouse.

Bay of Birds

A dead-end road from the village of **Sveti Nikola** (Свети Никола) drops steeply through ancient oak forest down to the peaceful holiday village of **Rusalka**, whose name means "mermaid". It lies on the islet-studded Taukliman, or Birds' Bay, with a shingle beach and huge, crumbling cliffs. Lookouts allow birders to spot some of the 300 species of birds found here, as well as dolphins and seals. The resort consists of 500 neat chalets – mostly occupied by German and French holiday-makers, along with restaurants and bars set amongst manicured lawns. Facilities include 15 tennis courts, a small football pitch and volleyball courts and organised activities include yachting, kayaking, diving and archery, with special activities arranged for children.

Off the beaten track

Kamen Bryag ⓭ (Камен Бряг) meaning "stone coast", is 5 km (3 miles) north of Rusalka between the wild Kaliakra and Shabla capes. Here, Yaylata Reserve is an extended kilometre-long bluff little more than a couple of hundred metres/yds wide with sheer cliff faces, making most of the area inaccessible. It is dotted with more than 100 caves, some of them man-made, together with 28 tombs and a church, all thought to have been built by local tribes between the 3rd and 5th centuries. They can be accessed along a track from the village, but a guide is advisable (make enquiries in the village). The area was once a sanctuary for Greeks.

Shabla

The unassuming city of **Shabla** ⓮, 20 km (12 miles) north of Kavarna, is made up of one-storey whitewashed houses. It was once a Thracian settlement, before becoming a Greek

Map on page 232

BELOW:
Kaliakra Castle.

Map
on page
232

colony and then a town in Roman times, when its harbour was built at Cape Shabla. Fishing and agriculture rather than tourism are the main industries here, although some archaeological excavations at Cape Shabla have uncovered foundations of a Roman fortress.

On the outskirts of the city is the freshwater **Shabla Lake**, visited by large numbers of birds, such as herons, ibises and grebes. It is the wintering site for a staggering 100,000 wild white-fronted geese and 50, 000 red-breasted geese – more than 60 percent of the world's population. Significant numbers of birds such as grebes, little bittens and crakes come here to nest and during spring and summer migrations, pelicans, egrets and herons can be seen. The lake, where there is a small beach and opportunities to fish, is also one of the biggest habitats of water lily and yellow pond lily in Bulgaria.

Border lands

The sleepy village of **Krapets ❶** 10 km (6 miles) north of Shabla and just a few kilometres south of the Roman-ian border, is made up of one-storey houses with livestock-filled court-yards. Surrounded by wheat and sun-flower fields, the coast here is fringed with sand dunes and low ochre-coloured cliffs. This is in a remote, rural area, with a strong appeal to those who want to get away from the commercialism of the coast further south. The magnificent 6-km (4-mile) curve of beach can often be enjoyed in splendid isolation.

Durankulak

Bulgaria's most northeasterly settle-ment, **Durankulak ❶**, is just 5 km (3 miles) from the border with Romania, and most visitors who have come this far north intend to cross the frontier. **Dourankoulak Lake**, 6m (4 miles) to the east is separated from the sea by pristing sand dunes. The glass-like waters of the lake are popular with windsurfers and sailors as well as swimmers, and there are opportuni-ties to fish for pike, catfish and carp. Attracting swans, pelicans and cor-morants, it is also a popular area for birdwatchers.   ❏

BELOW: climbing the cliffs, Kamen Bryagg.

RESTAURANTS & BARS

Restaurants

Albena

Arabella Restaurant
Albena Beach
Tel: (0579) 64082
This restaurant in a distinctive wooden "ship" on the beach is good value. A wide ranging menu features all the old Bulgarian favourites plus lots of seafood options. €€

Drobrudja Hotel
Tel: (0579) 62020
Enjoy French cuisine and first-rate service whilst taking in the panoramic views from one of the highest points in Albena. A romantic and memorable setting. €€€

Panorama Restaurant Flambe
Tel: (057) 22421
This is a traditional establishment that has remained popular for many years. Lots of meat, salad and fish and some international dishes to choose from. €€

Staria Dub
Tel: (0579) 62108
www.stariadub.com.
Family-run restaurant with traditional interior and vine-covered terrace offering a combination of Bulgarian and Mediterranean food. A folk-cum-cabaret show and live music are laid on most evenings. €

Balchik

White House
18 ul. Geo Milev
Tel: 579 73951
Terraced restaurant with views of the promenade. Typical Bulgarian fare. Air-conditioning in summer and a fire in winter. €

El Marinero
Of the handful of restaurants on wooden jetties overlooking the harbour, this is the nicest. Specialises in seafood (the smoked fish selection is excellent), plus good meat and pasta. €

Golden Sands

Dolphin
Popular option in centre of resort with live entertainment every evening. Lots of meat on the menu, plus local and international dishes. €

Old Lighthouse
Sv Nikolas
Tel: (052) 355 531)
www.prima.com
Good range of international standbys from salads and pasta to steak and seafood, and lots of fancy desserts. Beachside terrace, live music and friendly service. €

Taj Mahal
Next to the Admiral Hotel
Authentic Indian cuisine is served in this splendidly decorated restaurant. The three-course set menu is excellent value. €

St Konstantine

Figaros
In the centre, close to Grand Varna Hotel
English-run café/restaurant that is excellent value for money. €

Riviera

Imperial
Tel: (052) 386 811
This is a stylish and relaxing beachside spot. Eat on the decking, inside or in an individual "tent" on the sand. Good fish, cocktails and a paella special. €€

Oasis
Tel: (052) 3869
Formal terrace with a brief but good menu offering interesting twists on international dishes. €€

Bars

In Golden Sands, most bars have a happy hour lasting for several hours in the early evening. This typically offers two drinks for the price of one. In Riviera, the only places to drink are the hotel bars, and in smaller resorts such as Balchik and Albena drinking is mostly limited to small local bars.

PRICE CATEGORIES

Price categories are per person for thee courses:
€ = under 10 leva
€€ = 10–25 leva
€€€ = 25–50 leva
€€€€ = over 50 leva

RIGHT: beach bar at night.

SOUTHERN BLACK SEA COAST

From Cape Emine, where the Balkan Mountains sink into the Black Sea, all the way down to the border with Turkey, the coast is dotted with sandy bays, backed by the deeply rural Strandzha

The Balkan Mountains form a natural barrier between the north and south sections of the Black Sea coast. At Cape Emine, just south of Obzor, the high cliffs of the northern section give way to long, wide sandy beaches stretching all the way down to Bulgaria's border with Turkey. Inland, among rolling hills traditional rural life is barely affected by the international tourism nearby.

Sunny Beach and neighbouring St Vlas and Nessebar are major attractions, while Sozopol, further south, though popular with visitors retains the feel of a fishing village with traditional wooden houses and ancient churches. For a quieter experience, head for the undeveloped beaches around Sinemoretz, or drive inland to the Strandzha Natural Park and explore a different world of forests, pristine rivers, wildlife and few people.

Most visitors stay at one of the many beach resorts, and there are plenty to choose from, from big and brash Sunny Beach to the more refined St Vlas with its up-market holiday apartments and shiny new marina. Bourgas is the main city on the southern Black Sea Coast. While not obviously full of sights, it is worth a visit, if only as an antidote to the tourism elsewhere.

Reasonably reliable bus services run between the major resorts, but to reach the smaller towns and villages or to travel inland you will need to hire a car. From Bourgas, the main road hugs the coastline north and south. Alternatively, turn inland towards Malko Tarnovo to discover the Strandzha.

Byala

The first settlement on the coast south of the Balkan Range is **Byala** (Бяла), 45 km (28 miles) from Varna, but there is little reason to stop here. A mere couple of thousand people live in the village, but its population swells considerably with mostly Bulgarian visitors during the summer months. The village was founded in the 3rd

Map on page 232

LEFT: remains of the basilica, Nessebar. **BELOW:** beach-goers and windmill in Nessebar.

century BC and became wealthy thanks to the local production of Dimyat white wine. Like so much of the coast, there are new, modern developments here, and a small marina is being constructed. The prehistoric formation of the unusual "White Rocks" is explained in a small visitor centre (irregular hours; free).

Between Byala and Obzor is a small string of camp sites and the recently opened all-inclusive Luna Resort with its own water-sports complex, built to appeal to international visitors.

Obzor

Six km (4 miles) south of Byala, **Obzor** (Обзор) is dominated by the Stara Planina mountain range on its western side. To the south, vineyards and dense woodland stretch all the way to rocky Cape Emine, with the Dvoynitsa River forming the northern boundary. The E-87 main road skirts the small town, which lies roughly halfway between Bourgas and Varna.

Relatively quiet even in peak season, Obzor has mainly small hotels and family guesthouses, plus a few modern hotel complexes. However, extensive building work suggests that residents and tourists are due to increase dramatically. The 6 km- (4 mile-) long beach is the main attraction, along with a small park displaying remnants of a Roman temple. An important point on ancient sea trading routes, it was once guarded by a Roman fort.

Emona

The road from Obzor winds south for around 10 km (6 miles) through vineyards and forest, giving wonderful ocean views. An area of open coast just before Emona features almost vertical cliffs soaring 90 metres (300 ft) high. **Emona** (Емона), a small village on the southern slopes of the Balkan Range, takes its name from the ancient name of the Stara Planina range – Aemon. Cape Emine forms a huge nose of land jutting out to sea, topped by a simple lighthouse.

The village was the birthplace of the Thracian King Rez, who took part in the Thracian War and was slain by Odysseus and Diomedus in Homer's *Iliad*. Emona has not yet been

BELOW: gated holiday development at Sv Vlas.

developed for tourism, although land around it is being sold off to international and Bulgarian buyers.

Elenite and St Vlas

Just over 20 years ago, **Elenite** ❷⓿ (Елените) was uninhabited, but in 1985 construction began on a "holiday village". Tucked away to the east of St Vlas, and bypassed by the main road between Bourgas and Varna, this attractive development is a quiet spot with villas and hotels set in green parkland. Most visitors – many of them families – come on all-inclusive packages. Its private beach, sports facilities, shops, restaurants and nightly entertainment programme mean that some of them never leave the complex.

Beautifully situated between the mountains and the sea, **St Vlas** ❷❶ (Sv. Vlas, Св Влас), a couple of kilometres northeast of Sunny Beach, has been snapped up by developers. Originally a Thracian settlement, it was given its current name in the 14th century, and in the 1960s was used as a health resort. It is a quieter, much more desirable resort than Sunny Beach, yet within easy reach of its neighbour's attractions. Before long, St Vlas will merge with the long crescent of hotels that line Sunny Beach.

The resort's old town has been largely swallowed up by the upmarket development on the other side of the main road. This comprises a series of apartment complexes, each with its own restaurant and pool. Many of the properties have been sold to British buyers. There are two sheltered beaches with parasols and sunbeds for hire, and a marina completes the exclusive resort. Boats can be taken to Nessebar, or yachts hired for day trips.

Sunny Beach

Although the dramatic mountains of the Stara Planina lie to the north and the lovely island of Nessebar is a short distance to the south, **Sunny Beach** ❷❷ (Слънчев Брят) attracts many foreign visitors with its superb beach – an impressive 6-km (4-mile) curve of sand that is 60 metres (200 ft) wide in places and backed by high dunes and large hotels. In summer it is thronged with sun worshippers.

Map
on page
232

Water-sports equipment can be hired by the hour on most of the more popular beaches along the coast.

BELOW: fishing and sailing are just some of the activities on offer.

Nessebar is known for its lace and embroidery. Check out the stalls in the old town.

BELOW: Nessebar is connected to the mainland by a causeway but the best approach is by boat.

The beach has "free" and "pay" zones, although the division is not always strictly enforced. This means that placing your towel directly on the sand is permitted at the back of the beach only. In the so-called pay zone, next to the sea, sun loungers and parasols must be hired – at inflated prices and with restrictions on the number of people sharing.

The generally calm waters make Sunny Beach popular with families (lifeguards operate between 8am and 6pm in summer), although water sports, such as jet skiing and para-sailing, are on offer too. The large promenade behind the beach, lined with souvenir shops, restaurants and bars, is busy day and night.

At the back of the resort is **Action Aquapark** (daily 10am–7pm; admission charge; www.aquapark.bg), with slides, wave pools and a children's playground. The park operates a free shuttle bus from pick-up points on the main road along Sunny Beach as far as Sv Vlas (every 15 minutes between 9.30am and 4.30pm, and every 30 minutes between noon and 2pm).

Another attraction for children is a go-karting track on the main Bourgas to Varna road, east of the Aquapark (daily 10am–1am; tel: 899 907 998; www.varnakarting.com).

World Heritage Island

On an island 3 km (2 miles) south of Sunny Beach lies the picturesque old town of **Nessebar** ㉓ (Несебър), guarded by an unusual wooden windmill. It is connected to the mainland and the new town to the west by a narrow isthmus, though the best way to reach the island is by boat from Sunny Beach or Sv Vlas. Several companies have small vessels which leave from the pier near the Globus Hotel on Sunny Beach (every 20 minutes from 10am–10pm; it is advisable to buy a one-way ticket, so that you can take any boat back). It is also possible to travel by bus or taxi, and organised day trips are offered from most resorts along the Black Sea coast.

There are many hotels and restaurants in the new town, as well as a park with playgrounds and fountains. Another water park, **Aqua Paradise**

(www.aquaparadise-b.com) picks up along Sunny Beach. With 20 different attractions, it claims to be the biggest water park in Bulgaria.

Settlement on the tiny island (just 850 metres/yds by 350 metres/yds) dates back to Thracian times, and it was a thriving Greek colony and trading centre from the beginning of the 6th century BC. An acropolis, a temple for Apollo and a section of the ancient city wall can still be seen. It had ports on both sides and became a centre for shipbuilding and crafts, and even minted its own coins.

Successive occupations – by the Romans in the 1st century, and then the Byzantines from the 5th century – did nothing to halt Nessebar's development. It continued to thrive in the Middle Ages: notable buildings from this time include the 9th-century basilica. In the 12th and 13th centuries it established trade links with other countries on the Adriatic and the Mediterranean, such as Venice, Croatia and Turkey.

It is Nessebar's old town, however, that is of most interest to visitors. Its narrow cobbled streets are usually full of international and local tourists, and its many souvenir shops give it the atmosphere of an open-air market. Goods range from fake designer sunglasses and T-shirts to old Russian war medals, hand-made lace table-cloths and local pottery. Prices are generally much higher than on the mainland, but still good value.

Nessebar's distinctive houses and churches constructed in local style have made it a UNESCO World Heritage Site. Built of stone and wood in the late 18th and early 19th centuries, they are typical of the Bulgarian National Revival period. The ground floor was usually used for commerce, while the upper floor served as the living quarters. More than 100 of these buildings remain, all of them restored.

The **Ethnographic Museum** (daily 10am–5pm; admission charge) in the Moskoyani House (1840) has a fine decoratively carved wooden ceiling and displays regional textiles and costumes. **Captain Pavel's House**, on the southwest side of the island, has a distinctive front door with arched frame, and Zhelyo Bogdanov's House.

Map on page 232

Characteristic green and red clay decoration on one of Nessebar's many churches.

BELOW: the 11th-century church of St John the Baptist, Nessebar.

Nessebar's Churches

The narrow peninsula comprising Nessebar's old town once contained some 40 churches, built chiefly between the 11th and 14th centuries. A large number have been preserved, and it is worth taking in the most significant of these on a (roughly) clockwise tour of the island, beginning with the Old Metropolitan Church, also known as St Sophia Church, in the centre of the town. Built in the late 5th and early 4th century BC, it features three naves and a roof, although some of the walls are no longer standing. St John the Baptist Church, also constructed in the 11th century, is a cross-domed church typical of later Nessebar churches. It was once covered in frescos, but all that remain today are portraits of its 14th-century donors, a father and son. Close by is the 14th-century Church of the Holy Pantocrator, whose exterior marks it out as one of the finest medieval churches in Bulgaria.

Near the harbour, the well-preserved St Stefan Church, also sometimes called the New Metropolitan Church, dates from the 11th century, but has some fine later features, such as 16th-century frescoes, a 17th-century wooden chancel screen and a late-18th century pulpit. St John Aliturgetos Church, with its three naves and highly decorated facades, perched high above the harbour, is considered to be the most beautiful of Nessebar's churches.

The Spa Industry

Bulgaria's karst mountains spurt abundant springs, three-quarters of them warm to extremely hot (30–103°C/86°–217°F), while the lagoons along the Black Sea coast are famous for their mineral-laden mud reputed to have anti-inflammatory and anti-ageing properties. The health benefits of these natural resources have been valued since antiquity, when Roman emperors travelled to the region take the waters, and temples were built close to the springs. The tradition of thermal bathing continued under the Byzantines and later the Ottomans, whose *hammams* often took advantage of the thermal waters.

During Communist times, Bulgaria was eastern Europe's answer to Baden-Baden. Spa treatments were a staple of the national health programme. It was common for sufferers of bronchial, kidney and reproductive problems, as well as arthritis and skin complaints, to be prescribed a a course of treatment at a balneaological centre.

You will find thermal springs throughout Bulgaria (there are said to be some 1,600 springs in all), but the areas that are best endowed are the Rhodopes, Rila and Pirin mountains. Along the Black Sea, thalassotherapy, mud, clay and peat treatments are big business, and can be had for a fraction of the cost in the UK or other European countries. For example, the mud from Lake Pomorie on the southern Black Sea Coast, prized since Thracian times, is considered beneficial in the treatment of arthritis and other pain, pulmonary and reproductive problems, but also provides a wonderful purifying facial.

For the most part, the facilities harnessing the springs are functional and rather dated in character, patronised by patients seeking cures for chronic conditions. However, as developers cotton on to the growing interest in luxury spas, especially among wealthy foreign visitors, this is likely to change. There are already reports of developers buying up and renovating old spa centres.

Indeed, health spas offering the full range of pampering treatments from jacuzzis and whirlpools to oriental massage and up-to-the-minute beauty treatments are becoming essential facilities in the very top hotels. The Helios Spa, part of the Helios Spa and Resort Hotel in Golden Sands (www.helios-spa.com) is a good example of a spa facility that offers traditional medicinal therapies alongside pampering packages. An impressive centre with highly trained medical staff, it includes a diagnostic centre, infra-red treatment zones, traditional Chinese medicine and hydrobaths. It may not be long before cosmetic surgery and dental treatment – other lucrative sources of income for the enterprising Bulgarians – are also on the menu.

Spa tourism has the potential to become a high-earning branch of rural tourism. Crystal-clear air, peace and tranquillity and outdoor activities such as riding, hiking or skiing are even more appealing when combined with luxurious spa and beauty treatments. One of the top spots is the country's first ayurvedic spa at Kempinski Hotel Grand (www.kempinkski-bansko.com) in the ski resort of Bansko in the Pirin Mountains. Its Softouch Centre offers 20 different holistic body massages plus a large range of body scrubs, wraps, facials and other beauty treatments, as well as inspiring views through the valley.

To find out more about Bulgaria's spas, their medicinal properties and the range of treatments and facilities on offer, whether you are seeking medical treatment or simply want to be pampered, visit www.spalifestylebulgaria.com. The site details the best spas throughout the country and tailor-made advice on where to go. ❏

LEFT: the mud in the Black Sea lagoons is used to beautify as well as cure.

from the latter part of the 19th century is baroque with a lovely balcony.

The **Archaeological Museum** (2A ulitsa Messambria; daily 9am–5pm; admission charge) comprises four halls displaying Thracian coins from the 1st and 2nd centuries BC, Greek plates, sculptures and jewellery, and Roman ceramics, tombstones and pottery. Also on display are icons from some of the island's churches.

Lake Pomorie

Lying on a 5km- (3 mile-) long rocky peninsula, **Pomorie** ㉔ (Поморие) is a modern town 18 km (11 miles) south of Nessebar, best known for spa treatments and bird watching. The beach's black, iron-rich sand is unbearably hot in summer, and often litter-strewn.

Nearby **Lake Pomorie** has 70 percent salt content, making it four times saltier than sea water. The ancient Appollian town of Anhialo, as Pomorie was originally known, grew rich from extracting salt from the lake. It continued to prosper under the Romans, and by the time of its conquest by the Ottomans in 1453 was the most important town on the coast after Varna. The mud in the lake is used to treat problems such as arthritis and rheumatism, carrying on a long tradition of mud baths begun by the Romans.

Throughout the year, more than 200 species of birds can be seen around the lake, and birds on the Via Pontica migratory route stop off to consume the lake's brine shrimp in spring and autumn. Endangered birds such as the pygmy cormorant and the Dalmatian pelican may be spotted along with more common waders. The lake is also a significant breeding ground for little terns and avocets. In recent years the construction of artificial breeding platforms has proved successful.

Pomorie's wooden buildings would have rivalled those of Nessebar, but sadly little of the original structures remain, on account of a devastating fire in 1906. Most of the modern buildings are concrete and unappealing, although there is a small pocket of National Revival-style houses on the eastern part of the peninsula.

The **Monastery of St George** has medieval foundations, although the

Map on page 232

Nessebar's Archaeological Museum, on the edge of the old town, is worth a look.

BELOW: Nessebar's ancient city walls.

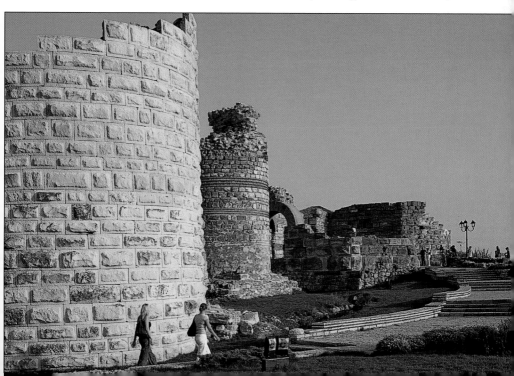

present building dates from the mid-19th century. It is still functioning and visitors are free to wander around and look at the well-preserved icons inside. Tsar Boris I, the main street in the pedestrianised town centre, is the scene of a nightly promenade for tourists and locals alike in season.

Bourgas by the Sea

Most visitors to the southern Black Sea coast will land in **Bourgas** ㉕ (Бургас), 18 km (11 miles) south of Pomorie, and then travel to resorts either north or south. But this is a bustling, friendly city that is worth a closer look. If you are travelling independently, consider spending a day or two here if only to get a glimpse of real Bulgarian life away from the resorts. Alternatively, squeeze in a few hours here before flying out from Bourgas airport.

Bourgas is the fourth-largest city in the country, but culturally somewhat in the shadow of Varna, its bigger, more beautiful sister up the coast. A small watchtower was built here in the Middle Ages, but it did not take off as a settlement until the 17th century, after which it evolved into an industrial port. It was the largest port south of the Balkan Mountains from the 18th century, and it has had the biggest oil refinery in the Balkans since the beginning of the 20th century.

Bourgas also has a beach, but the sea here is polluted, the seafront lined with dilapidated buildings and industrial cranes and there is no real vantage point. The city centre, however, is pleasant, with leafy boulevards and attractive old buildings with elegant wrought-ironwork.

It is worth wandering through the **Sea Gardens**, studded with statues, flower-beds and fountains, or taking a stroll along **Ulitsa Aleksandrovska**, a long, wide boulevard that cuts through the town, and stopping at one of its many pavement cafés. Other options include shopping in its competitively priced designer clothing shops or visiting one or more of its museums.

Bourgas's **Archaeological Museum** (21 ulitsa Aleko Bogoridi; daily 9am–5pm, until 9pm in summer; admission charge; be sure to ask for

TIP

While in Pomorie try its red wines, which are some of the best in Bulgaria. Also try the locally produced and very palatable grape brandy.

BELOW: taking a boat trip.

Map on page 232

the leaflet in English as most exhibits are only labelled in Bulgarian) occupies a fine old building that was the first school in Bulgaria (1889). It contains Thracian jewellery, pottery and 2,000 copper coins, all testament to Bourgas's importance as a trading centre in ancient times. Look out for the star exhibit – a Thracian chief in a wooden sarcophagus.

The **Ethnographic Museum** (69 ulitsa Slavyanska; Mon–Sat 9am–6pm; admission charge) is housed in the Brakalov House (1873), by which it is also known. It contains restored interiors and fashions from the 19th century, as well as traditional crafts and costumes, including *kukeri* masks.

There is also a **Natural Science Museum** (20 ulitsa Konstantin Fotinov; 9am–6pm; admission charge). The geographical displays on the ground floor have limited appeal, but the stuffed birds, fish and mammals, such as a jackal and wild boar, are a bit more interesting, especially for children.

Of minor interest is the **City History Museum** (31 ulitsa Lermonotov; 9am–6pm; admission charge), documenting the development of Bourgas in the 19th and 20th centuries and displaying examples of Bulgarian icons.

Like Lake Pomorie, the nearby salt lakes to the north and south of Bourgas are on the Via Pontica migration route. As such, they have been earmarked as an area for ecotourism, with information centres. However, the area is also being developed for properties targeted at the UK market, which may not bode well for the birds.

Chernomorets

The small town of **Chernomorets** ❷⁶ (Черноморец), 25 km (15 miles) south of Bourgas, lies in an inlet between the capes of Akra and Talasakra. Although it doesn't have much of a beach – it's really a rocky shoreline – fishing, swimming and surfing are all possible here. It's a quiet town with flower-filled gardens and some budget accommodation in new buildings.

To the south, the beach by the Gradina camp site is pleasant. The sands here stretch for several kilometres and the sea is generally calm, making it ideal for learning to windsurf.

A view over industrial Bourgas, the main port on the Black Sea.

BELOW: a bar in Bourgas.

Excavations in progress at the site of ancient Apollonia. A thriving port, Apollonia began minting its own silver coins, engraved with an anchor and a crayfish on one side and Apollo on the other, in 520 BC.

BELOW: Sozopol's enclosing walls.

Historic Sozopol

Sozopol ㉗ (Созопол), 35 km (22 miles) south of Bourgas, is the oldest town on the Black Sea coast. Combining a good beach and an attractive old town with plenty of history and culture, it is one of the nicest places to stay on the coast. Its hotels are all low-rise.

Sozopol was an island until the Thracians built a stone isthmus connecting it to the mainland. The first settlement on this site was Apollonia Pontica, whose inhabitants worshipped the Greek God Apollo, represented in the town by a 30 ft- (9 metre-) high bronze statue by Kalamis, a famous Athenian sculptor, which guarded the harbour. Nessebar, Varna, Kavarna and Balchik were all Apollonian settlements scattered along the coast; Sozopol was the capital.

The Apollonians – the first Greek settlers on the Black Sea coast – lived relatively peacefully with the Thracians and intermarried. However, the mixing of the populations led to disturbances significant enough to be mentioned by Aristotle.

From the River Danube all the way south to Istanbul and the Bosphoros, Sozopol was the only settlement with a protected port. Carts full of grain, timber, animal hides, dried meat and metal ingots were brought here from the rest of Bulgaria and loaded onto ships for export to Greece. The ships returned with decorative ceramics and bronze vessels.

At the beginning of the 1st century BC, the Romans attacked Sozopol, burned the city to the ground, and then annexed it. The emblematic statue of Apollo was shipped to Rome. The town was later occupied by the Byzantines and the Ottomans, eventually becoming part of newly independent Bulgaria in the 19th century.

Sozopol's old town

The atmospheric old town comprises 200 or more traditional wooden houses built between the mid-18th and mid-19th centuries. Typically, they have two or three floors, the lower ones designed to store nets and other fishing equipment. In the 19th and 20th centuries, some 90 percent of

the Bulgarian Black Sea catch was hauled in by fishermen from Sozopol. Many of these houses feature fine Turkish tilework.

Tours of the old town can be arranged by **Foundation Sozopol** (50 ulitsa Milet; tel: (0550) 22267; www.sozopol-foundation.com), where there is also an exhibition on the town's fortified wall and tower, built and rebuilt between the 4th and 14th centuries, and an ancient well dating from the 4th–2nd century BC. A leaflet in imperfect English guides visitors through an anteroom where there is a granary dating from the 5th century, when Sozopol was the biggest port on the Black Sea. Downstairs, the interior of an ancient well and the foundations of the watchtower are revealed.

Outside, a restored house in National Revival style contains the **Ethnographic Museum** (daily 8am–6pm; admission charge), displaying the clothing and handicrafts of the three ethnic groups who lived on the coast in the late 19th and early 20th century. The **Archaeological Museum** (2 ulitsa Han Krum; 10am–5pm; admission charge) is of limited interest except for its large collection of painted pottery and sea-eroded stone anchors found in the sea around Sozopol.

Sozopol's medieval churches were destroyed by the Ottoman Turks, but four historic churches remain. The church of **St George** was built on part of a 1st-century basilica when Christianity was declared the official religion in 1895; tiny 19th-century **St Zosim** in the town's central park showcases icons created by a talented local artist; the church of the **Virgin Mary** has fine wood engravings; and **Saints Cyril and Methodius**, near the Archaeological Museum.

Sozopol's beaches

The town has two beaches, both crowded in summer. The northern beach, near the old town, is narrower and marginally quieter, sloping gently into shallow water; **Harmanite Beach**,

behind the new town, is about 1 km (½ mile) long, backed by a noisy fairground and restaurants. The sand here is not very clean, and an ancient necropolis is being excavated on part of the beach.

A couple of kilometres northwest of the town, the Zlatna Ribka camp site lies alongside a lagoon. However, signs warn of underwater holes and reefs, although a lifeguard watches part of the beach. There are windsurfing boards and peddle boats for hire from a small hut next to a stagnant stream. Apart from camping, there is accommodation in basic huts catering mainly to Bulgarian and eastern European holiday-makers.

A new development is set to change this makeshift state of affairs. Opposite the camp site, pine trees have been felled to make way for a luxury complex called Santa Marina (www.santamarina.bg), which will contain around 400 apartments and villas, two large pools, restaurants and shops. At the time of writing they were attracting British investors and more apartments are planned.

Map on page 232

A fresco inside the church of Sveti Georgi.

BELOW: Sozopol's characteristic stone and timber houses.

One of the numerous bars in Sozopol, one of the best places for nightlife on the coast.

St John's Island

Just off the coast of Sozopol is the uninhabited island of **St John's** (Св Йоан), which has the remains of a 13th-century monastery and temple, as well as a lighthouse built in 1884 to mark the entry to Bourgas. Now a nature reserve, it is home to more than 70 species of nesting birds, as well as the underground hare and the monk seal. Boat trips to the island leave throughout the day from a point just north of Sozopol's port. Among them, the *Kleopatra* takes visitors on a sightseeing tour to Sozopol's beaches, the fortress wall and the islands; other boats take in the Ropotamo River or offer fishing trips.

Between Sozopol and St John's Island is an underwater forest of petrified bog cedars sunk 70 million years ago when the water level rose dramatically. It is possible to make dives from a ship to see this strange formation, as well as ancient anchors and everyday items from shipwrecks. The **Cape of St Toma**, 15 km (9 miles) south of Sozopol, is another good area for diving. The water level

was once around 10 metres (30 ft) lower, so ancient constructions that are now submerged, along with sunken ships and underwater flora and fauna, can be explored. One diving company operating trips in this area is Monisub, 1 ulitsa Simeon Gater-Ruse Volgrad; tel: 88 740 7027.

Waters ports and wildlife

The deep horseshoe of the south-facing beach at **Dyuni** ❷ (Дония) runs for several kilometres and is 100 metres/yds wide in places. It is an attractive spot, backed by dunes, with calm conditions and gently shelving sands. At the northern end, a breakwater runs parallel to the beach, creating an area of protected water that is perfect for learning to sail or windsurf; rentals and tuition are available.

Austrian-designed Dyuni Holiday Village was built in the late 1980s as a stylish resort set in attractive parkland. Though parts of it have definitely seen better days, it is popular with Dutch and German families in particular, and accommodation gets booked up quickly in summer.

BELOW: swimming and sunbathing at Sozopol

Map on page 232

South of Dyuni is a lovely stretch of road that, after a few kilometres, passes **Alepu**. An area of marsh and reed beds, it is home to a rich variety of bird, plant and animal life. In spring, wild flowers, including crimson poppies, cover both sides of the roads; and sand lilies flourish in the dunes. Further south, **St Thomas Island** lies several hundred metres offshore. Sometimes called Snake Island – although no snakes live there – the island used to feature a Hellenic sanctuary. Now uninhabited, it is of interest mainly for its collection of cacti, planted in the 1930s.

Drowned river

A few kilometres south of **Dyuni** is the estuary of the **Ropotamo River**, which rises in the Strandzha *(see page 259)*. The Ropotamo is a "drowned river" – its bed is below sea level 5 km (3 miles) from its mouth – so sea water mixes with fresh water. The surrounding swamps, dense oak forests and towering sand dunes form a nature reserve. Fishermen can be seen looking for catches of whitefish, grey mullet and carp, and seals sometimes visit the rocks and caves of Cape Maslen to the south. A climb to the top is rewarded by good views. It is well worth taking a boat trip along the estuary, through the reed beds and the glorious carpets of water lilies, for which the river is famous (take binoculars to observe the bird life). Accommodation is available in small hotels and guesthouses along the river; ask for further information from any of the travel agents in Sozopol.

Youthful ideals

South of the Ropotamo River are a string of small settlements, none of which need detain you for long. **Primorsko** ❷❾ (Приморско), a small town on a peninsula, is home to an International Youth Centre, which was once the largest of its kind in Europe. Thousands of young people from various Soviet bloc countries came here on holiday, sleeping in communal tents set in the woods and parkland. Young people still come here to camp, but these days they tend to be looking for cheap accommodation rather than political ideals.

Volleyball on the beach at Dyuni, with Dyuni Holiday Village in the background.

BELOW: a "noddy train" pauses for passengers in Sozopol.

New hotels, villas and apartments are proliferating along the Black Sea coast. Quiet and unspoilt areas may not remain so for long.

BELOW: the beach at Primorsko.

Mid-range hotels, guesthouses and camp sites, along with discos, snack bars and souvenir stands, cater to Bulgarian and international visitors alike. The resort is rather down at heel, but there is a long and magnificent crescent of sand. The sea at the northern end tends to be rougher, attracting surfers; families are better off sticking to the calmer conditions at the southern end.

Pretty peninsula

Kiten (Китен), whose name means "pretty", is another peninsula settlement just 5 km (3 miles) south of Primorsko, but with no real centre. A low-key place (it wasn't declared a town until 2005), it is mainly popular with Bulgarian holiday-makers, although increasing numbers of Czechs and Germans are discovering it. Atliman, the northern beach, tends to be more sheltered; the southern stretch has a camp site and beach cafés.

Growing resort

About 5 km (3 miles) further south, **Lozenets** ⓾ (Лозенец)is barely more

than a beach, with a few family-run hotels and a couple of camp sites. But, like so many other locations along the coast, the land here is rapidly being bought up by rich Bulgarians from Sofia or by foreigners, and it is likely to be a very different place in five years time. The village's first church was built just a few years ago – thanks to a donation from a wealthy newcomer from Sofia.

International port

Continuing south along the coast road for around 10 km (6 miles) will bring you to **Tsarevo** (Царево), the most southerly port on the Black Sea. It has evolved from a traditional fishing village and some handsome National Revival buildings, but these days serves large passenger and cargo vessels and yachts. It is situated on three small bays, with only a tiny area of sand. Even so, it is the subject of a fair amount of new development, including the building of small hotels and holiday villages, such as Crocodile Beach and Costa del Croco, as well as large hotel complexes.

South to the border

Ahtopol ③ (Ахтопол), the most southerly town on Bulgaria's Black Sea coast, lies at the foot of the Strandza Mountains 7 km (4 miles) southeast of Tsarevo and less than 10 km (12 miles) from the border with Turkey. It has one of Bulgaria's last functioning summer camps, where Bulgarian workers come for bargain breaks. Until recently this was a quiet fishing settlement, but a new holiday village has been built around the harbour and shingle beaches.

Excavations have unearthed evidence of occupation in Thracian times. In later years, the Byzantines and Bulgarians fought for control over the settlement, and it was regularly ransacked by pirates. The only remnants of former times are the ruins of a fortress and a fountain with a carved horseman. Walk up to the lighthouse for good views, especially at sunset.

The final enclave

South of here are some of Bulgaria's loveliest bays and beaches. Dense oak woodland separates Ahtopol from **Sinemoretz** ㉜ (Синеморец), which has only been open to visitors since 1990. Under Communism access was restricted to this sensitive border region and as a result it is one of the loveliest parts on the coast. To the north is a long swathe of sand and rolling green hills surrounding the mouth of the Veleka River. Accessed by a dirt track, it remains wild and unspoilt save for a nudist colony. The southern beach, backed by a rocky headland, has several cafés and can get quite full in high season. New luxury villas are being built.

The Strandzha Nature Park

The **Strandzha Mountains** (Страндж) form a natural park that stretches for more than 1,000 sq. km (386 sq. miles) over the far southeast corner of Bulgaria. This is a region of small mountain villages and undulating forests, which blankets much of the park. The main road from Tsarevo plunges deep into the wooded region, as does the inland road south from Bourgas.

The Strandzha is rich in animal, plant and bird life, which for many years was protected due to the inaccessibility of

Map on page 232

BELOW LEFT: beach-goers at Lozenets.
BELOW: Sinemoretz on the mouth of the Veleka River.

Detail on the village church of St George in Sinemoretz.

BELOW: coastal scene near Sinemoretz.

this border region. Declared a natural park in 1995, it is now protected by law. Wolves, wild boar, deer, jackal and wild cats are among the larger mammals in the park, and otters swim in its rivers.

The Strandhza also includes 50 percent of the species of flora found in Bulgaria. Beech trees make up most of the forests, and there are significant numbers of oak trees. Reeds and bulrushes are found in the swamps and riverbeds. The unique species that live here, such as wild jasmine, juniper and fig trees, are protected, as are endangered species such as the Strand-zanian blueberry, Istanbul chickpea and Strandzanian oak tree.

Relatively few tourists visit the Strandzha due to the lack of facilities, with improvements being slow and low-key. As a result it offers wonderful opportunities to get off the beaten track within close proximity of the coast. Plan to travel by car, as public transport is very limited. The adventurous may want to hire a bike from one of the resorts on the coast as the dirt tracks offer some wonderful,

solitary rides (although good-quality mountain bikes may be hard to find, so allow time to shop around).

For hikers, there are long-distance trails and shorter hill treks and river walks. Autumn is the best time for woodland walks.

Fishing is excellent in the Veleka river. Turbot, goby, red and grey mullet and carp can all be caught. On the coast, sea angling and spear fishing are also possible, with equipment available to rent in Sozopol. Horse riding is also popular here, with great rides through the forests, along the rivers and on the beaches.

Bird life of the Strandzha

The Strandzha is especially notable for its rich bird life. At certain times of the year, the number of bird species here is over 260, representing some 68 percent of the total bird population in the country. The BSPB, Bulgarian Society for the Protection of Birds (www. bspb.org), offers birding tours in the region thoughout the year, through mid-May to mid-June and September are considered the best times for

sightings, as migratory birds are also in evidence. The Poda Lagoon, south of Bourgas, has the only spoonbill colony on the Black Sea coast, and is a breeding site for glossy ibis, grey and purple herons and the little egret. The Veleka estuary offers sightings of little egret, black and white storks, woodpeckers, red-footed falcons and many other birds. There are some 40,000 birds of prey in the area, as well as 240,000 white storks, and over 30,000 white pelicans.

The villages of the Strandzha

Travelling southwest through the Strandzha from the Black Sea port of Tsarevo leads to a string of little villages where tourists are rarely seen and time seems to have stood still.

One fascinating local tradition that has endured through the centuries in several Bulgarian and Greek villages in the area is Nestinarstvo (fire dancing, *also see Festivals, page 48–9)*. This is an ancient pagan ritual, believed to date from Thracian times, in which participants dance barefoot on burning embers to the tune of bagpipes and drums. Dancing begins at sunset, with performers forming a circle before moving through the fire and often falling into a trance. The dance was traditionally thought to bring good crops and health, although nowadays it is more often performed to entertain tourists.

About 35 km (22 miles) from Tsarevo is the little village of **Gramatikovo**, surrounded by swathes of oak and beech forests. It was founded by monks in medieval times, hence its name – *gramatik* means "man of grammar". The church of the Forty Martyrs, dating from the 18th century, is the oldest church in the village, although it was burned to the ground by the Turks in 1877 and rebuilt after the Liberation. Gramatikovo's school opened its doors in the early 19th century, making it one of the first in the area.

The village has been the headquarters of the forestry board since the 1930s, a body that seeks to protect the existing forest of the Strandzha, as well as planting new species such as bamboo and eucalyptus.

Map on page 232

BELOW:
rock formations
near Tsarevo.

Map on page 232

TIP

While in Malko Tarnovo pop into the administration centre for the Strandzha Natural Park, which sells hiking maps for the area and can book accommodation in local guesthouses.

BELOW: traditional architecture in Brashlyan.

Rural "capital"

An hour's drive southwest of Tsarevo, **Malko Tarnovo** ❸ (Малко Търново) is the only town in the Bulgarian part of the Strandzha Mountains and the region's unofficial capital. Its name is said to derive from the Bulgarian word *truni* (prickly bush), alluding to the large number of thistles that grow hereabouts; the prefix "malko" was later added to distinguish it from the ancient Bulgarian capital of Veliko (Great) Turnovo in the northwest of the country. Its wealth was founded on the local marble, which was quarried for use in cities such as Adrianople and Constantinople.

Lying in a karst bowl surrounded by bare hills, it is of interest for its history rather than its scenery. A small group of National Revival houses near the main square forms a town museum, with ethnographic and icon collections and photographs and documents depicting traditional life in the region. The **Church of the Assumption of the Holy Virgin** was built in 1830 on the site of an earlier construction and today looks fairly modern thanks to a succession of repairs. However, it is well worth taking a look inside to see its stunning collection of over 100 icons in local style.

The surrounding region is dotted with the remains of ancient tombs, temples and settlements. A Thracian tomb can be inspected at **Propada**, 5 km (3 miles) northwest of Malko Turnovo, while Thracian tombs and a Roman villa are found at **Mishovka Niva**, 13 km (7 miles) southwest of town.

Revolutionary site

Those with a special interest in Bulgaria's revolutionary history may want to make a short detour to **Petrovo Niva**. On a hill-top above a bend in the Veleka River, 10 km (6 miles) northeast of Malko Turnovo, this is a significant place for many Bulgarians. It was here that Bulgarian revolutionary leaders gathered in 1903 to plan the uprising against the Turks. Known as the Preobrazhenie (Transfiguration) Uprising because it took place on 6 August, an Orthodox holy day known as Preobrazhenie, it is commemorated each year in national celebrations on the nearest weekend to that day.

Architectural ensemble

A kilometre (½ mile) off the main road north to Bourgas, 11 km (7 miles) northwest of Malko Turnovo, is the hamlet of **Brashlyan** ❹ (Бръшлян) designated an architectural and historical reserve in 1982 on account of its traditional peasant houses. At its centre is the sunken church of Sveti Dimitar, built behind a high wall according to Ottoman regulations, so it could not offend local Muslims. Next door is a small church school.

Brashlyan has an ageing population of just over 80 people, although with properties here being marketed at foreign investors that may change in the near future. At present, there are no hotels or restaurants here, with most visitors just passing through or coming on a day trip. ❏

RESTAURANTS & BARS

Restaurants

Bourgas

Fors
17 ul Konstantin Fotinov
Tel: (056) 828 852
www.hotelfors-bg.com
Part of the hotel of the same name. Italian restaurant with large garden open until the early hours. €

Chernemorets

Condros-Pri Kapitana
11 ul Vazrajdane
Tel: (0550) 72270
Family-run *mehana* serving traditional food on a flower-filled terrace. €€

Fantastico
1 ul Anton Strashimiro
Tel: (0550) 73057
Serves hearty Bulgarian cuisine in the hotel of the same name. Barbecues are sometimes held in its garden. €

Nessebar

Dionis
5 ul Kraibreshna
Tel: (0554) 42557
There are sweeping sea views from the terrace of this good value restaurant in old Nessebar. Excellent fish. €€

Europa 2007
Nessebar Harbour
Tel: (mobile) 898 635 800
Despite its opportunistic name, this is an established restaurant on the harbour, with a sunny terrace. Claims to serve 38 kinds of fish. €€

Monte Cristo
2 ul Venera Str
Tel (0554) 42055
A traditional house to the right of Sv Parakeva Church. On two levels, with plush interior, and garden. Bulgarian and international cuisine. €€

Primorsko

Pizza Bar and Grill Micra 1
3 ul Mart
Tel: (mobile) 0897 951 652
A simple restaurant with pavement seating. Serves Italian, Bulgarian and Serbian food. €

Sv Vlas

Manastira
Laguna Hotels and Resorts
Tel: (0554) 68 790
Most of the apartment complexes have good restaurants, but this is the best, serving regional food in a lovely setting. €€

Sozopol

Di Valli
35 Morski Skali
Tel: (mobile) 888 982 265
Excellent Italian food from authentic carpaccio to tiramisu, served on a scenic cliff-side terrace. €€€

Viatarna Melnitza
27 ul Morksi skali
Tel: (0550) 22844
Classic Bulgarian food served in a traditional wooden building. Folk music some nights. €

Sunny Beach

Condor
Two blocks back from the beach, next to the post office
Tel: (mobile) 0888 853 875
A lovely garden restaurant with great service and excellent food. One of the best options in the resort. €

La Perla
Next to Hotel Colosseum
No phone
Beach-side restaurant serving Italian and international dishes and steaks. €

The Windmill
Opposite Hotel Sunset
Tel: (0554) 228 12
Located in a traditional windmill and serving Bulgarian cuisine. Nightly folklore performance.

Bars

Sunny Beach is packed with bars. On the beach, the **Pirate Ship**, a "bed bar", serves good cocktails. Bars in Bourgas include the **Karaoke Bar** (2 ul Sv Kl Obridski), open until 4am. Also on this street (No. 113) is one of Bourgas's several casinos (9am–6am). In small resorts, nightlife can be a few local bars.

PRICE CATEGORIES

Price categories are per person for thee courses:
€ = under 10 leva
€€ = 10–25 leva
€€€ = 25–50 leva
€€€€ = over 50 leva

RIGHT: a sunny table awaits in St Vlas.

✦ INSIGHT GUIDES

T R A V E L T I P S

BULGARIA

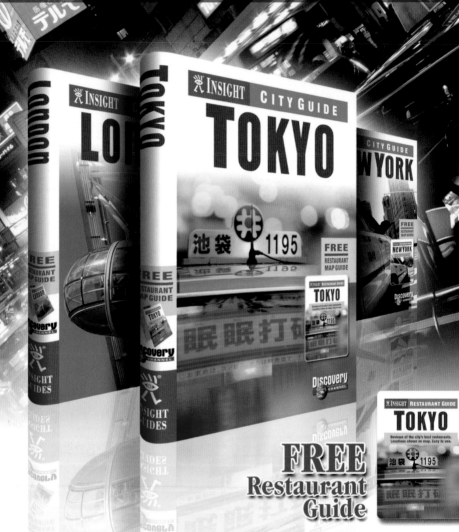

TRAVEL TIPS

Transport

Getting There **268**
  By Air from the UK **268**
  By Air from North America**268**
  By Boat **269**
  By Rail **269**
  By Car **269**
  By Coach **269**

Getting Around **269**
  By Air **269**
  By Rail **269**
  By Bus **269**
  City Travel **270**
  By Car **270**
  Taxis **270**
  Guided Tours **271**
  Tour Operators **271**

Accommodation

Choosing Accommodation .. **272**
Sofia **273**
Around Sofia and
  the Northwest **274**
Southwest, Rila and Pirin
  Mountains **275**
The Rhodopes **277**
The Balkan Range **278**
The Danubian Plain **279**
Northern Black Sea Coast.. **279**
Southern Black Sea Coast **281**

Activities

Music and Theatre.............**282**
Music Festivals **282**
Museums and Galleries **282**
Museum Opening Hours......**282**
Nightlife **283**
Children's Activities **283**
Festivals **283**
Shopping **283**
  Counterfeit **284**
  What to Buy **284**
  Where to Shop **284**
Sport and Outdoor Activities**285**
  Canoeing, Kayaking
  and Rafting........................**285**
  Caving............................**285**
  Climbing **285**
  Adventure Tour
    Companies **285**
  Cycling **286**
  Diving **286**
  Golf................................**286**
  Hiking **286**
  Horse Riding **286**
  Hunting **287**
  Sailing............................**287**
  Skiing **287**
  Wildlife Tours **287**

A – Z

Admission Charges **288**
Budgeting for your Trip **288**
Business Hours.................**288**
Children **288**
Climate.............................**288**
Crime and Safety..............**289**
Customs Regulations.........**289**
Disabled Travellers **289**
Electricity **289**
Embassies and Consulates **289**
Emergency Numbers **289**
Entry Requirements...........**290**
Etiquette...........................**290**
Gay and Lesbian Travellers..**290**
Health and Medical Care **290**
Internet **290**
Maps **291**
Media...............................**291**
Money **291**
Photography **292**
Postal Services **292**
Public Holidays **292**
Religion **292**
Telephones **292**
Time.................................**292**
Tipping **292**
Toilets **292**
Tourist Information **293**
Websites **293**
Weights and Measures **293**
What to Bring **293**

Language

Understanding the
  Language **294**

Further Reading

Recommended Background
  Reading **296**
Other Insight Guides **296**

TRANSPORT

GETTING THERE AND GETTING AROUND

GETTING THERE

By Air

The flying time from London is around three hours, depending on your departure airport and which airline you fly with. Bear in mind that there is a good range of options if you want to travel from a UK regional airport, with flights from Manchester, Cardiff, Glasgow and Birmingham amongst others, to Sofia, Plovdiv, Varna and Bourgas in Bulgaria.

Buying a package deal (including flight, accommodation, transfers and sometimes some meals) often works out cheaper than the price of a flight on its own, particularly when travelling to the popular Black Sea resorts, so it is worth considering this option. Thomson (www.flythomson.co.uk) offers holidays with flights to Bourgas (from 10 airports across the UK) and Varna (from Newcastle, Manchester, Liverpool, Cardiff and Gatwick) several times a week. Balkan Holidays (www.balkanholidays.co.uk) sells holidays to Bulgaria's beaches, as well as to its lakes and mountains.

From the UK

A handful of airlines – see the following list for details – currently fly directly between the UK and Bulgaria, but the number is growing all the time. In particular, look out for no-frills airlines starting up routes over the next few years.

Bulgaria Air
Rooms 39–42, 2nd Floor
Morley House
320 Regent Street
London W1B 3BD

Tel: 020 7631 1263
www.bulgaria-air.co.uk
www.air.bg
Formally Balkan Air, Bulgaria Air operates non-stop flights between London, Manchester, Dublin and Sofia, as well as flights from London to Bourgas and Varna in summer. If you want to book flights online you must use the www.air.bg site or use an online booking facility, such as www.travelocity.com or www.flightline.co.uk

British Airways
Tel. 0870 850 9850
www.ba.com
BA offers competitively priced flights from London's Heathrow and Gatwick airports to Sofia and between London Gatwick and Varna several times a week.

Hemus Air
www.hemusair.bg
Room 40, 3rd Floor
Morley House
320 Regent Street
London W1.
Tel: 020 7637 5654
In Sofia, tel: (02) 981 8330
In Varna, tel: (052) 501 039
This Bulgarian airline flies from London to Sofia several times a week.

Malev
Tel: 0870 909 0577
www.malev.com
The Hungarian airline flies from Heathrow to Sofia, Bourgas and Varna via Budapest. Prices are competitive, but the current route involves stopping in the Hungarian capital and extends the journey time considerably.

WizzAir
www.wizzair.com
This low-cost airline flies from London Luton to Sofia four times a week and to Bourgas several times weekly, for as little as £19.99 one

way plus taxes, although flight times are very inconvenient.

From North America

There are no direct flights to Bulgaria from the USA or Canada. Your best bet is to investigate eastern European airlines such as the Polish airline LOT (www.lot.com) via Warsaw or Malev *(see above for details)*, the Hungarian airline (via Budapest).

From the Airport

Sofia
Sofia's airport (www.sofia-airport.bg) is only about 10 km (6 miles) east of the city centre. If you take one of the taxis waiting outside the arrivals hall, make sure it is a licensed vehicle and the meter is used. The airport recommends that passengers only use the company OK Supertrans (Tel: 02-973 2121; www.oktaxi.net). Regular buses run to the city centre between 5am and 11pm from just outside the arrivals hall.

Varna
www.varna-airport.bg
Varna's airport is 9 km (5 miles) from the city, connected by a regular bus service throughout the day.

Bourgas
This is around 13 km (8 miles) from the city centre, and is served by regular buses. As with Sofia, if taking a taxi, take sensible precautions to ensure that you are not overcharged.

By Boat

Few passengers will choose to arrive by boat, as services are infrequent and lengthy. Bourgas (www.port-bourgas.com) and Varna (www.port-varna.bg) are both functioning Black Sea ports, albeit with limited

ABOVE: catching a tram in Sofia.

passenger vessels. There is an official entry point into Bulgaria at Vidin across the Danube River from Calafat in Romania, as well as a road bridge from Rousse to Giurgiu.

Cruise Liners

Nessebar and Varna are ports of call on some eastern Mediterranean/ Black Sea cruises. For details of the cruise lines offering Bulgarian ports in their itineraries visit www.choosingcruising.co.uk. The Bulgarian section of the Danube is visited by several river cruises (ports of call are Vidin Orehova and Rousse).

By Rail

There are frequent rail services between Sofia and the European capitals of Paris, Vienna, Munich, Berlin, Budapest, Belgrade, Bucharest and Istanbul. For details contact RILA (www.bdz-rila.com).

If you are planning to travel through other countries in the region it may be worth buying a pass. Bulgaria participates in the Inter Rail scheme (open to European travellers only), while US and Australian visitors are eligible for the Eurail Select Pass covering Bulgaria. However, remember that travelling by train within Bulgaria is inexpensive so do your sums before deciding what to buy.
www.interrailnet.com
www.eurail.net

By Car

If you are driving your own vehicle while in Bulgaria you will need to have your vehicle registration document to prove you are the vehicle's owner, and Green Card insurance to cover you for the duration of your stay (alternatively buy insurance on entering). On entering Bulgaria, motorists are required to pay a small tax and also purchase a "vignette" or road tax, both obtained at the border. It is also necessary to carry a fire extinguisher, first-aid kit and warning triangle. *(See also By Car in the Getting Around section, page 270)* for "Rules of the Road" in Bulgaria.

By Coach

It is possible to travel by coach from the UK, but the journey takes about 45 hours.
National Express
Tel: (08705) 808 080
www.nationalexpress.com.
Eurolines
Tel: (08705) 143 219
www.eurolines.com
Eurolines offers regular coach services from other European countries.

GETTING AROUND

By Air

Bulgaria is not a huge country, but air travel is an obvious option for some destinations as it is relatively inexpensive, with most journeys taking less than an hour. The national airlines, Bulgaria Air (www.air.bg), and Hemus Air (www.hemusair.bg) both operate

services connecting Sofia with the coast and main cities.

By Rail

Although Bulgaria has an extensive railway network (www.bdz.bg), lack of investment has meant the service is infrequent, slow and somewhat basic. Do make reservations and if possible travel first class for some kind of comfort and on an express train for reasonable speed.

If you are in the area around Bansko in southwestern Bulgaria it is worth taking the narrow-gauge railway from Septemvri to Dobrinshte via Bankso (three trains a day), a spectacular route climbing through deep forests and tobacco-growing country.

By Bus

Consider taking a bus when travelling on a major route rather than going on an organised excursion, not only to save money, but to get a taste of local Bulgarian life. Tickets are extremely cheap. As an example, a bus ticket between Sofia and one of the Black Sea resorts costs 8 euros and takes around six hours. Few bus drivers will speak English or any other foreign language, and destinations on timetables and on the front of buses will appear in Cyrillic *(see Language, page 270).*

Minibus services (for up to 15 people) operate on tourist routes – such as Sofia airport to the ski resort of Bankso and along the Black Sea coast. These offer a good compromise in terms of price and comfort between taxis and regular buses.

Hitchhiking

Safety is a major concern when considering hitchhiking anywhere in the world, but on top of this hitching is actually illegal in Bulgaria. If you do decide to travel around by this means, take sensible precautions.

Travel in Rural Areas

In rural areas, public transport (usually limited to buses) is often very limited. It can also be difficult for travellers to get information and make sense of timetables. However, taxis are inexpensive, even for relatively long distances and this may well be your best option if you haven't hired your own car.

ACCOMMODATION

ACTIVITIES

A – Z

LANGUAGE

ABOVE: an official taxi in Sofia.

Let others know where you are, don't take rides with anyone who seems remotely suspect and never hitchhike alone. Hitching over long distances can be a problem, as traffic tends to be restricted to local journeys. Also, the amount of traffic on the roads is limited, so hitchhikers in quieter areas may have to wait several hours just to see a car, and much longer for one that will offer a ride.

City Travel

Flat fares are charged on all local transport. Sofia has buses, trams and trolleybuses, tickets for which must be bought from nearby kisoks before boarding. Since 1998, a new Metro underground train system has opened. This is currently fairly limited but set to expand over the next couple of decades. Evenutally it will extend to the airport.

Trolleybuses also operate in Plovdiv and Varna.

By Car

If you are staying in one of the bigger resorts on the Black Sea coast, it is unlikely that it would be worth your while to rent a car, as bus services are good along the coast and taxis relatively cheap. Day trips, including transport, are easily arranged through holiday companies or local agents. But visitors with limited time or wanting to visit more remote areas, might decide to hire a car, for at least a few days. The minimum age for hiring a car is 18. You don't

need an international licence provided you have a European licence with a photocard. Other nationalities should obtain an international licence.

Car-hire prices are inexpensive compared with many other European destinations – from around 20 euros a day, plus insurance and payment of a deposit. Many international car hire companies are represented, along with a number of national operators, both with representatives throughout the country (see opposite for details).

Prices drop significantly when renting a car for more than 3 days, and outside of the ain peak season. Make sure the price includes VAT and local taxes. It will generally cost more to hire through a foreign agent. Normally, additional drivers can be put on the insurance at no extra cost. Cars can usually be returned to a

Taxis

Once an unregulated rip-off for foreigners, all taxis are now metered and drivers must provide clients with a receipt. That said, still exercise caution and only take taxis displaying the name of their company. Taxis can be hired from taxi ranks or ordered by phone (see Language, page 295). In Sofia:
Yellow Taxi: 02-911 19
EuroTaxi: 02-910 33
Sofia Taxi: 02-974 47 47
OK Supertrans: 02-973 21 21

location different from the pick-up point on payment of a small fee.

If you fancy hiring a car but don't like the idea of driving in Bulgaria, a good option is to hire a car with a driver. This need not be prohibitively expensive. Ask a taxi driver what his daily rate would be; if you are travelling for more than one day you would also be expected to pay for the driver's meals and accommodation.

Driving in Bulgaria

Driving in Bulgaria can be a real pleasure as the roads are generally straight and empty. With the exception of Sofia, which suffers from congestion like any big city, and the old town of Plovdiv – a labyrinth in which you could be lost for days – you should encounter few headaches. Do get a map with place names in both Cyrillic and English as many signs outside of major tourist areas are only in Cyrillic.

It may be helpful to hire a jeep; even if you don't use the four-wheel drive facility, the extra suspension can make for a more comfortable journey on mountain roads and if you hit the occasionally pothole – Bulgarian road surfaces can be patchy.

Fuel

The price of fuel (unleaded and diesel) is about a third cheaper than in the UK, and twice that of the US. Service stations are reasonably plentiful but not all accept credit cards, so be sure to have enough cash for emergencies. Leaded petrol is no longer sold. Be aware that red pumps at service stations are for service vehicles only. Note that it is

Car Hire Companies

Avis
www.avis.com
Avis has offices in Sofia, Sunny Beach and Varna
Sofia:
60 Bul. Vassil Levski
Tel: (02) 989 8800
Sunny Beach:
Hotel Oasis - XG2
Tel: (0886) 533 588
Varna International Airport
Tel: (052) 500 832

Hertz
47 bul. Vassil Levski
Tel: (02) 980 0461
www.hertz.autotechnika.bg

Renta Auto
44 ul. Sredna Gora
Sofia
Tel: (02) 988 1299
www.rentauto-bg.com
A Bulgarian company with reliable cars.

Sixt
East Park Trade Center
53A bul. Nikola Vaptzarov
Sofia
www.e-sixt.com
Tel: (02) 816 95 75
This competitively-priced, international company offering vans and limousines as well as standard vehicles. Has offices throughout the country.

Top Rent
www.toprentbg.com
Has offices in Sofia and Varna,
Sofia:
37 Bul. Hristo Botev
Tel: (02) 952 3 777
Varna:
17 bul. Tsar Osvoboditel
Tel: (052) 601 353

TS Travel
24 ul. Solunska
Tel: (02) 8864 43036
Sofia
www.tstravel.net
Has offices in all the major cities and in the Black Sea resorts and online quotes are emailed within 48 hours, but it is not necessarily the cheapest company around.

forbidden to carry a can of fuel in your vehicle.

Rules of the Road
The blood alcohol limit is 0.05 percent, so even one drink will invalidate any insurance claim and could have severe consequences. On-the-spot fines are common for all kinds of traffic offences. If you receive one, be sure to obtain a receipt. Seat belts must be worn in the front

seats of vehicles, and children under 12 years of age must travel in the back. Motorcyclists and their passengers must wear crash helmets and keep their headlamps on at all times.

Avoid driving at night as few roads are lit. Bulgarian drivers are generally considerate but have a kamikaze approach to overtaking; they rarely signal and will pull out despite oncoming traffic.

Speed Limits
50 kph (30 mph) in built-up areas.
90 kph (55 mph) outside built-up areas.
120 kph (75 mph) on motorways.

Guided Tours

Expert guides, who are usually multi-lingual, can be hired to show visitors around historic towns and cities. This is a recommended option for those with an interest in history, architecture or archaeology as unfortuately many of Bulgaria's museums and historic buildings have only limited information in English. As well as being a good way to soak up some local knowledge, a city tour is also a good idea if time is limited. Tours of cities such as Sofia, Bourgas, Varna and Plovdiv are easily arranged, either through local tourist offices or holiday companies. Depending on the destination, they usually last three hours and sometimes include lunch. Guided tours in Sofia take in the Aleksander Nevski Cathedral and Boyana Church, both UNESCO listed. Dinner in a traditional Bulgarian restaurant with fire dancing is an optional extra. The nearby village of Oreshak and its folk-art exhibition can be visited as part of the trip, with the chance to buy locally made souvenirs.

Most city tours will involve a fair amount of walking and some coach travel. For those who prefer something more personalised, tailor-made individual tours are not prohibitively expensive. A 10-day UNESCO tour (See Alexander Tour under Tour Operators, see right) takes in Bulgaria's UNESCO sites, including the Ivanovo rock monasteries, the Madara Horseman, Nessebar and the Rila Monastery, as well as some historic towns and cities.

Tour Operators

As a way of putting money directly into the local economy, it is a nice idea to use operators and agents based in Bulgaria when booking a

trip. Staff are almost invariably friendly and helpful, and prices tend to be lower than those of companies at home. Here are a few options.

Alexander Tour
44 ul. Pop Bogomil
1202 Sofia
Tel: (02) 983 3322
www.alexandertour.com
Good range of tours including themed options such as bird-watching, archaeology and folklore.

Brill Travel
1 ul. Khan Asparuh
1463 Sofia
Tel: (02) 8520764
www.brilltravel.com
Cultural tours and/or accommodation can be arranged for groups as well as independent travellers throughout the country. Self-drive holidays too.

Pandion
20A Bul. Cherni Vrah
1421 Sofia
Tel: (02)-9630436
www.birdwatchingholidays.com
This Bulgaria-based company specialises in nature holidays of all descriptions, such as bird-, mammal-watching and even dragonfly-watching tours.

Spa Life Bulgaria
7 ul. Sveta Gora
1164 Sofia
Tel: (02) 865 9354
www.spalifestylebulgaria.com
Provides a helpful, thoughtful service. Its programme includes a full range of luxurious up-to-the-mintue spa treatments, plus activities such as rafting, hiking and horse riding.

Rural Tourism
Rural tourism is gaining ground in Bulgaria, as Bulgarians realise the growing foreign interest in its unique rural heritage. Local tourist offices can provide information about accommodation in traditional homes, particularly in the mountain regions.

To book rural accommodation, visit www.ruralbulgaria.com. It alllows you to search type of accommodation (farm, hostel, house, apartment, etc.) and location (historic town, sea, lake, etc.)

Emotion Holidays
Baltantsi Ltd
31 ul. Khan Krum
Varna
Tel: (052) 631 745
www.emotionholidays.com
Organises tailor-made holidays in Bulgaria with accommodation in family guesthouses and rural lodgings, with the option to take part in an activity such as walking or fishing.

ACCOMMODATION

HOTELS AND GUESTHOUSES

Choosing Accommodation

Bulgaria has a wide range of of accommodation, from rural "home-stays" in the interior to large, brash hotels on the coast. Bear in mind that "five stars" may not mean the same as it would at home, especially when it comes to service. Although accommodation standards are being dragged into the 21st century – particularly along the coast –the remnants of Bulgaria's Communist days linger on in the form of concrete blocks and surly waiters, and some of the more traditional hotels have a somewhat faded grandeur with outdated decor and facilities. For this reason it is a good idea to book one or two stars higher than you normally would, particularly as prices are generally a lot lower than in western Europe.

BELOW: late night arrival in Veliko Tarnovo.

There are lots of all-inclusive deals to Bulgaria, but the food provided in these packages is generally of poor quality, although this is improving. The Bulgarian tourist industry has cottoned on to the concept of a "boutique hotel", which you may see advertised in some cities. Often these are small and modern, but not necessarily chic or stylish.

There are some good-value and friendly family-run hotels, many of which accept only cash. Rates in these kinds of establishments will usually be quoted in lev, while larger hotels will also quote, and accept, euros. An antiquated price structure means that a room can often cost a third more for foreigners than for Bulgarians. Prices rise dramatically in the peak season, when they double, or even triple.

Renting Accommodation

Thanks to the current property boom in Bulgaria, privately owned accommodation is increasingly available for rental directly from owners, through organisations such as Owners Direct, a UK-based company.
Owners Direct
58 The Street
Ashtead
Surrey, KT21 1AW
Tel: (01372) 229330
www.ownersdirect.co.uk/Bulgaria.

Both single and triple rooms are usually available across the country, and one-bedroom apartments with a sofa bed in the sitting room will usually sleep four. If travelling independently, it is a good idea to work out the name of your accommodation in Cryllic as this is how names often appear on signs, especially in rural areas (see Cyrillic alphabet, page 294).

Guesthouses

Consider staying in a small family-run establishment rather than anonymous blocks. This feeds the local economy, offering lower costs and a much more authentic experience. BAAT, the Bulgarian Association for Alternative Tourism, www.alternative-tourism.org. publishes a directory of small guesthouses chosen for their hospitality and exceptional quality. It can be ordered from 20-V Stamboliiski Blvd., Sofia, Bulgaria, Tel: (02) 980 76 85 or by e-mail: baat@spnet.net.

Another websites worth consulting is: www.thebackpacker.net/travelhostels/bulgaria/index.htm. Lists hostels and small guesthouses.

ACCOMMODATION LISTINGS

SOFIA

HOTELS

Grand Hotel Sofia
1 ul. Gurko
Tel: (02) 811 0800
www.grandhotelsofia.bg
Grand in both name and nature, this superb hotel situated opposite Sofia's National Theatre is one classy place. Impeccably attired doormen welcome you in, friendly reception staff meet you and greet you, and the sheer luxury and spaciousness of the rooms are well worth the splurge. €€€€

Hilton Sofia
1 bul. Bulgaria
Tel: (02) 933 5000
www.hilton.com
You will either love or hate the modernist Sofia Hilton, a glass and steel structure south of the city centre, just behind the NDK. It can at times appear unwelcoming, but that is only on the outside: inside you will find one of the most luxurious Hilton's in Europe. It has great restaurants too and serves the best Sunday Brunch in the city. €€€€

Kempinski Hotel Zografski
100 bul. James Bouchier
Tel: (02) 969 2222
www.kempinski.com
This hotel was originally built by Japanese investors, and many people visit it just to see its beautiful Japanese garden or to eat in its superb basement Japanese restaurant. It is now a Kempinski, and though some way from the city centre offers luxury at an affordable price. It has an excellent sport and fitness complex. €€€€

Radisson SAS Grand Hotel
4 pl. Narodno Sabranie
Tel: (02) 933 43 43
www.radissonsas.com
Pricey, but worth every penny. This is another shining glass edifice, only this time in the heart of the

city, just a stone's throw from the Alexander Nevski Cathedral. It offers a wealth of splendour and luxury throughout, with its fine rooms and restaurants, and the service is unmatched elsewhere in the city. It is a good choice for families. €€€€

Sheraton Sofia Hotel Balkan
5 pl. Sveta Nedelya
Tel: (02) 980 6541
www.starwoodhotels.com
The historic Sheraton is the oldest of Sofia's five star hotels, and is still the first choice of travellers for whom location matters most. Built in the early 1950s, it is a superb building, though the common areas on the ground floor do now look a little dated. Rooms have all been recently refurbished, however, and are genuinely luxurious. The suites on the top floor are especially stunning. €€€€

Art'Otel
44. ul. William Gladstone
Tel: (02) 980 60 00
www.artotel.biz
This is a new and stylish boutique hotel centrally (though noisily) located on a side street off Bulevard Vitosha. The rooms are all uniquely decorated, with taste and panache, though some are larger than others. If there are enough vacancies, ask to see at least a couple before choosing which one to take. The suites with their vast corner windows offer the best value. €€€

Holiday Inn Sofia
111 bul. Alexandar Malinov
Tel: (02) 807 07 07
Though the location of this new hotel, in the Sofia business park, is perhaps not the most convenient for tourists, quality is high and prices are lower than you might think, especially at weekends when the conference crowd is

absent. There is a huge swimming pool – we think the biggest in the city – and fitness centre, and it is a good choice for those with a car. €€€

Anel
14 bul. Todor Aleksandov
Tel: (02) 911 9902
www.hotelanel.com
The Anel is what happens when veneer meets futuristic kitsch: an enjoyable mélange of styles and a great-value hotel. Rooms are fine without being remotely luxurious, though the spa, complete with swimming pool, is great, and as bizarrely decorated as the rest of the hotel. €€

Crystal Palace
14 ul. Shipka
Tel: (02) 948 9488
www.crystalpalace-sofia.com
A superb lesson in how to build a new hotel with style and class. The faux classical facade is super, and the elegant lobby, with its *Titanic*-esque staircase a genuine treat. Rooms are modestly-sized but well furnished and bright. €€

Barcelo Festa Sofia
83 bul. Bulgaria
Tel: (02) 818 9618
www.barcelo.sofia.com
Not brilliantly located for the city centre, but for visitors looking to split time between Vitosha and the city this is nonetheless a great choice. Newly built in 2006, it is a simple looking hotel from the outside, a fact more than made up for by the plush interiors. Rooms are well sized and furnished. €€

Light
37 ul. Veslets,
Tel: (02) 917 90 90
www.hotels.light.bg
A few minutes' walk along a quiet side street from the city centre, the Light is, as the name suggests, bright and airy. Some of the singles are tiny, but rooms are otherwise well sized, and though breakfast can

be a disappointment, you get excellent value for money here. €€

Niky
16 ul. Neofit Rilski
Tel: (02) 952 3058
www.hotel-niky.com
This is a smart new hotel in a five-storey building that blends effortlessly with its surroundings. All the rooms – though not exactly big – boast plenty of natural light, comfortable beds and great bathrooms. €€

Olymp
110 bul. Simeonovsko Shose
Tel: (02) 962 0580
www.maxisofia.com
If you are prepared to forego a city-centre location, you can get yourself what is a five-star, luxurious hotel for relatively little money. Rooms are large, nicely furnished, and the common areas are stunning. Indoor and outdoor swimming pools too. €€

Rodina
8 bul. Totleben
Tel: (02) 917 9999
www.rodina.bg
Despite its dated decor and somewhat forlorn look, there remains a real charm to this place, which was one of the first high-rises to be built in Sofia. Many of the 500 rooms have been

PRICE CATEGORIES

Approximate prices **per person** per night in a double room in high season:
€ = less than 25 leva
€€ = 25–50 leva
€€€ = 50–100 leva
€€€€ = more than 100 leva

ABOVE: Sheraton Sofia Hotel Balkan.

recently refurbished, though these cost more than those which haven't. The huge indoor swimming pool and health spa are a bonus. €€€

Sofia Princess
131 bul. Maria Luisa
Tel: (02) 933 88 88
www.sofia-princess-hotel.com
From afar it looks more like one of Sofia's monolithic apartment blocks, but the Princess is in fact a decent hotel situated within walking distance of both the centre and the railway station. Large indoor pool, sauna, casino and dated but large rooms. €€

Sveta Sofia
18 ul. Pirotska
Tel: (02) 981 26 34
www.svetasofia-alexander.bg
We adore this little place,

situated on Sofia's one pedestrianised street. The baroque yellow facade, the charming lobby and bar, and the well-furnished, spacious rooms all make it a great choice. Staff are friendly and amongst the most helpful we've come across outside the five-stars. €€

City Best Western
6 ul. Stara Planina
Tel: (02) 915 15 00
Offering decent sized rooms at good value prices, like all Best Western hotels this is a no-frills establishment. It is located just north of the city centre is popular with business travellers during the week. There are only 36 rooms, so reservations are essential. €

Meg-Lozenetz
84 ul. Krum Popov
Tel: (02) 965 18 70
A nice little three-star hotel offering 17 good-value, tastefully decorated rooms in a quiet, residential part of the city close to the NDK. €

Scotty's
11 ul. Ezarkh Iosif
Tel: (02) 983 67 77
This is the best budget choice in Sofia. A renovated town house, it has 16 rooms, each with something to recommend it, be it quirky decor or wall art. The attic room (Auckland) with its sloped ceilings and wooden beams is the best. €

Serdika
2 bul. Yanko Sakazov
Tel: (02) 846 54 85
www.serdikahotel.com
With many rooms overlooking the Vasili Levski monument, the Serdika is well located for sightseers. It's a spartan place, with no real frills, but the rooms are well-sized. €

Triada
5 ul. Venera
Tel: (02) 970 67 67
www.hoteltriada.com
On the road in from the airport this place is a quiet, relaxed option ideal for those with families and their own transport. A well equipped health centre is

one perk, while the mildly luxurious rooms will have you wondering why they do not cost a lot more. €

Lozenetz
23 ul. St. Naum,
Tel: (02) 965 44 44
www.lozenetzhotel.com
Strikingly modern in design this place overdoes it slightly with the garish decor, but the rooms are large and all have great little en suite bathrooms. €

Pop Bogomil
5 ul. Pop Bogomil
Tel: (02) 983 11 65
www.bulgariabedandbreakfast.com
A good attempt to create a real bed-and breakfast in the heart of Sofia. It is family-run and the rooms all have a personal touch (the wooden beds are great), and the breakfast is how it should be: hearty and served at any time you like. €

Red Bed and Breakfast
15 ul. Lyuben Karavelov
Tel: (02) 988 81 88
www.redbandb.com
If it wasn't for the small, high windows that can make some of the rooms feel more like prison cells, Red Bed and Breakfast would be the best budget option in Sofia. But if you want a budget option with a central location, it is worth checking out. €

AROUND SOFIA AND THE NORTHWEST

Belogradchik

Madona Inn
26 ul. Christo Botev.
Tel: (0936) 5546
www.madonahotel.belogradchik.info
This hotel is a long-established family-run business, which puts great emphasis on rural charm. It has tiny rooms with minuscule bathrooms, but they come at extremely cheap prices and offer great value for large groups and families. There is also good little *mehana* on site too, serving up hearty portions of authentic Bulgarian food. €

Berkovitsa

Salvia
8 ul. Hrizantema
Tel: (0953) 885 13
www.hotel-salvia.com
The Salvia is a wonderful hotel, offering bags of genuine character at every turn, from the superb wooden floors in the antique furniture in the common areas. The owners of this place have clearly gone the extra mile to make their guests feel welcome and at home. There's also a sauna, and an open fire in winter and summer barbecues are held in the courtyard. €€

Koprivshtitsa

Koprivshitsa Hotel
40 ul. G. Benkovski
Tel: (07184) 833 1441
www.panoramahotel.com
The views from the eight panoramic rooms in this stunning National Revival house are what brings people here, as well as the good food in the adjacent restaurant. The rooms are in fact disappointingly rather plain, though the bathrooms are grand. If you want a room with a view make sure you specify this when making your reservation. €

Private Homes
This is the perfect place to stay in a private house. Contact the tourist office (tel: 07184 2191). Accommodation with breakfast costs around 20 leva per person per night. Most hosts will prepare evening meals at extra cost.

SOUTHWEST, RILA AND PIRIN MOUNTAINS

Bansko

Kempinski Grand Arena
98 ul. Pirin
Tel/fax: (0749) 88888.
www.kempinski-bansko.com
It is right next to the main gondola lift, and the location could not be better. Set over five interconnected buildings, it blends in perfectly with its surroundings, one of few new build hotels in Bansko that actually does so. The spa and wellness centre, with a huge indoor pool, will keep non-skiers occupied.
€€€€

Belle Vue
14 ul. Vardar
Tel:/fax (0749) 864 47/8
Newly built apartments close to the gondola with one of the best spas in Bulgaria, featuring two saunas, two steam rooms, three massage rooms and a Jacuzzi. Even if you are not staying here you can use the facilities, for 30 leva per day. One- and two-bedroom apartments and studios available. €€€

Alpin
8 ul. Neofit Rilski
Tel: (0749) 880 75
www.alpin.bansko.bg
Opened in 1992, the Alpin was one the first private hotels to be built in Bulgaria after the fall of Communism. With its traditional architecture, and super location next to the Sv. Troitsa Church, it fits in well with the rest of historic Bansko. Some rooms are on the small side. €€

Chateau Vaptzarov
23 ul. Solun
Tel: (0749) 882 81
In Sofia (02) 963 0230
www.chateau-vaptzarov.hit.bg
If the stunning architecture of the chateau is not enough to convince you that you want to stay here, then the large, comfortable rooms, suites and great value duplex rooms doubtless will. There is also a large health complex offering sauna, steam bath, hot tub and massage. Daily transport to the gondola lift is included in the room price. €€

Martin
28 ul. Neofit Rilski
Tel: (0749) 883 01
www.hotel.martin@bansko.bg
Modern and luxurious rooms in a superb villa close to the centre of Bansko. Bathrooms have only showers, no bathtubs, but there is a huge Jacuzzi in the on-site healh spa. €€

Pirin
68 bul. Tsar Simeon
Tel: (0749) 880 51
www.hotelpirin.bansko.bg
This is a historic hotel close to Bansko's central square. It offers large and well decorated rooms and plenty of extras, including an indoor pool, fitness centre, sauna, and solarium, steam room, and *mehana*, it is a good choice for families. The well-kept garden is a real bonus. €€

Tanne
7 ul. Georgi Nastev
Tel: (0749) 881 00
www.hotel-tanne.com
Glorious bathrooms with marble trimmings and large tubs. The bedrooms are a good size too, but if you can afford it go for one of the split-level maisonettes. Other features include a great pool, and we can recommend the on-site *mehana*. €€

Vihren
55–57 ul. Pirin
Tel: (0749) 80 99
www.hotelvihren.com
Expect unfussy, good-value rooms, all of which are decorated with some style. All bathrooms have bathtubs, while the suite has a wonderful open fireplace. There is a sauna and Jacuzzi in the basement which can be used at extra cost. €€

Avalon
Tel: (0749) 883 99
www.avalon.bansko.bg
Great value villa owned and run by an English couple. You can expect simple but tastefully furnished rooms done out in local wood. Has good bathrooms, and there is a sauna and Jacuzzi in the basement. Can also arrange ski school and guiding. €

Bansko
17 ul. Glazne
Tel: (0749) 88055
www.hotelbansko.bansko.bg
One of the largest hotels in the resort. The rooms are large if rather garishly furnished, but the host of extras, such as the big indoor swimming pool, more than makes up for that. €

Bulgaria
2 ul. Hristo Matev
Tel: (0749) 88010
www.hotelbulgariabansko.com
Low-rise hotel used mostly by package-tour operators. Close to the gondola lift station, with indoor pool, Jacuzzi, games room, fitness centre, sauna, solarium and steam bath. Rooms are not the largest in the resort, and most have twin, not double beds, but they are brightly decorated and offer good value for money. €

Hadjipopova Kashta
3 ul. Tsar Boris III
Tel: (0749) 821 31
www.hadjipopov.bansko.bg
Gorgeous large rooms in a splendid villa in a quiet location a short distance from the centre of the resort. It is owned and operated by a local family who make everyone welcome, but especially families. Free transport to the ski lifts included. €

Ida
1 ul. Lazar Trenchev Str
Tel: (0744) 38227
www.idahotel-bansko.com
Simple, good value rooms in a quiet location on the edge of Bansko, a 10-minute walk from the centre. Extras include what may be the smallest pool in Bulgaria and great local cuisine cooked by the owner's wife. €

Karol
21 ul. Tsar Kalojan
Tel: (0749) 880 88
www.karol.bansko.bg
Set in an original, National Revival-era house, this is a delightful little hotel, where antique furniture and polished wooden floors contribute to the atmosphere. Huge rooms. €

Sveti Georgi Pobedonosets
18 ul. Hristo Botev
Tel: (0749) 882 75
www.svgeorgi.bansko.bg
Though the decor is less than tasteful, everything else is wonderful. From the neo-National Revival exterior to the open fire that makes the on-site *mehana* such a cosy place. Minutes from the resort centre, and tremendous value for money. €

Blagoevgrad

Ezeretz
2 bul. P. Iavorov
Tel: (073) 88 66 11
www.ezeretz.com
A superb spa resort with indoor and outdoor pools, Jacuzzi, sauna and a great restaurant. Worth paying the extra for the much larger luxurious-class rooms. €€

Borovets

Samokov
Tel (0750) 32306
www.samokov.com
This resort-within-a-resort was one of the first (1990) to be built in the Bulgarian mountains with private finance. It is situated at the foot of the Yastrabets gondola, and offers large rooms, most with great views. It also has a pool, a fitness centre, shops and a good restaurant. €€€

Villa Stresov

PRICE CATEGORIES
Approximate prices **per person** per night in a double room in high season:
€ = less than 25 leva
€€ = 25–50 leva
€€€ = 50–100 leva
€€€€ = more than 100 leva

Tel (02) 980 42 92
www.villatresov.com
A fairy-tale, Swiss-style 19th century chalet in the perfect mountain setting; you would never guess it was actually almost new. Rooms are luxurious, and there is a sauna, Jacuzzi and leafy garden. This is the best accommodation in Borovets, though it comes at a price. Note that bookings are made through the villa's Sofia office, or online through the villa's website. €€€

Rila
Tel (07128) 44 16
The Rila is one of Borovet's "all-in-one" hotels, built in the days when the Communist regime wanted to keep tourists in one place for the duration of their stay. It is impressive in size, has loads of extras (sauna, health centre, shops, etc) but the rooms are on the plain side and the bathrooms are tiny. A good choice for families with children, though, as staff are really friendly. €€

Yastrebets
Tel (089) 671 5923
www.yastrebets.com
The terrace in front of this hotel has sublime views up to the Moussala peak, and sitting at the foot of the piste is prime posing territory. The rooms above have equally great views, though are less plush than hotels in the resort. €

Kyustendil

Strimon Spa
24 ul. Tsar Simeon I
Tel: (078) 55 90 00
www.strimon-spaclub.com
Utter indulgence is the order of the day here, at this fantastic self-contained spa resort. Every health and beauty treatment you could wish for is on offer, and the bedrooms match the opulence of the spa. The split-level suites even have their own Jacuzzis. Note that spa treatments are not usually included in room prices, but the spa does offer weekend all-inclusive packages which are well worth investigating. €€

Malyovitsa

Malyovitsa
2020 Govedartsi
Tel/fax: (07125) 22 22
Completely renovated in 2006, the Malyovitsa is a good choice in this small ski resort. It is attractively situated amongst the pine trees, the smell of which wafts into the rooms. Though a little isolated, the hotel is close to the ski slopes and offers a good range of facilities, from a hairdresser to a babysitting service. The rooms are excellent, although the bathrooms are a little on the small side. €

Melnik

Despot Slav
Tel: (07437) 248
Fax: (07437) 271
If you decide to spend the night in this "village museum", this wonderful stone house, with original features, is the best place to stay. It is situated in the village centre, and offers 30 eccentrically furnished rooms, some with stained glass windows. The excellent restaurant serves a selection of wines matured in the cellars below the hotel. €

Panichishte

Enorgoremont Hotel
2650 Panichishte
Tel: (0707) 2200
www.hotelenergoremont.com
Situated up in Panichishte, the small ski resort above Sapareva Banya, this is a startling high-rise offering fantastic views across the mountains from the top-floor café and bar. Rooms are large though somewhat simply furnished, and there is a large indoor pool, sauna and gym.

Sandanski

Interhotel Sandanski
2800 Sandanski
Tel: (0746) 311 62/65
www.interhotelsandanski.com
Set at the top of the town, inside the huge park devoted to the healing waters of Sandanski's springs, this enormous place looks much like a cruise liner. Inside you'll find everything ship shape, from the large rooms to the terrific views from the upper floors. The hotel has a great spa and health complex, though most treatments and services come at extra cost. €€

Edia
7 ul. Lilianska
Tel: (0746) 323 00
www.edia.hit.bg
As an alternative to the monolithic Sandanski, this little place is ideal. Its setting, at the foot of one of the town's many hills, is glorious, making the outdoor swimming pool particularly inviting in high summer. The rooms are clean and bright, with good bathrooms. There is also a Jacuzzi, sauna and fitness centre. €

Sapareva Banya

Villa Popov
15 ul. Germanea
Tel: (0707) 20 66
Located just a short spurt from the geyser in the centre of the resort, this charming, unfussy little villa offers six rooms, all with bathrooms (not just showers) and positively welcomes both children and pets – a real rarity in these parts. €€

Velingrad

Park Hotel Olymp
bul. Tsar Samuil
4600 Velingrad
Tel: (0359) 561 00
www.olymp.velingrad.com
Another of Bulgaria's growing band of spa resorts, the Park Hotel Olymp offers all the usual spa treatments, as well as drinking cures involving waters from the local spring. The rooms are spacious if not brilliantly furnished, and there is a lovely restaurant – its summer terrace is one of the best in the country. €€

BELOW: village in the Pirin Mountains.

THE RHODOPES

Devin

Devin Spa
2 ul. Dryzhba
Tel: (03041) 24 98
www.spadevin.com
The Devin Spa is situated in the centre of Devin, and offers a wide range of health treatments, from electro-baths designed to alleviate the pains of rheumatism to anti-cellulite massage. Rooms could be better furnished, but they are spacious and have great bathrooms. €€

Ismena
41 ul. Goritsa
Tel: (03041) 48 72
www.ismena-hotel.com
This is a wonderful hotel, built in National Revival style with taste and elegance featuring throughout. As with most hotels in this spa town there are health options available, including a slimming programme to help you lose 15 kg (32 lb) in two weeks. The hotel also owns a two-bedroom, self-catering villa in a secluded location 5 km (3 miles) outside town, which can be rented for the night. €

Pamporovo

Orlovetz
Tel/fax: (03095) 8417
The newest hotel in Pamporovo, this giant five-star hotel is as luxurious as you could hope for, with enormous rooms and elegant furnishings. Best of all is the top-floor bar that must have some of the best views in the resort, if not the country. There is a free shuttle bus to the ski area. €€€

Pamporovo
Tel: (03095) 81 22/85 55
www.victoria-group.net
This is Pamporovo's best five-star hotel, and was once the best hotel in the Bulgarian mountains. It is still a great place, with huge comfortable rooms, and everything from an Irish pub and casino to a Turkish bath to offer its

guests. Views from every window in the hotel are superb, and prices – especially on week days – offer great value. The resort's new Orthodox Church is next door. €€€

Finlandia
Tel:/fax: (03095) 8374
www.hotelfinlandia.com
The Finlandia remains a good choice for those seeking large, stylish rooms at an affordable price. Smaller than many of the resort's hotels, it has a great atmosphere and the staff are the friendliest we have come across in Pamporovo. Good indoor swimming pool. €€

Malina Village
Tel/fax: (03021) 8388
These cosy, two-level chalets in a remote part of the resort offer a back-to-nature way to enjoy Pamporovo. Most chalets have an en suite sauna, and there is a restaurant in the village. Each chalet sleeps up to six people, the ground floor has a lounge with sofa bed, television and small kitchenette suitable for preparing snacks and baby milk. There are two loft-style twin bedrooms on the upper level. €€

Snezhanka
Tel: (03021) 83 16
This is a good-value hotel known for its huge pool (the largest in the resort) but somewhat small rooms. Bathrooms have showers but no tubs. The on-site sauna, Jacuzzi and massage services are all available at extra cost. €€

Markony
Tel: (0309) 585 31
www.markony.com
For those looking for something a bit different from the standard package-tour hotel, this little place is ideal. Its lovely rooms are all furnished with wood and wicker, and there is a personal touch in each one. The sauna and Jacuzzi are free of charge for guests, as is the outdoor pool in summer. There is also a riding centre attached, with lessons for beginners. €

Murgavets
Tel: (03095) 8310
www.murgavets-bg.com
A sleek high-rise, the Murgavets has been recently fully renovated and now offers comfortable rooms, all of which have en suite bathrooms with tubs and showers. It costs extra to use the indoor pool, with skylights that are often framed with snow in winter, but it is worth it. €

Plovdiv

Novotel Plovdiv
2 ul. Zlatyu Boyadzhiev
Tel: (032) 93 44 44
www.plovdivhotels.com
Situated on the northern bank of Maritsa River, and overlooking the slopes of the lovely Rhodope Mountains, this sparkling five-star is Plovdiv's best hotel. It is close to the trade-fair grounds and as a result often full during May and September. Reservations at these times of year are therefore essential. €€€

Trimontium Princess
2 ul. Kapitan Raicho
Tel: (032) 60 50 00
www.trimontium-princess.com
Even people who do not stay at this hotel will see it: the grand, classically designed hotel facade dominates pl. Tsentralen, and its legendary casino is a favourite with visiting businessmen. Rooms are enormous, although the furniture betrays the somewhat faded grandeur of the whole place. €€€

Dafi
23 ul. G. Benkovski
Tel: (032) 62 00 41
www.hoteldafi.com
In the heart of Plovdiv, close to the Roman Stadium and Ottoman Mosque, this new hotel offers grandly furnished rooms – some even have enormous circular beds – and great-value suites with Jacuzzis as standard. €€

Elite
53 ul. Raiko Daskalov
Tel/fax: (032) 624 537
The Elite was first opened a

decade or so ago in a renovated National Revival-era house dating from 1871. The building is listed as a national heritage monument, though inside it offers all the mod cons you would expect in a modern three-star hotel. €€

Hebros
51A ul. Konstantin Stoilov
Tel: (032) 26 01 80
www.hebros-hotel.com
Another of Plovdiv's National Revival gems, with interiors that match the stunning facade. It is furnished with antiques and the rooms are decorated in period style – which may be a little over the top for some. €€

Bulgaria
13 bul. Evtimil
Tel: (032) 63 35 99
www.hotelbulgaria.net
Plush, historic hotel in the heart of Plovdiv, inside an ugly concrete box exterior. Rooms are large but fall short of being luxurious. There is also a casino and a trendy terrace café. €

BW Royal Plovdiv
6 ul. Belgrad
www.bestwestern.com
This is a modern place in the centre of the city, on the northern bank of the Maritsa River. A cut above most Best Westerns, it has large rooms with great bathrooms. Breakfast is a terrific buffet spread, but costs extra. €

TRANSPORT

ACCOMMODATION

ACTIVITIES

A – Z

LANGUAGE

ABOVE: a balcony in Plovdiv.

Imperial
1A ul. Arch. K. Petkov
Tel: (032) 600 730
www.plovdivhotels.com
Situated in a quiet part of the lower city, the Imperial is all concrete ugliness on the outside and does not make a terrific first impression. However, it does offer excellent value for money as well as large comfortable rooms. The service can be a bit on the surly side, but for the location and room size you will do no better in Plovdiv at these bargain prices. €

Noviz
55 bul. Ruski
Tel: (032) 63 12 81
hotel.noviz.com
Small but reasonably smart – if old fashioned – four-star opposite Budjarnik Park. All bathrooms have a tub: a plus in this part of the world, and prices include a good breakfast in the hotel's quite reasonable restaurant. €

THE BALKAN RANGE

Arbanassi

Arbanassi Palace
Tel. (062) 630 176
www.arbanassipalace.bg
The sweeping views over the surrounding countryside and large terrace bar are the highlights of this large, concrete building with dated interior, but full range of facilities, including a spa centre, a tennis court. It is the top hotel in the village. €€€€

Hotel Arbanassi
Tel: (062) 650 149
The Arbanassi is a traditional and intimate hotel in a delightful building. Offers tours. Summer garden and barbecue. €€

Bacho Kiro

Strinava Camping
Tel: (0676) 2332
Beds in simple wooden bungalows with shared bathrooms and camp site (seasonal) in a pretty location. €

Dryanovo

Dryanovo Hotel
Dryanovo Monastery
Tel: (0676) 2314
Good rooms, many with enormous balconies overlooking the monastery courtyard in a relaxing, riverside spot. Not to be confused with the hotel/restaurant across the river. €

Gabrovo

Balkan
14 ul Emil Manolov.
Tel: (066) 23474
Modern and somewhat anonymous, but central and well-established. €€

Kilifarevo

Kilifarevo Monastery
Tel: (06114) 2480
Suitably monastic quarters. The more expensive rooms have bathrooms. An unusual, atmospheric choice. Book ahead. €

Lovech

Hotel Tsariana
Tel: (068) 600995
www.tsariana.com
Well-run medium-sized hotel in central location. Recently renovated. €€

Sliven

Imperia
Tel: (044) 66 75 99
www.imperia.sliven.net
Luxury hotel, a 10-minute drive out of town, with all facilities from tennis courts and swimming pool to bar and disco. €€€€

Stara Zagora

Ezeroto
60 Bratia Jekovi
Tel: (042) 600 103
In a peaceful park overlooking a lake with bar, room service, laundry and business services. €€

Forum
94 ul Hadji Dimitar Asenov
Tel: (042) 631 616
This modern hotel markets itself as a boutique hotel, but really is a mid-sized operation with recently renovated rooms and a decent restaurant. €€

Uniqato
36 Sava Silov
Tel: (042) 661 155
www.uniqato.com
Small, mid-range business hotel with internet access in all rooms, good restaurant and parking. €€

Troyan

Troyan Plaza
54 P.R. Slaveykov
Tel: (0670) 64399
www.troyanplaza.com
Large four-star hotel with a range of rooms. Full spa including massage, restaurant and tavern.

Tryavna

Ralista
16a ul. Kaletok
Tel: (0677) 2262
Charming, well-priced hotel; many rooms with large balconies overlooking the town. Outdoor pool, sauna (extra fee), massage and shooting gallery. €€

Tryavna Hotel
46 Angel Kanchev
Tel: (0677) 3448
www.tryavna.bg
This modern three star close to the old part of town is popular with tour groups. There is a small

gym. 38 double rooms, 10 singles and 5 apartments, all with mini bar. €€€

Veliko Tarnovo

Grand Hotel Yantra
Tel: (062) 600 607
2 ul. Opalchenska
www.yantrabg.com
This newly renovated four-star is the best of the large hotels in the town, with great views, spa, restaurant and bar with real fire. Enjoy coffee and cake in the Viennese tea-room. €€€

Premier Hotel Complex
Tel: (062) 615 555
1 ul. Sava Penev
www.hotelpremier-bg.com
Comfortable hotel with spacious rooms and four-star facilities including sauna and pool.

Comfort
5 ul Paneyot Tipografov
Tel: (062) 628 728
Clean rooms – most with balconies with wonderful views over the fortress – make this a eal bargain although owners can be unfriendly. Breakfast is not included in the charge but can be arranged. €

THE DANUBIAN PLAIN

Pleven

Balkan
85 bul. Rousse
Tel: (064) 803 700,
www.hotelbalkan.com
Large, with basic rooms
and apartments 2 km (1
mile) east of the centre. €€

Interrostov
2 ul Osvobojdenie
Tel: (064) 801 095
Large, modern block, but
with lots of facilities. In
centre of town and better
value than the Balkan. €€

Rousse

Danube Plaza
5 pl. Svoboda
Tel: (082) 822 950
www.danubeplaza.com
Conveniently located on the
main square. Offers a
higher standard than most

of the other hotels in the
city. Several restaurants
plus room service. €€

Splendid Hotel
51 ul Alexandrovska
Tel: (082) 825 970
www.splendid.rousse.bg
Functional, with restaurant
and bar. Ten percent
discount is offered for
weekend bookings. €€€

Shumen

Bohemi
20 ul. Izvorna, Divdiadovo
Tel: (054) 828 110
www.bohemi.net
Large, modern hotel with
many amenities in a village
4km (2½ miles) west of
Shumen. Special offers
sometimes available.

Shumen
1 pl. Oborishte
Tel: (054) 879 141

Large, modern hotel with
Internet, pool and massage
service. The rooms on the
upper floors are the best. €€

Zamaka
17 ul. Vasil Levski
Tel: (054) 800 409
City centre three-star hotel.
Comfortable, with a
restaurant and a garden. €

Svishtov

Dunav
2 ul. Tzar Osvoboditel
Tel: (0631) 22361
www.hoteldunav.com
Located on the main
square. Nothing special, but
has decent restaurant. €€

Rest House Kaleto
2 ul. Toma Panteleev
Tel: (0631) 23247
In Kaleto Park with views of
the Danube. Has restaurant,
bar and coffee shop. €€

Vidin

Bononia
ul. Baba Vida
Tel: (094) 606031
Lots of facilities, plus a
good location next to
riverside park. €€

Ninov
28 ul. Dunavska
Tel: (094) 37360
A business-oriented hotel
on the river with good
standards of service and
cleanliness throughout. €€

NORTHERN BLACK SEA COAST

Albena

Diana
Albena Villa Zone
Tel: (0579) 64232
www.diana-hotelbg.com
Completed as part of an
environmental programme
to ensure Bulgarian
accession to the EU, the
Diana is a family operation
with six apartments and
eight double rooms on the
main road behind the
beach. €€€€

Balchik

Mistral
8B ul. Primorska
Tel: (0579) 71130
www.hotelmistralbg.com
A plush new hotel in a
perfect position overlooking
the marina. Most rooms
have large balconies with
sea views; spacious
apartments are also
available. €€

White House
18 ul Geo Milev
Tel: (0579) 73951
Intimate hotel in central
location. Mostly small
rooms with balconies and
sea glimpses. €€

Dobrudzha

Albena
Tel: (0579) 620 20
There are panoramic views
from many of the rooms
and the restaurants on the
top floors of this high-rise
hotel. All mod cons
including internet and
medicinal spa are provided
by this four star in the
heart of the resort. €€

Golden Sands

Helios Spa and Resort
Tel (052) 356 108
www.helios-spa.com
Set back from the beach
surrounded by forest.
Spacious, with a range of
rooms, many with large
balcony; pools, tennis
court and state-of-the-art
spa. €€

**Kempinski Hotel Grand
Hermitage**
1 Kempinski Alley
Tel: (052) 333 888
www.kempinski-varna.com
Splendid location and
wonderfully luxurious. Great
rooms, spa and service.
Several restaurants and
bars. €€€

Krapets

Yanitza
Tel: (057) 49324
www.yanitza-hotels.com.
This mid-size hotel opened
in 2000 and has been run
by a local couple with love
ever since. It's right on the
beach and there is a pool,
garden and terrace. €€

Villa Kibela
Tel/fax: (02) 718 878 (booking
office in Sofia)
www.villakibela.com
A hacienda-style villa with
seven rooms, flower
garden, pool and sauna. A
vegetable garden provides
produce for the hotel
restaurant. €€

Riviera

Imperial
Tel: (052) 386 811
www.rivierabulgaria.com
Five-star luxury, although
dated decor. Lovely location
and fascinating history. €€€

Riviera Beach
Tel: (052) 386 815
www.rivierabulgaria.com
A new five-star addition to
the Riveria offering modern
rooms – all with balconies

and sea views. Families will
feel particularly at home,
with a pool, sports facilities
and restaurants all on site.
sss

Oasis
Tel: (052) 38 69
www.rivierabulgaria.com
This 50-year-old classy
hotel would not be out of
place in the south of
France. There are plans to
turn it into a luxury
boutique hotel. €€

PRICE CATEGORIES

Approximate prices **per
person** per night in a
double room in high
season:

€ = less than 25 leva
€€ = 25–50 leva
€€€ = 50–100 leva
€€€€ = more than 100 leva

ABOVE: a typical resort hotel in Varna.

Sv Konstantin

Grand Hotel Varna
Tel: (052) 362 831
www.grandcasinovarna.bg
This 300-room hotel dominates the beach at Sv Konstantin, a 10-minute drive from Varna. Rooms are comfortable and luxurious facilities include indoor and outdoor pools, a spa, football field

and casino. The beach is a short walk away . €€€

Varna

Capitol
40 ul. Petko Karavelov
Tel: (052) 688 000
www.capitol.bg
Classy hotel with large stylish rooms and a splendid restaurant in a location close to the

entrance of the municipal beach. €€€
Musala Palace Hotel
3 ul. Musala
Tel: (52) 664100
www.musalapalace.bg
Luxurious and historic, this hotel was built over a century ago, but recently renovated. Just 24 rooms, plus bar and spa. €€€
Odessos
1 bul. Slivnitsa
Tel: (052) 608185
Enormous hotel on the

seafront, at the entrance to the sea gardens. Most rooms have great sea views. A little rundown these days and perhaps overpriced, but the location cannot be bettered. €€€
Antik
10 ul. Ohriad
Tel (052) 632 167
A smart little family-run hotel offering great value rooms, all with small en-suite bathrooms. Close to the centre and station. €€
More
33 bul. Slivnitza
Tel: (052) 232 115
Good-value high-rise in central location next to the sea gardens. Functional, but decent. €€
Reverence
58 bul. Osmi Primorski Polk
Tel: (052) 631 831
www.reverence.bg.com
This is a small and welcoming hotel on main boulevard. Trendy terrace bistro attracts a fashionable crowd for drinks and or dinner. €

SOUTHERN BLACK SEA COAST

Bourgas

Bulgaria
21 ul. Alexanderovska
Tel: (056) 842 610
www.bulgaria-hotel.com
Large, mostly business hotel, with a range of rooms and three suites. Rather dated decor, but pool and casino are among the various facilities. €€€
Plaza
42 ul. Bogoridi
Tel: (056) 846 294
www.plazahotel-bg.com
Smart new hotel in turn-of-the-century building on main boulevard. Spacious rooms, most with balconies. Disappointing breakfast but pleasant café open 7am–midnight. €€€

Chernomorets

Sezoni Yug Guesthouse
Tel: (056) 841 703
26 ul. Morska
Simple but comfortable family-run establishment.

Dyuni

Marina Hotel
Dyuni Holiday Village
Tel: 905514) 2347
All rooms with balcony, most overlooking the sea. €€

Elenite

Royal Bay Elenite Holiday Resort
Tel (0554) 68 940
www.victoria-group.net
A modern hotel with plenty of family rooms, and most with a sea view, right on the beach with sports, spa and children's club. Let down by its mediocre food which is offered on an all-inclusive basis. €€

Nessebar

Marina Palace
7 ul. Ivan Vazov
Tel: (0554) 20 600
www.marinapalacebg.com
Large, well-appointed, with spa. In good location in the new part of town. €€€

Aquamarin
3 ul. Krajbrezna
Tel: (0554) 43360
Lovely little hotel on the northern tip of Old Nessebar. Rooms are fairly basic but the views out towards Sunny Beach are excellent. Great seafood restaurant too. €€
Bora
7 ul Slaviansaka
Tel: (0554) 42225
Small, family-run hotel and restaurant in the centre of the Nessebar Peninsula, next to the only working church in the old town. Luxuriously furnished rooms are often booked up in high summer, so it is best to reserve well in advance. €€
Mistral
ul. Khan Krum
Tel: (0554) 7741
This is a modern, medium-sized hotel in the newer part of Nessebar, a five-minutes walk from the town's main beach. The

rooms are airy and well-sized. There is an on-site sports centre with Jacuzzi, hydromassage and sauna.
Monte Kristo
5 ul. Venera
Tel: (0544) 42055
In the heart of old Nessebar, this small, family-run establishment is one of the best hotels on the coast. Excellent restaurant too. €€
The White House
2 ul. Tsar Simeon
Tel: (0554) 42488
www.white-house-13.8k.com
Small, family-run hotel, with four rooms and four apartments and a roof terrace. €€

Pomorie

St George Hotel and Spa
15 bul. Yavorov
Tel: (0596) 24411
www.st-george-bg.com
New, with both a rooftop and a piano bar, plus spa. The "exclusive" rooms have internet, sea views and bath. €€€

Sozopol

Hotel Selena
7 ul. Yani Popov
Tel: (0550) 25200
www.hotelselena-bg.com
Friendly mid-range option, in the heart of the old town, overlooking the sea. Restaurant and swimming pool. €€
Lozite
Hamanite Beach
Tel: (0550) 23718
www.lozite.com
This is a small and friendly hotel; most rooms have balconies and sea views and all with air-conditioning. Pleasant terrace restaurant for breakfast and snacks. €€
Santa Marina
Head office:
Cherni Vruh 51B, Sofia
Tel: (02) 819 9193
www.santamarina.bg
New, swish holiday village

with 20 villas and several hundred apartments, in a quiet location on a hill 2 km (1 mile) from Sozopol. A pool, bar, restaurant and wellness centre are all part of the complex. €€€

St Vlas/Sv Vlas

Laguna
1 ul. Odessa
Tel: (0554) 68790/68791
Choose from 18 four-star apartment complexes next to the marina and beach, with swimming pools and restaurants. €€
Sky Hotel
h.e. Rousalka
Tel: (0554) 689 653
email: sky_hotel@hotmail.com
€€
This is a stylish boutique hotel; all the rooms have balconies with lovely sea views. There is also a restaurant and bar plus a lovely pool area.

Sinemoretz

Villa Fanny
Tel: (0887) 567 165
www.villafanny.com
Bright simple rooms, studios and one apartment; all with air-conditioning and minibar at this friendly place with a garden. The villa, run

by Fanny, is situated close to the beach and open all year round. €€
Villa Sinemoretz
Tel: (0550) 66 106
A six-roomed American-run "inn" with good sea views courtyard and café. A simple operation, but very clean. Tours can be arranged. €€

Strandzha

National Park Office
Malko Tarnovo
Tel: (0359) 595 2229.
The administrative centre for the national park can arrange simple accommodation in private houses. €
IRT Holidays
www.strandjavillage.com
This company offers characterful accommodation in houses in three villages in the Strandzha, with an online reservation facility. €€€€

Sunny Beach

Chaika Beach
Tel: (0554) 28 500/28 504
www.victoria-group.net/
This modern hotel in a prime beach-front location is one of the largest on the coast. The pools can get crowded and the service is often not up to

five stars, although it does include 24-hour room service €€€
RIU Helena Resort
Helena Park
Tel: (0554) 200 20
www.helenaresort.com
The resort includes the enormous Helena Park and Helena Sands, both five- star hotels, with hundreds of rooms, and five luxury villas. All facilities. €€€
Sunny Twins
Tel: (0544) 23545
Pleasant, medium-sized hotel in the villa zone. Some rooms have balcony. Nice pool.
Apartments
The resort has many apartments and villas that can be rented – usually for a minimum of a week but sometimes for shorter periods Most include maid service (not necessarily on a daily basis) and cooking facilities. €€

PRICE CATEGORIES

Approximate prices **per person** per night in a double room in high season:
€ = less than 50 leva
€€ = 50–100 leva
€€€ = 100–200 leva
€€€€ = more than 200 leva

BELOW: late afternoon in Nessebar.

TRANSPORT
ACCOMMODATION
ACTIVITIES
A – Z
LANGUAGE

A CTIVITIES

FESTIVALS, THE ARTS, NIGHTLIFE, SHOPPING AND SPECTATOR SPORTS

THE ARTS

Music and Theatre

Thanks to consistent investment during the days of Communism, most of Bulgaria's larger towns and cities have at least one theatre and many have ballet and opera companies. However, the current state of the economy has meant that art subsidies have suffered and some smaller local companies have been forced to close down.

Sofia, Varna and Plovdiv are the best places to see cultural performances.Often, trips to see arts performances are arranged as excursions (which includes transport) by major holiday companies. Look out for signs on the notice boards in the

BELOW: the National Theatre, Sofia.

receptions of major hotels. Local tourist offices may also be able to advise on where to buy tickets. Most theatres close down completely during July and August.

Music Festivals

Various musical festivals occur throughout the country. Varna Summer festival in June *(www.varnasummerfest.org; see under Varna, page 226)*, in particular, has an impressive programme of international classical concerts. Rousse has a March Music Days International Festival in late March; Sofia sees the Jazz Peak festival at around the same time, as well as the Sofia Music Days at the end of May. Bansko puts on the International Jazz Festival in August, and down south in Sozopol there is the August Apollonia Arts Festival, with a wide range of

musical acts. Most of the major festivals have their own websites, with information on where to purchase tickets.

Opera

The Sofia National Opera is the country's most famous opera, though the standard of performances depends on the singers on stage on any particular night. There are also opera houses in Blagoevgrad, Vana and Plovdiv. The country's best performers congregate in Plovdiv in the summer when they perform at the amphitheatre.

Museums and Galleries

Bulgaria's interesting history is well represented by its museums, which can be found throughout the country, along with local and regional art galleries. Part of the reason for this is the long tradition of trying to give Bulgarians knowledge and a sense of pride about their culture. Unfortunately, this means that in some cases, information is only provided in Bulgarian, and not in English, although this is changing, particularly in tourist areas. Most towns and cities have a local

Museum Opening Hours

The opening hours of galleries and museums are often frustratingly erratic. Even when an establishment advertises daily hours of 9am to 5pm, for example, these are not necessarily adhered to. When opening hours really cannot be . relied upon, this information has been given in the text. Many museums close for lunch.

museum, and may also have an archaeological museum. Visitors travelling around the country may also notice the large number of ethnographic museums, often housed in historical homes. Displays typically include traditional clothing, craft tools and domestic objects.

NIGHTLIFE

Restaurants often put on live music for free, although band members will usually ask for a tip. Clubs and bars with live music often charge a small entry fee. Predictably, most entertainment geared to tourists is to be found in the major tourist resorts – along the Black Sea and in the ski centres. It is worth bearing in mind that private enterprise in Bulgaria is still very much in its infancy; a fact reflected by the type of entertainment on offer. Don't expect the latest dance music or sophisticated jazz venues; what is big here is café culture and folk music, although techno clubs and Irish bars are increasingly popular.

CHILDREN'S ACTIVITIES

Bulgaria is generally child-friendly. Locals are likely to welcome children, whatever their ages, and there are plenty of activities to keep them entertained. The more developed resorts will have a few hotels with dedicated kids' clubs, as well as fair ground rides and electronic games. Rural Bulgaria can also be a good choice for families with children. Consider staying on a working farm and learning about traditional ways of life that have died out in many parts of Europe (see Rural Life pages 51–5).

Water Parks

On the coast, water parks with slides and waterfalls are a big attraction, appealing to everyone from small children to adults. They are often situated just outside the main hotel and apartment areas and therefore operate a free shuttle-bus pick-up from the resorts. Aquapolis just north of Golden Sands, has a climbing wall and shooting range specifically for children.

The three main water parks are:
Aqua Paradise
Nessebar
www.aquaparadise-bg.com
Twenty different kinds of water attractions.

ABOVE: there are several waterparks on the Black Sea coast.

Action Aquapark
Sunny Beach. www.aquapark.bg
Aquapolis
Between Golden Sands and Albena. www.aquapolis.net

Other Amusements

East of Action Aquapark in Sunny Beach, on the main Bourgas to Varna road, is a **go-karting** track (tel: 899 907 998; www.varnakarting.com). Further up the coast, Albena is a water-sports centre for adults, but has plenty to keep children entertained too, including a **mini-train**, **trampolines** and a children's **amusement park**.

Skiing

All of the major ski resorts have children's clubs, which cater for toddlers right through to teenagers, whether they have skied before or not. It is best to make enquiries and bookings before leaving home, as they tend to become booked up quickly during the season. Bansko also offers non-slope activities,such as **ice-skating** and **sleigh rides**.

SHOPPING

Many visitors to the country report that shopping in Bulgaria is one of its highlights. Almost all goods are competitively priced when compared to those at home and the choice is wide. Crafts, clothes and fake

Main Festivals

New Year's Eve/1 January.
Kukeri Festival This dramatic festival is celebrated in many towns and villages, but Pernik and Dupnitsa have particularly large and lively celebrations. Young men wearing costumes made of goat or sheep hides, dripping with bells, and brightly coloured masks, representing goats, bulls or rams, perform ancient dances to mark the beginning of spring and drive away evil spirits.
Beginning February. St Trifon Zarezan. Dedicated to the patron saint of wine, this ancient festival dates back to Thracian times. Celebrations, which are restricted to men, involve vine pruning, pouring and of course drinking. The vintner who has produced the largest quantity is crowned "king".
28 Feburary. Horse Easter A festival for fertility in rural areas. Young men compete in horse races to win the attention of young women, and women bake bread in the shape of horseshoes to give to new brides and horses in the hope of maximising fertility.
1 March. Granny Marta's Day Celebrates the beginning of spring, when people give each other martenitzi, little red and white tassels that they wear to bring health and happiness.
6 May. St George's Day This is an important church holiday in the Bulgarian Orthodox calendar. Traditionally, an icon of St George, the patron saint of farming and shepherds, is richly decorated, and many Bulgarian households sacrifice a lamb in his honour.
First weekend in June. The Festival of Roses Celebrated in Kazanlak, in the Balkan Mountains. Festivities include a beauty contest to find the "Queen of the Roses" as well as circus acts, dancing and general festivities.
4 June, or nearest weekend. Fire dancing in the Strandzha, on the Southern Black Sea coast.
8–13 August International Jazz Festival in Bansko.
September. International Folk Festival. Sandanski in the Pirin Mountains holds one of the top folk music and dance festivals in the country.
Mid-September Apollonia arts festival in Sozopol

TRANSPORT

ACCOMMODATION

ACTIVITIES

A – Z

LANGUAGE

Counterfeit

Counterfeit items, particularly designer sunglasses and DVDs can be found almost everywhere. While they may be a bargain, do bear in mind that the quality is likely to be very low, and when you get your film or accessory home it may turn out to not work or fall apart. The availability of such goods may change now Bulgaria has joined the EU. Copies of antique icons can be bought cheaply; just don't be fobbed off that you are buying the real deal. Those seeking authentic icons should only buy from a professional dealer.

designer goods such as clothes and sunglasses are particularly popular buys. Small, family-owned shops abound, particularly in tourist areas. Thankfully Western-style shopping centres are rare, with the country's first mall only opening in the capital in 2006. That said, do pay a visit to TZUM department store if you are in Sofia. Formerly state-run and selling very little, it is now a temple to international brand names.

Markets provide food and clothes at bargain prices, and some sell souvenirs. Good buys include rakia (a local firewater similar to schapps), pottery, glass ware and textiles (woollen rugs, cotton kilims, tablecloths, lace and embroidery).

Tax

VAT in Bulgaria is 20 percent. Tax-free shopping for EU citizens is no longer possible now that Bulgaria is a member of the EU.

What to Buy

Icons and Woodcarvings

Reproductions of Orthodox iconography and woodcarvings can be bought all over the county, with the best quality being found in Sofia in the art market outside the Aleksander Nevski Cathedral. However if you are after genuine antique icons, as opposed to reproductions, contact a professional art dealer. Exporting antiques is a difficult process and best left to a dealer to organise. There are a number of galleries is Sofia, clustered around the Radisson Hotel.

Embroidery, Lace and Textiles

Visitors to Bulgaria are often struck by the attractive brightly coloured textiles. The best places to buy these are Koprivshtitsa and Chiprovtsi. The latter has long been famous for its rugs and kilims, usually in reds, black, cream, brown and blue in bold geometric designs.

Varna is one of the best places to buy lace, especially around the Cathedral of the Virgin Mary.

Pottery

Bulgaria was once known for its fine pottery. The industry has largely died out but a few centres of excellence

remain such as Etura near Gabrovo (see page 201). Another place to find it is Veliko Tarnovo (see page 194).

War and Soviet Memorabilia

Old Soviet-style posters, statuettes, medals, uniforms, etc can be found in flea markets. One of the best places to look is the flea market outside the Alexander Nevski Cathedral in Sofia, but watch out for reproductions.

Where to Shop

Sofia
Bulevard Vitosha is the country's top shopping street. For souvenirs, try the second floor of the TZUM department store. Bulevard Graf Ignatiev is a good place to buy second-hand books and counterfeit CDs and DVDs. For atmospheric markets visit the Halite grocery market and the Zhenski Pazar (Women's Market), ulitsa Pirotska.
Plovdiv
The pedestrianised bulevard Aleksander I is the main shopping thoroughfare. Ulitsa Raichio, on the southern side of ploschad Tsentralen, is a good source of counterfeit clothes and accessories.
Varna
The shopping here is more upmarket than elsewhere in Bulgaria. Bulevard Knyaz Boris I, from ploschad Nezavisimost to bulevard Tsar Osvoboditel, has the best shops in Bulgaria, including designer boutiques. Lace and embroidery are sold outside the cathedral.

BELOW: picking through the bric-a-brac outside Alexander Nevski Cathedral, Sofia.

TRANSPORT

ABOVE: cycling is a great way to see the countryside.

SPORT AND OUTDOOR ACTIVITIES

Bulgaria's variety of landscapes makes the country a playground for all kinds of sport and adventure activities. Its long coastline, studded with marinas, offers sailing and surfing while pristine rivers cutting through the interior are ideal for rafting and canoeing trips. Rolling hills, meadows and great swathes of forest are a haven for wildlife. Native bears and other animals roam the interior where colourful wild flowers, birds and butterflies can be seen.

Snowcapped mountains provide a scenic backdrop for hiking and skiing, two activities that are, along with golf, growing in popularity, with new facilities opening all the time. The winter ski season usually runs from December to March, and sometimes longer, with snow walks and climbing also possible.

Canoeing, Kayaking and Rafting

Spring, when the mountain snows have melted and the rivers are augmented by the meltwater, is the best time for white-water rafting. The best areas for the sport are the Balkan, Pirin and Rhodope mountains, with the Arda and Ossam rivers providing the most exciting conditions. The languid waters of the Danube provide for more sedate activities, as do the lakes in the Rhodopes. Sea kayaking along the Black Sea coast is another possibility.

Kayak Safaris
www.kajak.dir.bg
Specialises in sea and white-water kayaking holidays, with short course available for the inexperienced.

Caving

There are approximately 5,000 caves in Bulgaria, many of them of historical and geographical interest, and some with ancient cave paintings. The website www.avalon.net/~vreloto/caving can provide contacts for local caving organisations as well as details of caving sites with maps.

Adventure Tour Companies

Alexander Tour
44 Pop Bogomil
Sofia 1202
Tel/Fax: 02-983-33-22,
983-23-71, 983-30-90, 983-55-68
www.alexandertour.com
This long established company specialises in activity holidays such as riding, biking and sailing, and offers a range of tours around the whole country, tailor-made options and cultural tours.
Odysseia In
20V bul. Aleksandar Stamboliiski
1301 Sofia
Tel: 02-9890538
www.odysseia-in.com
This leading Bulgarian operator has run adventure tours for over 15 years. Offers a range of active holidays, including cycling, hiking, mountaineering, kayaking, paragliding, caving, climbing, etc. It also arranges heritage and monastery tours, wine and gourmet

Insurance

If considering one of the more adventurous activities mentioned here, it is well worth taking out specialised insurance as accidents do happen. Personal liability cover should also be included. When skiing, look for a policy that includes mountain rescue and air-ambulance and covers off-piste skiing and piste closure.

Climbing

Bulgaria forms part of the Alpine-Himalayan mountain range and therefore has a lot of geological variations. Its two Alpine mountain ranges are Rila and Pirin, both reaching more than 2,900 metres (9,500 ft) above sea level, making these popular for climbing, along with the Stara Planina.

Within the Rila mountain range, Mussala has the highest peak at 2925 metres (9,500 ft) above sea level. It has more than 100 climbing routes, most of them in the Maljovitsa Ridge (Granite Paradise) some 90 km (56 miles) from Sofia, where the Alpine and Mountaineering School is based.

At lower altitudes, climbers can enjoy a backdrop of plunging gorges, clear lakes and fish-filled rivers. The website www.climbingguidebg.com is a comprehensive online guide to

trips and nature tours from bird to bear-watching. It offers environmentally sustainable trips by aiming to put money into local communities and at the same time minimise the impact on local life. Its office in Sofia has a good selection of maps and walking guidebooks.
Penguin Travel
Tel: 02-400 1050
www.penguin.bg
The Bulgarian branch of a well-established Danish operator that works with conservation projects. Choose from bird-watching, hiking, trekking, skiing and horse-riding tours.
Moto Roads
Dimitar Ivakiov, Sofia
www.motoroads.com
Offers an enormous range of activity holidays such as hang-gliding, paragliding, biking, skiing, hiking, climbing and rafting.

ACCOMMODATION

ACTIVITIES

A – Z

LANGUAGE

climbing in Bulgaria, detailing sites, maps, events, mountaineering shops, etc.

Cycling

With its quiet roads and lovely landscapes, Bulgaria is ideal for a cycling trip. Indeed, in some areas you are more likely to find yourself travelling alongside carts and animal herds than cars. As with driving, the main difficulty you will come across is trying to read road signs in Cyrllic, so get a map that details both.

In the small towns of Tryavna, Gabrovo, Apriltzi, Trojan and Teteven in the Balkan Ranges, marked cycling routes have been established as part of the "Way of the Sun" tourism project. Each is graded for difficulty and duration and may take in historical or cultural attractions or beauty spots. The local tourist offices rent bicycles, sell maps, and can provide local guides. For those who fancy a longer trip, www.cyclingbulgaria.com offers a variety of tours.

Diving

Bulgaria is relatively new to diving, although it is being developed all the time. Prime diving spots along the Black Sea coast are Kavarna, Nessebar, Varna and Sozopol, most of which are accessible from the shore or by small boats. The coastline is home to numerous shipwrecks; of note is the spectacular submerged ancient port near Varna.

Diving conditions are generally good in Bulgaria's temperate waters, although visibility can sometimes be poor. The ideal time of year for a trip is the summer because of warmer air and sea temperature.

Useful websites
www.dive-centers.net
Gives details of regional diving centres.
www.diving-bg.com
Has a range of diving trips, exploring shipwrecks and caves, including som that are suitable for children.

Golf

Bulgaria has three golf courses. Two of these – at Ihtiman, 40 km (25 miles) from Sofia and at Sliven, 90 km (56 miles) from the Black Sea, which opened in 2000 and 2004 respectively – are owned by Air Sofia. The third is the modern St Sofia Golf Club & Spa, 15 minutes from Sofia in the village of Ravno Pole. New courses are due to open at Ragrad in the northeast of the country, Kavarna on the Northern Black Sea coast and at Primorsko near Sozopol.
www.golf.bg has details of Bulgarian golf facilities.

Golf Club Ihtiman
Ihtiman
6 ul. Septemvri
Sofia

Tel: (02) 981 09 25
18-hole course with hotel and country club offering diversions for non-golfers, such as horse riding, tennis, football and swimming. The par 71.3 course also includes two putting greens. Coaching is available.
Sliven Golf Course
Sliven
Tel: (02) 981 0925
The country's largest golf course, Sliven is an 18-hole course with lovely views across the Balkan mountains.
St Sofia Golf Club & Spa
Elin Pelin Municipality
Ravno Pole
Tel: (0725) 68888
www.stsofiagolf.com
The first officially rated golf course in Bulgaria, St. Sofia's impressive facilities include an 18-hole course, putting green and teaching academy. The well-maintained 6,175-metre/yd course welcomes golfers of all abilities.

Hiking

Bulgaria has a long hiking tradition and new centres and trails are always being developed. The country offers some of the best walking in the world, from winter snowshoeing in the mountains to summer hikes through riverside meadows and forests. The Pirin, Rila and Rhodope mountains are the three main areas (also see page 134 for hiking in the

BELOW: Bulgaria has has a long equestrian tradition, and you will frequently see horses pulling carts or being ridden.

Hiking Holidays

Bulgarian companies

www.bghike.com
This recommended Bulgarian company that will tailor-make either a guided or self-guided walking tour, using local accommodation in the Pirin, Rila and Rhodopes mountains.

UK based Companies

Exodus
www.exodus.co.uk
Tel: (0870) 950 0039
All grades of hiking plus snowshoeing.
The Ramblers Association
www.ramblers.holidays.co.uk
Tel: (0170) 733 1133
Offers a mountains and monasteries walking tour which

combines sightseeing with hiking in moderate terrain. Four nights are spent in the Rila Mountains, six nights at Bansko in the Pirin Mountains and four nights in the hills outside Sofia.
www.responsibletravel.com
Tel: (01273) 600030
This ecotourism company organises walking and wildlife-watching tours. It donates a percentage of its profits to local, ongoing conservation programmes.
Easyways
Tel: (01324) 714132
www.easyways.com
Based in Velko Tarnovo and organises day walks to surrounding villages

Rila). Coupled with staying in local inns or private homes, hiking can provide a real taste of rural life.

There are thousands of kilometres of marked trails, using the European standard of red, blue, green, yellow and white trails. In snowy conditions, yellow and black markers are used to show the safest route. This means that it is possible to go it alone, although it is advisable to buy a good hiking map. Alternatively, experienced local guides can be hired at very reasonable rates.

Horse Riding

The first Bulgarians arrived on horseback and their army was famous for its equestrian skills. The country has excellent horse breeding traditions and horse-drawn carts and carriages are still common. For visitors, riding offers an ideal way to experience the Bulgarian countryside.

You can choose from short hacks with local stables to longer trips exploring mountains, rivers and the coast. Make sure you go on a tour that suits your ability; some require a certain level of fitness and experience.
Useful websites
www.ridingholidays.com/bulgaria.htm
This US-based company specialises in international riding holidays. It offers four different week-long trips in southeast Bulgaria from April to November
www.horseridingbulgaria.com
With offices in Plovdiv, this company organises horse-riding trips in the Valley of the Roses, Balkan Mountains and at a ranch just outside Sofia. It is a branch of the Danish holiday company Penguin (see page 285).

Hunting

Incredibly, in Bulgaria you can still legally hunt bears (with special licences), as well as deer, boar, wild goat, grouse, hare and pheasant. The country has a long tradition of hunting, with an unusually large variety of game often found in the same location.
Useful websites
www.bulgariahunting.com
The website of the National Forestry Board provides general information. The organisation also provides a useful brochure

The website www.bulgariatravel.org details hunting seasons and areas, the costs of the different licences, the complex hunting regulations, and lodges.

Sailing

Under Communism yachting was seen as a pastime for the idle rich, but now an increasing number of facilities are being built, such as the state-of-the-art marina in St Vlas. The Black Sea coast with its generally clear water, low salt content and calm waters runs for more than 370 km (300 miles). Sailing opportunities range from the serious to sporty, with choices including leisurely sea picnics and week-long Black Sea charters.
Useful websites
www.bg-sail.org/main.php
Lists marinas, sailing clubs, and locations offering boat charter (for which experience may be needed), as well as a detailed coast guide with local weather conditions.
www.bulsaf.bg
The Bulgarian Sailing Federation's website (English and well as Cyrillic)

features a calendar of events as well as contact information for all its members.

Skiing

Bulgaria's ski resorts are considerably less expensive than Alpine resorts. Although facilities are not as developed or as sophisticated, significant investment in recent years mean they are improving all the time.

The main resorts are Borovets on the northern slopes of the Rila Mountains, Bansko in the Pirin Mountains and Pamporovo in the heart of the Rhodopes. In addition, there is Vitosha, just a 45-minute drive from the capital. (For more information on skiing, see page 144). The season lasts from the end of December until mid-April.

Wildlife Tours

Bulgaria is one of the richest countries in Europe in terms of biodiversity. This is partly thanks to its variety of habitats, which are home to 80 native species of mammals and 400 of birds.

Around 700 brown bears and 1,000 wolves roam the interior of Bulgaria, along with golden jackals, wild cats and chamois (wild goats). At the other end of the scale, Bulgaria has many varieties of butterflies and dragonflies, many of them rare and endangered.

The National Parks

The country's three national parks – Pirin, Rila and Central Balkan – make up more than a third of all protected areas in Bulgaria. The Central Balkan National Park is a prime area for trips to see bears, wolves and golden and imperial eagles. For more information about the parks visit the website www.bulgariannationalparks.org.

When choosing a wildlife tour, it is important to assess a company's approach to conservation. The www.spatiawildlife.com offers a variety of wildlife tours from a sustainable perspective, including bear, butterfly and wolf watching trips. It is not always necessary to take part in a dedicated wildlife watching tour in order to spot animal life; often a walking or riding trip will allow for the chance to experience nature and spot some wildlife. Those with a serious interest in the country's fauna can join one of a number of volunteer wildlife protection projects (for further information about these visit the websit www.inaturenet.org.

A – Z

A HANDY SUMMARY OF PRACTICAL INFORMATION, ARRANGED ALPHABETICALLY

A Admission Charges 288
B Budgeting for Your Trip 288
　　Business Hours 288
C Children 288
　　Climate 288
　　Crime & Safety 289
　　Customs Regulations 289
D Disabled Travellers 289
E Electricity 289

　　Embassies & Consulates 289
　　Emergency Numbers 289
　　Entry Requirements 290
　　Etiquette 290
G Gay and Lesbian Travellers 290
H Health & Medical Care 290
I Internet 291
M Maps 291
　　Money 291

P Photography 292
　　Postal Services 292
　　Public Holidays 292
R Religion 292
T Telephones 292
　　Time 292
　　Tourist Information 292
W Websites 293
　　What to Bring 293

A dmission Charges

A two-tier system is in place in many tourist operations, such as hotels and museums, which means that foreigners pay a premium over locals. For example, for some attractions the entrance fee for tourists from overseas may be 3 Levs, for Bulgarian visitors, the price would be 0.5 Lev.

B udgeting for Your Trip

One of the main attractions of Bulgaria for westerners is the low cost of living. A week of sun and sea or skiing here can work out at a fraction of the cost for more obvious destinations such as Spain or France. Visitors looking for a bargain break frequently plump for the great value package deals, which are often all-inclusive. These options can offer great savings, but check the details carefully. Standards are most definitely improving, but at the bigger resorts on the Black Sea especially, food offered with all-inclusive details may not be up to much.

Eat in a tourist restaurant on the seafront in a major resort such as Sunny beach and you could find yourself paying several times more for the equivalent meal just two streets away. As in most countries in the world, stick to local products and you will keep costs down considerably. A cocktail made with an international spirit, rather than a domestic one can cost four times the price. Similarly, local brands of beer are predictably much cheaper than imports. Hiring a small car from an international company can easily cost you more than three times the amount of a local company, although do check insurance cover and car quality.

In a local bar, a "small" vodka (a double, a "large" is a quadruple) and soda is less than a euro. A decent bottle of plonk in a restaurant costs around 5 euros; a fairly decent one would be about 10 euros. A three-course meal for two with wine can easily be had for under 30 euros. Accommodation costs around 30 euros for a mid-range hotel, regardless of whether you have a double or a single room.

Business Hours

Offices are generally open Monday to Friday 9am–6pm, although those catering for tourists may well have extended opening hours. Banks are usually open Mon–Fri 9am–3pm. While shops in the interior are, as a rule, open Mon–Fri 9am–7pm, and Sat 9am–noon, outlets in tourist areas are frequently cater to customers until late in the evening and at weekends.

C hildren

As in much of southern Europe, children are welcomed in hotels and restaurants, whatever the time of day or night. Items such as baby food and nappies are readily available, but "training pants" for toddlers are less common, so you may want to bring these with you. Baby-sitting services are provided by some of the largers hotels on the coast. *For child-oriented attractions, see the Activities section, pages 283.*

Climate

Bulgaria's winters tend to be very cold, and its summers very hot. Probably the best time to visit the coast is late spring and early autumn, when the temperatures are cooler and there are fewer tourists. Many of the resorts on the Black Sea practically shut down in winter when the temperature plummets and even Bourgas airport closes.

Crime and Safety

Most visitors are much less likely to be a victim of crime in Bulgaria than in their home country and violence against individuals is rare. Some theft inevitably takes place and it is advisable not to make obvious displays of wealth and to consider leaving jewellery at home. Remove valuables from cars and lock them securely. The biggest crooks tourists are likely to meet are taxi drivers who may have rigged meters. Don't be fooled by the "dropped wallet" trick, which is designed to distract you while your pocket is picked.

Organised crime is still an issue in Bulgaria, but unlikely to directly affect foreign visitors. Some Bulgarians say that gypsies will rob you at any opportunity, which is more a reflection of their prejudice than any basis of fact.

Sadly, prostitution is a problem, and it is common to find prostitutes hanging around city centre hotels. Many are young girls who may be working against their will. Others operate with thieves targeting tourists.

Customs Regulations

Most travellers to Bulgaria are unlikely to want to import goods; quite the opposite, in fact. Visitors are allowed to bring into the country – without incurring import fees – any item necessary for their stay in Bulgaria. For non-EU citizens this can include duty-free goods, including 200 cigarettes and 1 litre of alcohol. .

Electricity

Electricity is 220 Volts AC. Bring an adaptor as two pin plugs are used.

Embassies and Consulates

Bulgarian Embassies and Consulates Abroad

UK
Bulgarian Embassy in London, 186–188 Queen's Gate London SW7 5HL
Tel: 020-7584 9400/020 7584 9433
Fax: 020-7584 4948)
Mon–Fri 9am–6pm.
www.bulgarianembassy.org.uk
Consular section:
Mon–Fri 9.30am–12.30pm (with an appointment); Mon–Fri 12.30–2pm (without an appointment); 24-hour automated booking system, tel: 090 6554 0750 (calls cost £1 per minute); 24-hour visa information service, tel: 090-6550 8950 (calls cost £1 per minute); 24-hour fax on demand visa application form service, tel: 090 6554 0819 (calls cost £1 per minute); individual enquiries on submitted applications: tel: 020-7589 3763 (1–3pm); consular section fax: 020-7581 9073.

Australia
4 Carlotta Road, Double Bay, Sydney, NSW 2028
PO Box 1000, Double Bay, NSW, 1360
Tel: (02) 932 77 581
Tel/fax: (02) 9327 8067

Canada
325 Stewart Street, Ottawa, Ontario K1N 6K5
Tel: (613) 789 32 15, 789 35 23
Tel/fax: (613) 789 35 24

Emergency Numbers

Emergency telephone numbers:
Police 166
Traffic police 165
Fire brigade 160
Emergency road service 146
Ambulance 150

France
1 avenue Rapp, 75007 Paris
Tel: (01) 45 51 85 90
Fax: (01) 45 51 18 68
Germany
11 Mauer Str., Berlin 10117
Tel: (030) 201 0922/23/24/25/26
Fax: (030) 208 68 38
Ireland
22 Burlington Road, 4 Dublin
Tel: (01) 6603293
Fax: (01) 6603915
US
1621 22nd S, NW, Washington DC 20008
Tel: (202) 387 0174, 387 0365, 483 1386
Fax: (202) 234 7973

Foreign Embassies and Consulates in Bulgaria

Australia
37 Trakia Street, Sofia 1504
Tel: (02) 946 1334
Fax: (02) 946 1704
Canada
11 Assen Slatarov St., 1st Floor, Sofia 1504
Tel: (02) 943 3704
Fax: (011 359 2) 946 1913
France
27–29 Oborishte Str., 1087 Sofia
Tel: (02) 946 03 80, 946 03 90, 946 15 79
Fax: (02) 946 1558

Disabled Travellers

The disabled in Bulgaria have traditionally had few facilities or support, which is reflected by the limited resources for visitors to the country. The good news is that with EU accession and the enormous amount of new hotels and holiday apartments being constructed, this is changing in some areas. In large resorts on the coast and in the popular ski resorts, disabled visitors can find an increasingly range of suitable accommodation. Other facilities will take longer to be set up.

BELOW: flying the flag at the annual Rose Festival in Kazanlak.

TRANSPORT

ACCOMMODATION

ACTIVITIES

A – Z

LANGUAGE

Germany
j.k. Izgrev, 25 ul. Freeric Julio Curie,
1087 Sofia
Tel: (02) 963 4518
Fax: (02) 963 1658
Ireland
Platinum Business Centre
26–28 ul. Bacho Kiro, 1000 Sofia
Tel: (02) 985 3425
Fax: (02) 983 3302
UK
9 ul. Moskovska, 1087 Sofia
Tel: (02) 933 9222
Fax: (02) 933 9250
www.british-embassy.bg
US
16 ul, Kozyak, 1407 Sofia
Tel: (02) 937 5100
Fax: (02) 937 5320
http://bulgaria.usembassy.gov

Entry Requirements (Visas and Passports)

Fellow EU citizens do not require a
visa to enger Bulgaria and may stay
in the country for up to three
months. They need show only a valid
passport or ID card.

Visitors from the USA, Canada,
Australia and Israel do not need a
visa for stays up to 30 days. Other
nationalities require a visa.

Visas are issued from the
Bulgarian embassy or consulate in
your home country *(see page 289)*.
Application processing usually takes
up to 10 working days. Children
travelling to Bulgaria need their own
passport (or a photo on their
parents' passport).

Etiquette

Standard greetings are applicable
and it is polite to learn hello, goodby
, please and thank you in Bulgarian
(see language, page 294). Hand

shaking is common in more formal
situations. Bulgarians are generally
very friendly, but relatively
conservative. You may be invited to
someone's house, in which case it
is common practice to bring a small
present. The main source of
confusion is that nodding your head
means "no" and shaking it means
"yes". Bulgaria is a nation of heavy
smokers but by law, all restaurants,
cafés and nightclubs have non-
smoking areas.

G ay and Lesbian Travellers

Like most other Eastern European
countries, Bulgaria is fast moving
from a restricted, Soviet society and
developing more liberal ideas.
Although homosexuals and lesbians
are increasingly tolerated, attitudes
are not as progressive as in
Western European. The gay and
lesbian age of consent was only
lowered to 16 to bring it into line
with that for heterosexuals in 2002.
In 2004 anti-discrimination
legislation was introduced banning
discrimination on the basis of race,
sex, religion, disability, age or
sexual orientation. Partnership
legislation is not likely to be
introduced in the near future.

Although gay clubs and bars can
be found in the capital, in the rest of
the country they are almost impossible to find. A number of websites
offer up to date information:
www.bg-lesbian.com is a very personal
site, offering support, a lesbian chat
room and news of events, with most
pages available in English.
GayGuide.Net tours. sofiagayguide.net
offer tours such as walking trips in
Sofia and car tours in the rest of
Bulgaria (or van in the case of
groups of more than three people),

as well as tailor-made tours for
seven or more days.
www.bulgayria.com covers gay and
lesbian life in Bulgaria, and requires
registration. It has a gay listings for
Sofia, Varna, Plovdiv, Rousse and
Bourgas, with further locations to be
added in the future.
www.queer-bulgaria.org is the website
for Queer Bulgaria Foundation, an
organisation that hopes to change
attitudes. It provides information on
legislation, media coverage and day
news.

H ealth and Medical Care

It is not only highly advisable to take
out medical insurance, but a pre-
condition of visa applications. It is
usually included in regular travel
insurance policies, but check that it
makes provision for adequate
emergency medical expenses. You
will be required to pay for any
medical service and then claim it
back on production of an invoice on
your return home. Take a copy of
your policy with you on holiday. Most
major hotels can provide contact
details of local doctors and
hospitals.

Mosquitoes can be a problem in
warm weather, although their bites
are annoying, rather than
dangerous. Either bring a reliable
repellent with you from home, or buy
an imported brand on arrival. Ticks
in rural areas can be disease
carrying, so cover up and avoid long
grass. The chances of being bitten
by a poisonous snake, or
contracting rabies (which does exist
in Bulgaria), is extremely unlikely,
but obviously seek immediate
medical attention if bitten by either
a snake or a dog. Be aware that
Sofia has a large stray dog
population. Though the dogs rarely
bite, they sometimes attack
passersby, and young children are
particularly at risk.

Water

Tap water is safe to drink, but
bottled water is considered
preferable and widely available.

I nternet

Internet cafes have sprung up in
towns and cities throughout the
country in recent years. In areas
little visited by tourists, they may be
a bit harder to find. Many Internet
outlets also offer a range of
services, such as scanning, printing
and webcams and have their own
website with a map of their location.
For example, in Sofia, Garibaldi

BELOW: read all about it on Sofia's newsstands.

Internet Cafe at 6 ul. Graf Ignatiev, 1st floor, pl. Garibaldi (www.garibaldicafe.net/indexe.htm) is open 24 hours and offers an hourly, all-day and all-night rate. Some libraries offer a free, limited service.

Increasingly, WiFi is becoming available in Bulgaria in hotels, etc, which means you can connect to the Internet directly from your laptop anywhere within the building. If you are bringing your own computer from home, you will need a European adaptor and possibly a different power pack.

Maps

When planning your trip, free online maps can be useful and printed out for reference. For example, http://get.info.bg/visit/maps has online maps, although not in great detail and of varying quality. Features covered include rivers, fishing and weather. For high quality and detail it is advisable to purchase a published map. When choosing, consider the scale, which will depend on whether you are planning a driving or walking holiday. If you are going even slightly off the beaten track, check that both Cyrillic and Latin place names are given for smaller places or you may find yourself getting very lost. Maps can be ordered online with both Amazon (www.amazon.co.uk)

Bulgaria published by Reise Know-How Verlag. Scale: 1:400,000. A detailed map showing places of interest to tourists, as well as scenic routes. Waterproof and easy to manage, it features an index and names of major settlements in both Cyrillic and Latin script.

Bulgaria published by ITMB Publishing. Scale: 1:375,000. A double-sided road map showing elevations and major roads. Larger towns are marked in both Latin and Cyrillic. An additional feature is a street plan of the capital, Sofia.

Bulgaria published by Cartographia. Scale: 1:750,000. A relief map with larger settlements in both Roman and Cyrillic alphabets, with other place names only in Roman script. Provides driving distances and features tourist attractions.

Bulgaria published by Freytag & Berndt. Scale: 1:400,000. A clear road map with road detail and some relief. Symbols indicate points of interest. All names on the map are given in both Latin script and Cyrillic. The index includes post codes and there is a plan of central Sofia.

Bulgaria published by GeoCenter.

ABOVE: ATMs are plentiful in large cities but scarce in rural areas.

Scale: 1:800,000. Main and scenic roads are shown, with some relief. There is an index and a basic street plan of Sofia, Veliko Tarnovo and Plovdiv.

Bulgaria Road Atlas published by Cartographia. Scale: 1:400,000 - 1:125,000. A spiral-bound atlas showing the whole country at a scaled of 1:400,000 and the popular Black Sea Coast area in more detail at 1:125,000. There are basic street plans of major towns.

Those travelling just to the Black Sea coast may prefer to get a map that covers just this area, such as one of the following:

Bulgarian Black Sea Coast published by Reise Know-How Verlag. Scale: 1:130,000. Waterproof and double-sided, showing the whole country in two sections. Minor roads and places of interest to tourists are shown, as well as some hotels.

Bulgarian Black Sea Coast published by Freytag & Berndt. Scale: 1:150,000. Good presentation and detailed, with some relief marked. Includes a street plan of Bourgas, which is probably irrelevant to most tourists, as well as a general map of Bulgaria.

Media

Newspapers and Magazines

English and German tabloids, with the occasional broadsheet can be found in the bigger resorts and in Sofia. American magazines such as *Time* and *Newsweek* are also available in some more developed tourist areas and in the capital. The *Sofia Echo* (www.sofiaecho.com) is a high quality, English-language newspaper, but you will only find this in Sofia.

Radio and Television

Bulgarian television is not generally of a high standard, and not likely to be of interest to tourists. Most large hotels offer a range of English-language programmes. The country's radio stations may appeal, as they often play foreign music, with Bulgarian chat in between. The BBC World Service can be listened to in Sofia, but is more difficult to receive in other parts of the country.

The website for Bulgarian radio, www.bnr.bg/RadioBulgaria/Emission_English, features lots of interesting, up-to-date articles about Bulgarian music and profiles of artists, including the latest CD releases. You can even listen to the Bulgarian entry to the Eurovision song contest. You can also listen to selected radio programmes in English.

Money

The Bulgarian currency is the Bulgarian Lev (plural Leva). A Lev consists of 100 stotinki (st). Leva notes come in denominations of 1, 2, 5, 10, 20, 50. Stotinki coins in use are 1, 2, 5, 10, 20 and 50. After the fall of Communism, new Leva notes were printed and all notes prior to 1974 made worthless. Since the Lev has been pegged to the euro, the rate of exchange has remained relatively stable, which was at the time of writing approximately 2 Leva to the Euro (slightly less to the US dollar), and 3 Leva to the pound. Bulgaria is set to adopt the euro in 2009, after accession to the EU, but many establishments already quote – and accept – euros.

There is no need to bring travellers' cheques as withdrawing

ABOVE: be aware that not all letterboxes are yellow.

money from cash points is as easy as at home, although ATMs may not always be available in rural areas. Cash is the only form of payment in many establishments, as credit cards are often not accepted. Visa/Plus, Visa Electron, MasterCard/Cirrus, Maestro, American Express and Diners Club cards are the most commonly accepted cards.

Bank opening hours

Banks are open Mon–Fri 9am–4pm; bureaux de change usually operate until 6pm or later; and larger hotels often offer exchange facilities.

Word of warning

Do not change money on the street, as you are highly likely to be given counterfeit notes.

Photography

If you use a digital camera, don't forger to bring a sufficient memory card, charger and adaptor and if necessary, spare batteries. It may be possible to buy these items when in Bulgaria, but they are not so widely available as at home. Camera film is generally on sale in tourist areas, but may be harder to find out of main centres.

Postal Services

Letters usually take around 10 days to reach the UK and up to three weeks to get to the US. At the time of writing a standard letter (20

grams or less) cost 0.85 Lev to other countries in Europe; a postcard costs 0.32 Lev. When sending packages, you are advised to use registered post or a courier service such as DHL as goods have a tendency to go astray. Public letterboxes are not standardised in terms of colour or size.

Public Holidays

1 January New Year's Day
3 March Liberation Day
Late March/April Easter Sunday and Monday (note that Orthodox Easter falls one week after Catholic or Protestant Easter)
1 May Labour Day
6 May St George's Day
24 May National Culture Day
6 September Union Day
22 September Independence Day
1 November Day of National Revival
24–26 December Christmas

Religion

The vast majority of the Bulgarian population is Eastern Orthodox, similar in almost every way to the Orthodoxy practised in Russia, Romania, Serbia-Montenegro and Macedonia, though somewhat different from (and frequently at odds with) Greek Orthodoxy. In addition, there are Muslim, Jewish and Catholic minorities.

Telephones

Pay phones in Bulgaria take either coins or – increasingly – cards, which can be bought from kiosks, shops and post offices. Most countries, including all European countries, America and Australia, can be called direct. If making a number of international calls, it is worth buying a low-cost call card, which can dramatically reduces charges. Most provide a dial-up number so check instructions are provided in English. Avoid making calls from hotel rooms, which, like most places in the world, involve a hefty surcharge. Telephone calls, telegram and fax services both in Bulgaria and abroad are also offered by Post Offices throughout the country. If you need to send a fax it is best to use the post office as hotels tend to charge a lot for this.

Mobile phones

Eighty-five percent of the population uses mobile phones. Most UK mobile phones will roam in Bulgaria,

but the cost of calls is usually very high, even just to receive calls. One of the cheapest options for mobile users is to buy a phone card that they can use in conjunction with their own mobile phone by dialling a special access code on the card.

Useful numbers

Operator 121
International operator 0123.

Area Codes

Sofia	02
Blagoevgrad	073
Bourgas	056
Pleven	064
Plovdiv	032
Rousse	082
Varna	052
Veliko Turnovo	062

Time

Bulgaria runs on Eastern European Time, which is UTC/GMT plus two hours. Daylight saving operates from the last Sunday in March to the last Sunday in October, when clocks are put forward one hour. There are no time zones within the country.

Tipping

Salaries in Bulgaria are very low – the national average is only around £100 per month. As hotel and restaurant staff rely heavily on tips just to feed their family, do budget for tipping waiters and hotel staff in particular (10 percent is usual in these cases). Taxi drivers do not expect tips, but of course welcome them, and it is usual to tip if you have taken a very short journey, simply to make it worth the cabby's time and trouble.

Toilets

Public toilets are practically non-existent, but anyone can use the toilets in a restaurant for a few coins. Indeed, even if you are eating at an establishment you may very well be asked to put some money in a saucer for the attendant. Although this may seem unreasonable, the recipient is likely to be elderly and very much in need of the cash. Attendants will normally supply you with a few sheets of toilet paper in return for some small change; it is not supplied as standard so if the toilets are unattended you will need to bring your own. In petrol stations and out of the main tourist areas, some toilets may be holes in the ground. Don't throw paper into the toilet as it may block the pipes; bins

ART & PHOTO CREDITS

akg-images 24, 30, 32, 34R
akg-images/Erich Lessing 22, 23
Julian Angelov/Travel Photo Gallery
114T, 119T, 133, 175, 176T, 241,
242, 262
Gyori Antoine/Corbis Sygma 37R
Archivo Iconografico, S.A./Corbis
27
Pete Bennett/APA 1, 2/3, 3BR,
4C, 7C, 7B, 8T, 9T, 9C, 16, 29,
40/41, 45R, 46, 47, 50, 53, 54R,
55, 56, 58, 59, 61, 71CL, 78L, 80,
81T, 82, 82T, 83, 84T, 85, 85T, 86,
87, 87T, 89, 91, 92T, 93, 94, 95L,
95R, 96T, 97, 103, 104, 111,
111T, 112, 113L, 113R, 113T, 114,
115, 116, 116T, 117T, 121, 121T,
122, 123, 129T, 131, 132, 132T,
147T, 148T, 150, 151T, 152, 156T,
157, 159, 160, 161T, 162, 163L,
163R, 175T, 176, 177T, 179T,
181L, 181R, 181T, 183T, 184, 185,
186, 195L, 195T, 196L, 196R,
196T, 197, 198T, 202T, 203, 223,
223T, 226, 227T, 230, 240T, 244,
247R, 251T, 254T, 255, 255T, 256,
257, 269, 270, 274, 278, 282,
284, 290, 291, 292, 295
The Bridgeman Art Library 25, 26,
38, 130
Wojtek Buss/Superstock 237
Nick Chaldakov/Alamy 228
Corbis 33, 250
Rosen Dimitrov/Alamy 261
Mary Evans Picture Library 28, 31,
34L, 35
Suzi Gibbons/Redferns 57
Hulton-Deutsch Collection/Corbis 36

Yevgeny Khaldei/Corbis 39
Chris Niedenthal/Time Life
Pictures/Getty Images 37L
Brigitte & Philippe Perdereau/
Photolibrary.com 126T
Valentina Petrova/AFP/Getty
Images 8B
Pictures Colour Library 135, 136,
144, 178T
Tom Schulze/transit/Still Pictures
18, 127
Gregory Wrona 4T, 5B, 6B, 7T,
10/11, 12/13, 14/15, 19, 21R,
51, 52, 54L, 62, 63, 64/65,
66/67, 68/69, 71TR, 101, 117,
120, 124, 125, 128, 129, 134,
140, 141, 143, 145, 146, 146T,
147, 148, 149, 149T, 151, 158,
162T, 166, 170, 171, 172, 173,
177, 178, 179, 180, 180T, 182,
182T, 183, 185T, 194, 215T,
218/219, 220, 221, 225, 231,
235, 240, 248, 251, 276, 281,
285, 286
Gregory Wrona/APA 5T, 6T, 20,
21L, 42, 43, 44, 45L, 60, 70,
71BR, 76, 77, 78R, 79, 79T, 81,
83T, 84, 88, 88T, 90, 90T, 92,
93T, 94T, 96, 98, 100, 100T, 102,
105, 106/107, 108, 109, 118L,
118R, 119, 137, 150T, 153, 154,
155, 156, 159T, 160T, 161, 164,
165, 165T, 167L, 167R, 168, 169,
187, 190, 191, 193, 193T, 194T,
195R, 197T, 198, 199, 200L,
200R, 200T, 201, 201T, 202, 203T,
204, 205, 206, 207, 208, 209,
210T, 211T, 212, 212T, 213, 213T,

214, 214T, 215, 216, 217, 222T,
224, 226T, 227, 229, 233L, 233R,
234, 234T, 235T, 236, 237T, 238,
239, 243, 245, 246, 247L, 247T,
248T, 249, 249T, 252, 253, 253T,
254, 256T, 257T, 258, 258T, 259L,
259R, 260, 260T, 263, 272, 280,
283, 289, 293

PICTURE SPREADS

48/49: Julian Angelov/Travel
Photo Gallery 49TR, 49BL; Jtb
Photo/Photolibrary.com 48/49,
48BL, 49CL; Image Register/Alamy
48BL; Gregory Wrona/APA 49BR

138/139: Pete Bennett/APA
138/139, 138TL, 138BC, 139TR,
139BL; Gregory Wrona 139CL;
Gregory Wrona/APA 138CR,
139BR

188/189: Pete Bennett/APA 188L;
Philippe Clement/Naturepl.com
189BL; Jose Luis Gomez de
Francisco/Naturepl.com 189CL;
Dietmar Nill/Naturepl.com
188/189, 188BR, 189TR, 189CR

Map Production:
Phoenix Mapping

2007 Apa Publications GmbH & Co.
Verlag KG (Singapore branch)

Production: Linton Donaldson

INDEX

Numbers in italics refer to photographs

A

Abdul Hamid II, Sultan 33
accommodation 272–81
admission charges 288
Adrian II, Pope 27
adventure tour 285
Agrarian Party 35, 205
agriculture 21, 51–5
agrotourism 55
Ahtopol 259
air travel 268, 269
Albena 230, 231, 235, 235–6, 243, 279
Aleko 100
Alepu 257
Alexander I Battenburg, Prince 32–4, 33, 90, 166
Alexander II, Tsar 32, 90
Alexander the Great 24, 168
Alexius Slav 150, 152
alphabet, Cyrillic 27, 28
amuesment parks, Sofia Land 96
April Rising 31, 121, 159, 181, 198
Arabs 26
Arbanasi 121, 196, 196–7, 207, 278
archaeological sites, Apollonia 254, 254
archaeological sites
  see also treasure
  Kazanlak Tomb 24, 202
  Madara Horseman 216
  Mishovka Niva 262
  Nebet Tepe Thracian citadel (Plovdiv) 157, 157
  Neolithic Dwellings (Stara Zagora) 203–4
  Nicopolis ad Istrum 197
  Nikopolis ad Nestum 147, 148
  Perperikon 186, 186
  Pliska ruined city 216, 216
  Propada 262
  Ritlite (Iskar Gorge) 112
  Roman Amphitheatre (Plovdiv) 157–9, 159
  Roman Forum (Plovdiv) 160
  Roman Theatre (Stara Zagora) 205
  Roman Thermae (Varna) 223–5
  Varna Necropolis 228
architecture, National Revival 121
Arda Gorge 186
area 19
art galleries see museums and galleries
arts, performing 282
  see also music; theatres
Asparouh Bridge (Varna) 228
Asparuh, Khan 26
Assen dynasty 29–30
Assenovgrad 173–5, 187
ATMs 292
Aurelian, Emperor 25
Axis Powers 36

B

Bachinovo 132
Bakshev, Bogdan 31
Balchik 231, 233, 236, 237–8, 239, 243, 279
Baldwin I, Emperor 29
Balkan Range 191–207
  hotels 278
  restaurants 207
Balkan Wars 34, 151, 239
Bansko 121, 141, 141, 142–6, 145, 153, 275
Barbarians 25
bars see restaurants
Basil I (the Macedonian), Emperor 27
Basil II, Emperor 28, 142
Batak 181
Batakshki Snezhnik 181
baths
  Former Central Bathhouse (Plovdiv) 164
  Former Central Bathhouse (Sofia) 82, 83
beer 63
Béla III, King of Hungary 130
Belmeken, Lake 136
Belogradchik 119, 123, 274
Berkovitsa 116–17, 123, 274
Berlin, Congress of 32, 32, 157
bird-watching 20, 188–9, 188–9, 287
  Arda Gorge 186
  Rila Mountains 125, 189
  Shabla Lake 189, 242
  Strandzha Nature Park 260–1
  Taukliman Bay 241
  Via Pontica migration route 188, 253
Bismarck, Otto von 32
Bistritsa (Mount Vitosha) 100
Bistritsa (Rila Mountains) 126, 132
Black Sea 19, 218–19
  Northern Black Sea Coast 231–43, 279–80
  Southern Black Sea Coast 245–63, 280–1
Blagoev, Dimitar 131
Blagoevgrad 128, 130, 131, 131–2, 132, 137, 275
Bogoridi, Alexander Stefanov 32–3
Boril, Tsar 29
Boris I, Khan 27, 216
Boris III, Tsar 35–6, 129–30
Borovets 20, 133, 135, 135, 136, 137, 144, 275–6
Botev, Hristo 113, 113
Botevgrad 120
Bourgas 231, 245, 252–3, 253, 263, 280
Bov 111
Brashlyan 262, 262

bribery 45, 46
Bulgarian Orthodox Church 47, 47, 139
Bulgarian Revolutionary Committee (BRCK) 31
Bulgars 25–6
Bunarjik Tepe (Plovdiv) 168
bunjee jumping 228, 228
bus travel 269
Byala 245–6
Byzantine Wars 28–9
Byzantium 25–9, 156, 216

C

car hire 271
castles and fortifications
  Assen Fortress (Assenovgrad) 175, 175
  Baba Vida Fortress (Vidin) 209
  Belogradchik Fortress 118, 119
  Fortress Gate (Plovdiv) 157, 162
  Kaliakra Castle 240, 241
  Shishman Fortress (Nikopol) 211
  Shumen Fortress 215
  Slav fortress (Melnik) 151
  Tsarevets fortress (Velika Tarnovo) 194, 195
  Urvich hill 102
cathedrals
  Alexsander Nevski (Sofia) 77, 78, 87, 87
  Cathedral of the Assumption (Varna) 220, 222–3, 223
  St Vissarion of Smolyan 180
caves 20, 285
  Bacho Kiro Cave 198
  Cave of St John of Rila 130
  Devetashka Cave 193
  Dyavolskoto Gurlo 182
  Kamen Bryag 241, 241
  Katakombite 235
  Ledenika Cave (Vratsa Gorge) 114
  Magura Cave 119, 119
Cerni Vrah 98, 101, 102, 178–9
Chepelare 179
Chernomorets 253, 263, 280
Cherven 214–15
Chervenkov, Valko 36
children 288, 46.283
Christianity 27, 47, 138
Christo 45
churches
  see also cathedrals; monasteries and convents
  Archangel Michael (Gotse Delchev) 148
  Archangels Michael and Gabriel (Arbanasi) 196, 197
  Archangels Michael and Gabriel (Haskovo) 184
  Armenian Church (Varna) 223
  Assumption (Gotse Delchev) 147–8

Assumption of the Holy Virgin (Malko Tarnovo) 262
Assumption of the Holy Virgin (Samokov) 133
Assumption (Shiroka Luka) 180, 181
Assumption of the Virgin Mary (Blagoevgrad) 131
Boyana Church (Sofia) 96–7, 97
Forty Holy Martyrs (Veliko Tarnovo) 195
Holy Godmother (Berkovitsa) 116
Holy Trinity (Assenovgrad) 174
Holy Trinity (Bansko) 145
Holy Trinity (Shishtov) 212
Holy Virgin of the Annunciation (Assenovgrad) 175
Nativity (Arbanasi) 197
Nessebar's Churches 244, 249, 249
Patriarchal Church (Veliko Tarnovo) 194, 195
Petrich Church of the Virgin Mary (near Assenovgrad) 175–6
Romanian Orthodox (Sofia) 83
Rotunda (Sofia) 78, 79
Russian Church of Sv. Nikolai (Sofia) 84, 85
Sv. Atanas (Varna) 225
Sv. Bogoroditsa (Koprivshtitsa) 121
Sts Constantine and Elena (Plovdiv) 162, 162
Sts Cyril and Methodius (Sozopol) 255
St Dimitar of Solun (Assenovgrad) 174
St Dimiter (Veliko Tarnovo) 195
St George Ambelino (Assenovgrad) 175
St George Metoshki (Assenovgrad) 174–5
St George (Sinemoretz) 260
St George (Sozopol) 255, 255
St John Predtecha (Assenovgrad) 175
St Mary of the Assumption (Assenovgrad) 174
Sv. Nedelya (Sofia) 81, 81
St Nicholas (Berkovitsa) 117
St Nicholas (Melnik) 151
St Nicholas (Pleven) 211
St Nicholas (Vidin) 210
St Nikola (Melnik) 151
St Nikola (Sepereva Banya) 127
Sv. Petka Paraskeva (Sofia) 82
Sv. Petka of the Saddlers (Sofia) 81–2, 81
Sv. Sedmotchislentsi (Sofia) 94, 95, 95
Sv. Sofia (Sofia) 86
Sv. Troista (Rousse) 213
St Zosim (Sozopol) 255
Shipka Memorial Church 201–2
sunken 78
Virgin Birth (Rila Monastery) 129
Virgin Mary (Dragalevtsi) 99–100
Virgin Mary (Haskovo) 184
Virgin Mary (Plovdiv) 161, 161
Virgin Mary (Sozopol) 255

Clement of Ohrid, St 89
climate 20–1, 288–9
climbing 285
clothing 293
coach travel 269
collective farms 51–2, 53
Communism 36–7, 44, 46, 138
erasing the Communist past 85
Former Headquarters of the Communist Party (Sofia) 79–80, 79
memorabilia 87, 284
place names 131
conservation 21
Constantine I (the Great), Emperor 86, 162
Constantine IV Pogonatus, Emperor 26
Constantine V, Emperor 26
Constantinople Patriarch 27, 29
counterfeit items 284
credit cards 292
crime 44, 45, 289
cruise liners 269
currency 291–2
customs regulations 289
cycling 286
Cyril, St 27, 81, 82, 89
Cyrillic 27, 28, 294

D

Dacia 19, 25
Danube, River 19, 21, 209, 212
Danubian Plain 19, 20, 209–17, 279
Delchevo 146, 148
democracy 37, 46
Devil's Bridge (near Ardino) 186
Devin 181, 187, 277
Dimitar, Hadzhi 206
Dimitrov, Georgi 36, 85, 183
Dimitrov, Vladimir 122
Dimitrovgrad 182–3
disabled travellers 289
Disraeli, Benjamin 32
diving 286
divorce 46
Dobrinishte 146–7, 153
Dospat 181, 183
Dourankoulak Lake 242
Dragalevtsi 99
drinks 63
driving 270–1
Drobudzha region 34, 36, 231, 231, 240, 279
Drumev, Vasili 120
Dryanovo 197–8, 278
Dupnitsa 125, 126, 137
Durankulak 242
Dyuni 256, 257, 280

E

earthquakes 21
eco-tourism 54
education 46, 53
electricity 289
Elenite 247, 280
embassies and consulates 289–90

emergency numbers 289
emigration 46, 53–4, 155
Emine, Cape 245, 246
Emona 246–7
Etar 201
ethnic groups 43, 44
etiquette 246, 290
European Union 37, 45, 46, 51, 55, 224
Ezeroto, Lake 205

F

fascism 35
Ferdinand I, Tsar 34, 34–5, 84, 90
festivals 48–9, 122, 282, 283
Festival of Roses (Kazanlak) 49, 49, 202–3, 203
gaidi festivals 181, 182
Horse Easter 48, 49
Kukeri festivals 48–9, 48, 122, 127, 131, 181, 283
St Todor's Day 48
Verdi Festival (Plovdiv) 158
fire dancing 48, 49, 261
First Bulgarian Kingdom 26–8, 138, 179, 216
fishing 186, 260
flora 20, 21
Rila Mountains 126, 133
Strandhza Nature Park 260
folk music 56–7
food 59–62
see also restaurants
fortresses see castles and fortifications
Franks 26–7
fuel 270–1

G

Gabrovo 200, 200, 207, 278
Gagarin, Yuri 89
gay and lesbian travellers 290
Gela 181
geography 19–20
George Terter II, Tsar 156
Georgiev, General Konstantin 35, 81
Germany, Nazi 35, 36
geysers 126–7
Golden Sands 231, 234, 243, 279
golf 145, 238, 239, 286
Gotse Delchev 141, 147, 147–8
Gramatikovo 261
Grand Hotel Balkan (Sofia) 80–1
Greben Canal (Plovdiv) 168
Greece 34
Greeks, Ancient 23–4, 239, 241
Gruenanger, Friedrich 83, 84
guesthouses 272
guided tours 271
gypsies see Roma

H

Haskovo 183–4, 187
health care 46, 53, 250, 290–1
Hermanite Beach (Sozopol) 255
Herodotus 23

hiking 286–7
  Mount Vitosha 101–2
  Pirin Mountains 147
  Rila Mountains 127–8, 132–3,
    134, 135–6
  Strandhza Nature Park 260
  Vratsa and Iskar gorges 115
Hilendar, Pasius of 31, 143, *143*
Hilton Hotel (Sofia) 92
historic buildings
  see also **archaeological sites;**
    museums and galleries;
    palaces
  Aleko Konstantinov House-
    Museum (Shishtov) 212
  Balabanov House (Plovdiv)
    159–60
  Captain Pavel's House
    (Nessebar) 249
  Central Military Club (Sofia)
    85–6, *85*
  Danov House (Plovdiv) 160
  Daskalov House (Tryavna) 199
  Dobri Voynikov House (Shumen)
    215–16
  Georgiadi House (Plovdiv) 159
  Hindlian House (Plovdiv) 160
  House of Lamartin (Plovdiv)
    158–9
  Kalinchev's House (Tryavna) 200
  Kaliopa House (Rousse) 214
  Kanchev Angel House (Tryavna)
    199
  Kirkov (Blue) House (Haskovo)
    184
  Konstantzaliev's House
    (Arbanasi) 197
  Kordopulov House (Melnik) 151
  Kurtpashova Tower (Vratsa) 113
  Kuyumdzhioglu House (Plovdiv)
    162–3
  Layosh Kossuth House (Shumen)
    216
  Meschii Tower (Vratsa) 113
  Michailov House (Montana) 118
  Nikola Nedkovich House (Plovdiv)
    159
  Old School (Tryavna) 199
  Oslekova House (Koprivshtitsa)
    121, *121*
  Panaiot Volov House (Shumen)
    215
  Pancho Vladigerov House
    (Shumen) 215
  Panov House (Belogradchik) 119
  Parliament Building (Sofia) 90
  Pasha House (Melnik) 151
  Presidency Building (Sofia) 79,
    80, *80*
  Prokopovata Kashta (Gotse
    Delchev) 147
  Sarafkina House (Veliko Tarnovo)
    196
  Velyanova House (Bansko) 145
history 23–39
hitching 269–70
Hitler, Adolf 36, 130
Homer 23, 246
horse riding 286–7
hot springs *see* **spas**

hotels 273–81
hunting 287
hydroelectricity 21

I

icons 139, 145, 161–2
independence 31–7
independent travellers 231, 233
insurance 285, 290
internet access 291
Isaac Angelos, Emperor 29
Iskar Dam 103
Iskar Gorge *109*, **109–12**, 123
Iskar, Lake 103
Iskrets 109
Islam 30, 43, 47, 163–4, 180
Ivan Alexander, Tsar 30, 156, 186,
  194
Ivan Assen I, Tsar *29*, **29**, 78, 130,
  175, 214
Ivan Assen II, Tsar **29–30**, 150,
  156, 175, 195
Ivan Shishman, Tsar 102, 112, 211

J

Jendem Tepe (Plovdiv) 168
John II Komnenos, Emperor 29
John Paul II, Pope 139
John V Palaiologos, Emperor 156
John of Rila, St 128, *130*, **130**
Jovanovic, Konstantin 90
Judaism *47*, 83, 164
Justinian I (the Great), Emperor
  25, *25*

K

Kaliakra Cape 231, 233, 239,
  240–1
Kaloyan, Tsar *27*, **29**, 195
Kamen Bryag 241, *242*
Kardzhali 185, *185*
Kavarna 233, **238–9**
Kazanlak 49, *202*, **202–3**, 207
**Kempinski Zografski Hotel
  (Sofia)** 92
Kilifarevo *197*, 278
Kiten 258
Klieidon, Battle of 28
Klisura Pass 121, 125
Klokonitsa, Battle of 195
Kobleshkov, Todor 121, *121*
Kokon Fountain (Arbanasi) 197
Kom, Mount 117
Konstantinov, Aleko 212
Koprivshtitsa 51, *120*, **120–1**, 274
Kostadinova, Stefka 45
Kostenets 136
Kostinbrod 115
Kovachevitsa 148–9
Kranevo 235
Krapets *242*, 279
Kremikovtsi 119–20
Krstevic, Gabriel 33
Krum, Khan 27
Kubrat, Khan 26
Kubrick, Stanley 24
Kutrigur 26

Kyivan Rus 28
Kyustendil **122**, 276

L

Lakatnik 111
Lamartine, Alfonse de 158
landscape 19–21
language 25–6, 28, **294–5**
Leo III, Emperor 26
Levski, Vasil **31**, 86, 88, 93, 111,
  115, 191–3, 198, *198*
libraries
  Ivan Vazov Memorial Library
    (Plovdiv) 166
  National Library (Sofia) 89
Lighthouse Golf Resort 238
Lipachov, Andrei 35
Lovech *191*, **191–3**, *193*, 207, 278
Lozenets 258, *259*
Lozenska Planina 102–3

M

Macedonia 24, 34, 35, 36
**Macedonian Revolutionary
  Organisation (IMRO)** 35
Madzehrovo 186
Malko Tarnovo 262
Maluk Rezen 102
Malyovista 128, **133**, 276
Manuel Komnenos, Emperor 29
maps 291
Marie, Queen of Romania 237
Maritsa Valley **136**, 189
markets
  Book Market (Sofia) 94–5
  Central Market (Stara Zagora)
    204
  Flea Market (Sofia) 86–7, *86*
  Halite (Sofia) 82–3
  Samovodende Marketplace
    (Veliko Tarnovo) 195
  Zhenski Pazar (Sofia) *83*, 84
Markov, Georgi 45
Melnik 51, 141, *149*, **150–1**, 153,
  276
memorials
  Communist Martyrs Memorial
    (Sofia) 85
  Mausoleum of Knyaz Aleksander
    Battenburg (Sofia) 90
  Mausoleum (Pleven) 210
  Pantheon of the Enlighteners
    (Rousse) 213
  Tomb of the Unknown Soldier
    (Sofia) 86
menus 60
Methodius, St *27*, *81*, 82, 89
Mezdra 113
Michael III, Emperor 27
Milev, Geo 205
Mladenov, Peter 37
Moesia 19, 25, 26
monasteries and convents **138–9**
  Aladzha Monastery 233, *234*,
    234–5
  Arapovo Monastery 177
  Bachkovo Monastery *139*, 173,
    177, **177–8**

Belashtitsa Monastery of St
George the Victorious 28,
176–7
Cherepish Monastery 112, *112*,
113, *139*
Chiprovtsi Monastery of St John
of Rila 118–19
Dervish Monastery (Obrochishte)
236–7
Dragalevtsi Monastery 99
Dryanovo Monastery 197–8, *197*
Glozhenski Monastery of St
George 120
Gotsedelchevski Monastery 148
Gradeshnitsa Monastery of St
John 118
Ivanovo Rock Monastery *138*,
214, *214*
Kilifarevo Monastery 197
Klisura Monastery of Svs Cyril
and Methodius 115–16
Kokolyane Monastery 103
Lopushanski Monastery of St
John the Precursor 118
Loven Monastery 103
Mouldava Monastery 177
Osenovlak Monastery of the
Seven Altars 111, *111*
Pancherevo Monastery 102–3
Prebrazhenski Monastery 196
Rila Monastery *124*, *128*,
128–30, *129*, *138–9*
Rozhen Monastery 152, *152*
St George Monastery at
Kremikovtsi 119–20
St George Monastery (Pomerie)
251–2
St John Prodromus (Kardzhali)
185
St Konstantine and Elena (St
Konstantine) 233
Sts Kirik and Yulita Monastery
(Gornovoden) 176
Vrach Monastery of Sts Kozma
and Damian (Kuklen) 176
Zemen Monastery of St John
122, *122*
money 291–2
Mongols 30
Montana 117–18
Montenegro 34
monuments
1,300 Years of Bulgaria
Monument (Sofia) 92, *92*
Assen Monument (Veliko Tarnovo)
194
Creators of the Bulgarian State
215, *215*
Gate of the Forty Maidens
(Kaliakra) 240
Monument of Freedom (Shipka
Pass) *190*, 201, *201*, *202*
Monument to Freedom (Rousse)
213
Monument to Freedom (Sofia) 93
Monument to the Virgin Mary
(Haskovo) 184
Red Army Monument (Sofia)
89–90
Russian Monument (Varna) 225,

226
Statue of Sofia Monument *78*, 83
Vasil Levski Monument (Sofia) 88
mosques
Bairakli Dzhamiya Mosque
(Samokov) 133
Banya Basha (Sofia) *79*, 82, *82*
Dzhumaya dzhamiya (Plovdiv)
160, *162*, **163**
Eski Mosque (Haskovo) 184
Eski Mosque (Stara Zagora) 204
Imaret dzhamiya (Plovdiv) **164**,
167
Osman Pazvantoglu Mosque
(Vidin) 210
Tombul Mosque (Shumen) 215
Moussala, Mount 20, 125, 136
Mugla 182
mummers 48, *48*
Murad II, Sultan 128–9, 130
museums and galleries 282–3
see also **archaeological sites**;
historic buildings; **palaces**
19th-century Town Life Museum
(Stara Zagora) 205
Academy of Fine Arts (Sofia) 88
Aquarium and Black Sea Museum
(Varna) 226
Archaeological Museum
(Bourgas) 252–3
Archaeological Museum
(Nessebar) 251, *251*
Archaeological Museum (Plovdiv)
167
Archaeological Museum (Sozopol)
255
Archaeological Museum (Svoge)
109
Archaeological Museum (Varna)
223
Archaeological Museum (Veliko
Tarnovo) 195–6
Archaeology Museum (Sandanski)
149
Balchik Art Gallery 238
Berkovitsa Ethnographic Museum
117
Bulgarian Contemporary History
Museum (Veliko Tarnovo) 196
Bulgarian National Art Gallery
(Sofia) 84
City Art Gallery (Plovdiv) 166–7
City Art Gallery (Varna) 223
City History Museum (Bourgas)
253
Education Museum (Gabrovo)
200
Ethnographic Museum (Bourgas)
253
Ethnographic Museum (Lovech)
193
Ethnographic Museum (Nessebar)
249
Ethnographic Museum (Plovdiv)
162–3, *163*
Ethnographic Museum (Sofia) 84
Ethnographic Museum (Sozopol)
255
Ethnographic Museum (Varna)
225

Ethnographic and National Revival
Complex (Vratsa) 114
Ethnographic Open-air Museum
(Etar) 201, *201*
Ethnographical Complex (Balchik)
238
Folk Art and Applied Crafts
Museum (Troyan) 194
Foundation Sozopol 255
Geo Milev Museum (Stara
Zagora) 205
Georgi Velchev Art Museum
(Varna) 223
Hadzhi Dimitar House-Museum
(Sliven) 206
Historic Museum (Stara Zagora)
205
Historical Museum (Balchik) 238
Historical Museum (Gabrovo)
200
Historical Museum (Rousse) 213
Historical Museum (Vidin) 210
History Museum (Assenovgrad)
175
History Museum (Blagoevgrad)
131, *132*
History Museum (Kardzhali) 185
History Museum (Montana) 118
History Museum (Samokov) 133
History Museum (Sliven) 206
History Museum (Vratsa) 24,
114
House of Humour and Satire
(Gabrovo) 200
Icon Exhibition (Bansko) 145
Icons Museum (Plovdiv) 161–2
Iskra Museum (Kazanlak) 203
Ivan Vazov Memorial Museum
(Berkovitsa) 116–17
Ivan Vazov Museum (Sofia) 91
Kableshkov House (Koprivshtitsa)
121
Kulata Ethnographical Complex
(Kazanlak) 202
Liberation Museum (Pleven) 211
Malko Tarnovo Town Museum
262
Medicine Museum (Varna) 225
National Gallery of Foreign Art
(Sofia) 88–9
National History Museum (Sofia)
37, **97–8**
National Liberation Museum
(Plovdiv) 159
National Museum of Archaeology
(Sofia) 24, **80**
National Museum of Earth and
Man (Sofia) 92
National Museum of Transport
and Communications (Rousse)
214
National Revival and Constituent
Assembly Museum (Veliko
Tarnovo) 195
National Revival Museum
(Assenovgrad) 175
National Revival Museum
(Plovdiv) 159
National Revival Museum (Varna)
223

National Science Museum
(Bourgas) 253
Natural History Museum (Plovdiv)
167–8
Natural History Museum (Sofia)
85
Naval Museum (Varna) 226, *226*
Neofit Rilski House Museum
145
Nikola Vaptsarov Museum
(Bansko) 143
Old Pharmacy Museum (Plovdiv)
161
Peyo Yavarov Museum (Sofia) 94
Prison Museum (Veliko Tarnovo)
196
Regional Historical Museum
(Pleven) 211
Regional History Museum
(Shumen) 215
Rila Monastery Museum 128,
130
Rose Museum (Kazanlak) 202
Sea Museum (Kavarna) 239
Slaveikov House Museum
(Tryavna) 199–200
Sofia Gallery of Art 91
Speleology Museum (Chepelare)
179
State Gallery of Fine Arts
(Plovdiv) 161
State Gallery (Stara Zagora) 205
Svetlin Rusev Gallery (Pleven)
210–11, *211*
Town History Museum (Gotse
Delchev) 147, *147*
Vasil Levski Museum and
Monument (Lovech) 193
Vladimir Dimitrov Museum 122
Vladislav Varnenchik Park-
Museum (Varna) 227
Woodcarving and Icon Painting
Museum (Tryavna) 199
Zahari Stoyanov House Museum
(Rousse) 214
music 56–7, 282

N

name days 45, 48
National Palace of Culture (Sofia)
91–2, *92*
national parks
Mount Vitosha 98–102
Rusenski Lom 214, *214*
National Revival 30, **31**, 57, 114,
121, 195, 223
see also **historic buildings**;
museums and galleries
Nebet Tepe (Plovdiv) 157
Nessebar *244*, 245, *245*, *248*,
248–51, *251*, 263, 280
newspapers 291
Nicopolis, Battle of 30, *30*
nightlife 283
Nikopol 211
Northwest Bulgaria 109–23
hotels 274
restaurants 123
Novi Iskar 109

O

Obrochishte 236
Obzor 245, **246**
Ognyanova 148
Omurtag, Khan 27
opening hours 282, 288
opera 57, 87–8, 158, 205, 227,
282
Orlov Most (Sofia) 93
Ottoman Yoke 28, 29, **30–1**, 32–3,
43, 44, 138, 157, 194, 262
outdoor activities 285–7

P

package tours 135, 233
Palace of Culture and Sport (Varna)
227
Palace of Justice (Sofia) 94
palaces
Battenburg Palace (Rousse) 213
Evksinograd Palace (Varna) 227
Former Royal Palace (Sofia) 84
Summer Palace of Queen Marie
(Balchik) 237–8, *237*
Pamporovo 144, *178*, *179*, **179**,
277
Pancherevo, Lake 102
Panichishte 127, 128, 276
Pannonia 27
Papasov, Ivo 57
parking 236
parks and gardens
see also **amusement parks**;
national parks; **water parks**
Ayazmo Park (Stara Zagora) 205
Botanical Garden (Sofia) **88**, 96
Botanical Gardens (Balchik)
237–8
City Garden (Sofia) 90, *90*
City Garden (Stara Zagora) 204
Doctors' Park and Memorial
(Sofia) 89
Knyaz Boris Garden (Sofia) 92–3
Penio Penev Park (Dimitrovgrad)
183
Primorski Park (Varna) 225
Sea Gardens (Bourgas) 252
Sea Gardens (Varna) 225–6, *225*
Skovelev Park (Pleven) 211
Stratesh Park (Lovech) 193
Tsar Simeon Garden (Plovdiv) 165
Vladislav Varnenchik Park-
Museum (Varna) 227
Yuzhen Park (Sofia) 91–2
Pasarel 103
passports 290
Penev, Penio 183
people 43–9
People's Republic of Bulgaria 36
Pernik 122, 123
Perperikon 24, *186*, **186**
Persia 24
Peter I, Tsar 28, 130
Peter II, Tsar 28
Peter IV, Tsar 29
Petrohan Pass 115
Petrovo Niva 262
Philip of Macedonia 24, 155–6,

157, *160*, 162
photography 292
Pirin 141
Pirin Mountains *18*, 130, *140*,
141–53, *148*, *276*
hotels 276
restaurants 153
Planetarium (Dimitrovgrad) 183
Pleven *209*, **210–11**, 217
Pliska 27–8, *208*, *216*, **216**
Ploschad *see* **streets and squares**
Plovdiv 121, *154*, **155–68**, *156*,
158
history 155–7
hotels 277–8
restaurants 169
politics 37
Pomaks 43, 180, 181, *182*
Pomorie, Lake 251–2
Pomorie peninsula 251, 281
Popina Luka 150
population 46
postal services 292
poverty 45
Predel Pass 141–2
Preobrazhenie Uprising 262
Preslav 28, 29, 216
Primorsko 257–8, *258*, 263
property, overseas investment in
54, **224**
public holidays 292

R

radio 291
Radoslavov, Vasil 35
rail travel 269
rain-making 49*49*
rainfall 21
rakia 63
Rakovski, George 31
Razlog 142
Red Army 36, 89–90, 168
religion 27, 30, 43, **47**, 138–9,
292
restaurants
around Sofia and the Northwest
123
Balkan Range 207
Danubian Plain 217
Northern Black Sea Coast 243
Pirin Mountains 153
Plovdiv 169
Rhodopes Mountains 187
Sofia 104–5
Southern Black Sea Coast 263
Southwest and Rila Mountains
137
Varna 229
Rhodopes Mountains 19, *19*, 144,
173, **173–87**
hotels 277–8
restaurants 187
Rila Mountains 19, 20, *125*,
125–36, 144
hotels 275–6
restaurants 137
Rilski, Neofit 143, 145
Riviera 231, **233–4**, 243, 279
road travel 269–71

rock formations 20, *261*
  Belogradchik Rocks 20, **119**
  Blue Rocks 206
  Katinski Pyramids 109
  Kurdzhali Pyramids 185
  Lakatnikishki Skali 111
  Miraculous Bridges 179, *179*
  Pyramids of Melnik 20, *150*,
    151–2
  Stob Pyramids 132, *133*
  Stone Forest 228
  Tsarevo *261*
  Zlatni Mostove **101**, 102
rock music 239
rock paintings 119, *119*
Roimitalkes III, King of Thrace 25
Roma 44
Romania 34, 237
Romans *24*, **24–5**, 148, 156,
  157–8, 197, 205, 223–5, 242,
  246, 262
Ropotamo River 257
roses 49, 202, **203**
Rousse 212, **212–14**, *213*, 217
Rozhen *151*, **152**
Rumelia, Eastern 32, 33, 157
rural life 51–5
rural tourism 54–5, 271
Rusalka 241
Russia 31, 32, 33
Russian Cultural Centre (Sofia) 89
Russo-Turkish War 201, 211, 223

S

safety 269–70, 289
Sahat Tepe (Plovdiv) 168
sailing 287
St John's Island 256
St Konstantine *233*, **233**, 243, 280
St Thomas Island 257
St Toma, Cape 256
St Vlas 245, *246*, **247**, 263, 281
Salzata, Lake 127
Samokov 133
Samuil, Tsar 142
San Stefano, Treaty of 31, *31*, 32
Sandanski **149–50**, 153, 276
Saxe-Coburg-Gotha, Simeon 36,
  37, *37*
sea travel 268–9
Second Bulgarian Kingdom **29–30**,
  138, 194
self-catering 272
Selo 52
Sepereva Banya 126–7
Serafin, Bishop 85
Serbia 33, 34, 35
Seuthes, King of Thrace 24
Seutus III, King of Thrace 203
Seven Lakes *127*, **127–8**, 132
Shabla 241–2
Shabla, Cape 241, **242**
Shabla, Lake 189, **242**
Shiligarnika 146
Shipka Pass 201–2
Shiroka Luka *172*, *180*, **180–1**,
  187, *188*
Shishtov 211–12
shopping 283–4

  see also **markets**
  Pirotska (Sofia) 83–4
  TZUM (Sofia) 82
Shumen *215*, **215–16**, 217
Simeon the Great, Tsar *26*, 27–8
Simeon II, King 36, 37, *37*, 84
Simeonovo 100
Simitli 141
Sinan Agha, Koca Mima 82
Sinemoretz 259, *259*, *260*, 281
Sitalkes, King of Thrace 24
Skifi, Nikifor 28
skiing 54–5, **144**, 283, 287
  Mount Vitosha **100–1**, 144
  Pirin Mountains 144, 146
  Rhodopes Mountains 144, **179**
  Rila Mountains **135**, 144
Slavs 25, 26
Sliven **206**, 278
Smolyan 179–80
Sofia 76–105
  airport 268
  around Sofia and the Northwest
    109–23, 274
  history 33, **77–9**, 91
  hotels 273–4
  restaurants and bars 104–5
Sokolovo 238
Southwest Bulgaria 125–37
  hotels 275–6
  restaurants 137
souvenirs 284
Soviet Union 36–7
Sozopol 245, *254*, **254–5**, *255*,
  256, *257*, 263
Spartacus **24–5**, 141
spas 250, 271
  Ardino 186
  Dolna Banya 136
  Gornovasilishki 136
  Kostenets Banya 136
  Narcahenski Bani 178
  Pchelin 136
  Sepereva Banya **126–7**, 276
  Tuzlata 238
sport 285–7
Stalin, Joseph 222
Stamboliski, Alexander **35**, 87, 120
Stambolov, Stefan 33, 34
Stara Planina 19
Stara Zagora **203–5**, *204*, *205*,
  206, *207*, 278
Stoichkov, Hristo 45
storks 150
Strandzha Mountains 245, **259–61**,
  262, 281
streets and squares
  Baba Yaga Square (Sofia) 89
  Battenburg Square (Rousse) 213
  Bazaar (Plovdiv) 163–4
  Boulevard Vitosha (Sofia) *76*, *93*,
    93–4, *96*, *104*
  Bulevard Kynaz Aleksander I
    Battenburg (Plovdiv) 166, *166*,
    167
  Largo (Sofia) 78, 80, 84
  Old Square (Tryavna) 199
  Pirotska (Sofia) 83–4
  Ploschad Aleksander Battenburg
    (Sofia) **84–5**, 90

  Ploschad Dzhumaya (Plovdiv)
    160, *164*
  Ploschad Makedoniya
    (Blagoevgrad) 132
  Ploschad Nezavisimost (Sofia)
    80, 84
  Ploschad Nezavisimost (Varna)
    222
  Ploschad Sv. Nedelya (Sofia) 79
  Ploschad Svoboda (Dupnitsa)
    126
  Ploschad Tsentralen (Plovdiv)
    164–5
  Ploschad Vazrazhdane (Bansko)
    145
  Slivnitsa (Varna) *221*
  Ulitsa Graf Ignatiev (Sofia) 94–5
Struma Valley 125–6
Studena, Lake 102
Sunny Beach 245, **247–8**, 263,
  281
Sveshtari 24
Sveti Nikola 241
Svoge 109
synagogues
  Plovdiv 164
  Sofia Synagogue 83
  Vidin 210

T

Taukliman Bay 241
taxis 270
telephone services 292
television 291
temperatures 20
Teres, King of Thrace 24
theatres 282
  Ivan Dimov Theatre (Haskovo)
    184
  Ivan Vazov National Theatre
    (Sofia) 91, *91*, *282*
  National Opera House (Sofia)
    87–8
  Opera House (Varna) 227, *227*
  Plovdiv Philharmonic Orchestra
    and Opera 165
  State Opera Theatre (Stara
    Zagora) 205
Third Bulgarian Kingdom 32–6, 84
Thompson, Major Frank 109, **112**
Thrace **24–6**, 97, 114, 202–3
Thrace, Plain of 19, 25, 155
Thracian Cliffs resort 239–40
time zone 292
tipping 292
toilets 292
Tomislav, King of the Croats 28
Topalov, Veselin 45
topless sunbathing 246
tour operators 271
tourism 54–5
tourist information 293
trade fairs, Plovdiv **164**, 165
transport 268–71
travellers' cheques 292
treasure
  Panagyurishte Treasure 97
  Rogozen Treasure *22*, 24, *114*,
    114

Thracian treasure *23*, 24, 97, 202–3
Trigrad 182
Trigrad Gorge 181–2, *183*, 189
Trimontium Princess Hotel and Casino (Plovdiv) 165
Troyan 193–4, 278
Tryavna *198*, **198–200**, *199*, 207, 278
Tsankov, Alexander 35
Tsarevo 258, *261*
Tsigov Chark 181
Turks *see* **Ottoman Yoke**
Tuzlata 238

U

unemployment 45, 46
UNESCO sites 96, 128, 133, 177, 216, 249
universities
Blagoevgrad 131
St Kliment Ohridski (Sofia) 89
urban migration 53–4
Utigur 26

V

Valley of the Roses 49, **202–3**
Valley of the Thracian Kings 202–3
Vaptsarov, Nikola 143
Varna 221–8, 231, 268
history 221–2
hotels 280
restaurants 229
Varna, Battle of 227
Varna, Lake 228

Varosha (Blagoevgrad) 131
Vasili Levski Stadium (Sofia) 93
Vazov, Ivan 86, **91**, 111, 116–17, 166
Veleka River 259, 260
Veliko Tarnovo 29, 30, 32, *194*, **194–6**, 207, 278
Velingrad 136, 137, 276
Vidin 209–10, 217
Vienna Award 36
Vihren, Mount 141, 142
villages 52
Vinitsa 227–8
visas 290
Vitosha, Mount 79, 97, **98–102**, *103*, 144
Vratsa 113–14, *114*, 123
Vratsa Gorge 114, *115*

W

War of Liberation 31, 239, 262
Warsaw Pact 37
water 52, 63, 291
water parks
Action Aquapark (Sunny Beach) **248**, 283
Aqua Paradise (Nessebar) **248–9**, 283
Aquapolis (near Golden Sands) 283
waterfalls
Boyana Waterfall (Sofia) 97
Kostenets 136
Polsko-Skakavishki Waterfall 122
Skakavnitsa Waterfall 127
Skaklya Waterfall 111

websites 293
weights and measures 293
wildlife 20, 287
Aquarium and Black Sea Museum (Varna) 226
Bistrishko Branishte nature reserve 98
Dolphinarium (Varna) 226
Golden Sands natural park 234
Parangalitsa Nature Reserve 133
Sofia Zoo 95–6
Strandzha Nature Park 259–61
wine 21, *53*, 63, 149, 150–1
women 46
World War I 35, *35*
World War II 35–6, 47, 79, 87, 91, 112, 164, 284

Y

yacht cruises 238
Yagodina 182
Yavarov, Peyo 94
Yugoslavia 35, 36

Z

Zemenski Gorge 122
Zhikov, Todor 36–7, 44
zoos
Sofia 95–6
Stratesh Park (Lovech) 193